30°E  60°  90°  120°  150°  180°

*OCEAN*

*Svalbard
(NORWAY)*

NORWAY
SWEDEN  FINLAND
EST.
LATVIA
LITH.
DENMARK
NETH.  BELARUS
GERMANY  POLAND
BELG.  CZECH REP.
ELG.  UKRAINE
ANCE  AUST.  HUNG.  MOLDOVA
SWITZ.  SLOV.  ROMANIA
BOSN. & HERZG.
ITALY  SERB.  BULG.
MONTENEGRO
KOSOVO  MACED.
ALBANIA  GREECE
MALTA
TUNISIA
CYPRUS  LEB.
ISRAEL
JORDAN

R U S S I A

KAZAKHSTAN

MONGOLIA

NORTH
KOREA
SOUTH
KOREA

JAPAN

GEORGIA
ARM.  AZERB.
TURKEY
TURKMENISTAN
UZBEKISTAN
KYRGYZSTAN
TAJIKISTAN

C H I N A

SYRIA
IRAQ  IRAN
AFGHANISTAN
KUWAIT
PAKISTAN
BAHRAIN
QATAR
U.A.E.
SAUDI
ARABIA
OMAN

LIBYA
EGYPT

NEPAL
BHUTAN
BANGLADESH

I N D I A

*PACIFIC OCEAN*

Northern
Mariana
Islands
(U.S.)

LAOS
MYANMAR
THAILAND  VIETNAM
CAMBODIA

PHILIPPINES

MARSHALL
ISLANDS

RIA
NIGER  CHAD  SUDAN  ERITREA  YEMEN
DJIBOUTI
NIGERIA
CAMEROON
CENT. AFRICAN
REPUBLIC
ETHIOPIA
SOMALIA
SRI LANKA
MALDIVES

PALAU  FEDERATED STATES OF MICRONESIA

BRUNEI
M A L A Y S I A
SINGAPORE

KIRIBATI
NAURU

AO TOME
PRINCIPE
BENIN
Q. GUINEA
GABON
CONGO
DEMOCRATIC
REPUBLIC OF
THE CONGO
UGANDA
RWANDA
BURUNDI
KENYA
TANZANIA

I N D O N E S I A

SEYCHELLES

*INDIAN OCEAN*

PAPUA
NEW GUINEA
TIMOR-LESTE

SOLOMON
ISLANDS

TUVALU

ANGOLA
ZAMBIA
ZIMBABWE
NAMIBIA
BOTSWANA
MOZAMBIQUE
COMOROS
MADAGASCAR
MAURITIUS

VANUATU

FIJI
ISLANDS

SOUTH AFRICA
SWAZILAND
LESOTHO

New Caledonia
(FR.)

A U S T R A L I A

NEW ZEALAND

0  2,000 miles
0  2,000 kilometers
SCALE AT THE EQUATOR
*Winkel Tripel Projection, Central Meridian 0°*

*Kerguelen Islands
(FR.)*

# SECRET
# JOURNEYS
## *of a*
# LIFETIME

### 500

## *of the World's Best Hidden Travel Gems*

# SECRET JOURNEYS *of a* LIFETIME

## 500
### *of the World's Best Hidden Travel Gems*

INTRODUCTION BY KEITH BELLOWS
EDITOR-IN-CHIEF, *NATIONAL GEOGRAPHIC TRAVELER* MAGAZINE

**NATIONAL GEOGRAPHIC**
WASHINGTON, D.C.

# Contents

Previous Page: In an image of timeless serenity, a herd of elephants crosses the vast African savanna. Opposite: Dancers from Zuni Pueblo perform traditional dances at Bandelier National Monument in New Mexico.

# YOUR NEXT JOURNEY STARTS HERE

Do you have a travel secret? Of course. We all do. Mine include the transfixing lake vista in Canada's cottage country, down a dirt road, past Bud's Dock, seen from an 80-foot-high (24 meter) granite ledge. The walk past Keith Richards's old place in London to a statue of Thomas Carlyle where you'll find one of a dying breed—a true neighborhood pub. The point in Chesapeake Bay that offers a front-row view of scudding sailboats and, at sunrise, a flotilla of skiffs pulling up pots bristling with blue crabs. The tucked-away, tiny loch in western Scotland ringed by palm trees. All my life, I've lived the philosophy of following the locals. And I've collected memorable finds throughout my travels.

That's what this book is about. It's a sequel to *Journeys of a Lifetime*, a showcase, I wrote when it was published in 2007, of "wonderful, indelible, life-changing journeys with terrific stops along the way." When readers asked me about the book, they inevitably wondered what we had left out. The short answer: Plenty. So now we're back with *Secret Journeys of a Lifetime*. This time, we decided to dig deeper into the fabric of the world to find little-known gems and discoveries. What we offer here is the product of the Society's deep experience of surveying the world and all that's in it, taking you beyond conventional guidebooks to reveal an insider's world. You'll find the Grand Canyon overlook few tourists visit; the best view of London; the place in Kenya's Amboseli National Park where the wildlife gather; Belize's Mayan ruins of Altun Ha; the breathtaking rail journey from Sarejevo to Mostar; the secret passage between the Pitti Palace and the Uffizi Gallery in Florence; the tastiest kebabs in Turkey; the lost-in-time Spanish villages south of Salamanca; the hidden Parisian garden of La Bagatelle; and the island that's the Caribbean's best-kept secret. Explore the places, tips, ideas, and insights on the following pages and you'll unearth a lot of what the locals like to keep to themselves. It's all here: hidden history, off-the-beaten track discoveries, little-known attractions and city secrets, obscure natural wonders, and forgotten cul-de-sacs. Welcome to a world truly less traveled.

*Keith Bellows*
*Editor-in-Chief,* National Geographic Traveler *magazine*

Opposite: Brightly painted old merchants' houses line the quay at lively Nyhavn, or old harbor, in Copenhagen's waterfront district.

# The World at Your Feet

The chance to look out on the world from its high places is one of the greatest joys that travel can provide. And while some vistas are so famous as to have become tourist-calendar clichés, others are less well known, on routes much less well trodden. And these, perhaps because they come as a surprise, are often the most rewarding. Some of the journeys that follow take you to sights that are downright astounding, such as the thousand-year-old Corsican town of Bonifacio clinging to a rock ledge overhanging the Mediterranean Sea. Another leads you gently but persistently uphill along a back road on the Tennessee–North Carolina border to a viewpoint over one of the most magnificent mountainscapes in the eastern United States. Others provide close-ups of some of nature's most elusive wonders, such as Peru's Colca Canyon, which brings you face to face with the Andean condor. And for explorers whose zest for new vistas is not matched by an appetite for exertion, there is an ascent by cog-railway to the heights of the Swiss Alps, where the only thing that takes your breath away is the splendor of the view.

The pretty village of Mürren in the Swiss Alps sits on a narrow plateau high above the Lauterbrunnen Valley and gives access to some of the most dramatic and vertiginous mountain views in the whole region.

# WATERTON LAKES

The crystalline calm of Upper Waterton Lake, in Alberta's southwestern corner, mirrors sheer granite peaks chiseled by nature.

NORTH AMERICA

ikers, bikers, bird-watchers, campers, and canoeists cannot fail to be energized by the pristine landscape that awaits their arrival at Waterton Lakes National Park, a three-hour drive south from Calgary. For this is where the Canadian prairies meet the Rocky Mountains, where jagged layers of Precambrian bedrock catch the sun in shimmering, mineralized red and green, and where gray crags soften to join gently sloping grassland and alpine meadows. It is also where glaciers have left their mark in a series of infinity-pool-like lakes cut high among the peaks. Named for the British naturalist Charles Waterton in the early 19th century, the park covers 195 square miles (505 square kilometers), with lakes as deep as 492 feet (150 meters), and mountains topping 9,580 feet (2,920 meters). When summer arrives, a profusion of wildflowers carpet the meadows, including bright yellow clumps of balsam root, lady slipper orchid, pink meadowsweet, and rock jasmine. Then, when a wintery hush descends on the park wrapped in a quilt of powdery snow, elk, mule deer, and Rocky Mountain sheep wander through Waterton village as curiously innocent visitors, and winter-sports enthusiasts take to their snowshoes, skis, or ice-climbing gear, stopping for hot cocoa or hearty soup at the Prince of Wales Hotel, a lone rustic chalet built on a bluff in 1927.

**When to Go** Waterton's climate is moist, windy, and quick to change. Temperatures can rise to 94°F (35°C) in high summer and plummet to -40°F (-40°C) in January and February, with frequent warm spells in winter around 50°F (10°C). June and April tend to be the wettest months; expect snow in winter.

**How to Find It** The park can be reached by car from Calgary, 164 miles (264 km) to the north, or via the Chief Mountain International Highway from the adjacent Glacier National Park, in Montana.

**Planning** Waterton is open year-round, although some facilities close during winter. You will find hotels and lodges in Waterton townsite, next to Middle Waterton Lake. There are several backcountry campgrounds in the park. Backpacking permits and maps can be obtained at the visitor center, open May through October.

**Websites** www.watertonpark.com, www.pc.gc.ca, www.travelalberta.com, www.canada.travel

### Blackfeet Reservation

Bounded by part of Waterton Lakes National Park, Blackfeet Reservation encompasses rolling plains, forests, and mountains that are now home to the once nomadic Blackfeet tribe.

■ The Northern Plains tribe's legacy lives on at the **Museum of the Plains Indian** in nearby Browning, MT. Permanent exhibits explain ceremonial and social customs and display life-sized traditional costumes.

■ Also in Browning, the **Blackfeet Heritage Center & Art Gallery** features beadwork, jewelry, pottery, rugs, kachinas, carvings, baskets, and paintings.

Waterton Lakes National Park in the Rocky Mountains encompasses a series of glacier lakes and pristine landscapes overlooking the Canadian prairies.

THE WORLD AT YOUR FEET

LAST WILDERNESSES   ISLAND GETAWAYS   THE ROAD LESS TRAVELED   SECRET HISTORY   SPIRITUAL HAVENS   HIDDEN TREASURES   UNDISCOVERED VILLAGES   CITY SECRETS

A peephole view of part of Raven Cliff Falls, which drops a total of 420 ft (128 m) in a series of thunderous cascades

SOUTH CAROLINA

# Caesars Head State Park

A lookout point at the top of a plunging escarpment
provides great views over the Appalachian foothills.

In the far northwest corner of South Carolina, rolling foothills suddenly give way to the 2,000-foot (610 meter) rise of the Appalachian Mountains known as the Blue Ridge Escarpment, or, as the locals call it, the "big blue wall." Sitting high atop this ridge is Caesars Head State Park, a rugged mountain wilderness that is treasured by locals but virtually unknown outside the state. In the 19th century, farmers would take their families to this lofty perch for summer picnics. Then, as now, the main attraction was the craggy granite outcrop that offers 200-degree views along the dramatic rise of the mountains. Early settlers thought the outcrop resembled the profile of a Roman emperor, hence the name. On a clear day, the vista can extend 60 miles (97 kilometers) across the foothills far below. Caesars Head is part of the Mountain Bridge Wilderness Area, which offers more than 50 miles (80 kilometers) of excellent mountain hiking trails. The most popular is the moderately strenuous 4-mile (6.4 kilometer) round-trip hike to Raven Cliff Falls, one of the highest waterfalls in the United States. A more demanding 8.6-mile (14 kilometer) loop takes hikers across a suspension bridge spanning the top of the falls to an overlook that offers the best view of the roaring, watery tumult.

**When to Go**  Low humidity in spring and fall often permits the best views. From mid-September through late October, Caesars Head is a great place for watching the annual southward migration of thousands of red-tailed, cooper's, sharp-shinned, and other hawks.

**How to Find It**  The park headquarters is about 35 miles (56 km) northwest of Greenville, SC, on U.S. 276.

**Planning**  Greenville is a small city with a busy little airport and is gaining a reputation across the southeastern U.S. for its charming inns and quality restaurants.

**Websites**  www.southcarolinaparks.com, www.wildernet.com

## Chapel on the Rock

A short drive from Caesars Head leads into North Carolina for a mile (1.6 km) and then back into South Carolina, through the grounds of the lovely Greenville Y.M.C.A. camp, to the cliff-top chapel known in a magnificently understated way as **Pretty Place.** This open-sided little church rests on a solid rock outcropping that juts out from the mountainside 2,000 ft (610 m) above the forested valleys below. Not surprisingly, it is a popular place for weddings and is often booked on summer weekends. But midweek you may have it all to yourself, especially at dawn, when the east-facing chapel provides a ringside seat for a glorious mountain sunrise.

# THE CHEROHALA SKYWAY

This winding, two-lane road across the Great Smoky Mountains offers ever changing views of ranks of forested peaks.

This little-known byway is also called the Mile-High Highway, and for good reason. Starting in the Tennessee town of Tellico Plains at the modest elevation of 990 feet (302 meters) above sea level, the road traces a serpentine route through lush, deeply forested foothills before climbing into the heart of the Blue Ridge, and descending again to Robbinsville, North Carolina. By the time the road reaches the Tennessee–North Carolina border, its elevation has reached 4,000 feet (1,219 meters), and for the next 15 miles (24 kilometers) it crosses several peaks in excess of 5,200 feet (1,585 meters). Completed in 1996 after 30 years of construction, this feat of engineering passes through one of the least developed areas of mountain wilderness in the eastern U.S. To the north lies the Citico Creek Wilderness and the celebrated Joyce Kilmer-Slickrock Wilderness. To the south is the Snowbird Backcountry and the Bald River Gorge Wilderness. An opportunity to experience the latter occurs early on the Tennessee side, where just 5 miles (8 kilometers) past the Skyway Visitor Center, Forest Service Road 210 leads to where the Bald River tumbles in a broad veil of mist 100 feet (30 meters) into a still pool.

**When to Go** In the first two weeks of October, the mountainsides are blanketed with foliage in a pallet of flaming reds, yellows, and oranges, and the usually crisp, dry air offers views far into the distance. Driving the Skyway in May and early June can also be a delight as springtime greens and firework-like displays of rhododendron, flame azalea, and mountain laurel burst in swathes across the steep hills.

**How to Find It** The Skyway is best driven from west to east. Starting in Tellico Plains, take Tennessee 165 to the beginning of the Skyway. Free maps are available at the visitor center in Tellico Plains.

**Planning** The Skyway is a smooth, well-maintained road, but it has no services, so make sure you have plenty of gas, water, and snacks before heading out. It takes about three hours to cover the 55 miles (88 km) at a leisurely pace, allowing time to enjoy the overlooks and visitor center. Add another three hours to hike the Joyce Kilmer-Slickrock Wilderness and you have a pleasantly full day.

**Websites** www.cherohala.com, www.cherohala.org, www.grahamcountytravel.com

## Poet's Memorial

Named for the poet and naturalist who penned "I think that I shall never see/ A poem as lovely as a tree," the **Joyce Kilmer Memorial Forest** protects one of the finest old-growth stands of timber in the southern Blue Ridge. Kilmer died in World War I, but the spirit of his poems is alive in this place. Here in a deep mountain cove, an easy, 2-mile (3 km), figure-eight trail leads through hushed stands of oak, hickory, and poplar. Some of these giant trees are 400 years old and more than 20 ft (6 m) in circumference.

The Skyway provides stunning views of the Cherokee and Nantahala National Forests as fall colors start to appear.

THE WORLD AT YOUR FEET

LAST WILDERNESSES | ISLAND GETAWAYS | THE ROAD LESS TRAVELED | SECRET HISTORY | SPIRITUAL HAVENS | HIDDEN TREASURES | UNDISCOVERED VILLAGES | CITY SECRETS

Dead Horse Point overlooks the arid, heavily eroded world of Canyonlands National Park.

UTAH

# DEAD HORSE POINT STATE PARK

Afflicted by a geology obsession? Give it full scope at
Dead Horse Point State Park near the small city of Moab.

The bones of the planet are fully exposed here: Red sandstone pinnacles and buttes, the products of ongoing erosion, stand arrayed against a sky overwhelming in its breadth. At sunset, the cliffs and mesas glow with an incarnadine light that seems to issue from within the rock, while 2,000 feet (610 meters) below, the Colorado River glimmers like quicksilver as it uncoils sinuously on its 1,400-mile (2,253 kilometer) run to the Gulf of California. The 5,200-acre (2,104 hectare) park was first exploited by local cowpokes seeking wild mustangs. At Dead Horse Point itself, a flat promontory accessible only by a narrow neck of land served as a natural corral for captured ponies. Today, the park constitutes a requisite side-trip for anyone visiting Moab, a recreational mecca for mountain bikers, rock climbers, and desert trekkers. Camping is available, and trails wend across the landscape, affording varied perspectives at every switchback. Watch where you're going, though; this is a place of extreme topography, and an accident, as locals say in their characteristically understated fashion, could ruin your day. Alternately, simply park at the Dead Horse Point overlook and stare in slack-jawed appreciation at a 150-million-year-old work-in-progress.

**When to Go** Summers are punishing in southern Utah, so go in spring or fall. Even then, midday temperatures can be trying. For the ultimate experience, visit at dusk or dawn, when alpenglow suffuses the cliffs and spires with fluorescent pink light.

**How to Find It** From Moab, drive 9 miles (14 km) northwest on U.S. 191, then head southwest on Utah 313 for as far as you can go (about 23 miles/37 km) to reach the park entrance.

**Planning** Salt Lake City, UT, Phoenix, AZ, Albuquerque, NM, Denver, CO, and Las Vegas, NV, are good starting points for an itinerary that takes in the park. Moab is the nearest town to stay, and car rental is a must.

**Websites** www.utah.com/stateparks/dead_horse.htm, www.moab-utah.com, www.discovermoab.com

### Mountain-bikers' Heaven

Dead Horse Point State Park is located in the heart of Utah's Red Rock Country, esteemed globally for its nonpareil mountain biking. You don't have to be an über-biker to enjoy the sport. Local bike- shop owners are free with advice and equipment and can recommend easy routes, while the park's **Intrepid Trail System** offers routes of varying difficulty.

For the proficient, the **Slickrock Trail** is a must: A 10.6-mile (17 km) route combining challenging terrain with vistas of earth and sky that trump any superlative thrown at them. The loop can take three to four hours. Conditions are arid, and often hot, so bring plenty of water.

NORTH
AMERICA

THE WORLD AT YOUR FEET

LAST WILDERNESSES · ISLAND GETAWAYS · THE ROAD LESS TRAVELED · SECRET HISTORY · SPIRITUAL HAVENS · HIDDEN TREASURES · UNDISCOVERED VILLAGES · CITY SECRETS

PERU

# Colca Canyon

This deep canyon carved through the Andes by the
Colca River has been inhabited since pre-Inca times.

It is hard to believe that so large a creature, with a wingspan of nearly 10 feet (3 meters), could even lift off the ground, let alone fly with such ease. Yet there it is: An Andean condor dancing in the thermal updrafts of southern Peru, oblivious to the earthbound creatures pointing and snapping its photo from the nearby *mirador* (viewpoint). The place is called Cruz del Condor, one of half a dozen miradors where you can peer into the depths of Colca Canyon. Originally formed by faulting during the final stages of the Andean uplift, the canyon takes its present shape from roughly 150 million years of erosion of the soft volcanic rock by wind and water. When American aviators first came across this huge trough in the 1920s, they dubbed it the Lost Valley of the Incas. A 2005 survey fixed the maximum depth at 13,648 feet (4,160 meters)—more than twice as deep as Arizona's Grand Canyon. The Colca's upper reaches are inhabited by indigenous groups who still farm stepped terraces built on the sides of the canyon by pre-Inca forerunners. The early inhabitants stored crops and buried their leaders in *colca* (niches) in the cliffs—from which the canyon draws its name. There are numerous ways to explore the canyon, including hiking, horseback riding, and mountain biking along primitive trails, or by running the Colca River by raft or kayak. Or you can simply relax in one of the many hot springs that bubble up from the canyon's volcanic depths, contemplating the natural magic that formed the canyon and the laws of physics that enable condors to fly.

**When to Go**  A high-altitude desert, the Colca region is marked by sunny days and cold nights throughout the year. The rainy season, such as it is, takes place during summer (January–March).

**How to Find It**  The deepest part of the canyon is the section between Chivay (near the canyon's upper reaches) and Cabanaconde (near Cruz del Condor), about a four-hour drive (125 miles/200 km) from Arequipa, which has daily flights to and from Lima. Most of the canyon's tourist services are on the south rim, especially in Chivay, Yanque, and Cabanaconde.

**Planning**  Places to stay range from modest guesthouses to upscale boutique hotels. Hotels along the rim can arrange just about anything you might want to do, from bird-watching at Cruz del Condor to week-long hikes into the wilds of the canyon.

**Websites**  www.pablotour.com, www.totallyperu.com, www.colcacanyontours.com, www.lascasitasdelcolca.com

SOUTH
AMERICA

## Geological Wonderland

Colca is far from being the only geological wonder in this region:

■ More like the surface of Mars than anything on planet Earth, the nearby **Valley of the Volcanoes** is scarred with 80 extinct cones and craters. Looming over the valley is the permanently snow-covered **Nevado Coropuna,** Peru's largest active volcano and, at 21,079 ft (6,425 m), the tenth highest in the Andes.

■ About 60 miles (100 km) south of Cabanaconde, and well camouflaged in the desert landscape of the Majes Valley (the Colca River changes its name to Majes as it descends toward the Pacific), **Toro Muerto** (Dead Bull) is a collection of more than a thousand pre-Inca petroglyphs. They are carved with geometric and zoomorphic designs that bear more than a passing resemblance to those found at the Nasca Lines.

Given their remoteness and difficulty to reach, both the Valley of the Volcanoes and Toro Muerto are best explored with a local guide.

Opposite: Villagers in remote Sibayo in the canyon's upper reaches  Above: A condor soars above the canyon.

Despite their height, the Fumaça Falls end in a wispy veil of water in a quiet, rocky pool.

BRAZIL

# FUMAÇA WATERFALLS

Hike along remote trails to the base of Brazil's highest waterfall,
then climb to the top of the falls for a great view over the treetops.

Edging forward on your elbows across a warm, flat rock, your shaking legs anchored by the firm grip of your guide, you peep over the 1,260-foot (384 meter) drop at Fumaça. The column of water is picked up by the strong wind and dispersed into a wall of mist, giving the waterfall its name: Fumaça, or "smoky." The falls are located in the Chapada Diamantina, or Diamond Highlands, a national park of distinctive mesas, valleys, rivers, and caves in Bahia, northeast Brazil. In the mid-19th century, the region was inundated with prospectors, or *garimpeiros,* seduced by the promise of diamonds. Today, the prospectors' mule trails form the basis for a three-day hike from the city of Lencóis, in the Capão Valley, to the base of the falls. Nights are spent camping in open caves or in the shells of old churches, and food is prepared over campfires under a twinkling sky. On the final day you arrive at a colossal pool at the base of the falls, where you can bathe and assess the climb ahead. The steep, three-hour ascent is part-meander, part-scramble, as you make your way to the precipitous clifftop and survey the valley from which you've just emerged.

**When to Go**  June to September are the coolest months, with daytime temperatures in the 70s (21-26°C). Skies are likely to be clear. The rainy period occurs from December through March, when the vegetation grows lush and the rivers and water holes are gushing.

**How to Find It**  Lencóis is the base for exploring the Chapada Diamantina. It is a short plane ride or a rather bumpy five hours on a bus from the city of Salvador, which is 255 miles (410 km) to the west.

**Planning**  Lencóis has all types of places to stay. Nearby villages, such as Mucugê and Capão Valley, are located deeper within the park and are less touristy. You can make day hikes under your own steam but are strongly recommended to hire a guide for longer trips as the trails can be very confusing.

**Website**  www.chapada-diamantina.travel

## Swimming Holes

An easy 2.5-mile (4 km) walk south of Lencóis awaits **Ribeirão do Meio,** a natural waterslide where the Lencóis River has smoothed out the rocks around a series of deep pools that descend in tiers to a larger swimming hole. The pools make glorious natural Jacuzzis—just sit back while the water, tinted by minerals and vegetation, bubbles up around you. Or you can sunbathe on the rocks alongside. For an adrenaline rush, and for those who don't mind the odd bruise, you can slide down the mossy, polished-rock waterslide— somewhat like a toboggan run—to land in the pool below.

SOUTH AMERICA

THE WORLD AT YOUR FEET

LAST WILDERNESSES    ISLAND GETAWAYS    THE ROAD LESS TRAVELED    SECRET HISTORY    SPIRITUAL HAVENS    HIDDEN TREASURES    UNDISCOVERED VILLAGES    CITY SECRETS

AUSTRALIA

# WINEGLASS BAY

A strenuous walk along the Freycinet Peninsula, part of eastern Tasmania's rocky coastline, takes you to this quiet, secluded bay.

AUSTRALIA AND OCEANIA

Descending walkers urge on puffing climbers: "Keep going, it's really worth it." Eventually, the steep, 45-minute haul from the Coles Bay parking lot reaches a boulder-flanked lookout point perched in a saddle between two of the pink granite peaks of the Hazard Range. Below, a sweeping arc of white quartz sand traces a perfect crescent between clear, turquoise waters and wooded slopes. This is Wineglass Bay, the gleaming jewel in the crown of Freycinet National Park, a sea-fringed strip of unspoiled wilderness and extraordinary beauty north of Hobart. The walk continues down to the pristine sands (about 30 minutes). Take provisions for morning tea on the shore, where you may be joined by an inquisitive wallaby. Watch for white-bellied sea-eagles wheeling overhead and the shining curve of a dolphin's back as it breaks the water's surface, then splash in the shallows or plunge in (the beach is safe for swimming, but is unpatrolled), before choosing a secluded picnic spot under the sheaoks. Walkers can return either by retracing their steps over the Hazards, or by crossing the low, marshy isthmus to tranquil Hazards Beach (about 30 minutes), and then taking the coastal track around the base of Mount Mayson, a further two to three hours' walk that involves some rocky patches and can be slippery when wet. The fastest way back is to arrange a pickup by aqua taxi.

**When to Go**  Although Tasmania's east coast has a mild marine climate, all outdoor activities are best between late spring and fall (November–April), when the weather is warmer and the days longer.

**How to Find It**  To reach Freycinet National Park from Hobart, take the Tasman Highway (A3) via Swansea to Coles Bay (86 miles/138 km). Stop at the park visitor center to buy an entry pass and pick up trail maps.

**Planning**  Wear good walking shoes and a hat, and take adequate food and water. Sign in and sign off at the start and end of your walk. The Wineglass Bay/Hazards Beach Circuit is 7 miles (11 km) long. Private companies operate guided tours, aqua taxis, lunch cruises, and charters; reservations are essential.

**Websites**  www.wineglassbay.com, www.freycinetadventures.com.au, freycinetseacruises.com, www.freycinetcoast.com.au, www.sealifecentre.com.au, www.freycinetvineyard.com.au

## Culinary Treats

■ At **Freycinet Marine Farm,** on the aptly named Great Oyster Bay, lobster, mussels, and oysters are specialties.

■ From spring through fall at **Kate's Berry Farm,** just outside Swansea, you can pick up fresh berries, jams, and ice creams.

■ Try **Coombend** and **Freycinet Vineyards,** just up the Tasman Highway between Swansea and Bicheno, for some of Tasmania's best cool-climate wines: Riesling, Sauvignon Blanc, Chardonnay, and Pinot Noir.

■ The **Sea Life Centre** at Bicheno has a seafood restaurant. If your timing is good, you can watch fairy penguins march up the beach as you dine.

Crescent-moon-shaped Wineglass Bay, outlined by a white, sandy beach, is tucked into the line of granite peaks known as the Hazards.

# OCEAN VIEWS

The high points where land and sea meet provide dramatic
vistas of craggy shorelines and pounding oceans.

## ❶ Mirador Escénico, San Carlos, Mexico

This scenic lookout, 4 miles (6 km) from San Carlos, gives a peerless view over the Gulf of California, dramatic Tetakawi—a volcanic hill jutting out of the sea—and the secluded coves of Playa Piedras Pintas. Mirador is also a world-class vantage point for spotting wildlife, including dolphins, pelicans, and whales.

Planning A good way to explore the Gulf of California (Sea of Cortes) is to rent a kayak or fishing boat in San Carlos. The best sailing and fishing weather occurs from November through May. www.visitmexico.com

## ❷ Kalaupapa, Moloka'i, Hawaii

A guided mule train down a near-vertical, 3-mile (5 km) trail in the Kalaupapa National Historical Park is the usual way to reach this hideaway, sheltered by the world's highest sea cliffs, which plunge 3,315 ft (1,010 m) into the Pacific. In the 19th century, the cliffs served as a natural barrier for a leper colony. Although the colony closed in 1969, some residents choose to remain here.

Planning Advance reservations are necessary as a maximum of 18 mules a day are allowed along the trail. The park is closed on Sundays. Visitors need permits. www.muleride.com, www.gohawaii.com

## ❸ Cape Leeuwin, Australia

At Australia's southwesternmost tip, where the Indian and Southern Oceans collide, Cape Leeuwin lighthouse safeguards one of the world's busiest and most treacherous shipping lanes. In summer, you can enjoy views of endless water; in winter, you feel the full force of the oceans crashing against the cape.

Planning Regular tours of the lighthouse precinct run throughout the day. The outlook is most dramatic in winter; whales are visible from June through December. www.westernaustralia.com

## ❹ Sur to Aija, Oman

At the town of Sur, on Oman's northeast coast, you can soak up the view across the creek to Aija, a village of low, pastel-colored dwellings and ornate merchants' houses and surrounded by rocky beaches. Fishermen's dhows bob on the water and several small boatyards still build these traditional sailboats.

Planning Sur is about 90 miles (145 km) along the coast from Muscat. The view is best at high tide. www.omantourism.gov.com

## ❺ Hornbjarg, Iceland

Iceland's most remote region, the West Fjords, is home to one of the world's greatest bird cliffs and its largest razorbill colony. At Iceland's westernmost point, the 1,457-ft-high (444 m) Hornbjarg also entrances its few visitors with misty views over white sand beaches and Snæfellsjökull glacier in the distance.

Planning  Boats to Hornbjarg sail from Isafjord and the northernmost settlements of the Strandir District. www.nat.is, www.visiticeland.com

## ❻ St. John's Head, Hoy, Orkneys, Scotland

Near the northern tip of the island of Hoy, St. John's Head is Britain's highest vertical sea cliff. Thanks to the fierce swell and tide, just reaching its base is a serious undertaking. For less courageous types, the best viewpoint is from the Scrabster-to-Stromness ferry, which leaves up to three times daily.

Planning The best time to view the cliff is on a summer evening when sunset turns it an ardent red. The ferry trip also provides views of the Old Man of Hoy, a 450-ft-high (137 m) seastack. www.hoyorkney.com

## ❼ Son Marroig, Mallorca, Spain

Tired of Viennese court life and enamored of the scenery around Son Marroig, on Mallorca's north coast, Austria's Archduke Ludwig Salvatore (1847–1915) bought a property here with sweeping vistas over the Na Foradada ("pierced rock") peninsula, which has a gaping 59-ft (18 m) hole at its center.

Planning For the best views of the peninsula, ask at the museum for permission to walk the 2-mile-long (3 km) path toward Na Foradada. www.illesbalears.es, www.dimf.com

## ❽ Sagres Bay, Portugal

For a whiff of historical romance and swashbuckling adventure, few outlooks outclass the one at Sagres, mainland Europe's most southwesterly community. In the 15th century, Prince Henry the Navigator came here to found his School of Navigation to train sailors and cartographers, in order to fulfill his quest to expand the known world's frontiers and open a sea route to India.

Planning The best way to explore Sagres Bay and Cape St. Vincent is by car or on foot, as there is no public transportation. www.sagres.net

## ❾ Dun Aengus, Aran Islands, Ireland

One of Europe's most splendid cliff forts, consisting of stone walls built in three semicircles, Dun Aengus sits atop an unclimbable sea cliff rising 328 ft (100 m) out of the ocean. The innermost court affords superb views over the island of Inishmore and the distant Connemara coast.

Planning Reachable by ferry from Doolin, County Clare, and Rossaveal, County Galway, Aran's main settlement is Kilronan. www.aranisland.info

## ❿ Coast Road, Western Sahara

One of the Paris–Dakar Rally's remotest legs, this artery cleaves seemingly endless sands and a rocky Atlantic coast. While the terrain initially appears monotonous, the tarmac road is far from featureless, passing glassy lagoons and palm-fringed oases.

Planning To avoid unexploded mines, drive off-road only with a local guide. Although camel-borne nomads outnumber vacationers, Western Sahara draws intrepid deep-sea anglers, and kite- and sand-surfers. www.mbendi.com, www.africatravelling.net

Opposite: The cliffs above Tonel Beach at Sagres provide dramatic views of the Atlantic Ocean and the western Algarve coast. The beach is popular with surfers.

# MOUNT JOHN

This mountain setting in the heart of South Island provides
spectacular views of Lake Tekapo and the Southern Alps.

It takes little more than an hour for a fit walker to climb the steep trail from the western shore of Lake Tekapo (meaning "place to sleep under the stars") through stands of larch trees to the golden tussock grasslands at the summit of Mount John, 3,382 feet (1,031 meters) above sea level. As you approach the summit, watch for the walkway that encircles the top of this ice-carved, dome-shaped mountain. The path passes the unmistakable shapes of the University of Canterbury's astronomical telescopes and leads to the modern, glass-sided Astro Café. From here the 360-degree view is breathtaking. Directly below are the vivid turquoise waters of Lake Tekapo, its intense color due to tiny rock particles in the glacial waters that feed it. In the distance you can see the Southern Alps, including a snowcapped Aoraki (Mount Cook), at 12,316 feet (3,754 meters) the highest point in New Zealand, and Mount Sefton just 1,640 feet (500 meters) lower. The summit walkway is a leisurely 45-minute stroll among clumps of porcupine shrubs, Muehlenbeckia (maidenhair), the thorny matagouri (wild Irishman), and two species of rare brooms. The kea—New Zealand's mischievous parrot—and the New Zealand falcon, or *kareareas,* can sometimes be spotted along with introduced birds, such as the Himalayan chuckor.

**When to Go** Year-round. The Astro Café is open from 10 a.m. to 5 p.m. in winter and from 9 a.m. to 6 p.m. in summer.

**How to Find It** Mount John is in the middle of New Zealand's South Island, a three-hour drive from Christchurch. The trail to the summit begins by the skating rink on Lakeside Drive in Tekapo village. Or you can dispense with the climb and drive to the summit.

**Planning** The round-trip hike from the lakeside to the top and back takes about three hours. Walking shoes or light hiking shoes are suitable, but the weather can be changeable, so a warm jacket or sweater is advisable (even on sunny days, when the wind can still be chilly). Day and night tours of the observatory are available.

**Websites** www.tekapotourism.co.nz/mt_john, www.earthandsky.co.nz (for observatory tours)

## Stargazing

On moonless nights, Mount John is one of the darkest places in New Zealand. The stability and transparency of the Earth's atmosphere in this area, together with the absence of intrusive city-light pollution, make the summit an ideal spot for observing the night sky, as a spectacular number of stars can be seen with the naked eye. To maintain the darkness, all lights are banned around the observatory, including car headlights, flashlights, and mobile phones. Stargazing tours are run for the public, during which the observatory's astronomers use laser pointers to identify the constellations.

Lake Tekapo at the foot of Mount John is famous for its turquoise color. The Church of the Good Shepherd on the lakeshore was built in memory of the area's pioneers.

THE WORLD AT YOUR FEET

LAST WILDERNESSES   ISLAND GETAWAYS   THE ROAD LESS TRAVELED   SECRET HISTORY   SPIRITUAL HAVENS   HIDDEN TREASURES   UNDISCOVERED VILLAGES   CITY SECRETS

A light sprinkling of snow turns the mountain scenery around Lu Shan into a winter wonderland.

CHINA

# GULING

Set up as a Chinese version of an Indian hill station,
Guling looks down from Lu Shan to the Yangtze River.

Reputedly the haunt of painters, poets, calligraphers, and mystics at least as far back as the fourth century, and rather less romantically of political enemies Chiang Kai-shek and Mao Zedong in the 20th century, Lu Shan (Mount Lu) offers unrivaled panoramas along the broad Yangtze River's south bank, about 455 miles (732 kilometers) upstream from Shanghai. The mountain owes its fame to an English missionary turned property speculator, who from 1895 created a high-altitude summer retreat for Westerners roasting in their coastal trading enclaves during China's sweaty summers. He artfully named the town Kuling. So the delights of a visit to Lu Shan include not only the pine-shaded paths that wind around the cluster of cloud-wrapped peaks and chairlift rides to the highest points, with views northward to the river, east to the vast Poyang Lake, and south across Jiangxi Province, but also the bizarre discovery of a high-altitude piece of England's Surrey, now known as Guling, all gable-ended, half-timbered bungalows and stockbroker-belt mansions nestling among tennis courts, churches, and China's first ever botanical garden.

**When to Go**  In summer, as the foreign residents did, to appreciate the benefits of Lu Shan's coolness, although from June through September, particularly on weekends, Guling hotels charge sums way beyond what they are worth: midweek is best. There's very little open in Guling from mid-October through early May, but in winter the mountain scenery recalls the most romantic classical Chinese painting.

**How to Find It**  One-day bus tours pick up at hotels all over Jiujiang city (below Lu Shan on the Yangtze), but for those who want to organize their own itineraries there are regular public buses to Guling. Maps of the area's walking routes are available in Guling, as are taxis for drives around the main loop of mountaintop road.

**Planning**  From mid-afternoon until mid-morning, the mountaintop is very quiet, and for those who want to overnight there's an assortment of modest places to stay, some built during the resort's heyday. Guling has numerous simple restaurants, but if you are making this a day-trip, take a picnic.

**Website**  www.china-lushan.com/english

### An Author's Childhood

Mervyn Peake, author of the 20th-century Gothic masterpiece *Gormenghast* trilogy, was born in Kuling in 1911. Childhood summers spent there—and particularly the steep, narrow, winding, and precipitous path up the mountain, along which he would be carried each summer in a sedan chair—left a lasting impression. In his first published piece of writing, he described the certain death that one misstep by a bearer would have brought him. Now there is a proper road, but even that has hundreds of sharp bends taken rather wildly by Chinese drivers, making a journey up Lu Shan little less dramatic today.

ASIA

Plumes of smoke rising from the heart of shattered Mount Bromo, on the left, do not deter the volcano's visitors.

INDONESIA

# MOUNT BROMO

Watch the sun rise over an unearthly landscape of sand, rock, and smoking peaks from the rim of one of Java's active volcanoes.

The paddy fields and villages of eastern Java are overlooked by the chain of volcanoes that extends along the length of this verdant island. Gunung, or Mount, Bromo is a small part of the ancient Tengger volcano, its precipitous-sided cone situated within the 6-mile-wide (10 kilometer) Tengger caldera. The road winds up from the lowlands over the rim of the caldera, then descends to the sand-covered caldera floor. The best time to make the journey to Mount Bromo is in the early hours of the morning, reaching the narrow rim of Bromo's crater—just a few feet wide in places—as the approaching sunrise reveals the surreal landscape all around in ever increasing detail: The broad, sandy plain ribboned with strands of mist, from which emerges a seemingly misplaced Hindu temple; the remarkable fluted ridges and pluglike form of neighboring Mount Batur; and, in the distance, the higher, greener slopes of volcanic Mount Semeru, Java's highest peak, complete with a curl of white smoke rising from the summit. Then look down into the cauldron of fire and brimstone far below. The vent at the heart of the crater usually emits only smoke and an evil, sulfurous stench, but every so often it bursts into flame, sending a thrilling blast of heat and steam spurting out from the subterranean maelstrom.

**When to Go**  The dry season runs from May through September and is generally the best time to visit.

**How to Find It**  The main access point is the small village of Cemoro Lawang, close to the northeast edge of the Tengger caldera. From here it is about 2 miles (3 km) to Mount Bromo. To reach the rim in time for sunrise, it is best to stay in Cemoro Lawang the night before. From here, you can walk or hire a horse or jeep to cross the caldera floor to the steps that lead up the side of the volcano.

**Planning**  If you prefer a guided tour, they leave from the town of Probolinggo on Java's north coast, 1.5 hours away. Most tours stop for sunrise at Penanjakan, a viewpoint on the edge of the Tengger crater, before continuing to Bromo

**Websites**  www.eastjava.com, www.petra.ac.id/eastjava, discover-indo.tierranet.com/volcano01.htm

## Dawn Horseback Ride

A wonderful way to experience the magical landscape of the Tengger caldera is to cross the sand sea to the edge of Bromo on horseback. If you arrive before dawn, you'll see the fires of the horsemen in the sand sea below the rim of the Tengger crater as they wait for customers. As the darkness lifts, you can wend your way with other riders across the dusty landscape and through the lava ripples, to the smoking cone to witness the sunrise. Within an hour it is likely that all tourists will be gone and you and your companions will have the entire landscape to yourselves.

THE WORLD AT YOUR FEET

LAST WILDERNESSES    ISLAND GETAWAYS    THE ROAD LESS TRAVELED    SECRET HISTORY    SPIRITUAL HAVENS    HIDDEN TREASURES    UNDISCOVERED VILLAGES    CITY SECRETS

INDIA

# Ranikhet Hill

Twisting mountain roads lead to this northern Indian hilltop resort surrounded by Himalayan peaks and verdant meadows and forests.

Perched 5,970 feet (1,820 meters) above sea level, on a ridge in the foothills of the western Himalaya, Ranikhet has stupendous views across the lower hills to the snowy peaks of the main Himalaya some 60 miles (97 kilometers) away to the northeast, with the twin summits of Nanda Devi (at 25,643 feet/7,816 meters, India's second highest mountain) clearly visible. Surrounding the town are fragrant wildflower meadows that are edged by dark pine, oak, and rhododendron forests, and enough well-maintained trails to occupy the most avid hiker. In 1869, the British army purchased land from local villagers at Ranikhet in order to set up a hill station where soldiers could escape the summer heat on the plains. And today, the genteel charm of the British colonial buildings still shines through. The town is now the home of the Indian Army's Kumaon Regiment, whose presence accentuates the air of tradition and heritage. Houses extend erratically along the ridge either side of the lively bazaar area, but just a short stroll along Mall Road takes you into areas of parkland and meadows with trees and flowers in abundance. Unlike the far larger former hill stations of Shimla or Dalhousie, Ranikhet lies blissfully undiscovered in its patch of Eden, engaging the visitor with an out-of-the-way quietness.

**When to Go**  From late February through late June and from early October through late November. The Nanda Devi Mela, an animated religious festival, is held in the region each September.

**How to Find It**  Ranikhet owes its peace and quiet to its isolation: It's a five-hour bus ride from Ramnagar, the nearest railhead and main access point for Corbett National Park; Ramnagar is reached by overnight train from Delhi. Buses run north from Nainital in two to three hours, Delhi in 12 hours.

**Planning**  Have warm clothes with you, even in summer. Places to stay, from hotels to private cottages, are available to suit all budgets. Keen golfers can enjoy one of the world's most scenic courses in the world just 4 miles (6 km) away at Upat.

**Websites**  www.hillresortsinindia.com, www.hill-stations-india.com, www.trekking-in-himalayas.com

ASIA

### Wildlife Safari

About a three-hour drive to the southwest of Ranikhet is **Corbett National Park.**

■ With a tiger population in excess of 130 individuals, this is one of India's prime tiger-spotting reserves. Your best chances of seeing a tiger are from April through June, although it is very hot then.

■ You also have a good chance of seeing elephants, impressively large monitor lizards, sloth bears, various species of monkey, and river crocodiles.

■ The scenery is spellbinding, particularly when observed on an elephant-back safari.

Several Himalayan peaks are visible from Ranikhet, which is perched on a ridge in the forested Kumaon hills.

THE WORLD AT YOUR FEET

LAST WILDERNESSES    ISLAND GETAWAYS    THE ROAD LESS TRAVELED    SECRET HISTORY    SPIRITUAL HAVENS    HIDDEN TREASURES    UNDISCOVERED VILLAGES    CITY SECRETS

INDIA

# Himalayan Pelling

Enjoy the mountain life and far-ranging views
in this small, picturesque town high in the Himalaya.

All it takes is a mountain with the august name of Khangchendzonga, with its highest peak reaching 28,208 feet (8,598 meters) above sea level, to bring people flocking to the tiny town of Pelling in the teensy northeast Indian state of Sikkim. The world's third highest mountain looms above the horizon, and no other vantage point affords such an exalted view. Pelling is the best spot from which to see Khangchendzonga, short of strapping on walking boots for a breathless trek. The sight is well worth the long ride by jeep to reach this little hamlet, which is not much more than a few switchback streets of shops and hotels among hills clothed in forest. The former Himalayan kingdom of Sikkim exudes an air of calm. Ancient ways persist in the hilltop Buddhist monasteries of Pemayangtse and Sanga Choeling (meaning the "island of esoteric teaching"), which stand like guards over Pelling. You can hike the rocky 2.5-mile (4 kilometer) path to Sanga Choeling, the state's second oldest monastery, built in 1697, along a path lined with a parade of prayer flags rippling in the wind. Or save your lungs (Pelling lies at an altitude of 6,200 feet/1,890 meters), and instead sit beside a snug fire in the lobby of the Elgin Mount Pandim Hotel, sipping a cup of tea and gazing at the view through a glass wall—and seeing the mountain smile back at you.

**When to Go**  Pelling is accessible year-round, but temperatures can drop to single digits in the heart of winter and most buildings have no central heating (though some hotels offer hot water bottles and space heaters). September through November and April through May are the best seasons for Sikkim.

**How to Find it**  Until the airport opens in 2011, travelers must reach Sikkim by road. Most tourists come by jeep from Darjeeling (allow an afternoon's drive along mountain roads) or Shiliguri, a transport hub several hours south in West Bengal. Prices are negotiable and arranged on an individual basis, but should be about $40-$50 for private transport from Darjeeling, $50-$60 from Siliguri.

**Planning**  A free special permit is required to visit Sikkim. It can be obtained through Indian Embassies abroad or through Foreigners' Regional Registration Offices in Kolkata, Mumbai, and Darjeeling. If you are arranging the permit in India, expect a day's worth of office visits and paper signings.

**Websites** www.elginhotels.com, www.sikkiminfo.net, sikkim.gov.in, www.east-himalaya.com

**My Secret Journey**

*Frigid Christmas Eve air sweeps through Pelling, where only a few buildings have central heating. It's the perfect time for a bonfire, blazing hot and high on the lawn of the **Elgin Mount Pandim Hotel.** A guard stands ready to chop more wood with his Gurkha knife. Travelers gather, singing carols and savoring complimentary cherry brandy served in crystal cordials that reflect the flickering flames. The evening progresses through Jingle Bells and old Bengali love songs. At 10 p.m., the crowd shifts inside to a dining room resplendent with chicken curry, Kerala fish, Kashmiri dum aloo, palak paneer, dal fry, Indian pickle, Jeera rice, and British-style Christmas crackers for a little bang. A decorated tree blinks near the door, and the hotel fills with the camaraderie of celebration. The air has lost its chill.*
**Karen J. Coates**
**Travel writer**

Opposite: Prayer flags line the path to the Sanga Choeling monastery. Above: Stupas on the monastery grounds

# VIEW OF THE ALPS

Test your head for heights among the mountain
peaks that surround the tiny village of Mürren.

EUROPE

Reached only by a cable car that breaches a vertical, gray cliff face or by a little mountain train from Grütschalp, the small, secluded farming village of Mürren is perched on a grassy shelf high above the Lauterbrunnen Valley in the Bernese Oberland area of Switzerland. In summer, hikers equipped with knapsacks and walking sticks pass through the quiet, car-free village and replenish their water bottles from mountain springs trickling into hollowed-log troughs. Throughout the village, traditional Alpine chalets are splashed with crimson geraniums, while their small glass windowpanes reflect the sheer walls of the forbidding trio of the Jungfrau, Eiger, and Mönch mountains across the valley. The sound of cowbells drifts through the village from the meadows above, each bell's tone recognizable by its herder. From the first snowfall of winter, walkers are replaced by skiers as the village transforms into an effervescent ski resort. Home to the first Alpine Skiing World Championships, held in 1931, the ski slopes above Mürren are the highest in the Bernese Oberland. Year-round, visitors tarry along the main walkway to the Restaurant Stäger Stübli, which serves hearty Swiss-German dishes of *schweinsbratwurst* (pork sausage) and *rösti* (grated potato) to sustain summer ramblers and fuel winter skiers.

**When to Go**  Summer hiking is best from June through October; winter skiing from December through April.

**How to Find It**  There are three ways to reach Mürren from the Lauterbrunnen Valley: by cable car from the village of Lauterbrunnen to Grütschalp (this route is recommended for those who are not comfortable with heights as, if you stand facing the hillside, you cannot see the drop below), then funicular to Mürren; by cable car from the village of Stechelberg, via Gimmelwald; or by hiking up from the valley floor (for the very fit), which takes about three to four hours.

**Planning**  If hiking, always make sure you are sufficiently equipped as mists and cloud can come down quickly and unexpectedly. There are 33 miles (53 km) of prepared ski runs around Mürren for all levels of skiers. Take notice of warnings for off-piste dangers and crevasses.

**Websites**  www.wengen-muerren.ch, www.schilthorn.ch, www.jungfraubahn.ch

## World of Snow and Ice

Take the cable car from Mürren via Birg to the summit of the **Schilthorn** mountain, at a height of 9,744 ft (2,970 m), to see ranks of icy peaks disappearing into the distance: the Jungfrau, Mönch, and Eiger; to the west, the Bernese Alps and Jura Mountains, and beyond them the Vosges in France. Sometimes it is possible to pick out Mont Blanc on the French–Italian border.

Perched on the Schilthorn's rocky summit is the revolving **Piz Gloria Restaurant,** where you can gaze down at the death-defying ski run that was featured in the opening sequence of the James Bond movie *On Her Majesty's Secret Service* as you relax over lunch.

The Piz Gloria Restaurant on the summit of the Schilthorn provides a ringside seat for the continuous drama being played out between weather and mountains.

The cliffs have been hollowed out so deeply that the houses of Bonifacio's old town look set to topple into the sea.

THE WORLD AT YOUR FEET

LAST WILDERNESSES  ISLAND GETAWAYS  THE ROAD LESS TRAVELED  SECRET HISTORY  SPIRITUAL HAVENS  HIDDEN TREASURES  UNDISCOVERED VILLAGES  CITY SECRETS

FRANCE

# BONIFACIO'S VISTAS

Perched on the southernmost cliffs of Corsica, the town overlooks the Straits of Bonifacio that separate this island from Sardinia.

From a boat...that is the best way to experience the extraordinary setting of Bonifacio. The medieval part of the town towers intrepidly above limestone cliffs that have been sculpted by wind and waves into a ruffled, extravagantly draped curtain that drops into the indigo sea. Yet as you walk up from the harbor and through the old town gates, any impression of precariousness disappears. Since the ninth century, Pisa, Genoa, Aragon, and France have at times fought over Corsica and molded Bonifacio's imposing character through the construction of massive stone fortifications, stoic churches, and a tightly knit web of narrow streets. Lookouts along the old town walls, as well as many of the old buildings, provide some of the best views of the Mediterranean. Below is the Grain de Sable (Grain of Sand), a massive lump of limestone that fell from the cliffs and juts out of the sea just off the Sutta Rocca Beach. A cliff walk runs from the old town to the Pertusato lighthouse (a 2.5-hour round-trip), providing a series of views toward Sardinia and back along the cliffs toward Bonifacio.

**When to Go**  Year-round, although the winter months are less recommended. The only month when the town gets busy with visitors is August, so avoid it if you prefer solitude.

**How to Find It**  The walk up to the old town starts at the harbor, where there is a parking lot and local bus stops. Cliff walks start at the top of the old town.

**Planning**  A single day is enough to explore Bonifacio. There are restaurants to suit all pockets in the old town and around the harbor.

**Websites**  www.bonifaciocorsica.net, www.bonifacio.fr, www.corsicatravelguide.com, www.visit-bonifacio.com

## Carved Coastline

Corsica offers another breathtaking spectacle for sailing fans and intrepid drivers who can handle narrow, twisty roads carved into frighteningly steep mountainsides.

■ On the western coastline, about 125 miles (200 km) north of Bonifacio, a group of extraordinary red granite formations known as **Les Calanches** emerges from the sea and rises to a height of 1,312 ft (400 m). Dog's Head, The Bear, and The Tortoise are the most photogenic. The crowning moment is to watch Les Calanches during sunset— seen from land or sea, the vista inspires awe.

■ Just below the copper-red cliffs of Les Calanches, another of Corsica's secrets lies tucked away. **Ficaiola** is one of the island's most beautiful beaches. In the morning, this tiny bay of white pebbles and intensely azure waters is drenched in sunlight; in the afternoon, as the sun descends behind Les Calanches, the bay is bathed in a shade of purple. The beach is accessible by foot, and though the path is a little tortuous, Ficaiola is worth the effort.

EUROPE

# CITY HIGH SPOTS

Cathedrals, columns, and observatories are among the buildings
that provide bird's-eye views of some of the world's greatest cities.

### ❶ Willis Tower, Chicago, Illinois

Short of performing a high-wire act, you will find no better
form of vertigo-aversion therapy than a visit to the glass viewing
platforms jutting out of the Willis Tower (formerly called the
Sears Tower) 1,353 ft (412 m) above ground. On clear days you
can see four states—Illinois, Indiana, Michigan, and Wisconsin.

Planning The tower is in the center of Chicago's financial district on
South Wacker Drive. www.willistower.com, www.choosechicago.com

### ❷ Camera Obscura, Havana, Cuba

Havana's Old Square is a fine place to admire the wonders of
Spanish colonial architecture as well as the Cuban style that
evolved in the 18th century. On the roof of the Casa de los
Condes de Jaruco, in the southeast corner of the square, is a
camera obscura. Inside the darkened room, panoramic views
of the city are projected onto the walls.

Planning The mansion is a perfect model of late-colonial architecture.
www.oldhavanaweb.com, www.gocuba.ca

### ❸ Cathedral of Christ the Savior, Moscow, Russia

The world's tallest Orthodox church is a reconstruction of the
cathedral that was founded to thank God for Russia's victory
over Napoleon in 1812 and subsequently destroyed in 1931 under
Stalin. Visitors can climb to an observation platform at the top
of the building for views across central Moscow.

Planning Visitors must take an organized tour to see the cathedral.
Check out the museum underneath the cathedral tracing its history.
The nearest metro station is Kropotkinskaya. www.moscow.info

### ❹ Bundestag dome, Berlin, Germany

Referred to by many people as the Reichstag after Germany's
first parliament building, the Bundestag was constructed after
German reunification. Peering down on the politicians in the
debating chamber below, the people remind them who is in
charge. With its marvelous panorama, the cupola is also the
perfect place from which to admire the city.

Planning To avoid the crowds, arrive shortly before the first entry
at 8 a.m. or the last at 10 p.m. or reserve a table at the rooftop
restaurant. www.bundestag.de, www.visitberlin.de

### ❺ Roof of St. Peter's Basilica, Vatican City

For a peek into the Vatican's private quarters, the roof of the
basilica's Michelangelo-designed dome and the lantern atop it
give those up for scaling 320 steps a pope's-eye view over the Holy
See and the city of Rome beyond.

Planning While an elevator leads to the gallery at the cupola's base, the
roof and lantern are accessible only by steps. You can skip Vatican lines
by reserving tickets online or taking a guided tour. www.vaticanstate.va

### ❻ Blackford Hill, Edinburgh, Scotland

The lookout at the Royal Observatory on top of Blackford Hill
has some of Edinburgh's headiest and greenest views, taking in
the suburb of Blackford, the King's Buildings Campus of the
University of Edinburgh, the Braid Hills and Hermitage of Braid,
and the Pentlands Hills—not to mention Edinburgh Castle, the
Royal Mile, St. Giles's Cathedral, and Holyrood Palace.

Planning Blackford Hill is 2 miles (3 km) south of the city center.
Several paths snake up to the observatory. www.edinburgh.org

### ❼ Monument, London, England

To commemorate the Great Fire of London (1666) and enable
posterity to survey his rebuilding of more than 50 churches,
architect Sir Christopher Wren helped design a colossal Doric
column with a 360-degree viewing platform. Planning restrictions
have protected vistas of his masterpiece, St. Paul's Cathedral, and
the 311-step climb well repays those willing to invest the energy.

Planning The Monument is a 15-minute walk east from St. Paul's. There
is no elevator, but a ground-level live video feed from the platform
enlightens those unable to tackle the stairs. www.themonument.info

### ❽ Cacilhas, Lisbon, Portugal

While Lisbon offers many celebrated vantage points, some of the
most dashing views of the city are from the other side of the Tagus
River, from Alameda's river port of Cacilhas. For the most scenic
approach, take the ferry from Cais do Sodré, which is also the best
way to admire the 4,740-ft (1,445 m) Ponte 25 de Abril, Portugal's
audacious retort to San Francisco's Golden Gate Bridge.

Planning Allow time to linger in Cacilhas, admiring the river views at
one of its fine seafood restaurants. www.golisbon.com

### ❾ Citadel, Cairo, Egypt

Cairo's fort was originally a 9th-century governor's pavilion built
for its clear vistas and fresh breezes, and it provides intoxicating
views of medieval monuments and the whole city. On a very
clear day, the outlook stretches to the pyramids at Giza.

Planning Two other Cairene viewpoints are the Cairo Tower on Gezira
Island and the minaret of the Ibn Tulun Mosque near the citadel.
www.egypt.travel

### ❿ Taj Talha Hotel, Sanaa, Yemen

The sixth-story café at this 18th-century former palace in Sanaa's
old town provides some of Arabia's finest visual frankincense.
Sanaa is one of the world's longest continuously inhabited
ancient cities, with mud-brick and stone skyscrapers vividly
adorned with geometrical stucco.

Planning If you're staying and don't mind the climb, look for a room on
an upper floor for the best panorama. www.taj-talha-hotel.com.ye

Opposite: The glass dome designed by architect Norman Foster for Berlin's Bundestag provides all-round city views.

In Las Médulas, Roman gold-mining techniques ate away the earth, leaving a scarred landscape of jagged peaks and ridges.

SPAIN

# Las Médulas

Once the Roman Empire's foremost gold mine,
this eerie, craggy landscape glows in the sun.

The remote mountain village of Las Médulas in northwestern Spain's El Bierzo region is ringed by a dramatic jumble of orange-red escarpments, tunnels, and peaks carved about 2,000 years ago by Roman slaves in search of gold. These ancient industrial waste-terrain sculptures are centered on a circular *castro,* or village, built by native Asturs during the Bronze Age. A fiercely independent Iberian tribe, the Asturs and the neighboring Cántabros were among the last inhabitants of the Iberian Peninsula to fall to the Romans in 25 B.C. Over two and a half centuries, the site became the Roman Empire's largest gold mine in its far-flung colony of Hispania Ulterior. By the third century A.D, for reasons still unknown, the Romans had abandoned the mines, leaving a bizarre moonscape of rust-colored cliffs and pinnacles that has endured largely unchanged for the last two millennia. The best overall view of the area is from the lookout point in the village of Orellán (Mirador de Orellán), a steep, 2,625-foot (800 meter) climb through a chestnut forest.

**When to Go** June or September for best temperatures.

**How to Find It** Las Médulas is 12.5 miles (20 km) southwest of Ponferrada in León's easternmost district of El Bierzo. From Ponferrada, take the N-VI west. At La Barrosa turn south on the N-536. At Carucedo turn off following signs for Las Médulas. Park at the edge of Las Médulas and start at the Visitor Reception Center.

**Planning** The Visitor Reception Center at the far end of the village of Las Médulas (437 yd/400 m from the parking area) offers a guided tour of Las Médulas. The Aula Arqueológica (Archaeological Information Center) at the entrance to the village explains the mining operation and provides maps for hikes of varying lengths through a hauntingly beautiful landscape. Bring good hiking boots and warm clothing.

**Website** www.fundacionlasmedulas.org

## Water Power

Roman army engineers remodeled the landscape around Las Médulas with seven aqueducts and highly advanced hydraulic mining techniques. The mining system, which was described by Roman chronicler Pliny the Elder as *ruina montium* (mountain ruin), used water power to blast away rocks and earth. Roads, dams, canals, locks, and sluices were constructed in order to store water in giant reservoirs and transport it to the mines via canals. Water pressure was created by gravity and released by opening the sluices at the lower end of the system to allow the rushing flow to wash dirt, rock, and gold deposits out to panning areas below.

During more than 250 years, the Romans removed millions of tons of topsoil here and amassed about 1,800 tons/1,830 tonnes (5 million Roman pounds) of gold.

EUROPE

EGYPT

# OLD CATARACT HOTEL

Enjoy old-world luxury and a view of one
of the world's most romantic rivers.

It is said that the view of the Nile from the terrace of the Old Cataract Hotel in Aswan, southern Egypt, provided Agatha Christie with part of the inspiration for one of her most famous novels, *Death on the Nile*. The truth of that is lost in literary history, but two facts are indisputable: The British crime writer most definitely lounged on this terrace, and the view remains one of the most iconic in Africa. Perched on rocky bluffs above the eastern bank of the Nile, near the first of six cataracts (stretches of rocky shallows) between Aswan and Khartoum in Sudan, the hotel (now owned by Sofitel) provides a sweeping panorama of river and desert that instantly defines Egypt's exotic allure. Nowadays, the old hotel, with its Moorish arches and ginger-colored facade, seems romantically quaint, but the view from the terrace remains essentially unchanged since the hotel opened in 1899—white-sailed feluccas flit up and down the blue water, *fellaheen* (peasants) go about their chores on Elephantine Island in the middle of the river, and the domed Mausoleum of Mohammed Shah Aga Khan (died 1957) rises on the river's western bank, while the vast Western Desert stretches beyond. Whether you take your brew in the English style or in the Egyptian way (with an inch of sugar in the bottom of the cup), tea on the terrace of the Old Cataract Hotel is certain to stir your imagination.

**When to Go** Aswan is best avoided in summer, when daytime temperatures often soar into triple digits; winters along the Upper Nile are sunny, mild, and nearly perfect for exploring Aswan and its environs by foot or boat.

**How to Find It** The Old Cataract Hotel is at the southern end of the town. Hotel guests have unlimited free access to the terrace and adjacent bar; nonresidents must pay a cover charge to gain access.

**Planning** Aswan is included on most Nile cruises, and can also be reached by train from Cairo. It is the jumping off point for visits to Abu Simbel on Lake Nasser, the Aswan dams, and the Temple of Philae.

**Websites** www.sofitel.com, www.all-about-egypt.com, www.aswan-art.gov.eg/english/index.php

### Agatha Christie in Egypt

Christie's first visit to Egypt was in the 1920s. While there, she visited the Cairo Museum and stayed at the Gezira Palace hotel (now the Cairo Marriott). Her interest in archaeology and ancient Egypt was sparked by trips to Egypt and Syria with her archaeologist husband Max Mallowan in the 1930s. They took a cruise up the Nile, visiting the main sites and staying at the Winter Palace in Luxor, as well as at the Old Cataract Hotel. In *Death on the Nile*, the characters take a cruise upriver from Aswan, through the First Cataract and into Upper Egypt, a journey that has not been possible since the building of the Aswan Dam.

The terrace of the Old Cataract Hotel provides a comfortable perch from which to watch as feluccas glide across the Nile.

# TEA AND COFFEE SHOPS WITH VIEWS

Location, location, location—these places where you can grab
a bite to eat or sip a soothing drink have it in abundance.

### ❶ The Yurt, Solitude Mountain Resort, Utah

Wintertime diners don snowshoes or cross-country skis and follow a guide for 0.75 mile (1.2 km) through snowclad conifers to a mountaintop yurt. Even summertime access is by group hike only. The eclectic international menu changes nightly according to what's in season.

Planning A five-course, fixed-price dinner is served daily, except Mondays and holidays, during the skiing season. Four-course dinners are served from mid-June through September. www.skisolitude.com

### ❷ Café Gourmet Mirador, Sucre, Bolivia

The leisurely service at this mountaintop garden terrace in Plaza Anzures, high above Sucre, allows patrons plenty of time to linger over a frappuccino. Few places compete as a vantage point to study Spanish colonial architecture at its finest—not to mention the adjoining botanical gardens.

Planning The café adjoins the Mirador de Recoleta, a 10-minute walk from Sucre's main square. www.boliviacontact.com

### ❸ Belvédère, Moorea, French Polynesia

Set in the heart of one of the South Pacific's most ravishing islands, this snack bar in a parking lot atop a volcanic remnant overlooks Opunohu Bay to the left, Cook's Bay to the right, and Mount Rotui between them. The journey there is half the point: The road pierces a valley of teak, mahogany, acacia, and mango forests and taro and pineapple plantations.

Planning The partially unpaved road from Cook's Bay is scarily steep, narrow, and winding. The other route, from Opunohu Bay, is easier. www.tahiti-tourisme.com

### ❹ Hotel Mountain Top, Manali, India

Parts of India remain serenely uncrowded. At Manali's summit, this hotel terrace peers over deodar-covered mountains on one side, snowclad peaks on another, and an emerald-green valley below full of musk-apple, pear, and cherry orchards.

Planning Manali has no railroad station. The nearest airport is at Bhuntar, 31 miles (50 km) away. www.mountaintophotel.com, www.himachaltourism.gov.in

### ❺ Pierre Loti Hotel, Istanbul, Turkey

This boutique hotel occupies a converted house in an enviable central Sultanahmet location midway between Hagia Sophia and the Grand Bazaar. Its rooftop bar proffers peerless prospects of the Blue Mosque, the Golden Horn, the Bosporus, the Marmara Sea—and two continents in one city.

Planning Why not kill two turkeys with one stone by also sampling the hotel's hammam (steam bath). www.pierrelotihotel.com, www.tourismturkey.org

### ❻ Solliden, Djurgården Island, Stockholm, Sweden

Comprising a restaurant, café, and tavern, Solliden is the main dining establishment of Skansen, the world's oldest open-air museum. Solliden also promises fine views over Djurgården Island and most of southern Stockholm, including the harbor. Expect classic Swedish specialties, such as gravlax (salmon cured with salt and dill) served with creamed potatoes.

Planning Solliden Matsal (Restaurant) is perfect for smorgasbord. Skansen hosts traditional celebrations on Swedish national holidays and singalong concerts on Tuesday evenings in summer. www.skansen.se

### ❼ M32, Museum der Moderne, Salzburg, Austria

Run by award-winning chef Sepp Schellhorn, the Museum of Modern Art's bar-restaurant delivers top-notch Austrian food and a magnificent baroque viewing platform over Salzburg's old town. In the unlikely event that the view grates, admire the intrepid light installation of 500 deer antlers.

Planning The restaurant is closed on Mondays. www.m32.at, www.museumdermoderne.at, www.salzburg.info

### ❽ Sonnenterrasse, Hotel Pilatus-Kulm, Switzerland

Switzerland doesn't lack for Alpine views magnificent enough to unleash your inner yodeler, but few outclass this spacious sun terrace in a 19th-century hotel 6,996 ft (2,132 m) above sea level. As you mainline fresh air and the heady view of 73 peaks, enjoy draft beer brewed with mineral water from the mountains.

Planning From early May through late November, the world's steepest cog-railway links Alpnachstad town with Pilatus-Kulm. An all-year cableway operates from Kriens, a Lucerne suburb. www.pilatus.com

### ❾ Joan Miró Foundation, Barcelona, Spain

Miró's friend Josep Lluís Sert built the museum as the world's largest showcase of the artist's sculptures and paintings. As if you need extra reasons to visit, its cozy garden terrace provides panoramic views of one of Spain's most eye-catching cities.

Planning The café is small and often full: Visit off-peak if possible. www.fundaciomiro-bcn.org, www.barcelonaturisme.com

### ❿ Café Hafa, Tangier, Morocco

Café Hafa commands a steep cliff overlooking the Mediterranean–Atlantic junction at Tangier Bay, with views toward the Rock of Gibraltar. As you sip mint tea and play backgammon, you join illustrious company: The shaded garden terrace has been a favorite of Jack Kerouac, Tennessee Williams, and the Rolling Stones.

Planning Arrive early if you want a seat to watch the sunset. www.visitmorocco.com

Opposite: The view from Mount Pilatus, in Switzerland, takes in several lakes and a vast array of mountain peaks.

The Merenid sultans, who once ruled much of North Africa, were buried in tombs perched high over their capital.

MOROCCO

# Fez from the Merenid Tombs

Climb to this hilltop at sunset for a magical view of Fez from the burial place of the city's ancient rulers.

On a hill to the north of Fez, and watched over by the city's Bab el Guissa (North Gate), the tombs of the Merenid sultans glow honey-colored in the shimmering heat. Few visitors linger on these sun-baked slopes, and you can often wander alone among the forlorn ruins. In the 13th century, the Merenids, a Berber tribe, made Fez their capital and took control of much of North Africa. They remained in power for 200 years, and many of their rulers were buried on this hill. Little is left of the tombs, but there is no better spot from which to look down on Morocco's spiritual heartlands, especially when the calls to prayer from the city below echo round the old walls and send shivers down your spine. Framed by arid hills and surrounded by an ancient wall, the medina (old town) spreads out at your feet, a tightly packed jumble of sugar-cube buildings interspersed with slender minarets. The green roofs of holy places glisten above white walls, the most easy to spot being the large Karaouiyine Mosque. Viewed up close, the medina is packed with architectural gems and crisscrossed by narrow streets lined with stalls selling brass, silver, and leather goods. Here, the air smells of mint tea and spices, and donkeys rattle along the crowded, tangled lanes.

**When to Go** In spring, when temperatures are pleasant. Visit the tombs early or late in the day, when the hilltop is quiet and cool.

**How to Find It** The Bab el Mahrouk gate in the walls of the medina leads to the road up to the tombs.

**Planning** Fez has a wide range of places to stay, from international hotel chains to riads, or boutique hotels, but it is wise to book well ahead. Restaurants cater to all budgets, and as long as you apply due care, food is safe and delicious. Tipping is expected, and bargaining is engrained in the Moroccan culture—aim to pay half the asking price when buying items such as carpets and craft goods.

**Websites** www.visitmorocco.com, www.vjv.co.uk/destinations/africa/morocco/royal-cities-morocco

### Mountain Strongholds

The Merenids came from the south across the wild Atlas Mountains, where few visitors venture, even today. Yet with high peaks and deep valleys, waterfalls, and lakes, the mountains offer a wonderful escape for nature lovers.

Drive south for about 40 miles (65 km) from Fez to explore the lake area and dramatic **Vallée des Roches,** near the town of Ifrane. Or head east for about 60 miles (100 km) to see the caves and forests of the **Djebel Tazzeka National Park** and **Taza,** a walled enclave beside a mountain pass and one of the oldest towns in Morocco, restored several times by the Merenids.

AFRICA

# BANDIAGARA ESCARPMENT

A trek in Dogon country brings a succession of spectacular views
from the crest of this 90-mile-long (145 kilometer) escarpment.

AFRICA

The sun blazes out of a cloudless sky, but on the top of the escarpment a breeze takes the edge off the heat. Standing on the 1,600-foot-high (488 meter) cliff, you gaze out over the great expanse of sun-baked savanna below—Mali's Séno-Gondo Plains, stretching as far as the eye can see into the neighboring country of Burkina Faso. Acacia trees grow scattered across the red earth of the plains, with occasional majestic baobabs rising like giants among them. Beneath you, tucked into the base of the escarpment, are the mud-brick villages of the Dogon people, famous for their carved wooden ritual masks and distinctive architecture. It is a view you will have several opportunities to enjoy during a three-day trek in the Dogon country. The escarpment marks the southeastern edge of the Bandiagara Highlands, a sandstone massif where the Dogon settled some time around the 15th century. Spending the nights in local Dogon homes or camping in their villages, you follow the line of the escarpment, sometimes trekking at its foot, sometimes striding along the rocky crest. As you clamber up the escarpment, be prepared for scrambles up tree trunks leaning against the rock face, with the stumps of sawn-off branches acting as the rungs of a ladder. If offered a cup of the local millet beer, don't forget to pour some onto the ground as an offering to the ancestors.

**When to Go** November to March are best, avoiding the rainy seasons and intense heat of summer.

**How to Find It** Most visitors fly into Bamako, Mali's capital, which is a good day's journey by road from Mopti, the nearest major town to Dogon country. The buses run by Bani Transport are good, as is the road between Bamako and Mopti. For a more leisurely journey, take an overnight break in Ségou.

**Planning** You need a visa and a yellow-fever vaccination certificate for Mali. Unless you're an adventurous and independent traveler, organize your trek in Dogon country through a tour operator.

**Websites** www.toungatours.com, www.sagatours.com, www.ambamali-jp.org, www.festival-au-desert.org

## Dogon Villages

At the heart of a Dogon village is an open-sided building with a thick thatched roof. Called the *toguna* (discussion house), this is where the *hogon* (the village's chief elder) and other men sit to discuss community affairs. As you walk through a village, you will also see narrow buildings with pointed thatched roofs. These are granaries, divided into male ones (used to store millet and other grain, and raised off the ground to keep their contents safe from rodents) and female ones (where the women keep their personal possessions). The number of granaries reflects the wealth of a village or family.

The flat-roofed houses of the escarpment village of Ende look out across the broad, dry plain below.

Elephants are regular visitors at the Enkongo Narok swamp below Observation Hill.

KENYA

# OBSERVATION HILL

For the best views of the wildlife in Amboseli National Park, southern Kenya, take an easy walk to this summit.

Towering no more than 100 feet (30 meters) above the surrounding plains, Observation Hill is not much to look at, especially compared to Mount Kilimanjaro looming in the distance. But this flat-topped volcanic bluff in Amboseli National Park might just offer the best view in all of East Africa. And as there is only a footpath to the summit, this is also that rare place in Kenyan safari parks where you can get out of your vehicle and walk. What makes the mesa so special is its location along the edge of the Enkongo Narok swamp, a sliver of bright green in a desertlike terrain. Created by snowmelt percolating down from Kilimanjaro, the swamp offers water—hence life—to creatures of every ilk, from millions of insects and tens of thousands of birds to the herds of elephant that can be spotted from the top of the hill. A pair of binoculars and a small dose of patience can yield incredible rewards—hippos basking in the swamp's larger pools, giraffe munching their way through the landscape, dust devils dancing across the plains. Early mornings on the hill are best for game-viewing and snapping photos of "Kili" before the clouds move in. But the view at sunset is hard to beat, too, especially if you've brought along camp chairs and cocktails to enhance your observations.

**When to Go**  Amboseli has two rainy seasons: from April through June and from November through December. Although the landscape is greener (and the temperatures cooler) during the rains, wildlife is much easier to view and photograph during the two dry seasons.

**How to Find It**  The quickest option is Air Kenya (40 minutes) from Nairobi to a small airstrip by Amboseli's Empusil Park Gate. The 148-mile (238 km) drive from Nairobi via Namanga on the Kenya-Tanzania frontier to the main park gate (the Meshanani Gate) takes about five hours. Observation Hill is in the park's southern section, near the airstrip.

**Planning**  Three full days is the minimum for touring; allow at least one early morning atop Observation Hill.

**Websites**  www.kws.org/amboseli.html, www.oltukailodge.com, www.oldonyowuas.com

## Newest Attraction

Amboseli's closest neighbor—**Chyulu Hills National Park**—is one of Kenya's newest nature preserves. With all of its volcanic cones and craters formed in the last 500 years, this is also one of the world's youngest mountain ranges. Much like Observation Hill, the park's primary attraction is its incredible vistas over a large swathe of south-central Kenya. But Chyulu also has its own natural wonders: Volcanic caves, 37 varieties of orchid, lush montane forest, and unusual animals such as the steinbok (rock antelope), as well as the elusive leopard.

THE WORLD AT YOUR FEET

LAST WILDERNESSES  ISLAND GETAWAYS  THE ROAD LESS TRAVELED  SECRET HISTORY  SPIRITUAL HAVENS  HIDDEN TREASURES  UNDISCOVERED VILLAGES  CITY SECRETS

UGANDA/KENYA

# MOUNT ELGON

Straddling the border between Uganda and Kenya, Mount Elgon offers a winning combination of rare plants and stunning views.

AFRICA

Uganda and Kenya share a secret—with uncrowded wilderness trails and few roads, Mount Elgon is the place to chill out. This extinct volcano has one of the largest intact calderas of any volcano in the world. The last major eruption was 12 million years ago, and today Mount Elgon offers an undemanding climb requiring no special equipment or expertise. The peaks on the Ugandan side are reached within three days, those on the Kenyan side in a few hours. While the Kenyan side has much to offer, if you have the time climb the Ugandan side. You'll ascend through several vegetation zones, with the chance to spot black-and-white colobus and blue monkeys, hyrax, and birds such as Jackson's francolin and the tacazze sunbird. At the top—after a short, steep scramble—the 5-mile-wide (8 kilometer) caldera falls away before you, its rim broken into jagged cliffs topped by sheer-sided peaks and crags. On a clear day you have panoramic views of the plains of eastern Uganda on one side and the bowl of the caldera on the other. The Suam River bisects the crater and marks the Uganda-Kenya border. Following the river, you'll come to a break in the caldera rim where the smell of sulfur betrays Mount Elgon's last vestige of volcanic activity—algae-filled hot springs. Here you can soak your tired feet in water that bubbles up at 118.4°F (48°C), before heading back down.

**When to Go** During the dry seasons—from June through August and from December through March

**How to Find It** The Ugandan side has several trails to the summit; you can reach them from the town of Mbale, about three-four hours' drive from Kampala on a good tarmac road. At Mbale, you can pay trekking fees and arrange guides. On the Kenyan side, drive to Kitale, 292 miles (470 km) from Nairobi, where you'll find the park's Chorlim Gate entrance.

**Planning** A trained ranger guide is required on all treks in the Mount Elgon National Park. By prior arrangement, you can ascend the Ugandan slopes accompanied by local guides, cross the border at the hot springs in the crater, and descend on the Kenyan side escorted by Kenya Wildlife Service guides (or vice versa). You can find places to stay to suit all wallets in towns and villages around the park.

**Websites** www.mountelgon.net, www.kws.org/mt-elgon, www.uwa.or.ug/elgon

## Salt Caves

At **Kitum Cave** (meaning "place of ceremonies") on the Kenyan side of Mount Elgon, elephants have excavated a cavern extending more than 656 ft (200 m) into the mountain. They go there to dig out salt to supplement their diet, and the walls, floor, and ceiling are scratched and furrowed by their tusks. They and other salt-seeking animals, such as buffalo and antelope, enter the caves at night. Passing through the waterfall that drops across the cave mouth, they follow a traditional path inside, finding their way in the dark among piles of rocks on the cave floor. Visitors can enter the cave, which is reached via a short nature trail from the park entrance.

The Mount Elgon crater is a great shallow basin covered with rare alpine and other plants, such as giant lobelia.

# LAST WILDERNESSES

There was a time when wilderness lay all around us, but now it seems nothing short of a miracle that wild and unspoiled places still survive. So the journeys on these pages are very special, offering privileged glimpses of rare and fragile locations where time seems to stand still. A glorious diversity awaits those who are willing to venture even slightly off the beaten track. Who would suspect, for instance, that Yellowstone Park conceals spectacular landscapes that few tourists ever see? Other journeys take you to the ends of the Earth—to the lava fields of Greenland or the breeding grounds of the legendary albatross in New Zealand. Some require meticulous timing, such as the expedition to witness the annual migration of 1.4 million wildebeest across Tanzania's Serengeti plain. Others bring you into a world that outsiders rarely penetrate—riding on horseback across the Mongolian desert in the company of nomads; or sleeping in the Louisiana bayou on a houseboat, with snakes and alligators for neighbors. Respect for these special places should always be paramount and they should be left as you found them.

Glacier-carved mountains and silent forests surround the clear, calm waters of the Yoho National Park's Lake O'Hara in the heart of the Canadian Rockies.

A distinctive whiff of bad eggs emanates from the colorful sulfur springs around Leirhnjúkur.

ICELAND

# Leirhnjúkur Lava Fields

In a far corner of Iceland hot springs and mudpots hiss and bubble and oozing lava solidifies into extraordinary formations.

Trekking at Leirhnjúkur is a bit like walking on the moon; in fact, some of the craters nearby were used as training sites for NASA's Apollo astronauts. This geothermal area is part of a 50-mile-long (80 kilometer) fissure zone associated with the ancient Krafla volcano in northeast Iceland. The great volcano may be resting, but its offspring are very much alive. There are bubbling mudpots, milky-white hot springs, spatter cones splashed with pastel-colored deposits, solfataras that spew out sulfur-tainted steam smelling of bad eggs, solidified lava ropes and pavements. Bands of lava stretch across the stark landscape; the older material has scrubby vegetation and patches of flowers, the younger flows black and hot. Cooled lava is tainted red with iron, as well as sulfur yellow, sulfite blue, and potash purple. Some of the lava is broken into blocks, while other formations resemble solidified tongues in an untidy pile. To see these features, a circular walking trail leads from the Leirhnjúkur parking area. Pegs mark parts of the route, and you are advised to keep to the designated areas—just a few feet (meters) on either side the crust can be thin, hiding fissures, where you could get severely burned.

**When to Go** The area is in a rain shadow, so summers tend to be relatively dry and the days long.

**How to Find It** Leirhnjúkur is an hour's drive east of Akureyri, in northern Iceland, and 9 miles (14 km) north of Rekjahlið, a village on the shore of Lake Mývatn. The active area is a 20-minute walk from the parking lot. In summer, regular buses serve Rekjahlið and cars and mountain bikes can be rented locally.

**Planning** You need stout walking shoes and waterproofs, as the weather can be changeable. In summer it's worth buying a head net to protect against midges and blackflies.

**Websites** www.icelandtouristboard.com, www.nat.is

## Fire and Water

■ Farther along the Leirhnjúkur access road, a path leads from another parking area to the blue-water lake of **Víti crater** (hell crater), on the western rim of the Krafla caldera. Hissing vents beside the slippery track betray a sleeping giant.

■ To the southwest, **Lake Mývatn,** meaning "midge lake" because of its annoying residents, is a stopover for migrating waterfowl that feed on the aquatic insect larvae.

■ In the Mývatn area you might spot glass doors set in the ground. These are the entrances to **underground ovens,** where volcanic heat is used to make a pumpernickel-like bread called *hverabrauð* (hot spring bread), which bakes for 12–24 hours.

EUROPE

CANADA

# NUNAVIK

This eerie, rocky, silent landscape in northern
Quebec bears the scars of Earth's dramatic past.

Hiking across the flat, boulder-strewn terrain toward Pingualuit Crater (formerly Chubb Crater) in the Parc national des Pingualuit, you may well spot caribou pawing the permafrost for moss and lichens as their calves frolic close by. In summer, the 600,000-strong Leaf River herd roams the 437-square-mile (1,132 square kilometer) park in Quebec's Nunavik region. Inuit still hunt here, traveling from Kangiqsujuaq, the nearest village, and from villages several days' journey away, just as their ancestors did. To generations of these indigenous people, the area is of great spiritual importance. Their name for it, Pingualuit—Inuktitut for "where the land rises"—refers to the park's 1.3-million-year-old impact crater, which formed when a giant meteorite crashed into the Earth and gouged a depression 1,300 feet (400 meters) deep and 2 miles (3.5 kilometers) in diameter. The crater rim rises more than 500 feet (150 meters) above the endless tundra, looking from a distance like a small hill on the horizon. Climb to the top, and you will be rewarded with the sight of Pingualuk Lake. Formed over the millennia from rain and snowmelt, the lake's water is intensely blue.

**When to Go**  Although the park is open year-round, longer daylight hours and better weather conditions make access easiest from mid-June through mid-September. March and April are ideal for visits by dogsled or cross-country skis via the park access trail from Kangiqsujuaq.

**How to Find It**  Kangiqsujuaq is about 1,120 miles (1,800 km) north of Montreal, with regular scheduled flights from Quebec City, Montreal, and Ottawa. Although experienced hikers may prefer to make the 55-mile (88 km) journey from Kangiqsujuaq to the crater on foot, most visitors book a flight from the village to Lake Laflamme, followed by a 45-minute trek.

**Planning**  Arrange accommodations and travel at least six weeks in advance. Be prepared for an arduous hike to the crater over very rocky ground that can also be wet and slippery.

**Websites**  www.nunavikparks.ca/en/parks/pingualuit, www.nunavik-tourism.com, www.cruisenorthexpeditions.com

### Inuit Village Life

The Inuit village of **Kangiqsujuaq** sits on the shores of Wakeham Bay, 6 miles (10 km) from the Hudson Strait. Although the community of 600 people has many modern facilities, including an Inuit-owned co-op hotel, as well as the park headquarters and interpretive center, it still retains several old traditions. Men hunt caribou and beluga whales to fill the community food locker. Women harvest mussels from under the thick winter sea ice and pluck eider ducks for down for outer garments. Girls learn *katatjaq*, or throat singing, imitating the sounds of nature, birds, and animals, from their mothers and grandmothers, just as they did from their elders.

Pingualuit Crater, whose sheer sides rise up from a rocky wasteland, contains one of the world's largest crater lakes.

ALASKA/CANADA

# WRANGELL-KLUANE WILDERNESS

This vast, remote wilderness of forests, mountains, tundra, glaciers, and shoreline is home to whales, bears, caribou, and more.

Take the old riddle about a tree falling in the forest, magnify the forest a million times, and the end result would be something close to the Wrangell-Kluane region. Every day in this vast wilderness spanning the southern end of the Alaska-Yukon frontier, nature thrives beyond the sight and hearing of human incursions. North America's largest glaciers are heaving and groaning, calving giant chunks of ice. The continent's biggest bear population is fishing for salmon and scrounging berries. White water is gushing down pristine rivers and streams. And countless trees are sprouting, soaring, swaying, and falling with no one around to witness the splendor. Taken as a whole, Wrangell-Kluane constitutes the world's single largest protected area—more than 50 million square miles (129 million square kilometers) of forest, mountains, tundra, glaciers, and shoreline—and encompasses eight sanctuaries, including Wrangell-St. Elias in Alaska and the Kluane National Park and Reserve in Canada's Yukon Territory. Nearly everything about the area is awesome and overwhelming. Wrangell-Kluane protects 2,000 glaciers fed by ice fields larger than several U.S. states. It contains more 16,000-foot (4,875 meter) peaks—including giants like Mount Logan and Mount St. Elias—than any other part of North America. And it supports one of the world's most diverse animal populations—grizzly bears and humpback whales, moose, trumpeter swans, Dall sheep, and timber wolves—in numbers not found anywhere else.

**When to Go** From early June through mid-September, the region is often blessed with blue skies and dry weather, but even then snow is possible, and nights can be very cold. Some facilities are open in winter.

**How to Find It** The main visitor hubs are the Alaskan towns of McCarthy-Kennecott in Wrangell-St. Elias and Gustavus village, near Glacier Bay; and Haines Junction on the outskirts of the Kluane National Park in Canada.

**Planning** Among the wide range of outdoor activities are kayaking and white-water rafting, mountain biking and bush-plane flights, hunting, and fishing. There are several historical sites, including the vast, deserted Kennecott Copper Mine near McCarthy.

**Websites** www.nps.gov/wrst, www.nps.gov/glba, www.pc.gc.ca/pn-np/yt/kluane/index_e.asp, www.steliasguides.com, www.ultimathulelodge.com

## My Secret Journey

*"You never seem to get jaded," says veteran ranger Mike Thompson as we kayak through water as smooth as glass. "I still get so excited about the glaciers, the mountains, the weather." And the place we're paddling at this moment? Icy Bay, a huge fjord on the Wrangell-St. Elias coast. Every way I look is untamed nature—Mount St. Elias glistening pink in the late afternoon light, a 600-ft-high (180 m) waterfall that doesn't even have a name, and the cotton-candy-blue facade of Guyot Glacier.*

*Pulling onto a rocky beach about half a mile (1 km) from Guyot, we make camp and start preparing dinner. Soon the calm is shattered by the explosive noise of a massive chunk of glacier calving into the bay. A pressure wave rolls out from the splash zone, building speed and height as it races across the water. "Let's go!" Mike shouts, shoving me toward the moraine where we've pitched our tents, and we scramble to safety just as the mini tsunami washes over the place where we'd been standing.*

**Joe Yogerst**
**Travel writer**

Opposite: The mountain wilderness of Wrangell-St. Elias National Park Above: Bald eagles on the Alaska coast

# LAKE O'HARA

Ringed by mountains and larch forest, O'Hara in British Columbia is one of Canada's most beautiful lakes.

NORTH AMERICA

Situated on the western side of the Rocky Mountains' Great Divide, in Yoho National Park, Lake O'Hara's crystal-clear waters are held in a gigantic rock bowl. All around are high, jagged peaks with vertical cliff walls, rock amphitheaters filled with clear mountain pools, thundering waterfalls, and ancient glaciers. This is prime alpine hiking country: Many trails of varying degrees of difficulty radiate out from the lake circuit like spokes from a hub. The walk around the lake itself is a gentle stroll, but the mountain trails are not for the fainthearted as they take you up steep, slippery terraces, along knife-edge ridges, and across scree slopes and boulder fields. Hazards along these challenging routes include avalanches and rock falls, but a more obvious concern is grizzly bears—restrictions apply on some trails at certain times of year, depending where the bears are feeding and on what food. Pikas and hoary marmots keep watch from their sunbathing rocks, and you might encounter porcupines on the trail or spot mountain goats on high ledges. During June and July, the area is carpeted by the most colorful floral displays in the Rockies. In fall the larches yellow, and by winter the entire region is blanketed with snow, to be explored on cross-country skis or snowshoes.

**When to Go** Yoho is open year-round, with July and August the busiest months. Hikes to the Burgess Shale run from July through September. The weather is very changeable so be prepared for all weather conditions, with snow on higher ground even in summer.

**How to Find It** The nearest town is Field, British Columbia, about two hours' drive west of Calgary. From there, Lake O'Hara is reached either by public bus or by a 7-mile (11 km) hike along the access road.

**Planning** Reservations are needed for the Lake O'Hara bus, which operates mid-June through early October. There is a daily quota of day visitors and overnight campers. A lakeside lodge and cabins are open year-round. The round-trip Burgess Shale hikes can take eight to ten hours, fossil collecting is prohibited

**Websites** www.pc.gc.ca/eng/index.aspx, www.field.ca/yohonationalpark/lakeohara, www.burgess-shale.bc.ca

### The Burgess Shale

In Yoho National Park, not far from Lake O'Hara, is Burgess Shale country. The rocks here contain the fossils of creatures that lived 500 million years ago, when the area was underwater. You can visit these historic sites at **Walcott Quarry** and **Mount Stephen** in the company of guides from the Burgess Shale Geoscience Foundation. The routes are quite demanding, so you need to be fit.

Pickup for both hikes is at the Yoho Trading Post at Field on the Trans-Canada Highway. The trailhead for the Walcott Quarry is close to the spectacular Takakkaw Falls, the second highest in Canada.

Lake O'Hara is fed by a number of high-level lakes that formed where glaciers retreated. Each is a stunning destination in its own right.

Fall colors tint Pisgah National Forest, with the peak of Cold Mountain rising in the background.

NORTH CAROLINA

# SHINING ROCK WILDERNESS

This little-known mountain wilderness encompasses
some of the highest peaks in the Blue Ridge Mountains.

Shining Rock and the adjacent Middle Prong form one of the largest wilderness areas in the eastern United States. Three peaks here break the 6,000-foot (1,829 meter) level, the tallest being Cold Mountain, made famous in the novel by Charles Frazier. This wilderness is one of the premier hiking areas in the Blue Ridge Mountains. It is a world of timeless forest, mountain streams, waterfalls, and natural high meadows, called "balds," that offer dramatic views across ranks of weathered mountain ridges. The Cold Mountain Trail is a strenuous 9.8-mile (16 kilometer) hike that leads to the summit of Cold Mountain and soul-lifting views of the ancient peaks and mist-filled glens of the Balsam Range. The route leads through a forest that has some of the highest levels of biodiversity found in America. At lower altitudes, hardwoods dominate, with hickory, oak, maple, and locust. As elevation increases, the understory hosts mountain laurel, flame azalea, and wild rhododendron that explode in a pallet of white, red, orange, and pink every spring. Above 5,000 feet (1,524 meters), the landscape shifts dramatically to a forest dominated by hemlock and fir.

**When to Go** From May through October is best; heavy snowfall is possible in winter.

**How to Find It** You can reach the Cold Mountain Trail from the Art Loeb Trail, which starts at the Daniel Boone Boy Scout Camp. Exit the Blue Ridge Parkway at milepost 423.2 and travel north on North Carolina 215; after 13 miles (21 km), turn right onto Little East Fork Road and continue 3.8 miles (6 km) to the Scout camp.

**Planning** The trail is steep and suitable only for experienced hikers; allow seven hours, plus rest stops. The District Ranger Station provides maps and advice on conditions: 1600 Pisgah Highway (U.S. 276), Pisgah Forest, NC 28768. Phone: 828-877-3265. Accommodations are available in Brevard and Waynesville.

**Websites** www.northcarolinaoutdoors.com, www.cs.unca.edu/nfsnc

## Fiction and Fact

Many of the scenes and characters in Charles Frazier's novel *Cold Mountain* were based on real people and events.

The fictional town of Cold Mountain was centered on the community of **Bethel,** south of Interstate 40 near Canton, and one of the oldest crossroad towns in the mountains.

Frazier's main character, Inman, was based on his great-great-uncle, W.P. Inman, who was born and raised in Bethel. The real Inman, like his fictional counterpart, served in the Confederate army and was wounded in battle. Disgusted with war, he escaped from his hospital bed and walked 300 miles (480 km) back home, only to be murdered in Bethel sometime after his return.

Every June, Bethel offers tours that visit Inman's gravesite; the Inman Chapel, founded by Inman's minister brother; and homes built by men who served alongside Inman in the Confederate army.

NORTH AMERICA

# WILDFLOWER DISPLAYS

Spectacular but short-lived displays of rare and colorful flowers can be found in every type of landscape, from deserts to high mountain meadows, volcano craters to forest floors.

## ❶ Diamond Valley Lake, California

Be there mid-morning. The natural displays of orange California poppies, deep blue Arroyo lupines, yellow brittlebush, baby blue eyes, Canterbury bells, and purple owl's clover are most spectacular at that time of day. It's a tight window, for the 1.25-mile (2 km) spring wildflower loop trail is open only during March, 6:30 a.m. to 4:45 p.m., while the spring flowers are blooming.

Planning The trail near East Marina is reached via the Domenigoni and Searl Parkways near Hemet, east of Los Angeles. www.dvlake.com

## ❷ Haleakala Volcano, Maui, Hawaii

This is one strange plant. The Haleakala silversword, or *ahinahina*, blooms from July through September on the higher slopes and in the crater of the Haleakala volcano. The 6.5-ft-tall (2 m) stalk with reddish-purple flowers grows up from a rosette of silver, sword-shaped leaves only once, at the end of the plant's 15-to-50-year life span. It then produces seeds and dies.

Planning The Haleakala summit is a two-hour drive from Kahului. With such a long gestation period, even experts cannot predict when plants will flower. www.nps.gov/hale/index.htm

## ❸ Southwest Botanical Province, Western Australia

Western Australia is a wildflower paradise. For six months, starting with the early rains in June, the rugged wilderness areas around Perth are packed with no fewer than 12,000 species of wildflowers, including red and green kangaroo paw, deep orange or bright red banksias, pink boronias, and yellow hibiscus.

Planning Check out the Pilbara region, Kalbarri National Park, and Coalseam Conservation Park. www.westernaustralia.com

## ❹ Annapurna, Nepal

Hillsides filled with color set against the stark white backdrop of some of the world's highest mountains—this is the prospect of a visit to the Annapurna Conservation Area during March and April, when nine species of rhododendron are in bloom. The largest forests are near Ghorepani village, which is reached by a two-to-three-day trek into the lower slopes of the Himalaya.

Planning A 30-minute flight or six-hour drive west from Kathmandu to Pokhara . . . then walk. www.dnpwc.gov.np/conservation-annapurna.asp

## ❺ Taurus Mountains, Turkey

Spring comes late to the mountains of southern Turkey. As the snows recede, snowdrops, wild crocuses, and tulips are everywhere, and during April and May the lower slopes are a riot of color, with wild cyclamen, purslane, purple vetch, blue cornflowers, red poppies, wild oregano, and a staggering 148 species of orchid.

Planning Isparta, in the lakes region of the western Taurus Mountains, is a convenient base and the center of rose-growing. www.goturkey.com

## ❻ Col du Lautaret, Haute-Alpes, France

The 6,561-ft-high (2,000 m) alpine meadows in this mountain pass in the Dauphiné Alps are filled with wild alpine flowers from mid-June until the end of July. Also on the Col is the Jardin Alpin, cared for by Grenoble University, with a collection of more than 2,000 alpine plants from all over the world.

Planning Northwest of Briançon on Route National 91. www.francetourism.com

## ❼ Forêt de Brotonne, Normandy, France

In a lazy loop of the Seine River in the heart of the Parc Naturel Régional des Boucles de la Seine Normande is the quiet and peaceful Forêt de Brotonne, a great forest with beech and oak, and a magnificent carpet of bluebells in April. It is a remnant of the vast, ancient forest of Arelaune that once covered the entire region.

Planning To the west of Rouen, reached via the tall and graceful Brotonne Bridge. brotonne.free.fr

## ❽ New Grove Meadows, Monmouth, Wales

Two of four adjacent meadows in this corner of southeast Wales are considered the best wildflower meadows in Britain. Cowslips and spring sedge bloom in April. Early purple orchids and green winged orchids appear in May. The fields turn pink in June with common spotted orchids, along with green-flowered twayblade orchids. Fall sees colorful grassland fungi appear, including red, yellow, and green waxcaps.

Planning Located south of Monmouth off the B4293 road near Loysey. gwentwildlife.org/reserves/NewGroveMeadows.htm

## ❾ Namaqua National Park, South Africa

In August and September the desert in the Namaqua National Park is transformed almost overnight into the most extravagant wildflower display in the world. Great swaths of orange Namaqualand daisies cover the ground where there was only dust before. Other desert daisies include the blue stars of *Romuleia*, light yellow blooms of white-eyed duiker root, and blue Karoo daisies.

Planning The park is off the N7 road to Namibia, 307 miles (494 km) north of Cape Town. www.sanparks.org/parks/namaqua

## ❿ Nieuwoudtville, South Africa

South Africa is blessed with not one but two spectacular wildflower areas. About 60 miles (100 km) south of Namaqualand is the Nieuwoudtville Wildflower Reserve, set in an area said to have the richest concentration of bulb species in the world. The endemic deep orange cat's tail, pink candelabra flowers, and carpets of pink *Hesperantha* and white *Cotula* spread as far as the eye can see.

Planning Nieuwoudtville Wildflower Reserve is 1.8 miles (3 km) from the town on the road to Calvinia. www.nieuwoudtville.com

Opposite: The desert floor in Namaqualand is carpeted each year with around 1,000 species of flowers that are unique to the area.

Steamboats once plied the Atchafalaya bayous, but they have become overgrown and form a haunting watery wilderness.

LOUISIANA

# ATCHAFALAYA SWAMP

This world of shimmering dark water and towering trees
in southern Louisiana is home to a rich diversity of creatures.

Located in the heart of Cajun Country, near Lafayette, Louisiana, and measuring 20 miles (32 kilometers) wide and 150 miles (241 kilometers) long, the Atchafalaya is the largest swamp in North America. In truth, it is not one body of water, but an interconnected maze of freshwater bayous; slow-moving, mirror-like rivers; darkly canopied, flooded forest; and salt marshes where the Atchafalaya River meets the tidal waters of the Gulf of Mexico. A true wetland wilderness, the swamp is a wonderland of birds, wildlife, and rare flowers and plants that can be seen only by getting up close and personal. Guided johnboat and airboat tours are available, but one of the best ways to experience this wetland playground is to rent a houseboat. The boat will be towed to a quiet place in the marsh where you can savor all the comforts of home amid the natural splendor of this watery wilderness. Sit on the porch overlooking the water as the sun sets and the swamp comes alive with a million sounds. Head out at sunrise in a skiff to fish, or watch the day break over the swamp as herons and egrets wade in the shallows and drowsy alligators lounge on the banks in the early sunlight.

**When to Go**  In late spring and early summer the water is high and wildlife is most active, the temperatures are moderate, and there is the greatest profusion of wildflowers in bloom.

**How to Find It**  The swamp can be reached via Interstate 10. Most boat tours of the swamp leave from one of the landings on Lake Henderson, just outside the town of Henderson.

**Planning**  Houseboat rentals are available through Houseboat Adventures; make a reservation well in advance. Boat tours of the Atchafalaya are available through McGee's Landing. Alligators and snakes are abundant in the swamp, but are reclusive and generally not aggressive unless provoked. Mosquitoes are relatively rare in daytime but can be plentiful after dark–bring strong repellent if you plan nighttime outings.

**Websites**  www.houseboat-adventures.com/index.htm, www.mcgeeslanding.com, www.cafedesamis.com, www.lafayette.travel

## Cajun Culture

■ When you are ready for a dose of civilization, Cajun-style, just head to **McGee's Landing** at Henderson or **Whiskey River Landing** at nearby Breaux Bridge where the weekends throb with the lively bounce of zydeco music, and young and old alike take a turn on the dance floor.

■ Breaux Bridge is a tiny Cajun town. On Saturday mornings, the **Café Des Amis** has a zydeco breakfast with live music that attracts locals and visitors of all ages. Everyone dances; the coffee is dark; the omelets are hearty; and the light, puffy beignets, deep fried and rolled in powdered sugar, are the stuff of legend.

NORTH
AMERICA

WYOMING

# HIDDEN YELLOWSTONE

Beyond the beauty of Old Faithful's predictable spoutings, there's a less visited area brimming with wildlife, waterfalls, and hot springs.

NORTH AMERICA

Tucked away in Yellowstone National Park's southwest corner is an area rich with meadows, forests, and waterfalls. Known as Cascade Corner, it encompasses the Bechler and Falls Rivers and their many tributaries that meander across the rugged Madison and Pitchstone plateaus and plunge over the sides in a series of spectacular cascades. Starting at the Bechler River Ranger Station, follow the banks of the fast-moving Falls River and you will hear the sound of water cascading down Cave Falls. Towering lodgepole pines frame this wide waterfall, while ospreys descend from above, fishing for trout. Then head northeast along the Bechler River. As you hike the trail through the expansive Bechler meadows, spectacular views of the Teton Range come into view to the south. A gentle breeze fans your cheeks and the scent of pine wafts on the air as you continue up the canyon through some of the area's lushest forest. Try the deep purple, tart huckleberries growing along the trail. You'll see thundering Ouzel Falls in the distance. Soon afterward are Colonnade Falls and then Iris Falls (9 miles/14.5 kilometers from the ranger station). A few miles farther on, at the Bechler River's Ferris Fork, you can watch steam rising from bubbling hot springs as you pause to take in the spectacular scenery. You will need to return by the same route.

**When to Go**  The best time to enjoy the Bechler area is from late August through September. In early summer, the meadows can be flooded and hungry mosquitoes abound.

**How to Find It**  The Bechler River Ranger Station is 20 miles (32 km) east from Ashton, Idaho.

**Planning**  Yellowstone is bear and buffalo country. Never hike alone, and always check at the ranger station for reports of recent bear activity. Go to the national park's website to learn about what to do if you encounter bears and how to use pepper spray. Bring mosquito repellent and wear waterproof boots. There are campsites along the Bechler Canyon, but you will need a permit.

**Website**  www.nps.gov/yell

## Natural Hot Tub

Although Yellowstone's thermal pools look inviting, they are filled with scalding water and it is illegal and dangerous to enter them, since this can lead to burns and even death. But about 16 miles (26 km) from the Bechler Ranger Station, you can enjoy a soak in a "hot pot" that is legal and generally safe (though check first with an official).

Spend a night in one of the campsites along the Bechler Trail. Next day, hike onto the **Ferris Fork side trail** where you'll come across a large, bubbling pool with softly rising steam. Before venturing into nature's very own hot tub, gently test the waters with your toes.

Off the beaten track in Yellowstone's Cascade Corner, the Colonnade Falls are just one of many stupendous waterfalls.

In the Salmon River maelstrom the only way for white-water rafters to go is downstream.

IDAHO

# THE "FRANK"

Whether you seek solitude or adventure, there are few better places for either than this wilderness area in central Idaho.

With few people and fewer roads, turbulent rivers, clear mountain lakes, deep canyons, vast tracts of forest, and wildflower meadows, the Frank Church-River of No Return Wilderness is the largest National Forest wilderness in the United States outside Alaska. It is named for Senator Frank Church, who introduced legislation to protect the area, and for the torrent that is the Salmon River, where conventional rivercraft (other than jet boats) have little chance of traveling upstream against its plunging rapids and swirling whirlpools. The Salmon River Canyon is deeper than the Grand Canyon. Rainbow and cutthroat trout are in the river all year, while spring and summer see steelhead trout and chinook salmon. Along the trail system you may well spot bighorn sheep and mountain goats on the most rugged terrain; moose and elk inhabit the forests and lower slopes, as do their predators: Mountain lions, wolves, coyotes, and wolverines. Black bears are present but tend to avoid people. There are also more than 2,316 square miles (6,000 square kilometers) without trails where you can find total seclusion.

**When to Go** Accessible year-round. In summer the temperature can soar above 100°F (38°C) in the valleys, and in the winter snows it can plummet to -49°F (-45°C) on the mountains, so be prepared for extreme weather as well as backcountry hazards and emergencies.

**How to Find It** Eighteen airstrips cater to small planes, and boat access is by jet boat on the Salmon River, but many people travel in on horseback or foot from the 66 trailheads reached from Forest Service roads.

**Planning** More than 90 companies organize outdoor activities in the area, and they can be contacted via the Idaho Outfitters and Guides Association. Guest ranches offer a less energetic wilderness experience. The Frank user's guide provides information on restrictions on numbers, permits, and other details. Mechanized vehicles, including mountain bikes, are not allowed in the area.

**Websites** www.fs.fed.us/r4/sc/recreation/fcronr/userguide.pdf, www.ioga.org

### The Sheepeater War

When the ice retreated after the last ice age, about 20,000 years ago, Native American tribes such as the Nez Perce and Shoshone settled in the **Salmon River** area. Dams and weirs for trapping salmon and trout, stone tools, and rock art are testament to their past presence.

In 1879, the Shoshone, who were called "sheepeaters" by European settlers, were accused of several murders, although there was no evidence to support the accusations.

During the ensuing conflict, known as the Sheepeater War, U.S. troops were ordered into the wilderness to pursue the Shoshone. Being at home in the extreme terrain, the Shoshone eluded the military, who lost mules, horses, and supplies over cliffs and down raging torrents, while the soldiers suffered from cold and exhaustion.

Eventually, despite their superiority in the mountains, the Shoshone tired of being pursued. They surrendered and were resettled at Fort Hall Reservation in eastern Idaho.

NORTH AMERICA

THE WORLD AT YOUR FEET

LAST WILDERNESSES

ISLAND GETAWAYS   THE ROAD LESS TRAVELED   SECRET HISTORY   SPIRITUAL HAVENS   HIDDEN TREASURES   UNDISCOVERED VILLAGES   CITY SECRETS

CALIFORNIA

# Mojave National Preserve

Enjoy the California desert in its most pristine state from the Preserve's hundreds of miles of dirt roads and hiking trails.

Like Death Valley, the 244,218-square-mile (632,522 square kilometer) Mojave National Preserve in southern California contains expansive vistas of eroded, naked landscapes made up of rugged mountain ranges, mesas and buttes, stark cinder cones, and vast, dry, lake beds studded with cactus. Following the network of paved and dirt roads, you can explore Cima Dome, a huge extrusion of eroded granite in the north of the preserve that supports the world's largest Joshua tree forest, and Hole-in-the-Wall's maze of gulleys and walls cut into the vivid red volcanic rock, called rhyolite, while Kelso Dunes in the southeast support more than 100 varieties of native plants. You can often spot roadrunners racing through the underbrush while golden eagles and red-tailed hawks soar overhead. Many mammals here, which include mountain lions, coyotes, bighorn sheep, and black-tailed jackrabbits, are nocturnal due to the daytime heat. Desert tortoises and several species of rattlesnake are also present. To experience the deep desert environment, camp if at all possible—a single night under the blaze of the Milky Way, far from the nearest artificial light, will yield a lifetime of memories.

**When to Go** Spring, when the desert floor is covered in wildflowers, and late fall are the best times. In midsummer, temperatures can climb to 120°F (49°C).

**How to Find It** The Mojave Preserve is located roughly 120 miles (190 km) northeast of Los Angeles, and can easily be reached by U.S. Highway 15 or 40. The two roads constitute the preserve's northern and southern borders.

**Planning** Plan at least one full day for your visit if you intend to stay in your car and on the roads. Any hiking or off-road exploration will extend your sojourn to two or three days. Dependable 4WD trucks and SUVs are the rule. Take a spare tire and know how to change a flat. Take at least 1 gallon (4.5 liters) of water per person per day, plus food and coolers and ice to keep it edible. Some of the wildlife is to be avoided. The Mojave rattlesnake is one of the most venomous snakes in the Americas: Its bite can be fatal, so watch where you put your feet and hands. There are two maintained campgrounds, and roadside camping is also permitted. If rooms are a must, Baker—a small town on Interstate 15—has a few motels.

**Websites** www.nps.gov/moja/index.htm, digital-desert.com/baker-ca

## Railroad Past

The ghost town of **Kelso** in the southeast of the preserve is a crumbling testament to the boom-and-bust economic cycles of the West. Founded in 1905 as a railroad stop between Los Angeles and Salt Lake City, Kelso was valued by the rail lines for its relatively abundant water supply. At its peak, the town had a population of more than 2,000. The arrival of diesel locomotives doomed Kelso, and the depot closed in 1986.

The mission-style depot building, constructed in 1924, has been restored and is now the preserve's visitor center. Most of Kelso's remaining structures are elegantly decayed and contribute a haunting melancholy to the site.

Joshua trees fill the desert landscape around Cima Dome in the Mojave National Preserve.

# SANTA ROSA NATIONAL PARK

The coral reefs, swamps, grassland, and forest of Costa Rica's oldest national park harbor a diversity of animals and plants.

American filibuster William Walker could never have guessed that his ill-fated 1856 invasion of Costa Rica would someday spawn one of the Western Hemisphere's great nature preserves. When you stand surrounded by so much pristine wilderness, it is hard to imagine that the bloody Battle of Santa Rosa against Walker's forces played out in this dry tropical forest. But thanks to Costa Rica's victory, the historic significance of the location helped in its protection and designation as a national park, founded in 1971. From that historic core, the park has expanded into something far greater—a sprawling reserve that now protects the entire Santa Elena Peninsula and its surrounding waters, 190 square miles (500 square kilometers) in total. Santa Rosa's landscapes vary from offshore coral reefs and miles of unspoiled beaches to savanna grasslands, mangrove swamps, and cactus-studded thorn scrub. Its wildlife is equally diverse—jaguars and ocelots, spider and howler monkeys, tapirs, sloths, coatimundis, and more than 300 bird species. Much of the 1856 battle took place at La Casona Hacienda, which is now preserved as a museum. Half a dozen major trails meander through the Santa Rosa wilderness, with Sendero Palo Seco considered the best for wildlife viewing. The peninsula has many great, often empty beaches, including Playa Naranjo, one of the region's best surf spots.

**When to Go** Wildlife is generally easier to spot during the dry season (from November through April), when animals gather around water sources and the vegetation is thinner.

**How to Find It** Santa Rosa lies 158 miles (255 km) northwest of San José on the Pan-American Highway. Visitors can fly in to the capital, rent a vehicle, and make the drive themselves (about four hours) or catch a domestic flight to Liberia International Airport, about an hour's drive from the park. Park maps and information booklets are sold at the entrance gate.

**Planning** Campgrounds are found at La Casona and Murciélago ranger stations. The nearest hotels are in Liberia. Santa Rosa can also be visited on day-trips from the beach resorts of the Papagayo Peninsula.

**Websites** www.costarica-nationalparks.com, www.monteverdeinfo.com, www.liberiacostarica.com

## Cloud Forest

The Pan-American Highway between San José and Santa Rosa is flanked by more than a dozen national parks and wildlife preserves, none more dazzling than **Monteverde Cloud Forest Biological Reserve.** This unspoiled patch of cloud forest is best explored on the 74 miles (119 km) of hiking trails. Formed by high humidity, almost constant precipitation, and low cloud cover, this habitat is off the charts when it comes to biodiversity: 1,200 species of reptiles and amphibians, 100 different mammals, and more than 400 bird species, including the quetzal bird, sacred to the ancient Maya.

A white-faced capuchin monkey with a baby on its back feeds in the trees in Santa Rosa. It is one of the most frequently spotted species in the park.

Boat tours offer a unique view of Montserrat's smoldering volcano and the largely off-limits south side of the island.

MONTSERRAT

# Soufrière Hills Volcano

Away from the devastation wrought by its volcano, this Caribbean island offers sun, sea, and wildlife in quiet surroundings.

It wasn't quite a repeat of the volcanic catastrophe that destroyed ancient Pompeii, but it came very close. Dormant for more than 200 years, Soufrière Hills volcano suddenly burst back into life in the summer of 1995. There was enough warning for those living around the 3,000-foot (914 meter) peak to evacuate the area before pyroclastic flows swept down the slopes, but Plymouth, the island's capital, largely disappeared beneath a wave of volcanic mud and ash. Subsequent eruptions affected the entire south side of the island, rendering it uninhabitable. Many of those who lost their homes migrated overseas and never returned, leaving the tiny pear-shaped island (39 square miles/100 square kilometers) with about a third of its pre-eruption population. There is no small irony in the fact that the smoldering dome—and the constant threat of another eruption—is now the island's biggest attraction. Visitors flock to the Montserrat Volcano Observatory to learn about the forces that sparked the eruption and rub elbows with world-renowned scientists. Excursions to Richmond Hill provide a dramatic bird's-eye view of devastated Plymouth. But Soufrière saves her best for night, when streams of bright orange magma flow down her slopes—best seen from the viewing platform at Jack Boy Hill.

**When to Go** Montserrat lets its hair down on St. Patrick's Day (March 17). For the rest of the year it is old-school Caribbean—empty beaches, laidback bars, and secluded jungle trails.

**How to Find It** Unless you have your own boat or plane, the only way to reach Montserrat is by scheduled flight via the nearby island of Antigua. WinAir offers several flights each day.

**Planning** There aren't many hotels on the island, but Gingerbread Hill and Tropical Mansions Suites count among the better overnight abodes. Green Monkey, the island's premier adventure sports outfitter, organizes boat trips to view the ruins of Plymouth, as well as scuba diving, kayaking, turtle-watching, guided nature hikes, and deep-sea fishing excursions.

**Websites** www.visitmontserrat.com, www.divemontserrat.com, www.fly-winair.com, www.mvo.ms

### The Other Emerald Isle

■ Many of the 4,700 islanders trace their roots (and surnames) to Irish Catholic settlers who arrived in the 1630s after a long trans-Atlantic journey.

■ **Montserrat** is the only place in the world besides the Irish Republic where St. Patrick's Day is an official national holiday. The day caps a week-long festival of Irish and island themed dinners, dances, and other activities.

■ The harp and Union Jack on the Montserrat flag, as well as the green shamrock that gets stamped in your passport upon arrival, derive from the days when both Emerald Isles were part of the British Empire.

NORTH AMERICA

Mighty buttress root systems support trees in the Manú jungle, providing a rich habitat for local flora and fauna.

PERU

# MANÚ NATIONAL PARK

Accessible only by boat, this unspoiled area of the Amazon Rain Forest is popular with wildlife enthusiasts and bird-watchers.

Sequestered on the eastern side of the Andes, more than 2,000 miles (3,200 kilometers) upriver from the Amazon proper, Manú National Park is about as remote as you can get. You need to organize what amounts to a mini expedition to explore the giant reserve, located on the Manú River, but the payback is priceless—a park that runs the gamut from chilly cloud forest to sweltering tropical lowlands, plush jungle lodges to primitive riverside camping, top-of-the-chain predators like jaguars and giant river otters to more than a million insect species. Only a tiny sliver of the park—along the banks of the Manú and Alto Madre de Dios Rivers—is open to the public. The remainder is set aside for scientific research, wildlife preservation, and an estimated 2,000 indigenous nomads. While vast stretches of the Amazon have been ravaged by logging, mining, and agriculture, Manú's remoteness has allowed it to pass into the 21st century virtually unscathed. "Manú provides an opportunity to see how things really work in nature," says U.S. zoologist Mercedes Foster. "Not how they work after you've cut down half the trees."

**When to Go** It's the Amazon—it rains year-round. Even during the drier months (May through September), expect daily showers. Throughout the year, daytime highs reach 85-90°F (29-32°C). Nights are at their most pleasant in June and July, when temperatures can drop to the low 60s (15-18°C).

**How to Find It** Most everyone organizes their journey from Cusco in the Peruvian highlands. You can either fly from Cusco to the tiny jungle airstrip near Boca Manú and then head into the park by boat; or drive over the crest of the Andes and down to Atalaya, where boats depart for the day-long journey to Boca Manú.

**Planning** If you are traveling independently, arrange river transportation before you leave Cusco. Primitive camping is the only possibility for staying overnight inside the park, but there are lodges on the park's eastern flank. Several adventure travel outfitters in Cusco can arrange transport to the park.

**Websites** www.inkanatura.com, www.manuwildlifecenter.com, www.pantiacolla.com

### The Heart of Darkness

In the 1890s, the Peruvian explorer and entrepreneur **Carlos Fermin Fitzcarrald** journeyed up the Ucalayi River, a main headwater of the Amazon, and discovered a land route across to the Manú River region and its vast tracts of rubber trees. He used workers and Indian slaves to cut a swathe through the jungle, disassemble a steamship, carry it piece by piece to the Manú, and reassemble it in order to explore the region. He then used the route to export rubber from the jungle. Several years later, Fitzcarrald drowned.

The rubber baron was immortalized in the 1982 film, *Fitzcarraldo,* by German director Werner Herzog.

SOUTH AMERICA

JAPAN

# AKAN NATIONAL PARK

This active volcanic landscape in eastern Hokkaido enchants
with clear lakes, virgin forests, bubbling mudpools, and hot springs.

Akan is all about water, some of it piping hot. The park has three main crater lakes set among volcanic peaks, surrounded by swaths of Ezo pine and Sakhalin fir virgin forest, home to brown bears and Ezo deer, and visited by the Steller's sea-eagle and the rare Blakiston's fish-owl. The Akan caldera is about 12 miles (19 kilometers) across and dominates the western part of the park. Here, Lake Akan is famous for its marimo algae, which accumulate in green spheres that, after a few hundred years, can reach the size of soccer balls. Sheer cliffs surround the lake, and all around there are signs of volcanic activity. At the hot springs resort of Akankohan Onsen, near the Eco Museum Center, a forest trail leads to bubbling mudpools, or *bokke*. Hiking trails cross two volcanoes—Mount Oakan, or Male Mountain, on one side of the lake, and the higher Mount Meakan, or Female Mountain, on the other. Mount Meakan has a triple crater with two crater ponds and emits sulfurous gases. The eastern part of the park has two crater lakes: Lake Kussharo is the largest in the park, with hot springs and hot sand baths along its shores; Lake Masshu is considered the most beautiful—when you can see it, for it is often hidden in dense fog—and its deep blue waters are claimed to be the clearest in the world.

**When to Go** Summers are drier and cooler here than in the rest of Japan, so June, July, and August are ideal for hiking. The mountain trails are accessible from June through October, but during winter they are covered by snow. Winter temperatures can drop to -22°F (-30°C).

**How to Find It** Flights from Tokyo to Kushiro city take 90 minutes. With infrequent buses and trains from Kushiro to the park, a rental car is recommended—the drive from Kushiro takes about an hour.

**Planning** A convenient base for visitors is Kawayu Onsen, a hot springs resort near Lakes Masshu and Kussharo. The trails around Mount Oakan and Mount Meakan take about half a day each and are relatively easy going, although you need to wear sturdy walking shoes. Check the status of the Meakan volcano before embarking on its hiking trail—it last erupted in 2006.

**Websites** www.lake-akan.com, japan-guide.com

### Dancing Cranes

Between Kushiro and Akan National Park is the **Kushiro Marsh,** which supports the only known population of Japanese cranes in the country. The birds are easiest to see in winter, when they gather at feeding sites. They are at their most spectacular in mid-February, when they dance in the winter sunshine. Pairs of birds throw back their heads, open their wings, and move in a series of bows, leaps, and kicks. Viewing for visitors is well organized. The Akan International Crane Center in Kushiro Shitsugen National Park is the main breeding center and museum; the adjacent Tancho Observation Center has a winter feeding ground.

Winter is the best time to see endangered Japanese cranes in the Kushiro Marsh.

CHINA

# The Three Parallel Gorges

In this remote corner of China, the Salween, Mekong, and Yangtze Rivers run in deep gorges through spectacular mountain scenery.

Close to the Myanmar (Burmese) border, in China's subtropical southwest, is a wild and remote region cut off from the outside world by the outlying spurs of the eastern Himalaya. And at the heart of this land of emerald-green mountains and jungles, a triumvirate of mighty rivers thunders through deep gorges, their waters brown with sediment washed down from the Tibetan Plateau, as they flow south and east to distant seas. This is the Three Parallel Gorges region, described by UNESCO as "maybe the most biologically diverse temperate ecosystem in the world." The gorges run north to south in parallel for some 200 miles (320 kilometers), as three of Asia's great rivers—the Salween (Nu Jiang) to the west, the Mekong (Lancang Jiang) in the middle, and the Yangtze (Chang Jiang) to the east—are forced into close proximity. The gorges may be close to each other as the crow flies, but they are separated by the near-impenetrable ridges of the lofty Hengduan Shan, with several peaks towering above 20,000 feet (6,100 meters). To fully appreciate the range of scenery in the region, from dramatic gorges to ancient forest, karst, and glaciated peaks, you need to set out on foot, which also gives the opportunity to explore the remarkable biodiversity: Around 6,000 species of plants and a rich variety of wildlife, including red pandas, snow leopards, black bears, and exotic birds.

**When to Go** The climate varies a great deal from one gorge to the next, and from north to south. As a general rule, any time between October and March is good for lower altitude treks. Areas below around 3,000 ft (915 m) are warm all year; the main trekking area around the northern part of the Salween Gorge is slightly cooler but still fine for trekking in the winter months at lower altitudes. The period from April through September is often wet.

**How to Find It** As you would expect in such a remote region, access is not easy. Trekkers mostly focus on the Salween Gorge, reached via the town of Fugong—a 12-hour bus ride from the nearest airport, at Dali, to the south. From Fugong, buses continue north along bone-shaking roads to the settlements of Gongshan and Bingzhonglou, starting points for treks into the best of the gorge scenery

**Planning** For a more accessible encounter with similar scenery you could visit Tiger Leaping Gorge near Lijiang on the Yangtze, 87 miles (140 km) as the crow flies over the mountains to the east of the Salween.

**Websites** www.chinatrekking.com, chinafittours.com/chinatours/best-of-yunnan.htm

### Record Rivers

Each river begins its journey high on the arid plateau of eastern Tibet, meandering south and east before plunging down to the lower altitudes of Yunnan province.

■ The **Salween,** or Nu Jiang (at 1,900 miles/3,058 km, the world's 24th longest river), continues through a series of gorges southward into Myanmar before emptying into the Bay of Bengal.

■ The **Mekong,** or Lancang Jiang (2,700 miles/4,345 km, world no. 11), surges southeast through Laos, Thailand, Cambodia, and Vietnam to reach the South China Sea.

■ The **Yangtze,** or Chang Jiang (3,900 miles/6,276 km, world no. 3), loops eastward to cross central China and enters the East China Sea close to Shanghai.

The region is home to an array of minority peoples whose way of life has remained largely untouched by the modern world. In the north are Tibetan communities. In the gorges region itself, tiny settlements of **Lisu, Dulong, Bai,** and **Yi** peoples are scattered in forest clearings along the river edges, often accessed by precarious wooden bridges.

Opposite: A local villager crosses the Salween in a rope basket. Above: The first bend of the Salween, near Fugong

# VIENG XAI

Well concealed in the jumble of karst hills of northeastern Laos, the Vieng Xai caves are the ultimate hideout.

ASIA

Set in a narrow valley amid fabulous scenery close to the Vietnamese border and the former Ho Chi Minh Trail, the Vieng Xai caves were the main base of the Pathet Lao communists in their fight for control of Laos in the 1960s and '70s. Each of the Pathet Lao leaders was allocated his own cave, a handful of which are open to the public. One of the most notable is that of Souphanouvong—the Red Prince, a member of the Lao royal family who became a freedom fighter. It is notably well appointed by jungle-hideout standards, its wooden walls and floors going a long way to disguise the fact that it is a cave. Outside the entrance is a house, complete with magnificently incongruous swimming pool and garden, built after the bombing threat receded in 1973. The cave of Kaysone Phomvihane, the supreme leader, who was to become the first president of the Lao People's Democratic Republic, is the largest of all. Extending 490 feet (150 meters) into the mountain, it was equipped with a library and a meeting room, and the original beds, items of clothing, and a portrait of Che Guevara remain. Elsewhere, one cave functioned as a military hospital, another sheltered 2,000 soldiers and featured an underground theater used by visiting performers from Vietnam, China, and Russia. Some areas could be sealed with aluminum doors and were equipped with oxygen pumps in case of chemical attack.

**When to Go** It's best to go during the dry season (November through May).

**How to Find It** The town of Vieng Xai is 40 minutes by bus or truck from Sam Neua, the regional hub, with daily flights from Vientiane. Most of the caves are a short walk from the town.

**Planning** Unless you organize a tour in Sam Neua, you will need to register at the Visitor Center in order to visit the caves, and will need to pay an entrance fee as well as a fee for the guide (compulsory). There is an additional fee if you wish to take photographs. Tours take around two hours and depart daily 9-11 a.m. and 1-4 p.m. There are a few guesthouses in Vieng Xai town.

**Websites** www.laotourism.org, www.tourabout.com/asia/laos/vieng_xai/tour_operators

## Bomb Shelters

In addition to their hideout function, the caves' other purpose was as shelter from the barrage of American bombs. From 1964 to 1973, the B-52 bombers of the U.S. Air Force are estimated to have dropped two million tons of bombs on eastern Laos, and some 23,000 people—not just Pathet Lao guerrillas—are thought to have sheltered in the caves.

A large number of bombs failed to explode, which leaves Laos with a terrible problem: Unexploded ordnance (UXO) kills and maims around 300 people each year. Visitors must keep to the paths when visiting **Vieng Xai** and other parts of Laos close to the Vietnam border.

Carved out of the limestone cliffs of Vieng Xai, a theater provided entertainment for the Pathet Lao leaders and their soldiers.

Mongolian horses, although temperamental, are the perfect form of transport in the far-reaching steppes of Mongolia.

# MOUNT TSAST

Explore western Mongolia's deserted steppes on horseback, encountering some of the world's last genuine nomads.

Mongolia is an unfenced green plain scored by the yellow lines of the jeep tracks that are the nearest thing most of the country has to highways, its emptiness broken up by the occasional braille of a group of *ger*, the circular tents of white felt that nomadic Mongols still call home. The provincial capital of Khovd, in the far west close to the Chinese and Russian borders, is a huddle of Soviet-era buildings in a sea of aching emptiness close to the Altai Mountains. From here it is about 60 miles (96 kilometers) to the base of 13,756-foot (4,193 meter) Tsast Uul, at the western end of the Tsambagarav massif. The mountain's lower slopes offer excellent trekking, best tackled the traditional way on locally rented horses, with their owners as guides. The pure air is complemented by the aromas from wild mint and garlic plants as they are brushed by the horses' hooves. Distant snowfields seem close enough to touch, and there's a digital clarity even to distant sounds—the grunt of a yak, the whistle of a marmot scurrying for its burrow, the wingbeat of a bird. This seems truly the middle of nowhere, until the sudden appearance of a camel-herder with a string of supercilious beasts, or marmot-hunters with small-bore, long-barrel rifles. Hovering kites are often an indication of a ger ahead, from which the occupants emerge to restrain a snarling mastiff and invite you in for fermented mare's milk.

**When to Go** From mid-May through September, with July the most popular month because of the traditional three-day *naadam* festivals of the "three manly sports"—horse racing, wrestling, and archery—which are held in regional centers. From October through April the weather can be extremely cold.

**How to Find It** Western Mongolia is usually reached via Beijing and Ulaanbaatar. There are regular flights between Ulaanbaatar and Khovd.

**Planning** Specialist companies such as the U.K.'s Steppes Travel or Australian-run Karakoram Expeditions run organized or tailor-made tours.

**Websites** www.mongoliatourism.gov.mn, www.steppestravel.com, www.gomongolia.com

## My Secret Journey

*Horseriding in Mongolia provides unadulterated pleasure for every nerve ending except those around the rear. Although 800 years ago it was the main tool in the Mongols' successful invasion of China, today's Mongolian horse is a little temperamental, and doesn't like those it carries to wear deodorants or take pictures from its back. Admittedly, cameras were not widely available in the 13th century, and legend has it that the Mongol invaders could be smelled long before they came over the horizon, but it is hard to imagine a beast as sensitive as this being the main tool in the creation of an empire stretching from the Black Sea to the Yellow Sea.*
**Peter Neville-Hadley**
**Travel writer**

ASIA

THE WORLD AT YOUR FEET

LAST WILDERNESSES   ISLAND GETAWAYS   THE ROAD LESS TRAVELED   SECRET HISTORY   SPIRITUAL HAVENS   HIDDEN TREASURES   UNDISCOVERED VILLAGES   CITY SECRETS

SUMATRA

# KERINCI SEBLAT

This is Earth as it was millions of years ago—jungle, swamps, volcanoes, and a food chain topped by giant plants and predators.

Located in one of the world's wildest places—the Indonesian island of Sumatra—Kerinci Seblat sprawls across four provinces and three major river basins. At the heart of the park are three large valleys surrounded by giant volcanoes, including 12,483-foot (3,805 meter) Mount Kerinci, Sumatra's tallest peak. Waterfalls and lakes abound, such as kayak-friendly Danau Kerinci in the main valley and Gunung Tujuh, a remote high-altitude crater lake. Despite the impressive geography, Kerinci is really about wildlife. The park is nearly three times bigger than Yellowstone and harbors many more species. Among its floral oddities are the world's largest flower *(Rafflesia)* as well as the world's tallest (Titan Arum), the latter also called the "corpse flower" because it stinks like rotting flesh. Asian elephants, Malay tapirs, Sumatran rhinos, sun bears, and clouded leopards are among the big animals that call the park home. But Kerinci is best known as the realm of the Sumatran tiger and an illusive creature called the *orang pendek* ("short person"), which, depending on who you chat with, is either a very rare primate or a Sumatran version of Bigfoot. Indeed, you really don't know what's down that jungle path. But that's a large part of Kerinci's allure.

**When to Go**  Almost astride the Equator, Kerinci has weather that is tropical throughout the year, with rain nearly every day, even during the so-called dry season (December–January). However, temperatures can be quite pleasant, the heat and humidity moderated by the park's altitude.

**How to Find It**  Fly via Singapore and the Sumatran west coast city of Padang. Whether you take the coast or inland route, the national park is about a six-hour drive south of Padang.

**Planning**  Most hotels and guesthouses are located in the town of Sungai Penuh, a drowsy hive of humanity in the middle of the park. Wedged between paddy fields on the edge of town, the Mahkota is the best hotel. The two-day trek to the summit of Kerinci volcano is the park's most celebrated activity, but there are numerous other hikes, including the rain forest trail to Gunung Tujuh crater lake. Given that it's extremely easy to get lost in the Kerinci jungle, no hikes should be attempted without a local guide. Book guides at the park headquarters in Sungai Penuh or in nearby villages.

**Websites**  www.bahasa.net/kerinci/kerinci.html, www.fauna-flora.org/tigers.php

ASIA

### My Secret Journey

*I found myself knocking on the door of a cinderblock house on the outskirts of Kerinci Seblat National Park, home to my old friend Debbie Martyr, caretaker of a conservation program. Over the next three days I explored Kerinci with Debbie and her conservation team, 20 young Indonesians with equal dedication. As the local maven for a British environmental group called Fauna & Flora International (FFI), Debbie has been consulting on wildlife projects with her Indonesian national park and forestry department partners. She has stalked elephant poachers, weaned orphaned sun bear cubs, intervened in conflicts between tigers and local farmers, and tried (unsuccessfully thus far) to capture the orang pendek on film or tape. Given that tiger numbers are on the rise in the park, her efforts seem to be paying off.*
**Joe Yogerst**
**Travel writer**

Opposite: Kerinci's tropical jungle, home to a vast range of flora and fauna  Above: The endangered Sumatran tiger

This giant tingle tree in the Walpole-Nornalup National Park has a trunk hollowed out by fire.

AUSTRALIA

# WALPOLE-NORNALUP

From forests of giant trees to deserted inlets and beaches,
this corner of Western Australia is a nature-lover's paradise.

The locals know where this gem ranks in the natural world order: "North Pole, South Pole, Walpole!" they say, with a smile. All around this small town on the southern coast of Western Australia, the distinctive scent of eucalyptus leaves fills the air. Ancient forests cover the hills where birds soar and dive, call and chatter. Coastal rainfall is high, and swift rivers run to quiet estuaries. Take an interpretive eco-cruise on a twin-hulled, covered boat to explore the shimmering waters of the Walpole and Nornalup inlets. The air is sweet and clean as you leave the town jetty and glide over the pristine waterways. The Frankland and Deep Rivers inlets are also in the national park. Later, you pause at a wooden jetty on the Nuyts Wilderness Peninsula before walking along a track through milk-white dunes leading to a wide, dazzling beach between granite headlands where the mighty Southern Ocean's waves crash ashore. Back to the boat and after a cup of tea and a piece of homemade "tingle" cake, the cruise takes you back toward Walpole. Black swans watch quietly as you pass by.

**When to Go** September through November (spring) is the time for wildflowers; in January (high summer) the red-flowering gums called *ficifolia* add splashes of bright color to the gray-green bush. All year, bird calls are everywhere—from honeyeaters, parrots, fly batches—and it is easy to spot gray kangaroos and bandicoots.

**How to Find It** Walpole is on the South Western Highway, 75 miles (120 km) west of Albany and the nearest airport. The Wow Wilderness EcoCruises leave from Walpole jetty; you need to book in advance.

**Planning** Walpole offers accommodations and cafés, an herb farm, and a parrot jungle. It is a popular destination for canoeing, fishing, and bush walking. Some walks, such as the Coalmine Beach Heritage Trail (1.8 miles/3 km), start in the town. For serious walkers, the Bibbulmun Track—at almost 600 miles (1,000 km) the longest walking trail in Western Australia—passes through the town.

**Websites** www.walpole.com.au, www.wowwilderness.com.au, www.bibbulmuntrack.org.au

## Valley of the Giants

■ Adults and children hang on to the safety rail as they make their way along the **treetop walkway** in the Valley of the Giants, part of the Walpole-Nornalup National Park, peering into the canopy of bright green leaves on swaying branches. The walkway sways slightly, too, so you become part of this ancient forest, which has tall *karri, jarrah,* and *marri* trees—pungent eucalyptus alive with birds and small animals.

■ The forest is most famous for the ramrod straight, towering **tingle trees** that grow only in this part of Australia. Here, just ten minutes from Walpole, you can listen to birdsong as you walk on the curved metal walkway 130 ft (40 m) above the ground.

■ At ground level is a **boardwalk** through the Ancient Empire Forest that is wheelchair accessible for the first section and offers another opportunity to discover some of the forest's secrets.

AUSTRALIA AND OCEANIA

THE WORLD AT YOUR FEET

LAST WILDERNESSES

ISLAND GETAWAYS · THE ROAD LESS TRAVELED · SECRET HISTORY · SPIRITUAL HAVENS · HIDDEN TREASURES · UNDISCOVERED VILLAGES · CITY SECRETS

AUSTRALIA

# THE OUTBACK BY CAMEL

Travel the outback in the manner of early explorers,
sleeping in a swag under the star-filled sky.

AUSTRALIA AND OCEANIA

A ustralia's lively coastal cities may glitter, but the country's interior remains both largely desert and largely deserted, and crossed by few roads. The best way to travel across the vast spaces in between is, as many of the original European explorers did, with a long string of pack camels. One of the places where you can do this is around South Australia's Lake Eyre, a region of vast, open beauty, all acacia-studded red sand and salt lakes, empty of people yet full of outback history. Here it is still possible to wander off into the void with camels as porters, startling kangaroos and emus used to having the arid landscape to themselves, the silence broken only by the calls of wagtails and magpies, and an occasional roar from a discontented camel. The passage of wild donkeys' hooves makes shallow trenches just deep enough to collect a little moisture and produce a wavering line of grass. But sometimes these tracks turn out to be long-forgotten human trails, revealed by the discovery of an ancient horseshoe, a miner's pick with his name still visible on the handle, or a litter of ceramic lemonade flasks and schnapps bottles, undisturbed from the day they were drained and dropped perhaps a hundred years ago.

**When to Go** The season for camel-trekking is the Australian winter, from late April through early September, when temperatures are tolerable.

**How to Find It** Trekking companies provide details on reaching trek starting points. These are often remote, so if you are without a vehicle you need to look into long-distance bus schedules or the company's pickup arrangements.

**Planning** Sleeping on camel treks is under the open skies, usually in swags (as in the "swagman" from "Waltzing Matilda"), an overcovering for the sleeping bag you need to bring. All other needs are usually included—not least, surprisingly good campfire meals that taste even better after a day in the open air, especially when washed down with a mug of good Australian red wine.

**Websites** www.austcamel.com.au, www.australia.com

### Ship of the Outback

The camel has been part of Australian life since 1840, when one known as Harry arrived from the Canary Islands and was used by John Horrocks to search the inland for new pastures. Unfortunately, Harry caused the explorer to accidentally shoot himself while unloading his gun. Despite the shaky start, hardworking camels became the unsung pioneers of the outback. Shipped from what is now Pakistan, camels carried freight to railheads, delivered mail, even provided police mounts. When they were overtaken by the internal combustion engine, more than 10,000 were turned loose, and bred themselves into the world's largest wild population, numbering 200,000.

Camel-riders make their way across a typical central Australian landscape of red earth dotted with eucalyptus trees.

The steep cliffs, tidal inlets, and rockpools of Taiaroa Head are home to a rich variety of seabirds, penguins, and mammals.

NEW ZEALAND

# TAIAROA HEAD

This wildlife sanctuary is home to a breeding colony
of the world's largest seabird, the northern royal albatross.

The coastal road to Taiaroa Head at the tip of South Island's Otago Peninsula twists and curves, offering teasing glimpses of cobalt blue waters and quiet bays dwarfed by towering rock cliffs. A northern royal albatross soars silently overhead on 10-foot-wide (3 meter) wings. It beelines back to its nest, hidden in the grass, where a fuzzy, snow-white chick waits eagerly for morsels of fish scooped from the cold Pacific waters. The headland has the only mainland breeding colony of the world's largest seabird, now protected through the Royal Albatross Centre nature reserve. Below the albatross viewing area, a colony of Stewart Island shags cling to the nearly vertical rock ledges. At dusk on a nearby beach, yellow-eyed penguins, the world's rarest penguin, surf to shore after their daily fishing trip. Resting briefly on the sandy beach, the penguins, called *hoiho* by the native Maori people, soon waddle off to their hidden burrows, their high-pitched trill piercing the air as they excitedly greet their mates. At Pilots Beach, another secluded inlet, blue penguins scamper past a pod of New Zealand fur seals, whose lazy slumbers are interrupted by a large bull clumsily hauling himself onto the slippery rocks.

**When to Go** Year-round, although from early November, when young albatross and penguins are born, through late March there is a greater abundance of marine wildlife to observe.

**How to Find It** Taiaroa Head is a 40-minute drive along the peninsula from Dunedin, the second largest city on South Island, overlooking Otago harbor.

**Planning** Accommodations and car rental are available in Dunedin. For up close viewing, visit the Royal Albatross Centre or Penguin Place (open year-round), a penguin conservation reserve. Advance reservations are essential. The center's albatross observatory is closed during the breeding season, from mid-September through late November. Several nature tour companies offer land or boat excursions.

**Websites** www.otago-peninsula.co.nz, www.albatross.org.nz, www.penguinplace.co.nz

### New Zealand's Castle

En route to the peninsula, detour to **Larnach Castle**—the country's only castle—constructed in the 1870s using the best imported marble, tiles, and glass, and wood harvested from native forests. Australian businessman William Larnach spared no expense when he built the 43-room mansion. The ornate wooden ceilings alone took 12 years to carve. In the 1930s, a subsequent owner added outdoor statues of characters and items from *Alice's Adventures in Wonderland,* a whimsical theme continued to the present day. Perched atop a hill, the castle tower has panoramic 360-degree views of Otago Peninsula, the ocean, and the town of Dunedin.

AUSTRALIA AND OCEANIA

INDIA

# Manas Wildlife Sanctuary

Enjoy elephant treks, river trips, and sightings of rare animals in this wildlife sanctuary in the Himalayan foothills of Assam.

ASIA

If you want to feel as close to nature as it is humanly possible to feel, spend a night at the forest bungalows at Mathanguri, on the banks of the Manas River, deep in the forest of the Manas Wildlife Sanctuary. The roar of the tiger, the screech of the golden langur—seen only here—myriad bird sounds, the startled "whoop whoop" of the rarely seen hoolock gibbon, as well as the constant rushing of the river, are just some of the exotic sounds you can hear as night begins to fall. Early next morning, you will see much more, especially from the back of an elephant. The animals obey the mahout's every command, crisscrossing the sanctuary's grassland plains, as the guide points out rare birds (from among the 450 species present), such as the great pied hornbill and the Bengal florican, swamp deer, hogs, and herds of wild elephant. The Indian rhino is a common sight, too, and if you are lucky you may see a clouded leopard, golden cat, or pygmy leopard. Tigers can be elusive, but sightings are not uncommon given the vastness and density of the sanctuary. Later in the day, boat trips take visitors upstream to view the thickly forested country along India's border with Bhutan.

**When to Go**  From October through April.

**How to Find It**  Barpeta Road, 25 miles (40 km) south of the park entrance, is the nearest roadhead and train station. The nearest airport is at Guwahati, the state capital of Assam, 109 miles (175 km) away. Buses and taxis run between Guwahati and Barpeta Road/Manas, and the journey takes about five hours.

**Planning**  You will need a permit, available from the park headquarters in Barpeta Road. There are two forest lodges near the park, one at Barpeta Road and Bansbari Lodge at the park entrance. Bansbari Lodge can arrange boat tours on the Manas River. The two bungalows at Mathanguri are operated by the state tourist department. If you are staying there you need to take your own provisions as there are no catering facilities, although you can engage a cook for a small fee.

**Website**  www.assambengalnavigation.com

## Nature's Treats

■ The vast variety of rare plants and flowers in Manas include *Reinwardtia indica, Pueraria subspicata, Exacum teres, Pygmaeoprema herbacea, Chiloschiosta junifera,* and *Mangifera sylvatica.*

■ In winter you might spot some of the migratory birds that visit here, such as ruddy shelduck, riverchats, cormorants, Indian hornbills, and great pied hornbills.

■ December through March is an ideal time for fishing as the river becomes an angler's paradise. Sit with a book, waiting for the fish to bite, with the sounds of the forest all around you.

Some of Manas's elephants relax after a day's work carrying visitors on tours through the park.

# CALL OF THE WILD

Enjoy close-up encounters with some of the
world's most remarkable animals.

### ❶ Right whales, Bay of Fundy, Canada

Northern right whales are on the brink of extinction, but survivors arrive in the Bay of Fundy each summer (May through October) to feed east of Grand Manan Island. They are recognized by a broad back, no dorsal fin, and white callosities on the head, which distinguish them from other whales entering the bay.

Planning Whale-watching tours operate out of Digby Neck peninsula on Nova Scotia and nearby islands, such as Brier Island, St. Andrews, Grand Manan Island, and Deer Island. www.bayoffundytourism.com

### ❷ Grizzly bears, Alaska

Grizzlies like salmon. In mid-July and again in mid-August and September, grizzlies make for Alaskan rivers to hook out the fish with their formidable claws. The bears gather in large numbers at rapids and pools, sometimes fighting for the best sites. MacNeil River State Game Sanctuary, Brooks Falls in Katmai National Park, and Fish Creek, near Hyder, have viewing platforms.

Planning Most fishing sites are accessed by chartered light aircraft and a hike. Hyder is off the Stewart-Cassiar Highway. www.explorenorth.com

### ❸ Monarch butterflies, Sierra Chincua, Mexico

Each fall, millions of North American monarch butterflies migrate thousands of miles to the oyamel fir forests of the Transvolcanic Mountain Range, in the state of Michoacán, to overwinter. They cluster together on tree trunks, bushes, and on the ground on Sierra Chincua and four neighboring hills that make up the Monarch Butterfly Biosphere Reserve.

Planning Chincua is one of two hills in the reserve open to the public from November through March. www.fs.fed.us/monarchbutterfly/index

### ❹ Community Baboon Sanctuary, Belize

Black howler monkeys are called "baboons" in Creole. Two hundred landowners have pledged to protect their local population, an initiative started at Bermudian Landing and now covering more than 19 sq miles (50 sq km) of rain forest along the Belize River. The community offers guided tours and night walks.

Planning Less than one hour's drive northwest from Belize City, or by boat from Ambergris Caye or Caye Caulker. www.howlermonkeys.org

### ❺ Humpback whales, Rurutu, French Polynesia

Snorkeling in waters with 98 to 196 ft (30 to 60 m) of visibility makes the island of Rurutu one of the best spots for whale encounters in the world. Between July and October it plays host to calving, nursing, and mating humpbacks. Boats leave regularly from the village of Moerai for three-hour trips to whale-watch and swim with mothers and calves.

Planning Rurutu is a 90-minute flight from Tahiti. The island has limited accommodations, so book early. www.tahiti-tourism.com

### ❻ Komodo dragons, Komodo Island, Indonesia

Landing on Komodo, you step back to a time when dinosaurs ruled the Earth for, as ancient maps reported, "Here be dragons!" This mountainous volcanic island is home to the world's largest living lizard—the Komodo dragon. You can hike to a viewpoint at Banugulung and watch as park rangers feed goat carcasses to the lizards, some of which are more than 10 ft (3 m) long.

Planning Komodo is reached by boat from Bima (on eastern Sumbawa) or Labuan Bajo (on western Flores). www.komodonationalpark.org

### ❼ Snow monkeys, Chubu region, Japan

Snow monkeys—Japanese macaques—sit in hot tubs to keep warm in winter. At Jigokudani Wild Monkey Park, in the central Japanese Alps, you can watch the monkeys taking advantage of hot mineral water bubbling into pools among the dark gray rocks. You can trek through the Nagano Woods to reach the site.

Planning Reachable by a train to Yudanaka town, a bus to Kanbayashi, and a 30-minute walk to Jigokudani. www.jigokudani-yaenkoen.co.jp

### ❽ Synchronous fireflies, Selangor, Malaysia

A sampan trip down the Selangor River on a clear night will bring you to one of the world's largest colonies of fireflies. The insects, which actually are beetles, flash their green-yellow lights so that the *berembang* mangroves along the riverside at Kampung Kuantan village resemble flashing Christmas decorations. Both males and females produce light, but it is the males that flash in synchrony.

Planning Kampung Kuantan is 5.5 miles (9 km) from Kuala Selangor town and 35 miles (56 km) from Kuala Lumpur. www.virtualmalaysia.com

### ❾ Giant pandas, Shaanxi province, China

With facilities at Wolong National Nature Reserve destroyed by the 2008 earthquake, there is an alternative at Laoxiancheng National Nature Reserve in Shaanxi, one of several reserves in the misty Qinling Mountains. An ecotourism project has guided treks into the bamboo forests here, where you might encounter giant pandas, golden snub-nosed monkeys, and golden takin.

Planning Laoxiancheng is 65 miles (105 km) east of Baoji. The best time to visit is May through September. www.wildgiantpanda.info/qinling.htm

### ❿ Wildebeest migration, Serengeti, Tanzania

Undoubtedly the world's most spectacular wildlife sight is the annual wildebeest migration, when 1.4 million wildebeest and 200,000 zebras and gazelles are on the move across the Serengeti plains. The animals chase the rain and fresh grass. Along the way, lions and hyenas stalk them, and crocodiles lie in wait.

Planning The herds migrate across Tanzania from December through July, and then pass through the Masai Mara in Kenya in August and September. www.tanzaniaparks.com

Opposite: Surrounded by a cold and rugged landscape, a pair of snow monkeys keep warm in the natural hot springs at Jigokudani Wild Monkey Park, Japan.

# YALA NATIONAL PARK

Sri Lanka's second largest national park is famous
for its exotic wildlife and unspoiled beaches.

ASIA

Even through binoculars you don't see the leopard until it finally moves. Nature's camouflage in action, black spots suddenly appear against the mottled brush as the big cat makes its way across a clearing in Yala National Park. Sri Lanka's largest conservation area, Yala sprawls across more than 386 square miles (1,000 square kilometers) at the island's southern end. From Asian elephants and sloth bears to crocodiles and wild buffalo, the park is home to varied big game. But its main claim to fame is its leopards—it is the best place on the planet to observe and photograph these big cats in the wild. Yala's Block One (the main visitor zone) supports a group of 30 to 35 and, unlike elsewhere, the leopards are not afraid to flaunt their spots. Visitors do the rounds in 4WD safari vehicles and sleep in tented camps or wilderness lodges. The landscape resembles the African bush, a mélange of scrub forest, savanna grassland, and water holes where the wild things gather to drink and bathe. Where it differs is in its beaches, as the park also has miles of unspoiled Indian Ocean coast framed by coral reefs and monolithic boulders. Park facilities were badly damaged by the tsunami of 2004; several dozen visitors and park employees were killed, but the disaster seemed to have had little impact on the wildlife.

**When to Go**  The main rainy season is April to May, when the northeast monsoon sweeps in from the Bay of Bengal. More rain can be expected between November and January. The January-April dry season is said to be best for seeing large mammals; the October–December period is best for birds.

**How to Find It**  The entrance to Yala is about 12 miles (19 km) southeast of the town of Tissamaharama, 190 miles (306 km) southeast of Colombo. It can be reached from Colombo by road, train, or bus. Tangalle is two to three hours west of Yala by road.

**Planning**  Three days is about right for exploring the park, primarily on early morning and late afternoon jeep safaris. There are five safari camps inside the park and several wilderness hotels on the western edge, including Elephant Reach Hotel and Yala Village resort. You can arrange jeep excursions through your hotel.

**Websites**  www.srilankaecotourism.com, www.elephantreach.com, www.amanresorts.com

## Tangalle

■ Set around a string of sapphire-colored bays, **Tangalle** town has talcum-powder-fine beaches framed by coconut palms. Its other charms include a fishing fleet and old Dutch colonial buildings, such as the courthouse and the old fort (now the local jail).

■ Tangalle also has fine resorts, including **Amanwella.**

■ Inland from Tangalle is the celebrated rock temple of **Mulkirigala,** with fabulous murals, an ancient library, and large reclining Buddhas. Spread through eight caves, the temple dates from the third century B.C.

Dusk is a good time for spotting Yala's leopards.

The Curonian Spit has miles of deserted sandy beaches and a mild climate.

LITHUANIA/RUSSIA

# Curonian Spit

## Forever on the move, the dune landscape on the eastern edge of the Baltic Sea will please beach lovers and bird-watchers alike.

After crossing the narrow strait from the Lithuanian port of Klaipeda, the entire Curonian Spit stretches before you, 60 miles (97 kilometers) in length—32 miles (52 kilometers) in Lithuania and the rest in the isolated Russian province of Kaliningrad Oblast. This long, thin, curved bar of sand separating the Curonian Lagoon from the Baltic Sea measures 2.5 miles (4 kilometers) at its widest point but just 1,312 feet (400 meters) at its narrowest. Strong winds roll the sand into dunes; those on the Baltic side are no more than 32-to-39-feet high (10 to 12 meters), but those on the lagoon side rise 195 feet (60 meters) or more. Forests of pine, spruce, and oak and groves of alder have been planted on many dunes to prevent nearby villages from being buried; other dunes, shaped like scimitars, are still moving. At 220 feet (67 meters), the highest dune on the spit is the Hill of Vecekrug, about a mile (1.6 kilometers) south of the village of Preila. The easiest way to reach it is via the bicycle track from the single road that runs the length of the spit. In spring and fall the spit is an important stopover for birds migrating along the White Sea–Baltic Sea highway, while others remain all year. White-tailed eagles breed in the more remote areas, and hobbies and black kites nest in the forest. The largest and oldest colony of gray herons and cormorants in Lithuania can be found at the village of Juodkrante.

**When to Go** The Curonian Spit is inviting year-round, its sandy beaches, dunes, and forests almost deserted. It is snow-covered in winter, but winters here are relatively mild, while summers are warm.

**How to Find It** Klaipeda has a half-hourly car-ferry service to Smiltyne on the northern tip of the spit. There is a bus service between Smiltyne and Nida, the spit's unofficial capital at the southern end of the Lithuanian section, stopping at Juodkrante on the way. The bus can be crowded, especially on Sundays in summer.

**Planning** One road runs the length of the spit, from Smiltyne to Nida, and car rental is available in Klaipeda. Bicycles are a good way to get about.

**Website** www.nerija.lt

### Amber Treasure Trove

In the 1850s, amber was found in the Curonian Lagoon, and over the next 30 years more than 496,000,000 lb (2,250,000 kg) was dug out. Mixed in with the raw pieces were amber amulets, brooches, figurines, beads, and buttons, which Professor Richard Klebs of Prussia's Königsberg University dated to the mid-Neolithic and Bronze Ages, making them among the oldest-known amber carvings.

During World War II most of the collection was destroyed or stolen, and only a few pieces survive, held at Göttingen University in Germany. The rest were so well documented by Klebs that craftspeople have made replicas, which can be seen at the **Amber Museum** in Nida.

BULGARIA

# BULGARIA'S MOUNTAIN RANGES

The Rhodope, Pirin, and Rila Ranges are filled with craggy peaks, glacial lakes, deep gorges, caves, and rare flowers and birds.

EUROPE

If you like mountains that are off the beaten track, then Bulgaria is the place for you. Three substantial ranges—the Rhodope, Pirin, and Rila—dominate the southwestern part of the country and are the oldest mountains on the Balkan peninsula. The Rhodope is karst country, a landscape carved by water into a series of knife-edged ridges and deep river valleys. Its limestone rocks are sculpted into fantastic shapes, such as the two huge, bridge-shaped boulders known as the Wonderful Bridges in the western Rhodope's Erkyupryia River Valley. The most spectacular gorge is undoubtedly the 4.3-mile-long (7 kilometer) Trigrad Gorge, a canyon with vertical marble walls about 980 feet (300 meters) apart for part of its length, but only 328 feet (100 meters) apart at the Wolf's Leap, where the sky is just a thin streak above you. Several rare bird species are found in the canyons, including the wallcreeper. To the west of the Rhodope is the Pirin Range, much of it contained in Pirin National Park, a mountainous area covered by thick forests of Macedonian and Bosnian pine and Bulgarian fir that hide wolves, brown bears, and almost every European bird of prey species, including the imperial eagle. Its northern end is linked to the Rila Range, the location of Bulgaria's highest peak, Mount Musala (9,596 feet/2,925 meters), glacial lakes, hot springs, and the Rila Monastery, the largest and most striking Eastern Orthodox monastery in Bulgaria.

**When to Go** Spring, after snowmelt, is the time to see the great waterfall in Devil's Throat cave at its most impressive, but June is best for wildflowers on the high alpine meadows. Winters are snowy, with snow lasting for more than six months on the higher slopes. Summers are warm.

**How to Find It** A good base for exploring the Rhodope is the mountain town of Chepelare, 143 miles (230 km) southeast of Sofia. The Trigrad Gorge, Devil's Throat, and Yagodina Cave are 30 miles (48 km) away. The mountain resort of Bansko provides good access to the Pirin Range; it can be reached by road via Blagoevgrad. The main hiking centers in the Rila can be reached via Samokov, southeast of Sofia.

**Planning** All three ranges are crisscrossed by marked hiking trails, and there are a number of huts in the mountains for overnight stays. Hiking and horseriding tours are available. Warm clothes are needed for cave visits as the temperature inside is only in the low 40s (around 6°C).

**Websites** www.bulgariatravel.org, www.bulgarianmonastery.com/rila_monastery.html

## Cave Country

■ In the Trigrad Gorge, the Trigrad River disappears down a vast cave system known as the **Devil's Throat** in which a roaring waterfall plunges 137.7 ft (42 m) into the abyss below—it is the highest underground waterfall in Europe. The first part of the cave is open to visitors.

■ On the other side of the road from the Devil's Throat is a cave more suited to the dedicated speleologist. The **Haramiiska Cave** is reached by climbing 65 ft (20 m) up to a gigantic gash in the vertical rock wall and then clambering 141 ft (43 m) down the other side into an enormous cavern 529 ft (160 m) long and 197 ft (60 m) high.

■ A two-hour walk (5 miles/8 km) from Trigrad village will bring you to the **Yagodina Cave** in neighboring Buynovsko Gorge. At 6 miles (10 km) long, it is the longest cave system in the country and was home to Stone Age people more than 6,000 years ago. The first of its several levels has electricity, and you can take a guided tour through tumbling stalactites resembling stone curtains and organ pipes, spirelike stalagmites, and nests of cave pearls. The walk takes 45 minutes or so.

Opposite: Glacial lakes high in the Rila Mountains   Above: Sculpted rocks in the Rhodope

Bialowieska is home to the continent's only remaining population of European bison.

POLAND/BELARUS

# BIALOWIESKA FOREST

This untamed wilderness is the last vestige of the once-vast woodland that extended from the North Sea to the Russian steppes.

Shafts of sunlight pierce the dense canopy, illuminating the mossy, fungus-covered remains of fallen trees that litter the forest floor. All around, ancient oaks, maples, hornbeams, and spruce recede into the shadowy depths. Other than the occasional drone of a passing insect, there is utter silence. This is Bialowieska, lowland Europe's last remaining primeval forest, sprawling across the marshy land on either side of the Poland-Belarus border. One immediately noticeable difference from other forests, and a clue to its unsullied authenticity, is the apparent "untidiness" of the landscape: Tree cover is variable, with areas of open woodland alternating with dense groves and airy glades. Trees are present in all shapes and sizes, lacking the degree of uniformity encountered in woodlands where planting (and felling) has taken place. Some of the oaks in Bialowieska are more than 400 years old and 120 feet (35 meters) tall. The protected area is divided into an inner zone and an outer zone—to visit the former (known as the "strict reserve") you must be accompanied by a registered guide, which is also the only way to fully appreciate the ancient magic of the forest. The outer zone is open to all and has numerous cycling and hiking trails.

**When to Go** From late March through early October, as winters are very cold and snowy.

**How to Find It** Most visitors access Bialowieska National Park on the Polish side, from the village of Bialowieska in the heart of the forest, about 60 miles (100 km) southeast of the city of Bialystok. There is a daily bus service between Bialystok and Bialowieska. The village offers various places to stay.

**Planning** The most popular way to see the forest is by a horse-drawn cart tour, which takes in the bison reserve and parts of the outer zone—reserve ahead in summer. There is an entrance fee to all areas.

**Websites** www.bpn.com.pl

### The European Bison

Few people are aware that there are bison in Europe, but Bialowieska is the last domain of the **wisent** (European bison). Even by 1914 the national park's population was down to 700. Most of these either died or were killed during World War I, and the last was killed by poachers in 1919. They were successfully reintroduced to the area in 1929.

The park is now home to around 750 of these heavyweights, which can weigh up to 2.5 tons (2.54 tonnes). There is a fair chance of spotting a wild bison in the inner zone of the park, but if you don't, there is also a special bison reserve, used for breeding, where the animals are kept in captivity.

Other notable wildlife includes elks, wolves, and beavers, as well as rich bird life—some 240 species have been recorded, and around 175 of them breed here.

FRANCE

# LE MARAIS POITEVIN

Tucked away just south of Brittany, on France's west coast,
this extensive marshland is best explored by boat.

EUROPE

A nature-lover's dream, Le Marais Poitevin in western France is a sprawling region covering 2,470 acres (1,000 hectares) of managed marshland *(marais)*. The city of Niort marks the eastern edge of the Marais, which stretches for more than 40 miles (65 kilometers) westward to the town of Marans, near the Bay of Aiguillon on the Atlantic coast, north of La Rochelle. On its northern edge, the verdant Marais starts around Fontenay-le-Comte in the Vendée and encompasses 2,485 miles (4,000 kilometers) of waterways. Since the 11th century, when local monks dug the first drainage canals in the area to allow floodwater to drain away, this unusual region has developed a canal-based system of agriculture and transportation. The *barque,* a flat-bottomed, wooden boat, has been used for centuries to haul lumber, grain, and livestock. Today, curious visitors explore the Marais on foot, by bicycle, or paddle a rented canoe. But to best observe this fragile ecosystem and its flora and fauna, reserve a barque and guide in advance for a canal ride in the filtered light of early evening: Everything from egrets to otters, kingfishers to muskrats, ventures out in their green world, and the frogs begin their nightly chorus.

**When to Go**  Boats can be rented from April through October. Wildfowl migrations pass through the Marais in spring and fall, the perfect time to visit the Parc Ornithologique (Bird Park) in St.-Hilaire-la-Palud, west of Niort. Yellow irises bloom along the canals in late spring.

**How to Find It**  For easy access to the dense maze of canals that make up the most interesting section of the Marais, head for Arçais. The village streets lead down to a row of canalside jetties where you can make boat reservations before enjoying a leisurely lunch. Maps for biking and boating are available at the tourism office facing the church. This area between Niort and Maillé is known as the wet marshes.

**Planning**  Car rental is available in La Rochelle and Niort. Allow a week if you want to tour the maritime and dry areas as well. Lists of accommodations are available at the tourist offices in Coulon, Arçais, and Niort.

**Websites**  www.la-venise-verte.com, www.visit-poitou.com

## Local History Tour

■ Visit **La Rochelle**'s Natural History Museum to see colorful displays and videos of the flora and fauna of the region's remarkable ecosystem.

■ Stop in **Coulon** (a short drive west of Niort) to tour the Maison des Marais Mouillés for exhibits on history, tools, and local folklore.

■ Arrive in **Maillezais** in time to tour the majestic St.-Pierre abbey ruins before taking an early evening, guided barque ride—with glimpses of the abbey as well as wildlife surprises. Boats can be reserved at Embarcadère de l'Abbaye.

Gliding peacefully along Le Marais Poitevin's labyrinth of canals, through a green, watery world

# BIRDING SPOTS

Experience some of the most intriguing sights in the bird world, from the colorful inhabitants of tropical rain forests to cliff-dwelling seabirds and migrating hawks.

## ❶ Point Pelee National Park, Ontario, Canada

A melodious symphony of birdsong fills the air as you meander through forests and marshlands at Point Pelee, which juts into the northwest corner of Lake Erie. The first landfall for neotropical migrants heading north across the lake, it's a major stopover for dozens of warblers and hundreds of other species, which often drop out of the sky from sheer exhaustion after the long water crossing.

Planning Peak migration occurs in mid-May. www.pc.gc.ca

## ❷ Quivira National Wildlife Refuge, Kansas

The raucous squawks and honks are deafening as migrating waterfowl and shorebirds gather in the marshes and mudflats of Quivira National Wildlife Refuge and nearby Cheyenne Bottoms in south-central Kansas. Nearly half of the Western Hemisphere's shorebird and waterfowl species stop here to rest and refuel.

Planning Visit in the spring or fall to view the greatest abundance of migratory species. www.fws.gov/quivira

## ❸ Asa Wright Nature Center, Arima, Trinidad

Hike through tropical rain forest on this former coffee-cocoa-citrus plantation in northern Trinidad and be dazzled by purple honeycreepers, golden-headed manakins, and many other brilliantly colored birds. The 1,500-acre (607 hectare) property is recognized for its commitment to tropical wildlife conservation.

Planning Access to the rare guacharo (oilbird) colony is available only to guests reserving a minimum of three nights' accommodation at the center. www.asawright.org

## ❹ Mindo, Pichincha Province, Ecuador

As you ascend Pichincha volcano's western slope into the high-altitude cloud forest of Mindo-Nambillo Protected Forest, you glimpse a flash of pumpkin orange plumage as an Andean cock-of-the-rock zips by. Nearby, golden-headed quetzals flit through the canopy. This 47,444-acre (19,200 hectare) nature reserve provides protection for more than 50 endemic bird species.

Planning Mindo is about 40 miles (65 km) northeast of Quito and can be reached by bus or taxi. Best birding is September through January, when migratory species are present. www.ecuador.com

## ❺ Roebuck Bay, Western Australia, Australia

Sandpipers, red knots, and other waders dart and bob on the rich mudflats of Roebuck Bay on Australia's northwest coast as they forage for food. Of the 300 species found in the Broome area, about 50 are shorebird species, a quarter of the world's total.

Planning Accommodations and guided birding tours are available at Broome Bird Observatory, a nearby education and research facility. www.broomebirdobservatory.com

## ❻ Shiretoko Peninsula, Hokkaido, Japan

The coast around the fishing town of Rausu, on the remote Shiretoko Peninsula in eastern Hokkaido, has the largest wintering population of the majestic Steller's sea eagle in the world, together with white-tailed eagles, glaucous, glaucous-winged, and slaty-backed gulls, Whooper swans, and northern pintail. At night, you might catch a glimpse of the rare Blakiston fish owl.

Planning Boat trips depart from Rausu for the edge of the pack ice for the best views of the Steller's sea eagle. www.japan-guide.com

## ❼ Çamlica Hill, Istanbul, Turkey

From the top of 860-ft-high (262 m) Çamlica Hill, Istanbul's highest point, you'll witness waves of black-and-white storks, honey buzzards, and other raptors cross the Bosporus from Europe. These diurnal migrants dip and soar on thermal lifts high above the meeting point of the Sea of Marmara and the Black Sea.

Planning Mid-morning to mid-afternoon in August and September is peak viewing time. www.tourismturkey.org

## ❽ Vega Archipelago, Norway

These windswept islands just south of the Arctic house one of the planet's densest populations of white-tailed eagles, and support migratory and resident seabirds, including black guillemots and greylag geese. Small, triangular shelters are built by villagers on Vega, the largest inhabited island, to protect nests of the common eider, whose down is collected for quilts.

Planning Transportation to the archipelago is by ferry from the town of Brønnøysund. www.verdensarvvega.no/english.htm

## ❾ Camargue, France

A flock of greater flamingos march across a shallow lagoon, turning in unison like a highly trained dance troupe. Watch as these pale-pink-feathered birds, heads submerged in the brackish water near the Camargue's Rhône River delta, scoop mouthfuls of brine shrimp before pausing to rest on one leg, the other tucked close to their bodies.

Planning Visit in January or February, the primary breeding months, to witness mating rituals. www.parc-camargue.fr

## ❿ Mkhuze Falls Game Reserve, South Africa

The diversity of habitats in Mkhuze Falls Game Reserve, KwaZulu Natal, including acacia savanna, swamps, and rare sand forest, attracts more than 400 of South Africa's 820 recorded bird species. Observe the country's only breeding colony of pink-backed pelicans or search for yellow-rumped tinkerbirds, lesser masked weavers, and purple-crested turacos.

Planning Use the park's eastern entrance to reach an array of habitats and the KwaJobe community, a Zulu village. www.sa-venues.com

Opposite: Greater flamingos perform a courtship display in the Camargue wetlands of southern France. Their pink color comes from the plankton on which they feed.

The Mawddach River runs through a wide, sandy estuary of great beauty and enters the sea at Barmouth Bay.

WALES

# Mawddach Estuary

Enjoy cycling, hiking, bird-watching, and miles of sandy beaches set against a backdrop of the Snowdonia Mountains.

Snowdonia National Park brims with stunning scenery spreading out over 800 square miles (2,070 square kilometers) in north Wales. Among its highlights is the soothing Mawddach Estuary, whose intense blue waters are surrounded by lush pastures and rugged mountains. William Wordsworth called Mawddach "sublime," and it continues to enchant visitors with its beaches of gold-flecked sands shining in the sun. For a short time, there was an actual gold rush in the area, but any remaining mines have long been abandoned. For a spectacular, traffic-free walk along the estuary, take the Mawddach Trail at the southern end of Snowdonia National Park. Considered one of the best trails in the U.K., the meandering route follows an abandoned railroad track and is perfect for walking or biking because much of it leads over flat expanses of countryside. Starting at the town of Dolgellau, the trail winds for 9.5 miles (15 kilometers) through fields dotted with wildflowers and ends at the beachside town of Barmouth. Dramatic backdrops are revealed at every twist and turn. The soft scent of salty air follows you, snowcapped Cadair Idris looms above, and wading birds and swift gulls frolic on the shoreline.

**When to Go** The Mawddach Estuary is lovely throughout the year, but in spring rhododendrons are bursting into bloom all around the area.

**How to Find It** To reach the estuary, fly in to Birmingham and take a train to Machynlleth. From there, take a bus to Dolgellau. Or take the train from Birmingham to Barmouth. For lovely mountain views, you can also take a quick ferry ride across the mouth of the estuary from Barmouth to Fairbourne.

**Planning** Along the way from the Mawddach Estuary to Portmeirion, plan a stop at Harlech, with its imposing castle set high on a hill overlooking the coast.

**Websites** www.travelwales.org

## Fantasy Village

Like a scene from a surreal dream of Italy, **Portmeirion Village** sits on a privately owned peninsula of golden beaches and sprawling subtropical gardens 13 miles (21 km) north of the Mawddach Estuary. The creation of Welsh architect Clough Williams-Ellis, the Italianate structures of Portmeirion were built on Snowdonia's southern shores to show that a place of natural wonder could be developed while still preserving the beauty of the site. Among an array of whimsical buildings, the Hotel Portmeirion features unique rooms, including one lined with gilded mirrors. Its Art Deco dining room reflects the ambience of a luxury ocean liner.

EUROPE

# Coffee Bay

This spotless stretch of coast on South Africa's southeastern seaboard is a paradise for hikers, surfers, abseilers, and bird-watchers.

Coffee Bay is in the heart of South Africa's Wild Coast, a relatively untouched haven in the Transkei region of Eastern Cape, birthplace of Nelson Mandela. The bay got its name, so the story goes, when a ship carrying coffee beans ran aground here in the early 19th century. Some of the spilled beans took root, although there is no sign of any coffee trees today. The sand beach here is pristine and edged by steep cliffs, and while surfing, beachcombing, or cliff walking you are more than likely to meet a domestic cow or two. They will be owned by the local Xhosa people, who live in the thatched huts dotted around the hillsides and who often invite visitors into their homes to give them something of the true African experience. Passing through the bay is the Wild Coast Hiking Trail, which in places is marked by white footprints painted on the dark rocks. A three-hour hike south from Coffee Bay through coastal bush and stands of aloe and euphorbia will take you to the Hole in the Wall, a massive sea arch set between the ocean and a lagoon at the mouth of the Mpako River. Along the way, you will come across Baby Hole in the Wall, a smaller sea arch dwarfed by sheer, 164-foot-high (50 meter) cliffs and the Hlungunwane Waterfall.

**When to Go** The subtropical climate is kind to visitors year-round, with few extremes. Winter temperatures (April through August) are 44°–68°F (7°–20ºC), and summer 60°–82°F (16°–28ºC), with a daily average of seven to eight hours of sunshine.

**How to Find It** Coffee Bay is a four-hour drive from the city of East London. Take the N2 north; shortly before the town of Mthatha (formerly Umtata), take the Viedgesville turnoff and follow the coastal road for 50 miles (80 km) down to Coffee Bay.

**Planning** Accommodations include two small hotels and two lively backpacker hostels. Hluleka Nature Reserve is 56 miles (90 km) southeast of Mthatha, off the R61. It is open all year from sunrise to sunset, and you can stay in rustic chalets in the reserve.

**Websites** www.sa-venues.com, www.ecparks.co.za

### Hidden Haven

Farther up the coast, between Coffee Bay and Port St. Johns, is the **Hluleka Nature Reserve.**

■ Impalas, blue wildebeests, and zebras wander among stands of exotic trees, such as stink ebony and coral trees. Look up to see Cape parrots and down for ground hornbills. Look carefully to spot the Knysna loerie, a green bird that flashes bright red wing feathers as it flies, and the bright yellow bill of the rare green coucal.

■ You are likely to see African fish-eagles and ospreys along the coast. Whales and dolphins may put in an appearance offshore.

Surf continually pounds the Wild Coast, creating a dramatic coastline of high cliffs, rocky shores, sea caves, and sheltered beaches.

# 3
# ISLAND GETAWAYS

Unspoiled tropical paradises, where crystal-clear turquoise waters lap against palm-fringed milky white sands, do still exist. Remote, self-contained, and laid back, these tiny pinpricks of sun-drenched land jutting out of the balmy waters of the Caribbean, the Indian Ocean, or the South Pacific seem to be the embodiment of heaven on earth. But island retreats come in many different guises. Isolated, icebound South Georgia, at the gateway to Antarctica, or Spitsbergen, known as the Arctic's answer to the Galápagos Islands, reward the adventurous traveler with life-affirming views of the natural world. Or for sheer otherworldliness, head for the island of Socotra off the Horn of Africa, where an alien-looking landscape harbors a collection of weird and wonderful plants found nowhere else on Earth. And in many parts of the world—from the Outer Hebrides to the coast of South America—it is the people themselves, with their unique history, culture, and folklore, who help to make their island such a truly magical and unforgettable destination.

All the ingredients for a sublime tropical island getaway—silver-sand beaches, pristine rain forest, and marine life inhabiting a cornucopia of coral—may be found in the remote El Nido archipelago, on Palawan, in the South China Sea.

# St. Helena Island

Steeped in history and strong on southern hospitality, this is the quaint, quiet home of the African-American Gullah culture.

One of the Sea Islands that string along the coast of South Carolina and Georgia, St. Helena is so different in culture and temperament from the mainland that it could well be another country. The Sea Islands are part of the Lowcountry, a vast coastal realm where precious little land rises more than 20 feet (6 meters) above sea level. Here thousands of tendrils of water, both salt and fresh, meander like a life-giving blood system through a landscape of wildlife-filled marshes and dry hummocks, or "marsh islands," shaded by giant live oaks festooned with Spanish moss. Before the Civil War this was some of the richest farmland in America, where untold wealth was generated through slave labor in the cultivation of rice, indigo, and later, cotton. When the land was exhausted, it was given to freed slaves, who created their own culture and language called Gullah. While the Civil War was still raging, the first school for freed slaves was started on St. Helena. Today, on the site of the school, the Penn Center preserves the history of the Sea Islands and the unique Gullah culture. Spend your days climbing the historic lighthouse and combing the beach at Hunting Island State Park, kayaking the marshes, visiting the Penn Center, or shopping for Gullah crafts, including finely woven seagrass baskets.

**When to Go** The best time to visit is in the spring and fall. April and early May offer warm but not too hot days, and a palette of blooming azaleas, magnolias, wisteria, and other flowers. In the fall, the marsh grasses turn golden and kayak touring is delightful.

**How to Find It** The nearest airports are Savannah/Hilton Head (48 miles/77 km) and Charleston (88 miles/142 km). U.S. 21 connects St. Helena with the county seat of Beaufort.

**Planning** Good accommodations can be found just off-island in Beaufort. Fripp Island, near Hunting Island State Park on the ocean side of St. Helena, offers an upscale private community of rental beachfront cottages. Nature lovers can rent a marsh-front cottage at Palm Key, located on the wildlife-filled wetlands of the Broad River, 27 miles (43 km) inland from Beaufort.

**Websites** www.southcarolinalowcountry.com, www.beaufortsc.org, www.rhetthouseinn.com

## Antebellum Gem

Located on the shores of the Intracoastal Waterway, **Beaufort** was once a center for plantation and shipping commerce. Today, elegant Greek Revival homes with stately white columns line the waterfront. The town's charm has made it a popular location for movies such as *Forrest Gump* and *The Big Chill*.

From late spring through early fall, you can clip-clop under moss-laden oaks through the historic town by horse-drawn carriage, or for a truly southern experience, enjoy Sunday brunch on the porch of **Rhett House Inn,** an elegant townhome built by plantation owner Thomas Smith in 1820.

Freshly caught shrimp, in season from May through December, can be bought straight off the boat.

Palms grace the uncrowded, pristine sands of the 2-mile-long (3.2 km) crescent of Sun Bay.

PUERTO RICO

# VIEQUES ISLAND

With its military past behind it, laid-back Vieques
is reinventing itself as an ecotourist destination.

Selected in World War II as the site for a U.S. Navy weapons-testing range, tiny Vieques, 6 miles (10 kilometers) from Puerto Rico's southeast coast, was for a long time largely off-limits. An unexpected legacy of the Navy's occupation is that today around two-thirds of the island remains entirely undeveloped, forming the Caribbean's largest, most ecologically diverse wildlife refuge. Here are coastal lagoons, coral reefs, palm-lined beaches, mangrove swamps, and forests rich with banana, mango, and aptly named *flamboyant* (flamboyant) trees. Wild horses roam freely. Yet Vieques's environmental beacon is Mosquito Bay, the world's biggest, brightest bioluminescent lagoon. Its rare ecosystem harbors dinoflagellates—plankton emitting light to deter predators. Splash hands underwater at sunset and they fluoresce. Vieques's history is equally incandescent. Archaeologists found some of the Caribbean's oldest human remains here at Puerto Ferro, a little-visited mini-Stonehenge, proving humans have lived here at least since 1900 B.C. When the conquistadores arrived around A.D. 1500, they savagely subjugated the indigenous Taíno people, whose culture almost perished. The fort—the last the Spanish built in the New World—and the nearby Punta Mulas lighthouse are reminders of Spain's four-century-long rule.

**When to Go** Vieques is warm all year. Avoid the relatively crowded high season–May through August.

**How to Find It** Ferries to Vieques ply from Fajardo, scheduled flights from San Juan and Ceiba, and charter flights from Culebra.

**Planning** Public transportation on Vieques is poor. Many roads and some of the best beaches are accessible only by 4WD. The best way to explore is to rent a jeep or horse. Expect to dodge wild horses after dark. Some areas remain off-limits because of road upgrades or unexploded ordnance. Most facilities are in Esperanza, on the south coast, or the administrative center of Isabel Segunda, on the north coast. Except for the low-rise, luxury W resort, accommodations are low-key. An ultrahip place to stay is Hix Island House. The best way to experience Mosquito Bay is a sunset tour with Abe's Snorkeling.

**Websites** www.gotopuertorico.com, www.vcht.com, www.vieques-island.com, www.isla-vieques.com

## Culinary Hot Spot

■ Vieques's gastronomy has rapidly risen from ill-lit to bioluminescent. The island is now a beacon for Nuevo Latino, a cuisine unafraid to fuse local ingredients and international techniques. *Ceviche,* a citrus-infused Latin American sashimi, *mofongo,* plantain mush, and *tostones,* twice-fried plantain chips, are well-known Puerto Rican dishes.

■ Unique to Vieques are arepas *fritas,* white-flour fritters, served with *arroz con habichuelas* (rice and beans) and fried fish. The signature alcoholic drink is *bilí,* a mix of white rum, seasonal fruit—perhaps *quenepa* (mamoncillo), *pajuíl* (cashew fruit), tamarind, or passion fruit—and white sugar.

NORTH AMERICA

# ISLANDS IN THE SUN

These tiny specks in the ocean might be difficult to find on a map,
but once there, you'll feel as if there is nowhere else on Earth.

### ❶ Eleuthera, Bahamas

English puritans landed in 1648 and named the island after the Greek word for "free," which is exactly what today's visitors feel when they set foot on the glistening pink and sugar-white beaches that ring this 110-mile-long (177 km) ribbon of land. Peace reigns over this colorful island of colonial villages, rolling acres of pineapple plantations, red-rock cliffs, and bougainvilleas in a palette of fiery shades.

Planning There is no public transportation, so it's best to rent a car at one of the island's three airports. www.bahamas.com

### ❷ Bonaire, Netherlands Antilles

Divers flock here to see underwater wonders that include rainbow frogfish, parrot fish, sea cucumbers, dolphin pods, volcanic slopes, and shipwrecks. On land, the aptly named Pink Beach plays host to hundreds of flamingos and big blue lizards. Lac Bay on the eastern side of the island is a mecca for windsurfers.

Planning Every diver must purchase a Marine Park tag, valid for one year. www.tourismbonaire.com

### ❸ San Blas Islands, Panama

A short (20 minute) flight from Panama City transports you to the islands of the Kuna, which have maintained their distinct way of life for centuries. The men still fish for crab, snapper, and lobster off the reefs in boats dug out of tree trunks, while the women in the thatched-roof villages wear traditional handcrafted fabrics in a rainbow of colors and decorated with geometric patterns, fish, birds, and animals.

Planning The Kuna are a reserved people, so a tip is expected and appreciated if you photograph them. www.visitpanama.com

### ❹ Ilha Grande, Brazil

Treks into protected pristine rain forest reveal rarities such as brown howler monkeys, maned sloths, red-browed Amazon parrots, and broad-snouted caiman. Offshore you might spot Magellanic penguins and southern right whales. There are more than 100 unspoiled beaches on the vehicle-free island, including Lopes Mendes with strong surfing waves.

Planning The best places to stay are in the forest away from the main villages. www.ilhagrande.com.ar

### ❺ Rangiroa, French Polynesia

Hundreds of tiny islets wrap around a large, deep lagoon like a pearl necklace. Along the few roads are small villages, coral churches, and over water bungalows. The lagoon's turquoise waters can be explored by glass-bottomed boat.

Planning Sign up to tour a black pearl farm or sample the island's wine at the Rangiroa Vineyard. www.tahiti-tourisme.com

### ❻ Koh Rong, Cambodia

Deserted beaches, one small fishing village, and a few thatched-roof huts flank the calm, clear waters of this rarely visited island, accessible by boat from Sihanoukville. The sands on Snowdrift Bay are so powder soft that they squeak underfoot.

Planning There are no guesthouses on the island, so take a tent and provisions. www.tourismcambodia.com

### ❼ Cocos (Keeling) Islands, Australia

The 600 or so inhabitants of ethnic European and Malay origin live in splendid isolation in the middle of the Indian Ocean, with coconuts their only cash crop. North Keeling Island is home to the only surviving population of Cocos buff-banded rail, the islands' only endemic bird.

Planning Rent a car or bike to explore West Island. www.cocos-tourism.cc

### ❽ Lakshadweep, India

Meaning "one thousand islands" in Sanskrit, Lakshadweep in fact comprises just 36 islands, ten of which are inhabited. This emerald cluster, off the coast of Kerala in the Arabian Sea, is India's only coral reef. Lagoons rich in marine life make it a beacon for fishing and water-sport enthusiasts. Uninhabited Bangaram is the ultimate get-away-from-it-all destination.

Planning The best time to visit is from October to mid-May. Permits to visit the islands are issued in Kochi. Consumption of alcohol is prohibited except on Bangaram. www.lakshadweep.nic.in

### ❾ Sífnos, Greece

Picture-postcard villages of dazzling whitewashed buildings perch on hillsides or nestle beside the cobalt sea. There is a church for each day of the year, including the Chrysopigi monastery on a rocky precipice just outside the village of Faros. Visit during *paniyiri,* a traditional festival to celebrate the name day of a saint. A church service is followed by a fiesta of local food and wine, music and dancing.

Planning The local buses are good and serve the main villages and many of the beaches. www.visitgreece.gr

### ❿ Frégate Island, Seychelles

Tales of buried pirate treasure add to the romance of this tropical paradise with just 200 permanent residents. The island is named after the frigate birds that perform their aerial acrobatics overhead. There are no fewer than 50 species of bird on the island, including the rare magpie robin. Giant tortoises and the world's only population of the giant tenebrionid beetle are other attractions.

Planning Swimming and snorkeling are particularly favorable April/May and October/November. www.seychelles.com

Opposite: Rangiroa, the largest atoll in French Polynesia, is one of the world's great dive destinations.

# St.-Barthélemy

Bon vivants are drawn to this tiny sliver of rocky,
hilly land that oozes French sophistication and style.

The mouthwatering aromas of freshly baked bread and just-brewed coffee waft on the balmy breeze as you stroll down the narrow streets lined with cafés and bakeries, chic boutiques, and art galleries. Gustavia is the capital of St. Barth and, like the rest of the island, is incontrovertibly French—although its name (after Gustav III) is a legacy of the near century the island spent under Swedish rule from 1784. Today, the island is a collectivity of France, with French the dominant language, culture, and cuisine. Some islanders still speak age-old Norman or Breton dialects, and at the fishing village of Corossol older women don traditional starched white sunbonnets known as *quichenottes*. Catch the waves at Baie de St. Jean on the opposite side of the island from Gustavia, a haven of designer boutiques, gingerbread cottages, beachside bistros, vividly painted bungalows, and brightly colored skiffs. Devoid of high-rises, mega-resorts, or casinos, serene St. Barth's nightlife consists of strolling moonlit beaches, stargazing, savoring French cuisine, or listening to the local beguine music—either beguine with drums and *tibwa* rhythm sticks or orchestral beguine with vocals usually sung in Creole.

**When to Go** St. Barth enjoys year-round warm temperatures, with cloudy days few and far between. High season tends to be mid-December to mid-April and peak holidays. In summer, the beaches are less crowded and villa rentals less expensive. A few restaurants close in September. June and November are a bit more humid. Rainstorms pass quickly.

**How to Find It** Take the high-speed ferry from St. Martin, arrive on a yacht, or fly into St. Barth's airport. There are direct flights or charters from the United States and Europe to Guadeloupe or the airport on the Dutch side of St. Maarten (St. Martin). Flights from St. Maarten take about 10 minutes.

**Planning** Rent a jeep or scooter to traverse the island's narrow and curvy roads. Driving is on the left-hand side. Be prepared for switchbacks and few guardrails. Although there are 22 intimate hotels, including the glitzy Eden Rock, many visitors rent villas.

**Websites** www.franceguide.com, www.frenchcaribbean.com, www.st-barths.com

## Bumpy Landing

Flying directly in to **St. Barth** can be an adventure. Because the runway at the small airport is just 2,170 ft (660 m) long, the strip can accommodate only a 20-seat (or smaller) plane. The real challenge comes as the plane almost skims a mountain peak and then immediately drops down to the runway. If it's windy, the plane shivers.

No nighttime flights are allowed, and any pilot who lands on the island must have special training. But even the best of pilots can overshoot the runway and land in the shallow water beside the airport. Passengers might get their feet wet, but otherwise a water landing is relatively harmless.

Traditional fishing boats rub shoulders with luxury yachts in this beautiful far-flung corner of France.

A river cruise through lush rain forest affords a glimpse of some of Dominica's remarkable flora and fauna.

DOMINICA

# DOMINICA

Getting away from it all is still possible on an island that has changed little since Christopher Columbus first landed in 1493.

It's first thing on a dazzling weekend morning and there's nobody else but you on the trail—a meandering path through pristine rain forest that peters out on the banks of the Emerald Pool. Stripping down to your board shorts, you slip into the chilly water and swim to a waterfall tumbling over the entrance to a rocky grotto on the far side. An emerald isle if ever there was one, Dominica boasts a larger percentage of land given over to national parks and forest reserves than any other major Caribbean island. Throw in secluded black-sand strands, mountains cloaked in lush vegetation, lakes, and hot thermal springs, and a different river to swim in or fish for every day of the year, and this is as close to a tropical Eden as you'll find. There is also a rich Creole culture that is evident in the island's cuisine, carnivals, and festivals—with the World Creole Music Festival taking place here every October. But still the major attraction is clean, green fun. Whether you are searching for the endangered Sisserou parrot along the Syndicate Nature Trail, clambering up the 4,747-foot (1,447 meter) Morne Trois Pitons peak, or getting up close and personal with humpback whales, this is nature at its unalloyed best.

**When to Go**  The island's tropical climate means that showers are possible at any time of year, the wettest months being from August through October. Sperm whales inhabit the waters around Dominica year-round, but the season for migratory humpbacks is from November through March.

**How to Find It**  There are no direct flights to Dominica from North America or Europe. The most convenient waystations are San Juan (Puerto Rico), Antigua, and St. Lucia. French-owned l'Express des Isles offers a high-speed ferry service from Martinique, Guadeloupe, and St. Lucia.

**Planning**  The Fort Young Hotel nestles inside the walls of a ruined 18th-century British colonial fort overlooking the waterfront in Roseau, the national capital. Or get back to nature at Beau Rive on the secluded east coast. Ken's Hinterland Adventure Tours offers guided hikes, waterfall safaris, and other nature activities.

**Websites**  www.dominica.dm, www.fortyounghotel.com, www.beaurive.com, www.expressdesisles.com

## My Secret Journey

*In amongst the ginger lilies and bright-red anthuriums flanking a mountain road on the secluded east side of Dominica, I encounter half a dozen local children, their light-brown skin and almost Asian faces unlike anything I've come across in the Caribbean before.*

*They are members of a tiny ethnic group called the Kalinago—the last of the Carib Indians who once inhabited all of the Windward Islands before the arrival of the Europeans. They live in eight villages in the highlands above the island's eastern shore, around 2,000 people on a small reserve set aside by the Dominican government.*

*The children agree to take me to their thatched-roof homes, about a mile away and almost hidden by the thick jungle. The Carib I meet are friendly but shy. Their Creole-accented English is too thick for me to understand, but by using mainly hand signals, I manage to learn a little about how they live: weaving, calabash carving, making clay pottery, and hunting birds with bow and arrow. This impromptu diversion into Carib territory on my way to the east coast has introduced me to a culture that has changed little since pre-Columbian days.*
**Joe Yogerst**
**Travel writer**

NORTH AMERICA

Fishing enthusiasts and divers can hire boats to explore Margarita's turquoise waters.

VENEZUELA

# ISLA DE MARGARITA

Venezuelans call this the pearl of the Caribbean, where
white beaches are bathed in sunshine nearly year-round.

Photographers are poised for another unforgettable golden sunset as generous brushstrokes of yellow-gold and wisps of pink paint the sky at Juan Griego, a town on the island's north coast. For the best views of this picturesque bay, climb up to La Galera, the fortress where the islanders fought a fierce battle for independence against the Spanish in the early 19th century. To get a flavor of life past and present on the island, venture inland to the charming village of Santa Ana, where you can see women at age-old wooden looms making the traditional netlike hammocks. At nearby La Vecindad, the distinctive hammocks are made from multicolored fabrics. In the village of El Cercado, you can watch artisans working clay by hand to create their characteristic pottery. Another slice of Caribbean life awaits at Punta de Piedras, a fishing port chock-full of bobbing boats, tangled nets, and colorful local houses. On the narrow isthmus separating this eastern side of the island from the arid, largely undeveloped Macanao peninsula to the west is the Laguna de la Restinga National Park, a stretch of sand, marsh, mangrove, and coral sandy beach that is home to more than 100 species of bird, including flamingos, scarlet ibis, white ibis, great white heron, pelicans, and hawks.

**When to Go** Margarita is busiest during Christmas and Easter and from July through mid-September. There is no rainy season. Most days are sunny, with average temperatures around 80°F (27°C).

**How to Find It** There are direct flights to Caracas from Houston and Miami, and charter flights from Europe. Then take the ferry or a 30-minute flight to the island. The express ferry takes two hours.

**Planning** Rent a compact car or scooter. Roads in the countryside are narrow; watch out for potholes. Siesta time prevails, so generally stores are open from 9:30 a.m. to 1 p.m., and again from 3 p.m. to 8 p.m.

**Websites** www.caribbeantravel.com, www.venezuelavisitorsbureau.com, www.margarita-island.com, www.margarita-island-venezuela.com

### Creole Flag

Venezuela's national dish, *pabellón criollo*, is a hearty concoction of shredded beef, white rice, black beans, and fried plantains—a combination that is said to resemble the national flag. Sometimes a fried egg is served on top, known as *pabellón a caballo* (meaning "on horseback"). The stacked plate is accompanied by arepas, a flat, round bread made from cornmeal. During Lent, *chigüire* (capybara) meat makes it onto the menu alongside fish. The story goes that, in the 17th century, Creoles were able to convince the Catholic Church that this large guinea-pig-like rodent was in fact a fish!

SOUTH AMERICA

BRAZIL

# FERNANDO DE NORONHA

One of Brazil's hidden treasures, this is the
only visible part of a submerged volcanic mountain.

On the shore, magnificent frigate birds swoop to steal the catch of red-tailed tropic birds on their way back from fishing at sea. Alongside these pirates of the air are pelicans, noddies, terns, and boobies. Jutting up from the turquoise ocean some 200 miles (320 kilometers) off the northeast coast of Brazil, this archipelago—consisting of one main island, from which the group gets its name, along with 20 small islands—is home to one of the largest island colonies of seabirds in the tropical south. In November, flocks of migrating birds, including ruddy turnstones, stop off on their journey from the Northern Hemisphere to South America. November is also mating time for green turtles off the beach at Leão Bay. The females haul themselves ashore between December and May to deposit their eggs in the sand. Golphinos Bay is closed to swimming, diving, and boating since it is a daytime resting site for spinner dolphins. In late afternoon, their activity rises to a crescendo, with dolphins leaping clear of the water and spinning through 360 degrees, before they all go to sea to hunt at night. Below the waves, snorkelers and scuba divers are privy to a vibrant underwater world of corals, sponges, and brightly colored fish. Lemon, nurse, and Caribbean reef sharks seem friendly enough, and flying fish take to the air. Above the water, volcanic rocks dominate the landscape, including the phallus-shaped Morro do Pico, the island's highest point.

**When to Go**  The rainy season is from January through August, with the heaviest rains from March through July. October is the driest month, and January through March are the hottest months.

**How to Find It**  There are daily flights to the main island from São Paulo, with a brief stop at Recife, or direct flights from Natal.

**Planning**  Only a limited number of tourists are allowed at any one time. An environment protection tax is collected from all visitors, and the longer you stay the more you pay. Don't forget to pack insect repellent.

**Website**  www.noronha.pe.gov.br

### Checkered Past

Portuguese explorer Fernão de Noronha is credited with discovery of the archipelago in 1501. Its strategic position in the South Atlantic is reflected in the number of times it has been invaded: The English, French, Dutch, and Portuguese have all occupied it at some stage.

When Charles Darwin visited in 1832, he found an "island covered with wood," but later all the trees were cut down to prevent prisoners on the island from escaping on rafts.

As well as being a fortress and a penal colony, **Fernando de Noronha** has served as a stopover for early trans-Atlantic flights, a World War II airbase, and a U.S. missile-tracking base.

A mature green turtle returns to mate and deposit eggs at Leão Bay, the beach where it entered the waters as a hatchling many years before.

# Isla Grande de Chiloé

Distinctive wooden churches stand testament to the days
when Jesuits made it their mission to convert the local people.

A low, warm mist hangs over the sea at Castro, the island's capital, and slated wooden *palafito* houses rise from the water on spindly legs. Herded by a noisy flock of gulls comes a small fleet of yellow trawlers, low in the water and heavy with fish. Isla Grande de Chiloé is the largest in the Chiloé Archipelago; it lies a few miles from the Chilean mainland and is just 118 miles (190 kilometers) long and, at its broadest point, 40 miles (64 kilometers) wide. Most people live on the eastern side of the island, which is dotted with small fishing and farming communities and hundreds of simple wooden churches painted in arresting colors. These are the result of zealous Jesuit activity in the 17th and 18th centuries, and it is this fusion of Christianity and indigenous beliefs, based on tales of the sea, trolls, ghost ships, and monsters, that makes the island's folklore so rich. The inhabitants, known as Chilotes, have forged a path largely separate from that of the mainland. The island was the last Spanish stronghold in South America, and the Chilotes' rural and seafaring traditions have evolved separately from those of their sovereign state. Chiloé National Park on the island's western shore is home to the Chilote fox and the *pudú*, a miniature deer. Walking trails lead visitors through miles of Valdivian temperate rain forest and along unspoiled coastline.

**When to Go** The summer months (November through February) are the best time to visit, although there is something of a microclimate here, with weather tending to be humid and cool. The Costumbrista Festival held each February in Castro is a celebration of all aspects of the island's culture.

**How to Find It** Fly from Santiago to Puerto Montt. From here travel southeast toward Pargua (a journey of 35 miles/56 km) and take the ferry across the Chacao Channel to the island. The crossing takes half an hour.

**Planning** Allow four to five days on the island to explore the main towns of Castro and Ancud, and to spend some time exploring the flora and fauna of the Chiloé National Park. A longer trip could involve visits to some of the less populated outlying islands that form the archipelago.

**Website** www.chiloestories.org

## Chilote Cuisine

■ *Curanto* is a type of seafood stew in which the main ingredients—shellfish, fish, meats, sausages, potatoes, and vegetables, each separated by a layer of rhubarb, fig, or cabbage leaves—are heated in a large earthenware pot over hot coals in a hole in the ground.

■ Another culinary specialty is potato bread, such as *chapalele* and *milcao,* which is used to mop up the rich curanto sauce.

■ *Licor* de oro (gold liqueur) is a toothsome fruit liqueur made from apples, berries, and lemon peel. Production is centered around the picturesque seaside town of **Chonchi.**

Colorful *palafito* houses built on stilts hover above the tide in Castro, the island's main cultural and tourist center.

King penguins crowd the beach at Salisbury Plain on the island's north coast. More than 200,000 king penguins breed here.

ANTARCTICA

# South Georgia Island

Intrepid travelers to this icy paradise at the gateway to the Antarctic are rewarded with a spellbinding natural pageant.

Isolated in the Atlantic Ocean's farthest southern reaches, this long, narrow island, together with its surrounding islets and rocks, is one of the world's last true wildernesses. Stormy waters lash the coastline and blizzards can appear out of nowhere even on seemingly quiet days. Access to the island is by cruise ship, and as you approach land, steep, ice-capped mountains come into view. Patches of black rock peek out from the stark whiteness in this pristine landscape. Glaciers, gleaming like blue-tinged diamonds, hug the coast, while jagged peaks and steep mountain ranges line the interior. It seems extraordinary that life could flourish in this forbidding landscape, but it does—and in concentrations unequaled almost anywhere else on the planet. Waddling king, macaroni, and gentoo penguins congregate in vast colonies; roaring elephant seals and fur seals crowd the beaches in the thousands. Overhead come the calls of courting seabirds like the wandering or royal albatross—some with 11-foot (3.5 meter) wingspans. Reindeer, introduced by Norwegian whalers in the 20th century, now roam the island. Gigantic whales, which enticed fortune seekers to establish a now long gone whaling industry in the early 1900s, cavort in the deep waters offshore.

**When to Go** Cruises generally sail during the southern summer—from November through January.

**How to Find It** The city of Ushuaia, at the extreme southern tip of South America, is a key access point for Antarctic cruises. There are regular connecting flights from Buenos Aires and Santiago.

**Planning** The journey is not for the fainthearted. You'll be traveling through extremely rough water, where 30-ft (9 m) swells are not uncommon, so expect to get seasick. There are no medical facilities or search-and-rescue operations on the island. The weather is severe and highly unpredictable. Some of the wildlife, such as fur seals, can be aggressive, so keep your distance. Wear waterproof, polar expedition-weight clothing and heavy boots. Bring sunscreen and sunglasses.

**Websites** www.hurtigruten.us, www.sgisland.org

### Ernest Shackleton

A simple stone in the whalers' cemetery at **Grytviken** marks the grave of one of the world's greatest explorers. In 1914, Ernest Shackleton set sail from South Georgia on the final leg of his expedition to cross Antarctica. His ship, H.M.S. *Endurance*, was destroyed by ice in the Weddell Sea, and after several months camping on the ice, the crew reached inhospitable Elephant Island. From there, Shackleton and a few of his men set out on the 800-mile (1,290 km) return voyage to South Georgia in a small lifeboat. Weeks later, they landed on the uninhabited south coast of the island, and after an epic 36-hour trek across the uncharted interior, Shackleton finally knocked on the door of the Stromness whaling station.

SOUTH AMERICA

# KIRIBATI

Not even a precarious future from the threat of rising
seas can dampen the joie de vivre of the I-Kiribati.

AUSTRALIA AND OCEANIA

The people "sing with a certain lustiness and Bacchic glee," wrote Robert Louis Stevenson about the inhabitants of Kiribati (pronounced KEER-ee-bas), a sprawling South Pacific archipelago that stretches across an area larger than the continental United States. In Stevenson's day, the chain of coral atolls was a British colonial possession called the Gilberts. While waves of progress have swept across the isolated islands, they maintain much of the amity and innocence that made them such a joy to visit in bygone times. All together there are 33 landfalls in the chain, including Tarawa, the national capital and home to more than a third of the archipelago's population. It was here that one of the bloodiest battles of World War II took place, and rusting tanks and other relics are still visible today. Farther north is the isle of Makin, home of the legendary Gate of Eternity, through which all I-Kiribati must pass on their way to the afterlife. The national drink is *kaokioki,* a potent, fermented toddy made from coconut juice, the recipe a secret passed down from generation to generation for hundreds of years. Another vital national art form is dance, including the vigorous *Te Buki,* with its gyrating hips and heavy palm-frond skirts.

**When to Go** Kiribati is always warm and sunny, with a breeze to soothe daytime temperatures that range from 77° to 91°F (25° to 33°C). The biggest holiday falls in the middle of July, a week of revelry that includes Kiribati National Day (July 12) and three other celebrations.

**How to Find It** Air Pacific flies twice weekly between Fiji and Tarawa.

**Planning** As tourism is relatively new to these islands, there are not many places to stay. Mary's Motel, Tawara, provides basic accommodation with air-conditioning and a good restaurant. Another option is Tawara's 40-room Otintaai Hotel, which has a car-rental service and can arrange boat trips to other islands and transport to local dance performances. English is widely spoken.

**Websites** www.kiribatitourism.gov.ki, www.airpacific.com, www.otintaaihotel.com

## Making the Headlines

■ With land that rises no more than 6 ft (1.8 m) above sea level, **Kiribati** has been pinpointed as one of the first places that will disappear if sea levels start to rise. Erosion of the coastline is already a serious problem, and the government is in ongoing talks with nearby nations (like New Zealand) to accept Kiribati refugees in the wake of full-scale submergence.

■ In 2000, Kiribati's easternmost island, **Caroline** (also known as Millennium Island), ushered in the first sunrise of the new millennium. The celebrations on the normally uninhabited island were televised around the world.

As a result of its warm climate and myriad lagoons, Kiribati is an ideal place to cultivate seafood for commercial purposes.

The mysterious ruined city of Nan Madol covers numerous artificial islets in a shallow lagoon.

FEDERATED STATES OF MICRONESIA

# Pohnpei

Despite its natural and man-made attractions, this volcanic island continues to fly beneath the radar of South Seas tourism.

Big, wet, and wild, Pohnpei is the largest of the many scattered islands that make up the FSM, a sprawling western Pacific nation that gained independence in 1986 after more than a century of largely benign colonial rule under Spain, Germany, Japan, and finally the United States. The island gets more rain (300 plus inches/7,620 millimeters per year) than just about any other place on the planet, water that nurtures an emerald-green nirvana with more than 40 rivers and streams, and myriad waterfalls that plunge into cool, blue swimming holes. Largely roadless and undeveloped, the island's rugged and remote interior is best explored on hiking trails that meander through thick tropical forest and along ridges that lead to the nation's highest volcanic peaks. Also known for its biodiversity, local forests harbor several bird species found nowhere else in the world, including the Pohnpei lorikeet and the Pohnpei fantail, and the island's wraparound lagoon is one of the region's most pristine. With marine life galore, Pohnpei's jagged, mangrove-studded coastline offers excellent diving and fishing.

**When to Go**  Relatively hot, wet, and humid throughout the year, with temperatures hovering around 80°F (27°C). For surfers, the season for the island's Palikir Pass, a hot spot for adventurous surfers, is October through April, when huge breakers roll in from the north Pacific.

**How to Find It**  Continental Micronesia airlines touches down in Pohnpei on its aerial "bus route" between Honolulu and Guam. Flight time is 10 to 11 hours.

**Planning**  Pack a light raincoat and waterproof shoes, especially if you're going to be doing much walking in the interior. The best place to stay is the Village Resort Hotel, a family-run establishment with thatched-roof bungalows beneath coconut palms on one of the small outer islands overlooking the Pohnpei lagoon. There are a handful of restaurants and bars on the island.

**Websites**  www.visit-fsm.org/pohnpei, www.continental.com, www.thevillagehotel.com

## The Venice of the Pacific

A 45-minute boat trip from Pohnpei's main town, Kolonia, takes you to **Nan Madol,** a magnificent lagoon city where you can see stone palaces and temples linked by canals rather than roads. According to ancient legend (partially verified by recent archaeological finds), the inhabitants worshiped sacred eels and sacrificed sea turtles as part of their religion.

First discovered by German explorers in the 19th century, Nan Madol's megalithic architecture remains one of the great mysteries of Micronesia. Nobody knows for sure where the huge stone building blocks came from or how they were transported to the site.

AUSTRALIA AND OCEANIA

# CORAL REEFS

Around many an island lies an underwater landscape of dazzling beauty—irresistible to divers and snorkelers—where fish and sea creatures weave through extraordinary coral sculptures.

## ❶ Andros Island, Bahamas

The barrier reef, 1.5 miles (2.5 km) offshore, marks the edge of a 2,000-ft (610 m) drop into the vast depths of the ocean. In the reef, underwater caves and blue holes thread through giant tube sponges, sea whips, finger coral, smooth star coral, and sea fans up to 5 ft (1.5 m) in height. Watch out for fire coral and incrusting stinging coral, as they burn the skin.

Planning There are two daily flights from Nassau to Andros, and a boat once a week. www.bahamas.com

## ❷ Palancar Reef, San Miguel, Mexico

Forty different dive spots are a magnet to winding canyons, narrow crevices, archways, tunnels, caves, and deep ravines filled with black and red coral. Coral heads form a natural U-shape at the top, making the area of Horseshoe a favorite for divers.

Planning San Miguel is on Cozumel island, 12 miles (19 km) east of the Yucatán. Fly to Cozumel International Airport. October through June is the best time to visit. www.visitmexico.com

## ❸ San Pedro, Belize

Hundreds of sand cays, mangroves, coastal lagoons, and estuaries touch the limestone coral island. Dive centers offer trips to 10 different sites amid soft, hard, and fleshy coral in hues of gold, red, orange, green, brown, and yellow. Nocturnal marine life makes for outstanding night dives.

Planning Although English is the official language, Spanish and Creole are widely spoken. June is the rainiest month. www.travelbelize.org

## ❹ Cahuita National Park Coral Reefs, Costa Rica

Zebra-striped fish, lacy tubipora, frondlike gorgonians, sea cucumbers, and fluttering sea fans pave the way for light yellow brain coral, elkhorn, and blue staghorn coral. Explore two sunken ships, one from the 18th century, replete with visible cannons and ballasts. On land, watch for capuchin monkeys, sloths, iguanas, and a birding route of curassow and Swainson's toucans.

Planning Buses depart daily from San José for the four-hour drive east to Cahuita. There is a regional airport at Limón, about 30 miles (48 km) north of Cahuita. www.visitcostarica.com, www.tourism.co.cr

## ❺ Grand Central Station Coral Reefs, Fiji

Submarine gardens of soft lavender, red, orange, and vivid yellow coral intersperse with giant clams, octopuses, squid, and clownfish. The towering coral of Grand Central Station is so named because of the mind-boggling number of sea creatures swimming about. Shallow waters make it easy to dive, stroll on the beach, swing in a hammock, and snorkel again.

Planning The best time to go is during the cooler season, from May through August. www.fijime.com

## ❻ Ningaloo, Australia

Walk directly from the beach onto this coral reef off the coast of Western Australia—a rare experience. Lavender, cabbage, and brain are among nearly 300 species of coral in the shallow, white-sand lagoon where 500 species of exquisitely colored and patterned fish dart around your toes. The protected marine park is home to green, loggerhead, and hawksbill turtles.

Planning Lodging is available in the nearby towns of Coral Bay and Exmouth. www.australia.com

## ❼ Tubbataha Reefs, Philippines

Endangered species, including Napolean wrasses and green turtles, inhabit the multicolored coral reefs of Tubbataha Natural Park. Since it can take ten hours or more to reach the underwater sanctuary by boat, opt for a live-aboard trip.

Planning Regular flights from Manila serve Puerto Princesa City, on Palawan, from where dive boats sail to the park. March through June is the best time to go. www.tubbatahareef.org, www.palawan.gov.ph

## ❽ Andaman Sea Reefs, Thailand

Fringing reefs dominate hundreds of islands off Thailand's west coast. Around the Similans, dive Beacon Reef to explore a recent wreck under the scrutiny of inquisitive batfish, or East of Eden where soft corals resemble an underwater Japanese garden. Translucent waters, white beaches, caves, and coral walls await those who secure a four-day live-aboard diving cruise.

Planning Depending on the boat, Similan National Park is between 45 minutes and three hours by sea from Phuket. The best diving is from October through May. www.tourismthailand.org

## ❾ Maldives

An archipelago of some 1,100 small coral islands and 26 natural atolls forms an infinite underwater mountain range. Three-fourths of the world's reef fish species are dotted around the islands. Some resorts feature a "house" reef where the short distance between beach and reef is safe for children.

Planning All resorts have a professional dive school. www.visitmaldives.com, www.themaldives.com

## ❿ iSimangaliso Wetland Park, South Africa

Formerly known as Greater St. Lucia Wetland Park, the reserve has been renamed iSimangaliso—"a marvel" in Zulu. The underwater seascape is home to coral canyons, overhangs, table and plate corals, and mushroom rocks. Snorkel Cape Vidal, Black Rock, or Kosi Bay; serious divers head for Sodwana Bay.

Planning St. Lucia is a 3.5-hour drive north from Durban Airport. The dry season, April through September, is the best time to go. Stay in a rustic bush camp, or a lodge. www.southafrica.net, www.stlucia.org.za

Opposite: Clown anemonefish inhabit a psychedelic world among the reefs of the Andaman Sea, a paradise for underwater adventurers.

PHILIPPINES

# PALAWAN ISLAND

With vast tracts of unspoiled land and sea harboring a multitude
of species, this has been called the last frontier of the Philippines.

For underwater explorer Jacques Cousteau, Palawan was one of the most beautiful places he had ever visited. With crystal-clear waters teeming with wildlife, this is a divers' paradise. On terra firma, the best way to experience the virgin wilderness of this long, thin island is to set out on foot into the ancient forests that cover much of the interior. The small, postcard-perfect village of Sabang lies where the jungle meets the South China Sea, about two-thirds of the way along the west coast. A number of rewarding treks start here, taking in waterfalls, caves, and pristine rain forest. Walk east along the beach for a short distance before a well-marked trail heads into the trees. The noise of the wind and waves quickly disappears, the light changes from dazzling yellowish white to dim bluish green, and the earthy smell of the jungle washes over you. The trail climbs through a forest of supersized trees draped in moss and liana, a haven for wildlife, including monkeys, monitor lizards, and various exotic birds. A few miles farther on, the entrance to a cave leads down to St. Paul's Subterranean River—thought to be one of the longest subterranean rivers in the world. The boat trip along its 5-mile (8 kilometer) length is an unforgettable experience, taking in cathedral-like caverns and domes, before emerging into the warm, turquoise waters.

**When to Go**  The dry season runs from late November to early May.

**How to Find It**  The capital, Puerto Princesa, is the main point of entry, with several flights a day to and from Manila. Buses and jeepneys (originally U.S. Army jeeps left over after World War II) travel from Puerto Princesa to most towns on the island, including Sabang. The roads are extremely bumpy.

**Planning**  Pay the entrance fee to St. Paul's Subterranean River National Park at the pier in Sabang before you leave. There are two marked trails from Sabang to the underground river—the Monkey Trail and the Jungle Trail—so you can walk there by one route and head back a different way. Alternatively, you can take a boat (banca) in one direction. Keep some time free to enjoy Sabang's magnificent beach and scuba diving. For most of the year it is possible to reach the resort of El Nido from Sabang by boat: a six-to-eight-hour trip. Otherwise, you can travel by bus via Puerto Princesa. El Nido is also accessible by plane direct from Manila. Malaria is widespread on the island, so take the necessary precautions.

**Website**  www.palawan.gov.ph

### Bacuit Bay

Farther up the west coast from Sabang is the spellbinding scenery of **El Nido,** a small resort set around island-studded Bacuit Bay.

■ The immense limestone cliffs that rise out of the tropical sea around Bacuit Bay are home to a species of swiftlet, whose nests (called *nido* in Spanish), perched on ledges hundreds of feet up, have long been used to make the famous Chinese delicacy—bird's nest soup. Spun from the birds' saliva, the cup-shaped nests, which are reputed to be nutritious and have aphrodisiac properties, fetch sky-high prices.

■ The waters around El Nido are protected as part of the Philippines' largest marine sanctuary, with coral reefs harboring more than 200 species of fish, as well as hawksbill and olive ridley turtles. Spectacular underwater drop-offs make for some superb diving.

Opposite: El Nido's skyscraper cliffs tower over the Church of St. Francis of Assisi. Above: Dawn breaks over Bacuit Bay.

# AMAKUSA ISLANDS

A pearl-like archipelago, the Amakusa Islands are as precious to travelers today as they were to Christian refugees 400 years ago.

ASIA

The tiny aircraft covered in blue dolphins starts descending almost immediately after taking off—and minutes later wobbles to a halt on a small hilltop runway on Amakusa. A fragmented archipelago of 120 islands, Amakusa is a blink-and-you-miss-it 20-minute flight from Japan's southern Kumamoto prefecture. With a jagged coastline flecked with small rocky islets, fishing villages, dense green forests, and cloudy mountain peaks, its landscape is as enchanting as its location is remote. As with most islands, the best way to acclimatize is on the water—ideally, cruising under each of the five bridges that link the three main islands beneath a blood-orange sunset sky. Amakusa may excel at producing white pearls, citrus fruits, figs, and sweet potatoes, but its biggest claim to fame is its spiritual heritage: It was here, among its inland hills and saw-toothed coastlines, that Japan's persecuted Christians sought refuge when the religion was banned in the 17th century. Today, the islands' spiritual tourists may be eclipsed by those intent on fishing, sea kayaking, fossil-hunting, and dolphin-watching, but Amakusa's sunsets seduce everyone. With its west coast facing the East China Sea, its skies produce some of Japan's most beautiful, Turkish Delight-colored sunset performances day after day.

**When to Go** Amakusa is a year-round destination, but the best times to visit are during the more temperate spring and fall. Winter days are often crisp, with blue skies, but can be very cold, while summer months can be uncomfortably humid.

**How to Find It** Amakusa Airlines operates daily flights from Kumamoto Airport (20 minutes) and Fukuoka (35 minutes), both of which connect to Tokyo's central Haneda Airport in less than two hours. Arrange car rental and reserve accommodations in advance.

**Planning** Avoid peak season holidays such as New Year and Golden Week in early May. Use local sea taxis to travel between the islands.

**Websites** www.t-island.jp, www.seejapan.co.uk, www.jnto.go.jp

### Christian Chic

■ A white church surrounded by green hills and a glistening sea is an unlikely image for rural Japan. Although most residents of Amakusa today are Buddhist or Shinto, two pretty churches remain—**Sakitsu,** in the Gothic style, and Romanesque-inspired **Oe.** They fuse Eastern and Western cultures, with shoes slipped off at the door as if entering a Japanese house.

■ The island's luxury hotel, **Gosoku no Kutsu,** embraces a religious theme. Sprawled across a forested mountainside, with epic sea views, it has long, candlelit stone corridors, Mexican Catholic artifacts, and monastery-style wooden doors.

An unusual sight in a Japanese fishing village: the church of Sakitsu in Amakusa, rebuilt in 1934

Cradled in the dunes are rain-fed sand-perched lakes, such as Lake McKenzie, where you can swim in the clear water.

AUSTRALIA

# Fraser Island

Uninterrupted white beaches, crystal-clear lakes, and rain forest are just some of the draws of this unique island.

It takes only ten minutes by ferry to reach this low, green island off Hervey Bay on the Queensland coast. Most visitors cross from the north to Kingfisher Bay resort, but by taking the punt barge from Tin Can Bay to Hook Point on the southern tip of the island, you can experience the wild ocean side of the island first. A breeze blows as the ferry carries more than a dozen 4WDs loaded with tents and fishing gear. Once ashore, you get a taste of 4WD sand-driving—you're on the sea-misted, 62-mile (100 kilometer) "highway" along the island's east coast to Indian Head. The beach is a shared zone: Flocks of terns take off and scatter from the shining sands as the vehicles approach. From high masts, the flags of beach fishing camps are stretched taut in the wind. At low tide, the beach serves as a landing strip for light planes. Stretching for 75 miles (120 kilometers), this is the world's largest sand island, now almost entirely national park, and one of the few where rain forest grows. Vast dunes are constantly shaped and reshaped: Hammerstone Sandblow is one of the largest. There is no surfing or swimming on the ocean side for fear of sharks and dangerous currents, but there is a choice of stunning, sand-perched lakes to enjoy.

**When to Go** Fraser Island has a temperate climate all year. Go July through September for wildflowers, July through October for whale-watching (tours from Hervey Bay or Kingfisher Bay).

**How to Find It** Flights from Brisbane to Hervey Bay take 45 minutes. The journey north by road from Brisbane takes about 3.5 hours.

**Planning** Kingfisher Bay and Eurong Beach resorts offer comfortable eco-resort accommodations. One, two, or three-day tours offered by 4WD operators include rain forest walks from Wanggoolba Creek, the old logging camp at Central Station, Lake McKenzie, Eli Creek, and the multicolored cliffs called the Cathedrals.

**Websites** www.fraserisland.net, www.kingfisherbay.com, www.eurong.com, www.sunrover.com.au

## Floating Down

■ South of Indian Head on the east coast is Maheno Beach, where **Eli Creek**—the island's largest waterway—forms a natural waterslide. The shallow, fast-flowing, sand-filtered water—so crystal clear that you can see the sandy floor of the channel as if there were no water—floats you effortlessly downstream to a wide ocean beach. Boardwalks on each bank lead to the head of the creek, where you get into the water. Set back a little way, bright green pandanus palms and wispy casuarinas offer shade from the Queensland sun.

■ Two miles (3.2 km) north of Eli Creek lies the wreck of the **S.S. Maheno,** built in 1905 as a luxury passenger ship. In 1935 it was hit by a cyclone while being towed to Japan for scrap metal and grounded on Fraser Island, where it has been rusting in the sands ever since. The shipwreck is a popular tourist attraction, but climbing on it is not permitted.

■ A little farther north up the coast you can explore the red, brown, and ocher spires of **The Pinnacles,** rocks that have been shaped by wind and water, their colors the result of iron oxides leaching from the rock.

AUSTRALIA AND OCEANIA

# PERHENTIAN ISLANDS

For the adventurous there are jungle treks and snorkeling, while those in search of more sybaritic pleasures head for the beaches.

Paradise has no roads, only trails beneath a canopy of ancient jungle and balmy waters circling the islands' lonely shores. Monitor lizards pad through thick, hot sand and sea-eagles soar over craggy cliffs. At night, bungalow doors stay open as a much coveted breeze returns with the tide. The only noise comes from crickets singing a lullaby accompanied by the lapping sea. Here there are no rowdy backpackers occupying the starlit beach as there are on some other islands in the region. The Perhentian Islands—Perhentian Besar (the big island) and Perhentian Kecil (the small island)—provide a different venue for personal discovery. Take a book, nap in a hammock. If you are feeling more adventurous, rent a snorkel and swim with parrotfish, their big buck teeth chomping on coral. Hike to a little Muslim fishing village—the islands' only permanent habitation—and order a lunch of mutton curry with a side of fried plantains. Hop in a kayak and work your arms in a jaunt across the water. When the wind stalls, the surface turns to glass, giving you a bird's-eye view of the vibrant underworld of fish and anemones.

**When to Go** Although the Perhentian Islands are still relatively quiet in comparison with other islands in the region, tourism is growing; reserve rooms ahead in the peak season of July and August. Don't even think of traveling during the monsoons, October through February, as everything closes down then.

**How to Find It** The Perhentians are accessible by speedboat (about 45 minutes, leaving several times a day) from the jetty in Kuala Besut on Peninsular Malaysia's east coast. Slow boats are also available for charter, as well as to and from nearby Redang and Lang Tengah islands.

**Planning** Perhentian Besar features a few air-conditioned chalets, while Perhentian Kecil is more geared toward budget travelers who don't mind mosquito nets. Both islands have bungalows and restaurants, as well as secluded hideaways where you might be the only guest for a few days. The Perhentians are part of a marine park and visitors are charged a conservation fee. There are no banks or ATMs on the islands.

**Websites** www.perhentian.com.my, www.florabaydivers.com

### My Secret Journey

*The alarm buzzes at midnight, just in time for a moonlit trek through the forest to a beach on the other side of the island. A tractorlike trail marks the sand. The female green turtle has come, as she does each year in May, almost to the date. It takes hours of labor for her to lay her eggs in a pit near the tree line. She grunts and snorts, flinging sand about and heaving her body in wild effort. By the time she finishes, the tide has left, leaving her with a difficult journey back to sea over sharp coral and jagged rocks. It is a trip she knows by instinct, just as her mother and grandmothers did.*
**Karen J. Coates**
**Travel writer**

When the water is clear in Coral Bay on Perhentian Kecil, you can see straight through to the seafloor.

Sleepy fishing villages and yellow-sand beaches fringe the quiet eastern shoreline of Koh Lanta Yai.

THAILAND

# KOH LANTA YAI

Set out on your own motorcycle journey and discover a tropical corner of paradise in the Andaman Sea after all the tourists have gone home.

All that remains on southwest Thailand's Koh Lanta Yai in the off-season are a few smiling Bob Marley-loving locals and countless motorcycles to rent. Arriving at tiny, dusty Baan Saladan from Krabi, head for the Lanta Emerald hotel, home to eclectic heaven—the Ting Tong bar. Order a Leo beer and take a seat on a rusty stool with a friendly crowd of Lantians listening to the whimsical Thai siren perform melodramatic island music. Birdsongs will have you up early the next day to rent your motorcycle and start south. After about 15 miles (24 kilometers) along the island's eastern road, break at Baan Lanta or "Old Town." The city of stilt-houses built out over the sea originally served as a safe harbor for Arabian and Chinese vessels. Today's diverse population includes Muslims, Thais, and modern-day "sea gypsies"—expats avoiding the more touristy western coast. One such resident runs the Hammock House. Grab his free Lanta Biker Map while admiring hammocks made by indigenous hill tribes. After tea at the boutique hotel Mango House, it's only another 6 miles (10 kilometers) to Sang Kha Ou Resort & Spa. The hotel is not really open at this time of year but its owner, Dtong, is not the type to turn away new friends. Sleep in your own tree house, with a view of the water, and in the morning share a meal of fried rice with Dtong and his staff, then let the Lanta Biker Map and the smell of salt be your guide.

**When to Go** The off-season, also the rainy season, is April through June, and September and October. The daily showers are often short, the temperature is cooler, and you'll have the island to yourself.

**How to Find It** The closest airport is at Krabi, 43 miles (70 km) to the north. In the off-season, you can reach Koh Lanta from Krabi by public minivan and car ferry; allow three hours.

**Planning** Carry a raincoat and be ready to experience refreshing showers. You will find that many hotels and activities are closed in the off-season but that the best hotels that are open offer 50 percent discounts.

**Websites** www.lantaoldtown.com, www.kolanta.net

### Thai Street Food

One way to greet people in Thai is to ask, "Have you eaten?" Food—spicy, meaty larb; fluffy molded cups of white steamed or sticky rice; and soupy or fried noodles—is ever present along the streets of Thailand. The menus are in Thai script so look at what's being made and eaten, then point to what you want. Learn to pronounce a few favorites—even if you can't read Thai you can ask for *Tom Yum Gai*, a mild chicken soup; *Somtam*, a spicy papaya salad with crunchy peanuts; and *Paa Thai*, the popular fried-noodle dish. Try at least one of the desserts: Ice-cream sandwiches in hot-dog buns or coconut milk-soaked rice with beets or taro root.

ASIA

St. Mark's Cathedral belfry provided the inhabitants of Korcula's strongly fortified town with a good vantage point.

CROATIA

# KORCULA

This tranquil Adriatic island has an old town center
in the style of Dubrovnik, but without the crowds.

Lying just 4,000 feet (1,220 meters) off Croatia's Dalmatian coast, Korcula is a breezy island of pine forests, quiet beaches, and vineyards, and has one of the best preserved old towns in the Mediterranean. Boats from the mainland coming into the harbor at Korcula town pass the defensive walls encircling its historic center. Built on a little peninsula jutting into the sea, much of the old town dates from the 15th to 18th centuries. Entering through the single, fortified gateway, you follow the narrow streets that climb uphill, your senses assailed by the scent of pine, the warmth of the local ocher-colored stone, and the brilliant pinks and purples of flowers hanging from balconies and in nooks and crannies. A riot of decorations, including coats of arms, shells, frogs, faces, figures, and winged lions, carved by local stonemasons, embellish the walls of the palaces, houses, and churches that cluster together on this rocky outcrop. Small bridges across the streets link houses at first-floor level—the only way some households could expand. Towering over the old town is the cathedral of St. Mark, whose elegant belfry doubled as a watchtower. And around the corner is the building where, islanders claim, the explorer Marco Polo was born, and which now houses a small museum with wonderful views.

**When to Go** From spring through fall. Even in the hottest months, there is usually a cooling breeze.

**How to Find It** Korcula is about 2.5 hours from Dubrovnik by hydrofoil. It can also be reached by car ferry from Orebic and Split.

**Planning** You can explore Korcula town in a day, or spend a week on the island enjoying its beaches—Lumbarda, near the town, is sandy, the others are pebbly—and visiting the vineyards around Vela Luka. Cars and bicycles can be rented near the marina. There are regular bus services to the villages and main beaches.

**Websites** www.korcula-croatia.com, www.mediterano.hr

### Moreska Sword Dance

For more than 400 years, the islanders have performed the Moreska, a sword dance that tells the story of a battle between the Red King (known locally as the White King) and the Black King when the Red King's fiancée, Bula, is captured by the Black King's army. The ritualized battle, danced with real swords, is performed with the Red soldiers in a circle around a circle of Black soldiers, the two armies facing each other. Both circles rotate, as the soldiers attack each other with sword thrusts and parries, with increasing speed. Eventually, the Black King is defeated and Bula returns to the Red King. During summer the dance is performed once a week in the old town.

EUROPE

SWEDEN

# SANDHAMN

An air of otherworldliness pervades this laid-back gem,
even in summer when Stockholmers arrive in number.

The sailboats and pleasure cruisers in Stockholm's bustling harbor gradually recede from view as the ferry plies its way through Sweden's archipelago of more than 20,000 islands. Gulls gently circle in the air above the ferry, and islands big and small appear at every turn. Finally, after an hour and a half, at the outer reaches of this tranquil archipelago, the island of Sandhamn (meaning "sand harbor") looms into view. Toward the end of the 19th century the island became popular with artists and writers, including Carl Larsson and August Strindberg, who described it as "a place of natural beauty, surrounded on three sides by water and on the fourth by the sea." Sandhamn has long been one of Sweden's main sailing centers, with regattas held here since the late 1890s, and today, in high summer, the harbor is full of boats. There are few cars and people walk or bike along the island's sandy paths, making for a relaxed, easygoing atmosphere. In the quaint town center there are pastel-colored, wooden cottages and small seafront cafés. Just a short stroll away lies a shady, secluded pine forest and a quiet, white-sand beach, where irresistibly blue water beckons. You soon begin to appreciate why this is one of Sweden's best kept secrets.

**When to Go**  Although Sandhamn is beautiful in any season, summer brings sunnier skies and warmer weather. But bring a raincoat, umbrella, and an extra layer of clothing just in case.

**How to Find It**  From Stockholm you can travel through the archipelago with ferry companies like Waxholmsbolaget and Cinderella. Waxholmsbolaget also offers the *Båtluffarkort*, a special five-day island-hopping card, during the summer.

**Planning**  Facilities at the island's only hotel, the Seglarhotellet, include a restaurant, bar, pool, hot tub, and fitness rooms.

**Websites**  www.archipelagofoundation.se, www.waxholmsbolaget.se/en/default.aspx

### Flower power

Another jewel in the archipelago is the isle of **Idö,** where the modern world has few footholds and nature reigns. There are no longer any permanent residents on the island and no cars. A few bright-red cabins stand out against the lush landscape, but they have long been abandoned. You can quench your thirst with water from pumps near the cabins, but there are no restaurants or shops.

Nature lovers will relish roaming the ancient paths that crisscross the forests, marshes, and meadows. In spring, there are wildflowers in abundance, with delicate white wood anemones carpeting the forest floors and wild garlic and cowslips growing in profusion in the fields.

In summertime, Sandhamn is a mecca for pleasure boaters.

NORWAY

# Spitsbergen

This Arctic outpost of northern Europe is remote but far from desolate, with awe-inspiring landscapes and nature aplenty.

EUROPE

Floating in the Arctic Ocean between 74° and 81° north, Spitsbergen is the largest island of Norway's supersecluded Svalbard archipelago. For a few months each summer the Gulf Stream releases the island's western shore from the clutches of polar ice, transforming it into a "Galápagos of the North." Here, against a hauntingly beautiful backdrop of icebergs, fjords, and snowy peaks, you can see birds in profusion along with mammals such as polar bears, reindeer, arctic foxes, walrus, and whales. There are no trees, only bushes, and a variety of wildflowers, mosses, and lichen. This northernmost habitable place on Earth is rich in minerals, especially coal, and its capital, Longyearbyen, was named after American industrialist John M. Longyear, who founded the town in 1905 as the operations center for his nearby coal mine. In recent years, Longyearbyen has metamorphosed from chilly backwater into an ultramodern wilderness outpost, with everything from cyber cafés and satellite TV to an art gallery and indoor heated pool. To experience Spitsbergen's ultrawild side you need a boat. Some hardy seamen sail their own across the treacherous Barents Sea, but most people opt for passage on the small expedition cruise ships that ply the archipelago in summer. Landmarks include the spectacular Monaco Glacier, the ruins of a 17th-century whaling station at Gravneset, and rust-colored Bock Fjord (where NASA trains for future Mars missions).

**When to Go**  Summer (July and August) is by far the most pleasant season, marked by blue skies and long days with highs around 45°F (7°C). June and September are also quite pleasant, although a bit cooler. Yet even during the height of summer, nighttime temperatures can easily plunge below freezing.

**How to Find It**  SAS Braathens, the domestic branch of Scandinavian Airlines, flies several times daily between Oslo and Longyearbyen (via Tromsø in northern Norway).

**Planning**  The capital's Spitsbergen Hotel is located in a rambling wooden building that once housed coal mine managers and their families. For more down-home digs, try Mary-Ann's Polarrigg, a modern B&B with shared showers and toilets. Spitsbergen Travel arranges guided activities around Longyearbyen, including dogsledding, snowmobiling, hiking, ice caving, camping, and kayaking. Norway's Hurtigruten line offers voyages around Spitsbergen on the 200-passenger MS *Nordstjernen* and MV *Polarstar*.

**Websites**  www.svalbard.net, www.spitsbergentravel.com, www.polarriggen.com, www.hurtigruten.com

## Seeds of Time

On the outskirts of Longyearbyen, buried nearly 400 ft (130 m) inside a sandstone mountain, is the world's most important bunker: the **Svalbard Global Seed Vault.** Opened in 2008, the nine-million-dollar facility will eventually harbor millions of plant species from all around the globe.

With a goal of preserving the planet's biodiversity and food sources, the vault was funded by the Norwegian government and created by the Nordic Genetic Resource Center (NORDGEN) as a high-tech sanctuary for rare and endangered flora, food crops, and any other plants vital to the future of both planet Earth and the human race.

Spitsbergen was chosen for the cutting-edge project because of its pristine environment, thick permafrost, and relative lack of tectonic activity. Fashioned much like an ancient Egyptian tomb, the vault contains three chambers accessed from the surface via a long underground corridor. The interior is off-limits, but visitors are allowed into the sleek, modern entrance structure.

Opposite: A yacht cuts through the Arctic ice. Above: Spotting polar bears is a highlight of any trip to Spitsbergen.

# TEXEL

Visitors return year after year to savor the wide-open spaces,
as do migrating birds, who return in much larger numbers.

EUROPE

The West Frisian Islands are one of the last surviving areas of wilderness in the Netherlands. In the far north of the country, five long, thin islands raise their heads above the shallow Waddenzee—remnants of an ancient chain of sand dunes that once stretched from France to Denmark. The largest of these is Texel (pronounced "Tessel"), an undulating, windswept lozenge of 62 square miles (160 square kilometers), with the 13,000 or so islanders clustered mainly in the island's seven villages. Sheep pastures crown the central uplands, but all around lies a fretwork coast rimmed by coastal marshland and polders (reclaimed land), and high, white sand dunes. Long, low tides expose acres of *wadden,* nutrient-rich mudflats that host fish and mud-loving shellfish and worms—a copious source of food for seals and for the thousands of seabirds and waders that flock here on their migration routes and to nest. Spoonbills, avocets, and black-tailed godwits all breed on Texel. In the 1,100-acre (445 hectare) marshland nature reserve of De Slufter, the tide surges into the creeks twice a day, lapping against salt-tolerant plants, such as sea lavender, thrift, and samphire. The sea is gradually pushing the island southward, sweeping sand relentlessly from round the lighthouse at the northern end and depositing it in the south—a dynamic that mankind, with dams, dikes, and seawalls, has been battling against for more than 700 years.

**When to Go** Texel is mostly visited in summer (late May to early September), with bird migrations peaking in August. The warm months are most conducive to the outdoor activities on offer, including guided tours of the mudflats. Winters can be bitterly cold.

**How to Find It** Texel is linked to the mainland port of Den Helder by a car-and-passenger ferry, which leaves every half hour from 6 a.m. to 9:30 p.m. No reservations necessary.

**Planning** There is a full range of accommodations, including hotels, bed-and-breakfast, holiday cottages, and campsites. Although cars are permitted, many visitors prefer to travel by bicycle, on foot, or on horseback.

**Website** www.texel.net/en

### The Texel Pilots

For centuries, ships sailed north out of the protection of the **Zuiderzee inlet** from **Amsterdam** and other ports, and anchored off Texel to await favorable winds. Texel pilots posted lookouts on the **Loodsmansduin** ("Pilot's Dune"), the highest dune overlooking the channels, then raced out to meet incoming ships and win the commission to steer them through the sandbanks of the Waddenzee.

For fantastic views out to sea, climb the 153 stairs of Texel's imposing red lighthouse. An exhibition recounts the importance of the lighthouse for shipping.

A thatched-roof windmill stands sentinel over the Texel landscape.

Accordionists entertain customers at a local hotel bar in Castlebay during the Barra Fest music festival.

SCOTLAND

# BARRA AND VATERSAY

Steeped in ancient history and Gaelic tradition, this rugged and remote corner of the Western Isles has been called "Barradise."

A rriving on Barra by air is a unique experience. The island has the world's only commercial beach airstrip (on Tràigh Mhòr Beach), and at high tide the runway is underwater. Barra is the larger of the two southernmost inhabited islands of the Outer Hebrides. The smaller Vatersay is linked to Barra by a causeway completed in 1991. Prehistoric dwellings, about 4,000 years old, have been excavated at Allt Chrisal, near the causeway, and the rest of the islands are thick with archaeological sites, including Iron Age forts and roundhouses and Bronze Age burial cairns and wheelhouses. The coast is dominated by the *machair*, a fertile, low-lying coastal plain, which in summer is filled with wildflowers, including orchids and ladies' bedstraw. On Vatersay there is a rare pink convolvulus, known locally as Bonny Prince Charlie's flower because it is said that the prince scattered the seeds when he landed on nearby Eriskay in 1745. The island is a birdwatcher's paradise—on the road to Scurrival you can hear corncrakes in summer, and there are snipe, plovers, ravens, gannets, and eiders. You might spot whales, dolphins, and basking sharks out at sea, while along the shore you are sure to see otters and seals, with harbor seals dropping their pups in June and July and gray seals pupping in October and November. The miles of white beaches are empty, save for the occasional sheep or cow, or low-flying Twin Otter aircraft coming in to land.

**When to Go** The weather and wildflowers are best in summer. Barra Fest music festival is at the end of July.

**How to Find It** There are daily flights from Glasgow. The car ferry from Oban on the mainland to Castlebay, Barra's main town, takes five hours. There are bus routes on the island, and both car and bike rental.

**Planning** There are hotels, guesthouses, and rental cottages on the islands, all with magnificent sea views. A small boat takes visitors over to Kisimul Castle, which is open from April through October, weather permitting. Several heritage trails guide you toward many of the islands' archaeological sites.

**Websites** www.isleofbarra.com, www.calmac.co.uk

### History Trail

■ Standing on a rocky islet just off Castlebay is **Kisimul Castle,** stronghold for centuries of the Clan MacNeil. Its strategic position surrounded by sea meant that the castle never fell to an enemy. A fish trap and freshwater wells enabled the castle to be self-sufficient in times of siege.

Kisimul was abandoned in 1838, but an American, Robert Lister MacNeil, acquired the site in 1937 and set about restoring the castle. Today you can see its chapel, with a baptismal font made of Irish sandstone; a watchtower and dank pit of a dungeon; the great hall; the Tanist House, which has the private quarters of the present clan chief; the great tower; the kitchens; and medieval toilets that are flushed twice a day by the tide.

EUROPE

# ISLANDS WITHIN CITIES

Looking for an escape from the turmoil of the metropolis? Many waterfront cities have island havens where nature beckons, just a quick step across a bridge or a short ferry ride away.

### ❶ Georges and Spectacle islands, Boston, MA

Fort Warren, built in 1847 as part of Boston's defenses, is the landmark on Georges Island in Massachusetts Bay. A Frisbee is not essential, but a lot of them get thrown in the fields here. Currents are too strong to swim, but you can have a dip on Spectacle Island, which has 5 miles (8 km) of trails, fine views over Boston Harbor, and free jazz concerts in summer.

Planning One ferry ticket will take in the two islands; leave before midday to catch both. There are five departure points around Boston Harbor. www.bostonislands.org/georges

### ❷ City Island, New York City

A touch of New England in New York City, this 1.5-mile-long (2.4 km) island in the Bronx has a nautical air, with marinas and seafood restaurants. Yachts competing in the Americas Cup have been built here, and you can hire sailboats or set out on a fishing trip. The small lanes of late 19th-century wooden mansions have made City Island a backdrop for many films.

Planning A road bridge connects the island to the Bronx. www.cityisland.com

### ❸ Bowen Island, Vancouver, Canada

A 20-minute ferry ride from West Vancouver brings you to this wooded island where life is friendly and unhurried. There are no hotels or campsites, so a bed-and-breakfast will bring you into contact with locals. You can enjoy the beaches, lakes, and Bridal Veil Falls, or rent a bike, kayak, or sailboat.

Planning Ferries leave Horseshoe Bay for Snug Cove every hour; you can take your car or board as a foot passenger. www.bowenisland.org

### ❹ Ilha de Paquetá, Rio de Janeiro, Brazil

In the middle of Rio's Baia da Guanabara, this romantic tropical island is a local favorite that fills up on weekends. On weekdays, though, it can seem a long way from the clamor of the city. Its colonial buildings are part of the well-worn charm, while the absence of cars ensures a leisurely pace: Horse-drawn carts and bikes are the way to get about.

Planning From Praça Quinze de Novembro in Rio's Centro take a ferry (one hour) or hydrofoil (25 minutes). www.riodejaneiro-turismo.com.br

### ❺ Matiu Somes Island, Wellington, New Zealand

Set at a strategic point in Wellington Harbour, Matiu Soomes Island been a Maori fortified settlement, the site of New Zealand's first lighthouse, and a military site. Now, under the Royal Forest and Bird Protection Society, the island has returned to nature. Bird life includes the cute Little Blue Penguin.

Planning Boats leave from Wellington's Queen's Wharf and take about 20 minutes. Take your own food and water. www.wellingtonnz.com

### ❻ Cockatoo Island, Sydney, Australia

Where else can you pitch a tent by the water in the heart of a city and watch the sun rise and set over its skyline? As a former penal colony and the largest shipyard in Australia, Cockatoo Island has a legacy of dry docks, industrial buildings, and warehouses that provide ideal venues for art and performance.

Planning The island is a ten-minute ferry ride from Sydney's Circular Quay. A café serves meals. www.cockatooisland.gov.au

### ❼ Pulau Ubin, Singapore

The last rural refuge in this modern city-state, Pulau Ubin is home to fishermen and prawn farmers. The 5-mile-long (8 km) granite island has areas of jungle and mangrove swamps with abundant wildlife, and mudflats where endangered flora and fauna flourish. There are mountain bikes for hire.

Planning Bumboats from Changi Point Jetty take 15 minutes and carry up to 12 passengers, departing when full. www.wildsingapore.com/ubin

### ❽ Margaret Island, Budapest, Hungary

When the mighty Danube reaches Hungary's capital, it is divided in two by Margaret Island (Margitsziget), named for a 13th-century princess. Caught between the two halves of the ancient city, the island provides escape and recreation, with a jogging path, restaurants, theater, and thermal springs. Ruined monasteries add to the romantic air that has inspired writers.

Planning The island is reached by Árpád Bridge and Margaret Bridge. Only taxis and Bus 26 are allowed on the island, but you can rent four-wheel cycles and electric cars. www.budapest-tourist-guide.com

### ❾ Kampa Island, Prague, Czech Republic

By day or night, this is a delightfully tranquil corner of the Czech capital. Slip down the double steps from the Charles Bridge, and you will find yourself on an island on the River Vltava where "the Devil's Stream" once powered flour mills. Sova's Mill is now a museum of modern Czech art. Mellow Renaissance and baroque houses surround a central square of cafés and restaurants.

Planning Kampa Island is accessible by steps from the Malá Strana (Lesser Town) side of Charles Bridge. www.prague-guide.co.uk

### ❿ Île des Cygnes, Paris, France

For a quiet stroll in Paris, head for the Île des Cygnes (Isle of the Swans). This narrow, tree-lined strip, half a mile (0.8 km) long and barely wider than its central path, is in the middle of the Seine near the Eiffel Tower. Facing New York like a ship's figurehead is a Statue of Liberty, a quarter the size of the original and a gift from the French community in America.

Planning You can reach the Île des Cygnes via the Pont de Grenelle or the Pont de Bir-Hakeim (Bir-Hakeim, Métro Line 6). www.paris.fr

Opposite: In the heart of Prague, the Grand Prior's Mill on secluded Kampa Island has retained its 26-ft (8 m) wheel.

Great Sark and Little Sark are joined by the narrow, razor-edged isthmus known as La Coupée.

CHANNEL ISLANDS

# SARK

Visitors to this small but beautifully formed island will soon feel the cares of the modern world slipping away.

There are no cars on Sark (even the fire engine and ambulance trailers are pulled by tractor) and radios are banned in public. Life on the smallest of the four main Channel Islands moves at a slower, quieter pace, all the better to appreciate the island's outstanding natural beauty. Walkers exploring the headlands and cliff tops along the 40 miles (65 kilometers) of spectacular coastline will see seabirds, including puffins. Out at sea, dolphins, porpoises, and basking sharks can be spotted. The cliffs are riddled with dark sea caves, including Jewel Cave with its multicolored sea anemones, sponges, and sea squirts. There are numerous sandy bays, inlets, and tidal pools to explore, and in spring and summer the wildflowers grow in profusion. Bluebells, red campion, and wild garlic dominate the valleys and woods, along with primroses, celandines, dog violets, and oxeye daisies. On the cliffs there are carpets of thrift, thyme, and samphire, along with pockets of foxgloves and patches of gorse—its delightful coconut scent wafting in the summer air. The clear coastal waters rich in fish, crabs, and lobsters ensure that Sark's restaurants serve the freshest seafood imaginable. There are several first-rate hotels and guesthouses on the island, as well as campsites, reached along narrow roads lined by exceptionally neat hedgerows that are inspected by the local constable, with fines for scrappy appearance.

**When to Go** "Wildflower Fortnight" takes place in the last week in April and the first week in May.

**How to Find It** Fly to Guernsey or Jersey. There is a daily boat service to Sark from Guernsey's St. Peter Port (45 minutes); a boat service operates most days from St. Helier, Jersey, April through September (50 minutes).

**Planning** If you are staying on Sark, local "carters" will carry your luggage. A tractor-drawn trailer takes you up Harbour Hill to the village. You can then walk, cycle, or travel by horse and cart to your accommodation.

**Website** www.sark.info

## Seigneurs of Sark

Up until 2008, Sark was one of Europe's last bastions of feudalism, with a nonelected council led by the Seigneur, the feudal lord. Today the island has an elected parliament—the Chief Pleas—but has retained the Seigneur, who still has sole right to a dovecote, an unspayed bitch, and anything washed up between the high and low tidemarks.

Since 1730, the Seigneurs of Sark have lived at **La Seigneurie.** The magnificent garden is open daily to visitors (except in winter). A bronze cannon in the grounds was presented to the first Seigneur, Helier de Carteret, by Queen Elizabeth I in 1572.

# PONZA

The well-heeled Italians who enjoy low-key summers
here have kept this island getaway close to their chests.

EUROPE

Lapped by the blue-green waters of the Tyrrhenian Sea, Ponza is the largest of the volcanic Pontine Islands. Circe, the enchantress who turned Odysseus's men into pigs, is said to have had a hideaway here. Later on, Roman nobility were banished to the island, but today they arrive in yachts and sailboats to spend the August vacation swimming in the secluded *cale* (bays) and exploring the island's numerous grottoes. Mere plebeians arrive by ferry at Porto, where buildings in shades of Neapolitan ice cream spill down toward the sea, filling the crescent-shaped port. Across the port, Cala Frontone is a small bay where trendy beach clubs front a small sandy strand. The Romans excavated a 180-foot-long (55 meter) tunnel through solid rock that links the port to Spiaggia Chiaia di Luna, the largest beach on the island, where a curving shoreline is backed by cliffs of yellow tuff. Most of the island's secluded bays and grottoes are accessible only by sea. If you don't have your own yacht, rent a small boat in the port and circumnavigate the island. Bathe in the cerulean glow of the Grotte Azzure (Blue Grottoes) or make like a Roman and dip in the Grotte di Pilato (Pontius Pilate's Grottoes). Or walk down to the Piscine Naturali near Le Forna, a bay so calm its waters are like a swimming pool and where it is difficult to imagine exile on Ponza as having been any type of punishment.

**When to Go** Easter to the end of September is the best time to visit. Most restaurants and hotels close from October until the week before Easter, and ferry connections to the mainland are limited at this time.

**How to Find It** There are boat services to Ponza from Anzio (1 hour 45 minutes), Formia (ferry 2 hours 30 minutes/hydrofoil 1 hour 15 minutes), and Naples (hydrofoil 2 hours 50 minutes).

**Planning** You can rent a small outboard boat from one of the many kiosks in the port. The Cooperativa Barcaioli Ponzesi in the port offers trips around Ponza and excursions to the uninhabited islands of Palmarola and Zannone. Dinner reservations are a must at most restaurants, especially in August.

**Websites** www.maredellazio.it, www.infoponza.it

## Local Specialties

■ Lentils and cicerchie (a sort of chickpea–lentil hybrid) have been cultivated on the island since antiquity and are used in hearty soups. The meaty *murena* (moray eel) is served fried or marinated in vinegar, and local Tyrrhenian fish are simply grilled.

■ **Da Gerardo** above the beach at Cala Frontone serves authentic *Ponzese cucina* (Ponza cuisine) beneath a leafy pergola. The owner has created a "museum" of the island's ethnographic history, which he proudly narrates after the meal.

■ The Assumption of the Virgin is commemorated on August 15 with the *sagra del pesce azzurro* (blue fish festival) in Le Forna.

The Grotte di Pilato beneath Porto is where Roman nobility would swim, shaded from the sun so as not to get tanned skin like the working classes.

# SOCOTRA

To step foot on Socotra is to embark on a botanical odyssey around one of the most alien-looking places on Earth.

ASIA

This island off the Horn of Africa and its smaller neighbors are the most isolated islands in the world not of volcanic origin. They were left behind when the African and Asian landmasses, both parts of the supercontinent Gondwana, split apart 23 to 34 million years ago and today they exist like some kind of lost world. Scientists call Socotra the Galápagos of the Indian Ocean, with around one-third of its plant species unique to the island. In the first century B.C., Greek historian Diodorus of Sicily described Socotra as supplying the entire world with all manner of aromatic and medicinal plants, and it still does. Among the bitter aloes, frankincense, and myrrh, there is the alien-looking dragon's blood tree, shaped like an umbrella blown inside out and complete with "spokes" underneath that attach to the vertical trunk. The tree is named for its bright red sap, which for centuries has been used in medicine and as a dye. When fully grown, the strange Socotra fig can best be described as looking like a fat snail with a multipronged headdress climbing up a vertical rock. Equally bizarre is the bottle-shaped desert rose, whose antler-like branches sprout pink flowers. All these plants are designed to store water or maximize its collection. Socotra also has its very own species of starling, sunbird, sparrow, bunting, cisticola, warbler, and grosbeak, and there are several important seabird-breeding areas. Seasonal upwellings in the surrounding seas attract species in their droves—dolphins, sea turtles, whales, sharks (including whale sharks), manta rays, marlin, and myriad small fish.

**When to Go** October through April is the best time to visit, avoiding the strong winds, high seas, and intense summer heat of the seasonal monsoon.

**How to Find It** There are 50-minute flights once a week from Aden and Sanaa on the mainland, and five times a week from Riyan Mukalla (not Wednesdays or Sundays).

**Planning** The tourism infrastructure is rudimentary, with no taxis or public transport. Camping is recommended, and 4WD vehicles can be rented with a guide, driver, and cook. Guides can understand English. A 3-month visa can be obtained at Yemen airports. U.S. dollars are acceptable. Be respectful of local traditions and dress codes. Areas of Yemen are considered unsafe for travel—check ahead for government warnings.

**Website** www.socotraisland.org

### Hoq Cave

During the first three centuries of the Common Era, Socotra was an important stop for traders on the eastern trade routes. Frankincense, cinnabar, aloe, and dragon's blood were important commodities acquired from the island, with travelers arriving from the Middle East, East Africa, and India.

Evidence of the island's past importance is found at **Hoq Cave,** a subterranean labyrinth near the northeast coast. Inside the cave, 1.2 miles (2 km) from its entrance, there is an ancient place of worship, which was in use until the third century A.D. Archaeologists have discovered two wooden tablets with Aramaic inscriptions, one of them dated A.D. 258, as well as pottery and painted murals and writing on the cave walls dating back to the time of Christ.

The artifacts—all of which have been well preserved in the cave's atmosphere—suggest that secret religious ceremonies may once have taken place here.

You can visit Hoq Cave with an experienced local guide. Tours last for around two hours.

Opposite: Desert roses are among the island's curiosities. Above: Dragon's blood trees can reach 33 ft (10 m) tall.

# SÃO TOMÉ AND PRÍNCIPE

Two volcanic islands 190 miles (300 kilometers) off the west coast of Africa offer everything, from rain-forest hikes to deserted beaches.

For two hours you trek through rain forest…and then you walk on water. This is the Obô, the high-altitude forest that still covers much of the island nation of São Tomé and Príncipe (STP). Your guide points out the wonders of the plant and animal life around you—factors including their position and volcanic origin mean that the islands have an unusual number of species unique to them. You taste wild cinnamon and wild raspberries, and watch giant sunbirds with iridescent starling-black plumage as they flit from flower to flower, using long, curved bills to probe for nectar. Finally, you reach São Tomé's extinct, water-filled volcanic crater of Lagoa Amélia. A mat of vegetation has formed on top, allowing you to walk over the water, although you may wobble a bit. And that is just one day's excursion. Next day you may opt for a trip down São Tomé's east coast, passing sandy beaches (*praias*), empty except for a few fishermen. In Água Izé, visit a cocoa plantation. At Boca do Inferno (Hell's Mouth), watch Atlantic waves crash skyward in fountains of spume through a blowhole. On the estate of Roça de São João, with a plantation house dating back to Portuguese colonial times, see how coffee is grown and processed. Then, having admired a waterfall near the fishing village of Riberia Peixe, take a swim from Praia das Sete Ondas (Beach of the Seven Waves) before heading north again.

**When to Go** For trekking and enjoying the rich wildlife, the two dry seasons—June through September, and mid-December through February—are best.

**How to Find It** TAP Air Portugal and the local STP Airways both fly between Lisbon, Portugal, and São Tomé. Most days you can catch a flight between São Tomé island and Príncipe island.

**Planning** Navetur in the capital, São Tomé city, is an excellent tourist agency that will help with everything from hotel reservations to trekking. Accommodations include guesthouses in old plantation houses (roças) and the boutique comfort of Omali Lodge on São Tomé and Bom Bom Island Resort on Príncipe.

**Websites** www.navetur-equatour.st, www.saotome.st, www.saotomeislands.com, www.africas-eden.com

## Island Sights

■ A two-day guided trek takes you to and from **Pico de São Tomé,** at 6,640 ft (2,024 m) the islands' highest point. The early morning views of the island from the peak are worth all the effort of getting there.

■ From September through April, **leatherback turtles** lay their eggs in the early morning on **Praia Jalé** in the south of São Tomé. You can join the guards who patrol the beach to watch the turtles laying.

■ If you make it to **Príncipe,** don't miss **Praia Banana** and **Baía das Agulhas,** two stupendous beaches on the west coast, where the rain forest comes down to the shoreline.

From bananas to breadfruit, anything you eat is likely to be locally grown and gloriously fresh. Fish is a particular specialty—fresh, salted, smoked, or sun-dried.

Traditional wooden *ngalawas* ply the rich fishing grounds off Pemba.

**Off the Beaten Track**

Ask at your guesthouse, in the market, or at a café if you can borrow or rent a small *piki-piki* (motorbike) to explore the island. Head out along the dirt roads through the villages to **Ngezi Forest** (home to the Pemba flying fox) in the northwest of the island. Follow the sandy track through the forest to **Verani Beach** along the bay beyond. This long, sandy beach is rarely visited and an ideal place to go snorkeling.

TANZANIA

# PEMBA

Unlike its southern sister, Zanzibar, this equally exotic spice island remains largely undisturbed by the outside world.

The heady aroma of cloves drying on coconut mats alongside the road drifts into the wooden, open-sided buses bringing passengers from Wete to Chake Chake. Early Arab sailors named this island in the Zanzibar archipelago Al Huthera (Green Island), and today the fertile, hilly terrain is covered with a patchwork of thick clove plantations and coconut groves, with paddy fields filling the hollows and valleys. Mangroves and sandy beaches protect the coastline where another world exists under the clear waters of the Indian Ocean. The coral reefs support an abundance of fish life off the many smaller islands to the west of Pemba, where wind-filled sailcloths propel wooden sailboats (*ngalawas*) across the reef. The fishermen cast their nets for the day's catch, which will be sold at the evening market or dried in the afternoon sun. In the busy marketplace, men in colored *shukas* (cloth wrapped around the waist) meet in chai (tea) houses to pass the time over cups of sweet, milky cardamom tea and *mandazi* (small, fried donut bread). As the sun dips behind the waving fronds of coconut palms, the call to prayer of the muezzin summons the men along the narrow, winding streets to the mosque.

**When to Go**  Visit from December through March to avoid the rainy season.

**How to Find It**  Fly from Zanzibar island, Dar es Salaam, or Tanga; there are usually daily flights to the airport near the capital, Chake Chake. Airport tax on departure needs to be paid in Tanzanian currency. The boat journey from Zanzibar takes from three to six hours; or sail by dhow from Tanga (times are erratic).

**Planning**  Eat at roadside stalls or cafés where the food is cooked as you wait—to avoid the risk of an upset stomach don't eat salads or have ice in your drinks. Stay at the Kervan Saray Beach lodge in the north of the island for diving and stunning beaches; Pemba Crown Hotel in Wete for the budget traveler; or the luxurious Fundu Lagoon on the west coast. Take antimalarial tablets and bring plenty of mosquito spray.

**Websites**  www.kervansaraybeach.com, www.fundulagoon.com

# THE ROAD LESS TRAVELED

4

**M**apped out on the following pages are those off-the-beaten-path highways and byways with fascinating stories to tell: Hidden waterways, picturesque train journeys, leisurely hikes along quiet trails, and challenging expeditions into some of the world's wildest places. Aficionados of classic road-trip movies will relish the solitude of the little-used Nevada stretch of U.S. Highway 50—nicknamed "the loneliest road in America." Fans of bluegrass, gospel, and old-time music might prefer the infinitely more convivial delights to be found along Virginia's Heritage Music Trail as it wends its way through the Appalachian heartlands to the tiny rural venues where the purest versions of traditional country music are still performed. Denmark's tranquil coastal roads are cycling heaven, while hikers in the Basque country in northeastern Spain will discover the region's many culinary delights. Intrepid wilderness-seekers can traverse the Guyanese jungle to reach one of the world's most spectacular waterfalls or join the Larapinta Trail for an unforgettable journey into the heart of Australia.

In Kenya's Great Rift Valley, a dusty, deserted road snakes toward Lake Nakuru shimmering in the distance. Millions of flamingos and other birds congregate at the lake, making this one of the greatest ornithological spectacles on Earth.

Expect wild animals and bumpy surfaces, but few fellow travelers, on this drive through Yukon Territory.

CANADA

# THE SOUTH CANOL ROAD

It is little more than a dirt road, but in summer it provides access to the pristine wilderness of South Central Yukon.

As you head north from Johnson's Crossing, a sign warns you that the next services are not until Ross River—at the end of the 143-mile (230 kilometer) South Canol Road. Slow, careful driving is the order of the day as the deserted road gradually narrows and rough patches and potholes appear. The unpaved road winds through a landscape that alternates between deep, dense forest and high mountain ridges, with stunning views of snowcapped peaks, even in summer, and shimmering creeks, rivers, and lakes. The views enthrall and invite regular stops—all the better to catch a glimpse of the abundant wildlife, including black bears and grizzlies, wolves, moose, mule deer, woodland caribou, porcupines, foxes, lynx, and bald eagles. At around the halfway point, you reach the shoreline of picturesque Quiet Lake, where you can camp, hike, fish, canoe, or simply soak up the tranquility. After crossing the newly opened bridge at Rose River—the waters are calm in summer, but in 2008, spring torrents washed away the bridge—the route continues to dip and soar as it skirts the Rose River, the Lapie lakes, famous for the trout that live in their cold, clear waters, and the beautiful Lapie River Canyon to reach the settlement at Ross River.

**When to Go** Summers are short, so plan your trip between mid-June and the end of August.

**How to Find It** Johnson's Crossing is an 80-mile (129 km) drive east from Whitehorse, where you can rent a 4WD. You can return from Ross River to Whitehorse along the Robert Campbell Highway—a 253-mile (407 km) drive via Carmacks or a 506-mile (814 km) drive via Watson Lake.

**Planning** The South Canol Road can be driven in a day, but be prepared for weather conditions that may hamper your schedule. It might be hot, but snow on elevated sections of the road, even in July, is not uncommon. At Johnson's Crossing you'll find a gas station, a bakery, and a small RV park, while at Ross River there is a grocery store and even a hotel. There are a few basic campgrounds en route.

**Websites** www.naturetoursyukon.com, www.travelyukon.com, www.visitwhitehorse.com

## Oil Supply

In order to safeguard the transportation of oil during World War II, a pipeline and supply road were constructed linking **Whitehouse,** Yukon, with the oil wells at **Norman Wells,** Northwest Territories.

Workers on the Canol (short for Canadian Oil) Project suffered terrible conditions—even recruiting posters warned that the work could be life-threatening. Oil flowed for just one year until 1945, with the road reopening in the 1950s as a seasonal access route. Today, the abandoned trucks from the 1940s that dot the route serve as rusting reminders of the road's past.

NORTH AMERICA

# THE CROOKED ROAD

Hit the winding road through the mountains of southwestern Virginia to discover the state's musical and cultural soul.

At the first plunk of the banjo strings, bluegrass devotees in the packed auditorium vault from their seats and begin flat-footing or clogging to the music. It's a familiar scene all along the Crooked Road—Virginia's Heritage Music Trail. The trail corkscrews for 253 miles (407 kilometers), linking traditional mountain music and bluegrass venues and attractions. Begin in Ferrum at the Blue Ridge Institute & Museum, a repository for mountain music and culture. Then join the toe-tapping, knee-slapping crowd in Floyd, a one-stoplight town whose tiny population swells on Friday nights as locals and visitors gather at the Floyd Country Store to hear gospel, old-time, and bluegrass bands. Farther down the road in Galax, listen in as a traditional bluegrass and country music radio show broadcasts live from the historic Rex Theater. The route then snakes past the Blue Ridge Music Center and through Bristol, where you tour the Mountain Music Museum, honoring Appalachian music pioneers. On Saturday nights, the Carter Family Fold in Hiltons carries on the musical traditions begun by A.P. and Sara Carter. End your musical pilgrimage in Clintwood, where the legendary Dr. Ralph Stanley and the Clinch Mountain Boys are celebrated at the Ralph Stanley Museum and Traditional Mountain Music Center.

**When to Go** Performances are held at various venues throughout the year. Check local schedules for dates and times. The Old Fiddler's Convention in Galax takes place in August.

**How to Find It** The Crooked Road is easily accessible from Interstates 81 and 77.

**Planning** Some performance sites, including the Carter Family Fold and the Floyd Country Store, are open only one night a week, so schedule your time accordingly. Arrive early to get a seat. Advance room reservations are recommended, especially in summer and on festival weekends.

**Websites** www.thecrookedroad.org, www.crookedroadvirginia.com

### Talent Scout

The music of Appalachia might have remained hidden in the hills and hollers had it not been for Ralph Sylvester Peer. In July 1927, this talent scout for the Victor Talking Machine Company in Camden, New Jersey, traveled to Bristol to record local music, many of the tunes having been passed down for generations. Establishing a makeshift recording studio in the Taylor-Christian Hat Company's warehouse, Peer encouraged local people to share their songs with him in what became known as the Bristol Sessions. When he left 12 days later, he had more than 70 recordings of hillbilly music, as it was called.

A jam session is in full swing at the Old Fiddler's Convention, which has been held in Galax every year since 1935.

# Umpqua Trail

This corridor of wild natural beauty follows the twists and turns of the North Umpqua River on its westward journey.

The trail begins 6,000 feet (1,829 meters) high in the Oregon Cascades, at a limpid lake that spawns a trickle where tiny minnows dart through shards of sunlight amid feathery grasses and patches of colorful lichens. Here, too, begins the trail that tracks this downhill course as it becomes the North Umpqua River. For 79 miles (127 kilometers), this path—which is divided into 11 segments, each with its own trailhead—leads you past old forest fires, where silvery snags stand parched from sun and wind, and through the rough lands that early Oregon pioneers homesteaded. The river cascades over piles of rock and picks up tributaries, growing ever wider, stronger, louder. The forest evolves, too—taller, thicker, wetter. Cedars rot on the riverbank beneath sky-scraping old-growth trees. A small sign marks the site of a Zane Grey fishing camp, where a fan has left two of the author's cowboy books in a Ziploc bag with a note: "Take one. Bring one back, partner." The trail ends along Oregon 138, not far from a bend in the road called Idleyld. But the waters keep flowing, joining their southern branch and continuing another 111 miles (179 kilometers) to a windswept bay, where the Umpqua tumbles into the Pacific.

**When to Go** Summer is most popular and fall most brilliant. Inclement weather can prompt trail segment closures, especially in winter when the higher elevations receive snowfall and the lower elevations are susceptible to heavy rain, washouts, and flooding. Forest fires are not uncommon in the dry summertime.

**How to Find It** All of the trailheads are accessible by vehicle except Maidu Lake at the far east end of the trail, which is a 4.75-mile (7.6 km) hike from Digit Point Campground.

**Planning** The trail segments range from 3.5 miles (5.6 km) to 15.7 miles (25.3 km) and vary in difficulty. Many of the trailheads offer campgrounds and picnic areas with drinking water and restrooms. Alternatively, take a road trip along Oregon 138, exploring the various North Umpqua trailheads en route to Crater Lake National Park. Spend the night in the historic Crater Lake Lodge.

**Websites** www.blm.gov/or/districts/roseburg/recreation/umpquatrails, www.fs.fed.us/r6/umpqua

## Open to All

You don't need to hike for days to enjoy the North Umpqua. The trail also welcomes equestrians, cyclists, paddlers, fishermen, and Sunday strollers. In the fall, visitors to the westernmost **Tioga segment** are treated to a remarkable natural spectacle. Park at the **Swiftwater Trailhead,** and walk the short distance to **Deadline Falls.** Here you can watch salmon as they rocket through the air, facing the falls head-on, mightily trying to beat the thundering water. Sometimes they fail, flopping against rock. Sometimes they disappear in the current's swift swirls. But they try again, suddenly launching from the depths, ready for another fight.

The emerald-green waters of the North Umpqua River gouge a path through steep canyon walls.

The highway crosses a series of snowcapped mountain ranges that break up the Nevada desert.

NEVADA

# Highway 50

Expect to have the road to yourself as you pass through the remote Nevada stretch of the epic coast-to-coast highway.

The western United States is replete with places where you can savor the Big Wide Open, but none are more readily accessible than the Nevada leg of U.S. 50, known as "the loneliest road in America." Highway 50 is an intercontinental road running more than 3,000 miles (4,800 kilometers) from Sacramento, California, to Ocean City, Maryland, and driving the 408-mile (657 kilometer) stretch of high desert through Nevada is indeed an exercise in solitude—you're apt to see more jackrabbits and ravens than people. Only four small towns mark this route—Fallon, Austin, Eureka, and Ely— each retaining relics of the Old West, from abandoned buildings to piles of mine tailings. The highway, which follows the original route used by the Pony Express mail service, provides an absorbing tutorial in Nevada's "basin and range" topography: Chains of rugged cordilleras separated by wide, low valleys. The flora and geology shift constantly as you drive from pinyon pine-clad summits down through slopes of sagebrush, past swales blanketed with willows to desolate, stark-white salt pans.

**When to Go** Nevada bakes in summer, while winters are bitterly cold and often raked with snow; go in late spring or early fall.

**How to Find It** The most popular access point for the Nevada leg is California. From San Francisco, take the Bay Bridge to Interstate 80 at Oakland, go north 90 miles (145 km) to Sacramento, then take U.S. 50 approximately 100 miles (161 km) to the Nevada state line.

**Planning** You can make the drive in one long day, or break it into a two-day trip, staying overnight in Fallon, Austin, Eureka, or Ely. Gas stations are not common, so fill up at every opportunity. Bring water and blankets in case you get stranded. Small family-run Mexican restaurants are often the best bet for meals.

**Websites** www.byways.org/explore/byways/2033, www.nevadatravel.net

## A Gem of a Town

In Nevada's remote center, Highway 50 rolls into **Austin.** Today, the former silver-rush town is quiet, real quiet, but once you've filled up with gas, it is worth taking a look around. Most of its historic buildings have been preserved, including Stokes Castle, a three-story stone keep built in 1897 by a local eccentric.

Austin is also a center for turquoise production, with several mines providing local jewelers with high-quality stone. As you stroll down the main street (Highway 50), you'll see several shops selling all things turquoise—from raw chunks of the sky-blue stone still in matrix to polished cabochons, and from small rings designed for a child's finger to heavy turquoise-and-silver squash blossom brooches and necklaces.

# SALT MISSIONS TRAIL

Crumbling adobe churches tell of a short-lived
European mission to convert the local Pueblo Indians.

For 75 years from around 1600, Franciscan friars established a string of religious outposts in the salt-rich valley that the Spanish named Salinas. The ruins of these red-rock churches are now protected within the confines of the Salinas Pueblo Missions National Monument, one of the least-known units of the sprawling national park system. The quiet, two-lane Salt Missions Trail starts in the tiny mountain town of Tijeras, just east of Albuquerque. Northernmost of the missions is Quarai, once the seat of the dreaded Spanish Inquisition in New Mexico. The 40-foot-tall (12 meter) red sandstone walls of La Purísima Concepción church hint at just how grand the mission must have been in its heyday. The national monument visitor center and museum are in the rough-and-tumble town of Mountainair, where the frontier spirit lives on in local institutions like the Rosebud Saloon. Abó Mission and its own grand church are just ten minutes west of town; the sprawling ruins of Gran Quivira are 25 miles (40 kilometers) farther south along New Mexico 55. Largest of the Salinas pueblos, Quivira was abandoned in 1672 in the wake of famine, drought, and Apache raids— a stark reminder that European incursions did not always prevail.

**When to Go** There really isn't a bad time to visit the Salinas Valley. Come in spring to catch the wildflowers. Summer temperatures can reach triple digits, and winter can bring a sprinkling of snow.

**How to Find It** Follow Interstate 40 east from Albuquerque to the turnoff for Tijeras. New Mexico 337 leads south toward the missions. Alternatively, you can take Interstate 25 south through the Rio Grande Valley to Belen and then follow the signs east to Mountainair and the park visitor center.

**Planning** The Shaffer Hotel in Mountainair (established in 1923) is one of the few places to stay along the actual trail. Most people tour the missions as a long day-trip from Albuquerque, where the many accommodation options include the modern and comfortable Embassy Suites overlooking downtown. Stock up on water and snacks for the journey.

**Websites** www.nps.gov/sapu, www.newmexico.org, www.shafferhotel.com

## Testing Site

Some 50 miles (80 km) south of Gran Quivira is the **Trinity Site,** where the world's first atomic bomb was detonated on July 16, 1945. Developed as part of the Manhattan Project at the Los Alamos labs in northern New Mexico, the plutonium-based device was a prototype of the "Fat Man" bomb that destroyed Nagasaki less than a month later. Now a National Historic Landmark, Trinity is open to the public twice a year (on the first Saturday in April and October). Visitors can see bunkers, base camp, and the old ranch house where the bomb's plutonium core was assembled.

Christian and Pueblo sacred buildings sit side by side at Abó. The circular structure, known as a *kiva,* is the remains of a Pueblo ceremonial chamber.

Sea kayakers navigate the island's caves, inlets, and rocky coastline.

MEXICO

# Isla Espíritu Santo

Glide through the calm waters of the Gulf of California for a kaleidoscopic view of one of the world's richest ecosystems.

As you raise your paddle, the warm, salty ocean water trickles down your arm, while alongside your kayak a shoal of gliding manta rays undulates beneath the ripples before surfacing and leaping through the air. You don't get much closer to nature than on this weeklong circumnavigation of Espíritu Santo, a deserted island in the Pacific, off the coast of Mexico's Baja Peninsula. Mornings are spent paddling around the island. On the sheltered western coast, the ocean is pond-flat and laps gently onto white-sand horseshoe bays, while the eastern shoreline is craggy and steep, buffeted by winds, and punctuated by the open mouths of caves. The island is a magnet for territorial and marine birds, and around 500 species of fish swim in the surrounding coral reefs. Each afternoon you pull up onto a beach and spend the rest of the day exploring the island's arid, copper-colored interior, studded with solitary cacti and surreal rock formations. Or you can submerge yourself fully into the ocean to explore underwater caves and to swim with playful sea lions. A hike through the shady gorges of the island brings you to a natural shower where you can wash off the sticky salt water that will have turned your skin white after a few days at sea. At sundown, sip cocktails and dine on freshly caught fish before camping beneath a sky full of stars.

**When to Go**  Organized trips run throughout the year, but October through December is the ideal time, with warm weather and calm seas. The winds increase from December through March or April. It seldom rains.

**How to Find It**  Most trips leave by motor skiff from La Paz on the Baja Peninsula, a two-hour flight from Los Angeles. You should arrive at least a day before your kayaking trip begins.

**Planning**  Experienced guides are on hand throughout and will instruct kayaking beginners. A supporting motor skiff carries camping and cooking equipment (including the all-important chemical toilet).

**Websites**  www.kayakinbaja.com, www.bajatravel.com

### Whale-watching

Each winter, female gray whales can be seen swimming in the shallow, temperate waters of **Magdalena Bay** on the Pacific coast of Baja California. They come here to calve and nurse their young, making the epic journey from their feeding grounds near Alaska.

A tour of the lagoon by small motor skiff will bring you within touching distance of these barnacled gentle giants as they swim alongside the launch.

The boat journey from La Paz to Magdalena Bay takes about 3.5 hours, and there is cabana accommodation on the shore.

NORTH AMERICA

# PERFECT BEACHES

There are no jostling crowds in paradise, just
miles of empty, sun-kissed golden sand.

### ❶ Coast Guard Beach, Massachusetts

Summer swimmers make a beeline for this stretch of Cape Cod National Seashore, where the *Mayflower* Pilgrims first spotted land back in 1620. A landscape of sweeping sand dunes, marshland, wild cranberry bogs, and the nesting grounds of threatened plovers beckons hikers.

Planning A lifeguard stays on duty from late June to the end of August. Beach entrance fees apply from late June through early September. www.capecodchamber.org

### ❷ St. Joseph Peninsula State Park, Florida

Bounded on the west by the Gulf of Mexico and on the east by St. Joseph Bay, this spit boasts towering dunes flecked with sea oats and mile upon mile of pristine sugar-white beach, where loggerhead turtles come to nest in summer. Take photographs of the stunning sunsets and sunrises, or zoom in on one of the many species of bird (more than 240) that have been sighted.

Planning The park operates a no-spray policy, so be sure to bring insect repellent. www.floridastateparks.org/stjoseph

### ❸ Descanso Beach, Catalina Island, California

A stone's throw from throbbing Los Angeles is this blissful refuge, where dolphins and whales can often be seen jumping out of the crystal-clear waters of the Pacific. Hop on a golf cart or bike to explore the island; or kayak, canoe, swim, or dive the shipwrecks offshore.

Planning The island is a one-hour ferry journey or a 15-minute helicopter ride from Los Angeles. www.catalinachamber.com

### ❹ Grace Bay Beach, Turks & Caicos Islands

With more than 10 miles (16 km) of soft white sands, secluded bathing is guaranteed in this northeast corner of Providenciales, or Provo for short. A coral reef fringes the shore, which keeps warm turquoise waters calm for swimming. No water skis or jet skis are allowed. Instead, you'll spot bottlenose dolphins frolicking in the low waves. You can expect around 350 days of sunshine a year.

Planning Flights from Miami take 1.5 hours and from New York 3.5 hours. www.turksandcaicostourism.com

### ❺ Canouan, St. Vincent & The Grenadines

Famous for the Raffles Resort and Trump International Golf Club, this small, verdant island, daubed with the vibrant hues of bougainvillea and wild orchids, is ringed by calm emerald waters that extend like a vast, salty swimming pool. The many secluded bays and coves are home to an abundance of marine life. Savor the view from Mount Royal, the island's highest peak.

Planning The ferry from St. Vincent takes about 2 hours. Flights arrive from San Juan, Barbados, and Grenada. www.discoversvg.com

### ❻ Morro de São Paulo, Brazil

The village of Morro de São Paulo, on the island of Tinharé, a 1.5-hour boat ride from Salvador, boasts five beaches, each with its own distinct personality. The soft white sands, restaurants, and *pousadas* (inns) of First Beach are closest to the village, while the Fourth and Fifth (the Beach of Enchantment) are much quieter, with stretches of deserted beach and natural pools.

Planning Visitors must pay a $6.50 island preservation tax. www.morrodesaopaulo.com.br

### ❼ Cable Beach, Broome, Western Australia

A few miles from the pearling town of Broome, this 14-mile (22.5 km) stretch of pristine sand is washed twice daily by the tides. Attractions include daily sunset camel treks. At low tide at Gantheaume Point, you can see dinosaur footprints thought to be 130 million years old.

Planning Broome is a 2.5-hour flight from Perth; the beach is 4.5 miles (7 km) from town along a good road. Be wary of box jellyfish between November and March. www.westernaustralia.com

### ❽ Cala Luna, Sardinia, Italy

Overhanging caves and limestone climbing crags tempt the adventurous to this beautiful half-moon-shaped beach on the east coast, while shallow, crystal-clear waters bursting with marine life provide superb conditions for snorkeling and a safe haven for children to swim.

Planning The beach is a short boat ride from Cala Gonone. www.sardegnaturismo.it

### ❾ Agios Georgios, Corfu, Greece

The Ionian island has some of the Mediterranean's most gorgeous beaches, many of them with Blue Flag status. Fragrant with sage and lemon and enveloped by olive groves, Agios Georgios at the northern end of the west coast is a secluded gem, its sweeping golden sands wrapped around a horseshoe-shaped bay. Fresh winds make it popular with windsurfers.

Planning Agios Georgios is a 45-minute bus ride from the town of Corfu. www.corfuvisit.net

### ❿ De Hoop Nature Reserve, South Africa

Situated near the southern tip of Africa, about 160 miles (257 km) east of Cape Town, this protected area lies on a stunning stretch of coastline, with huge sand dunes and quiet, cliff-framed bathing bays. Trek the Whale Hiking Trail and watch the awesome mammals leap out of the water. On land, look for baboons, zebras, yellow mongoose, and leopards.

Planning Whale season is from June to November, with peak viewing during August and September. www.sa-venues.com

Opposite: Glorious Cable Beach in Western Australia gets its name from the underwater telegraph cable that was laid from here across to Singapore in the 1880s.

The 17th-century church and bell tower of Hacienda Santa Bárbara

MEXICO

# Tlaxcala Haciendas

Two hours from the bustle of Mexico City, the hacienda route takes you on a tour of the region's historic estates.

On the other side of the mountains east of Mexico City lies the world of the Spanish rancheros. Here in Tlaxcala, Mexico's smallest state, with its sprawling ranches and fields of maguey and nopal cactus, the estates called haciendas flourished for 300 years. At their heart was an imposing home, where the *hacendado* and his family lived. Some haciendas now lie crumbling and abandoned, while others are inhabited by descendants of the original families, who will open their doors and share their history. In recent years, uninhabited haciendas have been restored and now provide lodging, where you can sample regional cuisine seasoned with local herbs and wild mushrooms. From Hacienda Soltepec, you can ride horses through the wildflower-dotted countryside dominated by snowcapped peaks. Several haciendas still breed the fine fighting bulls for which Tlaxcala is famous. Hacienda de Atlangatepec, a 23.6-mile (38 kilometer) drive from Hacienda Soltepec, gives beginner lessons in bullfighting and takes guests to local bullfights. A number of haciendas, notably Hacienda Xochuca, still produce *pulque,* the fermented juice of the maguey, and run demonstrations and tastings.

**When to Go** The temperate climate makes Tlaxcala a year-round destination. The mid-August festival of Asunción brings flower carpets and fiestas to the city of Tlaxcala and the running of the bulls through the streets of Huamantla.

**How to Find It** There are frequent buses between Mexico City and Tlaxcala (2 hours). Huamantla is 16 miles (26 km) from Tlaxcala. Begin the route at Hacienda Soltepec 3 miles (4.8 km) from Huamantla.

**Planning** The hacienda route is flexible, with options for day-trips, regional dining, or overnight stays. You can rent a car or hire a guide/driver at the tourism office in Tlaxcala, one block northeast of the plaza at Juárez and Lardizabel avenues.

**Websites** www.descubretlaxcala.com, www.bestday.com/tlaxcala/attractions, www.haciendasoltepec.com

## Tlaxcala and Beyond

■ The small colonial capital city, also called **Tlaxcala,** is built around a flower-filled central plaza and remains unspoiled by modern buildings. A walk up the hill from the plaza leads to the 16th-century **Templo de San Francisco,** with its Moorish ceiling of inlaid wood and a mural of the baptism of the indigenous chiefs of the ancient kingdom. Across the cobblestone patio is the bullring, one of the oldest in Mexico and still in use.

■ Only 11 miles (18 km) outside town is the archaeological site of **Cacaxtla,** dating to A.D. 650. Here you'll see still-vivid murals depicting the battle between the Mexican eagle warriors and the Maya jaguar warriors, as well as the Bird Man and Scorpion Man.

■ The **Altiplano Zoo** in the village of San Pablo Apetatitlan is dedicated to the conservation of endangered animals, with a breeding program aimed at reintroducing species back into the wild.

# KAIETEUR FALLS

A jungle trek through Guyana's lush interior culminates in one of the world's most spectacular waterfalls.

SOUTH AMERICA

It's dusk at the Tukiet camp, and you are surrounded by the towering wet walls of the Kaieteur Gorge. The clamor of the water tumbling from the falls is constant, and the sky is cloudy with thousands of swifts, which dart like arrows behind the cascade to nest in the rocks behind. The trek to Kaieteur is not for the fainthearted. The expedition begins with a bumpy, potholed ride from Guyana's capital Georgetown, through bauxite mining country to the put-in on the Potaro River. Here a motorboat zips you through the waterways, impenetrable jungle on either side, to camp on a white sandy beach at Amatuk Island. Hammocks are slung up between trees, and fresh fish and cassava bread are cooked on an open fire while trekkers bathe at the bank. The trail follows the river through dense forest, crossing creeks over log bridges and snaking over dark, slippery boulders. The final day's push is a precipitous four-hour climb to the top of Kaieteur Falls, where the Potaro River plunges over the limestone lip into the frothy pool below. With a drop of 741 feet (226 meters), the waterfall is five times the height of Niagara and twice that of Victoria. A small, noisy biplane lifts you for a final bird's-eye view of the falls and the never-ending canopy of the rain forest as you head back to Georgetown.

**When to Go**  Most trips run between July and November.

**How to Find It**  The three to five-day treks leave from Georgetown. The first full-day's travel is by bus, then 4WD to the put-in on the Potaro River.

**Planning**  Your luggage is transported by boat for the majority of the trek, but on the final day, for the steep climb, you must carry your own equipment, so bear this in mind when packing. Remember to take something with long sleeves as mosquitos and sand flies are voracious. The flight back to Georgetown takes just over an hour.

**Websites**  www.wilderness-explorers.com, www.geographia.com/guyana

## Wildlife-watching

Guyana's forests teem with wildlife. Flashes of vibrant color overhead signal macaws and toucans, while the distinctive mating calls of the cock-of-the-rock can be heard for miles around. These bright orange birds with prominent crests make their precarious nests within near-vertical cliff faces. Keep your eyes peeled for the beautiful sunset morpho, the continent's largest butterfly with a coffee-colored wingspan measuring up to 8 in (20 cm). You might even be lucky enough to catch a rare sighting of an ocelot resting in the lower branches of the forest.

With around 23,400 ft³ (663 m³) of water plunging down each second, Kaieteur Falls is one of the most powerful waterfalls in the world.

# ACROSS THE ANDES

From Salta in Argentina to the desert oasis town of San Pedro de Atacama in Chile, this is a bus ride of contrasts and extremes.

As the bus leaves the bustling, colonial town of Salta behind, the foliage becomes dense with hanging palms and bromeliads, the result of an incongruous subtropical microclimate at 3,930 feet (1,198 meters) above sea level. The flora soon thins out as you emerge into the mountainous valley around the village of Purmamarca, where the rock faces are spliced with golden, ocher, and russet hues. From here the road corkscrews up the precipitous Lipan Slope around a series of hairpin bends that takes you into the clouds as the lush foliage is replaced by spiky cacti. Here the driver slows to peer through the mist, and it's a relief not to be able to see the steep drop that falls away from the roadside. The cloud disperses to reveal the vast, parched salt flats of the Salar Grande, which glimmers, white and cracked, as far as the eye can see. The landscape is bleak and bright beneath a dome of clear sky as you approach the Argentinean border—a tiny outpost at the Paso de Jama, at a head-spinning altitude of 16,000 feet (4,877 meters). From here a lunar landscape unfolds as you continue into Chile: Lagoons of sapphire blue and emerald green fringed with rings of salt beneath rust-colored Andean peaks and volcanoes dusted with snow. Then, as you swoop down into the Atacama Desert in the shadow of the Licancabur volcano, a puddle of green appears in the distance— the adobe oasis of San Pedro de Atacama, 7,900 feet (2,400 meters) above sea level, beckons.

**When to Go**  The trip is best undertaken during Salta's dry season, from April to October.

**How to Find It**  There are flights to Salta from Buenos Aires. The Nueva Chevallier Bus Company runs a daily service from the capital (17 hours).

**Planning**  The Pullman bus service from Salta to San Pedro de Atacama currently runs on Tuesdays, Fridays, and Sundays, departing at 7 a.m., but timetables may change. The trip takes 12 hours. For a more leisurely ride, you can arrange the trip privately and spend a night along the way. Be prepared for altitude sickness.

**Websites**  www.welcomeargentina.com/salta, www.sanpedrodeatacama.com

## Salta

■ An alternative to the bus is the **Tren a las Nubes** (Train to the Clouds), which leaves Salta three times a week for the Argentina-Chile border. The track crosses bridges, switchbacks, and vertiginous viaducts to reach the terminus at **La Polvorilla.**

■ About a four-hour drive from Salta is the colonial town of **Cachi.** Its 16th-century church is a national monument.

■ From Cachi you can hike through a landscape straight out of a cowboy movie. Camps are basic, with log fires and *yerba mate* (a tea-like infusion drunk from hollowed gourds) to keep you warm at night.

The little village of Purmamarca nestles in the foothills of the polychromatic Cerro de los Siete Colores (Hill of Seven Colors).

A rope connects the Hatago Iwa on the peninsula's west coast. The two rocks are thought to represent lovers.

JAPAN

# Noto-hanto Peninsula

A remote finger of land, where life moves at a slower pace and artisanal traditions are preserved, juts out into the Sea of Japan.

From Noto airport near the center of this peninsula on Honshu island's northern side, it is a short drive to the rugged west coast, where the outer road tunnels through mountains and spits out suddenly onto spine-tingling cliff edges with expansive sea views. Curious rock formations and islands dot the coastline, including the Hatago Iwa, two rocks that, because they are considered sacred, are linked by a *shimenawa*, or rope, and Ganmon Rock, a naturally eroded gate onto the roaring ocean. Locals live in concert with the sea, gathering seaweed at low tide, scattering seawater on clay fields to produce salt, and maintaining 13-foot-high (4 meter) bamboo fences, or *magaki*, along the seafront to "soften" the force of wind and waves in winter. In the small northern town of Kamiozawa, the magaki is constructed with 10,000 bamboo stalks and insulates the traditional wooden homes from the Siberian winds that volley between the cliffs surrounding the village. Just past the magaki, and about 15 miles (24 kilometers) from the peninsula's tip, is Wajima City, where artisans still create the famous Wajima-nuri lacquerware, as exquisite as it is durable and showcased in two museums. The bustling morning market, dating back 1,000 years or so, is a good place to buy some and also sells an exotic range of seafood. The hillside of terraced paddy fields a little farther along the coast at Senmaida (literally "a thousand paddy fields") is a sight to behold.

**When to Go** The weather is best in summer and fall, but winter brings fresh, fatty seafood and waves and winds that blast the coastline to dramatic effect.

**How to Find It** Noto airport is a one-hour flight from Tokyo. The train journey from Tokyo takes six hours.

**Planning** Public buses are infrequent—rent a car at the airport or station, or a bicycle, which is a good way to explore the peninsula. Wajima's morning market is from 8 a.m. to noon daily. Kiriko festivals are held in summer, when giant lanterns are paraded and then set alight.

**Website** www.jnto.go.jp

## My Secret Journey

*His face crinkles as he stretches for the English phrases that he memorized years ago. We wash our hands with silver dippers and he asks me to bow, "only as an exercise," before entering the Shinto shrine, Keta Taisha, in the peninsula's southwest corner. He is the Guji (head priest) and 77-year-old guardian of the shrine's virgin forest. Only priests can enter the forest-sanctuary, but he tells me of a time, 27 years ago, when he took the emperor to see the old-growth forest. "He was so glad, so glad, that he gave a poem!" He rises and recites the haiku: "Going into the unaxed woods of the shrine, We found—how rare!—the karatachibana growing there."*
**Katrina Grigg-Saito**
**National Geographic Traveler**

ASIA

AUSTRALIA

# The Larapinta Trail

This bushwalking track takes you through
the rugged heart of central Australia.

The steady climb up the iron-stained ridge soon leaves behind the ocher-colored cliffs, mirror-surfaced waters, and bustling bird life of Ormiston Gorge for sweeping views across mulga and spinifex-dotted hills to the mauve ramparts of Mount Sonder. This is one of the final stretches (section 10 of 12) of the Larapinta Trail in the Northern Territory, a remote walking track that runs for 138 miles (222 kilometers) west from Alice Springs to Mount Sonder along the timeworn spine of the West MacDonnell Ranges. Each section of the trail is vehicle-accessible, so hikers can do as much or as little of the trek as they want. Even so, numbers thin out as the trail wends west, and beyond Ormiston Gorge you may not meet another soul. Ahead, the sandy bed of the Finke River (*lara pinta* in the local Arrernte language) makes a timely lunch spot, and for day-trippers a side track farther on leads off to the outpost of Glen Helen, with food, cool drinks, and campsites. For millennia, water holes in the string of gaps and gorges cleft through the range have been oases for humans and wildlife. At Simpsons Gap, reached at the end of the first (two-day) section, rock wallabies bask in the sun on umber rocks, while kites and cockatoos wheel overhead. Farther west, the track squeezes between the cool walls of Standley Chasm. At Ellery Creek, Big Hole walkers are welcomed by a deep pool flanked by silver-trunked ghost gums and shaded by steep red-rock faces, while at cycad-fringed Serpentine Gorge a flock of tiny zebra finches flutter and dip at the water's edge.

**When to Go** Walkers are strongly advised to tackle the trail (in groups of at least three people) between April and October, when daytime temperatures are less intense. Nights can get chilly.

**How to Find It** There are flights out to Alice Springs from the major Australian cities. Alice Springs is also connected by the Ghan railway, which runs between Adelaide and Darwin.

**Planning** To walk the entire length of the trail takes two weeks. Each of the 12 one- and two-day sections is graded for difficulty. A number of local companies offer guided tours with road transfers between trailheads to avoid the longer and more difficult sections. Glen Helen Resort at the end of section 10 offers food drops and transfers to and from trailheads at the western end of the track.

**Websites** www.nt.gov.au/nreta/parks/walks/larapinta, www.treklarapinta.com.au

AUSTRALIA AND OCEANIA

### Albert Namatjira

The vivid palette of Arrernte watercolor artist Albert Namatjira brilliantly captured the landscape of his West MacDonnell homeland. Born in 1902, Namatjira began painting in the "western style" in 1936 after being inspired by visiting artist Rex Battarbee.

Two years later Namatjira's first exhibition, in Melbourne, was a sellout, as were later exhibitions in Adelaide and Sydney. But his success came at a terrible price. At the time Aboriginal people were not even recognized as Australian citizens, but an exception was made for Namatjira and in 1957 he was awarded citizenship. As a citizen, he could now buy alcohol, but under tribal obligations he was expected to share it with his fellow Aboriginals. It was against the law to supply liquor to an Aboriginal, and in October 1958 Namatjira was found guilty and sentenced to two months in prison. The experience broke his spirit and he died the following year.

Namatjira's work is showcased at his birthplace **Hermannsburg** (about 77 miles/124 km west from Alice Springs on the sealed Larapinta Drive) and in the Albert Namatjira Gallery in the **Araluen Arts Centre** in Alice Springs.

Opposite: Hikers explore Standley Chasm. Above: A solitary ghost gum with Mount Sonder in the distance

# FERRY JOURNEYS

All aboard for some of the most exhilarating
crossings on the planet.

## ❶ Labrador Straits, Canada

During the 90-minute crossing from Blanc-Sablon on the Quebec-Labrador border to St. Barbe in Newfoundland, you will probably spot Labrador eider duck, which stay in the area year-round. Fall migration of shorebirds is a sight to behold, with greater yellowleg sanderlings or white-rumped sandpipers. In summer and early fall, follow the roll and dive of whales.

Planning Ferry service runs daily from mid-April to mid-January. www.tourismlowernorthshore.com, www.tw.gov.nl.ca

## ❷ Homer to Unalaska, Alaska

Meandering beside glaciers, the ocean-class boat calls in at half a dozen fishing ports in the Aleutian chain of volcanic islands, most of which comprise Aleutian National Wildlife Reserve. Photo opportunities are plentiful, including numerous eagles, the rare whiskered auklet, and the summer wildflowers that cloak Unalaska in color.

Planning The four-day journey runs from mid-April to the end of September. www.homeralaska.org, www.unalaska.info

## ❸ Tortola to Jost Van Dyke, British Virgin Islands

A 20-minute or so glide across turquoise Caribbean water on the aptly named *Paradise Express* delivers you to laidback Jost Van Dyke, named after a Dutch pirate and also known as the barefoot island. Lounge around in a beachfront café, snorkel, take a taxi tour around the island, or hike to White Bay beach.

Planning The last ferry back to Tortola usually leaves between 4:30 and 5 p.m. www.bvitourism.com

## ❹ Cruce de Lagos, Argentina to Chile

Starting in Bariloche, the lake-hopping adventure by bus and ferry traverses Lago Nahuel Huapi, Lago Frío, and Lago Todos los Santos, and ends at Puerto Varas. The scenery is worth every bump and wave, with scenic vistas of the Andes, crystal waterfalls, blue-green waters, snowcapped peaks, and sheer forest walls.

Planning This all-season trip can be made in one long day or broken up with an overnight stay in Peulla. www.visit-chile.org, www.turismo.gov.ar

## ❺ Kusu and St. John's Island, Singapore

A vehicular bridge crosses from mainland Singapore to Sentosa, where you can see a replica of the Merlion, the half-lion, half-fish symbol of Singapore. The ferry departs Sentosa for a 45-minute ride to the southern islands of St. John's—an ideal getaway for a picnic or a swim in the lagoon—or a 30-minute crossing to Kusu, where you can explore Da Bo Gong Temple and Kramat Shrine.

Planning Visit during weekdays, or in off-peak hours during the annual Kusu Pilgrimage from mid-October to mid-November, to avoid the crowds. www.visitsingapore.com, www.sentosa.com

## ❻ Lake St. Clair, Tasmania, Australia

Savor a peaceful, 30-minute cruise from Cynthia Bay across this translucent lake, against a backdrop of coves, beaches, and moraines, to Narcissus Bay at the southern end of the Overland Track walking route. You can hike back to Cynthia Bay among tea-tree thickets, rain-forest ferns, lofty dead standing eucalyptus, and buttongrass. You may see shy wallabies, wombats, or platypuses.

Planning Camp or stay in Alpine-style huts at Cynthia Bay. www.discovertasmania.com, www.parks.tas.gov.au

## ❼ Cook Strait, New Zealand

The three-hour ferry ride from Wellington on North Island to Picton on South Island passes green rocky slopes, lush forests, golden beaches, and the historic Cook Strait lighthouse. Seals, dolphins, and whales frolic in the sometimes extremely choppy waters. Picturesque Picton gives way to waterfront cafés, boutiques, and museums.

Planning Hop on the shuttle bus from Wellington station to the ferry terminal. www.newzealand.com, www.interislander.co.nz

## ❽ Strömstad to Koster Islands, Sweden

A scenic, 40-minute crossing takes you to car-free Koster Islands, Sweden's most westerly populated islands. Cyclists and hikers can explore the rocky landscape, fjords, moors, and forests. Opt for guided walks, seal safaris, or boat trips. The dramatic North Koster is filled with heather moors, fields of cobblestone, and remnants of the Ice Age.

Planning The best time to go is between early May and late September. www.visitsweden.com, www.kosteroarna.com

## ❾ Rostock, Germany, to Gedser, Denmark

For more than 100 years, ferries have crossed the 28-mile (45 km) stretch of Baltic Sea that separates the historic Hanseatic town of Rostock and the small village of Gedser at the southern tip of the Danish island of Falster. In fall, bird-watchers catch sight of flocks of migrating birds.

Planning The crossing takes 1 hour and 45 minutes. www.cometogermany.com, www.visitdenmark.com

## ❿ Cornwall to the Isles of Scilly, England

From Penzance on the mainland you sail to Hugh Town on St. Mary's, one of the 56 islands that jut out of the sparkling green water. Yellow daffodils abound, thousands of which are exported to the mainland. Pick ripe blackberries in August, or scuba dive the reef and shipwreck areas brimming with marine life.

Planning Ferry times may be altered due to extreme tides or to special events taking place on the islands. www.visitcornwall.com, www.visitbritain.com

Opposite: Ferry passengers experience the remote beauty of Alaska's Aleutian Islands.

# ALPINE LAKELAND

Take a pleasant drive through the Salzkammergut, a region
of lakes, mountains, and Alpine villages bedecked with flowers.

Traveling south from Mozart's birthplace of Salzburg, the first lake you come to is Lake Fuschl, one of the smallest, but arguably most picturesque in the area. On your descent into the next valley you are greeted by the sight of sailboats rocking on the much more touristy Lake Wolfgang. Enjoy the views, but press on farther south into the very heart of Austria and the Alps. As you approach Lake Hallstatt (site of a prehistoric settlement that gave the early Iron Age its name), you understand why even until well into the last century, this site was accessible only by ferry. The road gets narrower, the mountain ranges ever steeper, and in winter the tiny settlement of Hallstatt is often completely cut off from the world. Today, a road has been tunneled through the rock to the town, but you can still cross the fjord-like lake by ferry. Travel early in the morning, when the often heavy mist rises above the water and the sun brings a few hours of warmth to this secluded village. The original pile dwellings have gone, but the houses built into the steep mountainsides are unique in style. Take the funicular or hike up the steep mountain path to the 7,000-year-old salt mines. Also not to be missed is the ossuary at the Catholic church, with its hundreds of painted human skulls.

**When to Go** May through October are the peak months. Hallstatt can be difficult to reach in winter, when many things (including the salt mines) close down.

**How to Find It** You can rent a car in Salzburg or inquire about tours at your hotel. Or you can take a bus from Salzburg Hauptbahnhof to Bad Ischl, then a train to Hallstatt station and a ferry to Hallstatt village.

**Planning** Plan your visit to coincide with the region's many festivals, the most memorable being the Corpus Christi boat procession on Lake Hallstatt in late spring and the Almabtrieb on Lake Wolfgang in early fall, when the cattle return from their summer Alpine pastures.

**Websites** www.salzwelten.at, www.fuschlseeregion.com, www.wolfgangsee.at

### Three-lake Panorama

The **Bartl-Hütte** is a popular filling station for hikers who come to admire the crystal-clear turquoise waters of the surrounding lakes from high above. On the menu is traditional hearty Austrian fare, including dumplings and pig roasts, as well as desserts, cordials, and schnapps made from locally harvested elderberries. Come by road from **Faistenau** (12 miles/20 km east of Salzburg)—the chalet is a five-minute walk from the car park; or take the cable car up the **Zwölferhorn** from **St. Gilgen** and brave the half-hour descent to the Bartl-Hütte.

St. Wolfgang by the shores of Lake Wolfgang is one of Austria's most popular lake resorts.

Lübeck's impressive Gothic Marienkirche is a symbol of the city's status as "Queen of the Hanseatic League."

GERMANY

# Hanseatic League Cities

Soaring Gothic spires, medieval redbrick gables, and
harbors are reminders of a once powerful trade alliance.

From Bremen the road winds north toward the Baltic coast to Lübeck, where the monumental Holsten Gate stands testimony to the city's prominence in the Hansa, a powerful trading association of medieval cities. Soak up the atmosphere of the old town with its brick and stone patrician houses dating from the 15th and 16th centuries, or seek out a quiet corner in a myriad of hidden courtyards, where well-manicured private gardens are open to visitors. Farther east along the coast, in Wismar, which has Swedish gabled houses, a neoclassical town hall, and a Dutch Renaissance-style pavilion, the pleasant aroma of smoked fish wafts through the air. Passing charming Baltic spa towns you reach Rostock, its massive gates, fortifications, and imposing gabled houses bearing witness to its importance as a Hansa city. Completely surrounded by water, Stralsund is known as "red town" for its redbrick Gothic architecture, every single clay brick having been formed by hand. Canals, warehouses, fortification ruins, a medieval abbey, and dozens of other historic buildings—including the 13th-century *rathaus* (town hall) with its distinctive arcades—are among the town's highlights.

**When to Go** Each season has its appeal. Colorful Christmas markets brighten the chilly winters, while springtime brings festivals and Easter fires in northern Germany. With long warm days and short cool nights, summer is busier and a little more expensive.

**How to Find It** The cities are easily accessible by train or car. Rostock, for example, is three hours from Berlin, two hours from Hamburg.

**Planning** You will need at least three days to cover the route of around 310 miles (500 km).

**Websites** www.cometogermany.com, www.historicgermany.com

### Farmyard Cafés

■ Sip on freshly brewed coffee in one of the region's 90 or so Farmyard Cafés (with alluring views of the Baltic thrown in). After serving the steaming coffee, the farmer's wife or daughter proudly doles out homemade cakes and pies, often baked from recipes handed down from generation to generation. A number of farms allow you to pick ripe raspberries and strawberries from the fields in summer.

■ While you're traveling the Hanseatic region, try Rote Grütze, a traditional red-fruit dessert that makes excellent use of the local fruit. Cooked in the fruits' natural juices, the thickened mixture overflows with black and red currants, raspberries, and sometimes cherries or strawberries. Rote Grütze is served with cream or vanilla sauce.

EUROPE

The Louisiana Museum of Modern Art is the most visited art museum in Denmark.

DENMARK

# The Danish Riviera

Not only is this stretch of Zealand coast beguilingly scenic,
it is also quiet and virtually flat—in other words, cycling heaven.

North of Copenhagen lies a lesser-traveled stretch of coastline known as the Danish Riviera, where hiking and biking paths follow the sinuous shores of serene, sandy beaches. Leaving Copenhagen behind, you can meander through harbor towns and expanses of woodlands. Vistas of sapphire-blue waters appear at your side as you inhale the heady scent of salt air. As you continue, upscale seaside homes, cozy inns, and quiet villages come into view. Pull up at Rungsted to visit the former home of *Out of Africa* author Karen Blixen, filled with memorabilia and surrounded by a bird sanctuary. Then take a detour inland to visit the gardens of the 18th-century Fredensborg Palace, still in use as a residence by the Danish royal family. In Klampenborg, you can visit Dyrehaven (the Deer Garden), once a royal hunting ground and now a sprawling forest where more than 2,000 deer still roam free. Back on the cycle path, your final destination as you head north is Helsingør (Elsinore), home of the imposing Kronborg Slot, also known as Hamlet's Castle, where Shakespearean legends swirl among the majestic halls of this stately 17th-century building.

**When to Go** Summers are warm but not sweltering. Denmark is delightful in spring and fall, but winters are windy and chilly. Always be prepared for rain.

**How to Find It** Cycle paths link Copenhagen with Helsingør, 25 miles (40 km) away. Alternatively, take your bicycle by train from Central Station in Copenhagen to Helsingør station. You can then pedal back to Copenhagen or stay the night before returning.

**Planning** A Copenhagen Card entitles you to free admission to scores of museums, as well as unlimited travel on buses, the metro, and S-Tog trains. Within Copenhagen, you can rent a City Bicycle for free (with refundable deposit), but you are not allowed to take it outside the city limits.

**Websites** www.visitdenmark.us, www.louisiana.dk

## Louisiana

Perched on a bluff overlooking the Øresund in Humlebæk, just south of Helsingør, is the **Louisiana Museum of Modern Art,** with works by many leading artists, including Picasso, Warhol, Ernst, and Giacometti. The multiwinged complex, set in spacious parkland, was originally built in 1855 as a country house for Alexander Brun, the Master of the Royal Hunt, who dubbed it Louisiana to honor his three successive wives—all named Louise.

Stroll through the sculpture park, where you'll spy a magnificent reclining figure by Henry Moore, and gaze out over the sound, with Sweden visible in the blue-hazed distance.

EUROPE

ITALY

# Puglia's Valle d'Itria

Explore the layers of history that are woven into the bucolic landscape of this picturesque valley in the heel of Italy.

An early morning fog hangs over the undulating hills, which are cloaked in centuries-old olive groves and vineyards and peppered with white conical structures that seem to have stepped out of the pages of a fairy tale. The Valle d'Itria is famous for these ancient stone buildings known as *trulli,* which were designed to keep their occupants cool in summer and warm in winter. Just southeast of the busy tourist center of Alberobello, quiet trulli-strewn country roads lead to pristine, centuries-old villages. In Locorotondo, named for its circular layout, concentric rings of whitewashed houses encircle the Chiesa Madre (Mother Church), a triumphant blend of neoclassical and baroque styles. Continuing a little way south, Martina Franca stands as a reminder of the region's centuries of Spanish domination, its elegant center dominated by baroque architecture, while in Cisternino the town's Arabic roots are preserved in the labyrinthine layout of its streets and in the pointed arches of its buildings. The valley's winding roads and well-trodden paths give way to rolling landscapes intersected by dirt paths that lead even farther afield to pastures where sheep graze, farmers harvest their produce, and trulli stand alone or in clusters. Food festivals in summer and fall celebrate the region's many culinary highlights, which include rustic durum-wheat pastas, hard and soft cheeses, and the good Locorotondo white wine.

**When to Go** Though July and August tend to be very hot, there are many cultural events, including the Valle d'Itria Opera Festival.

**How to Find It** The closest airports are at Bari and Brindisi. There are also trains to Bari from Rome and other Italian cities.

**Planning** The valley's many B&Bs and *agriturismi* (farm accommodations) are ideal for visiting nearby towns such as Castellana-Grotte, Bari, Trani, Castel del Monte, Ostuni, and Matera. Public transport connections are infrequent and unreliable, so you will need to rent a car.

**Websites** www.viaggiareinpuglia.it, www.andantetravels.co.uk, www.grottedicastellana.it

### Grotte di Castellana

Some 9 miles (15 km) north of the Valle d'Itria is a 1.8-mile-long (3 km) system of caves created by millions of years of sedimentary deposit and water flow. The caves are a natural wonder that draw scientists, spelunkers, and tourists alike. Stalactites and stalagmites fill the extensive caverns, including the **Tower of Pisa Cave,** so-named for its large stalagmite; the **Cave of the Monuments;** and most spectacular of all, the **White Cave,** with its brilliant white calcium formations. There are daily guided tours lasting either 50 minutes or two hours.

Thousands of trulli pack the winding, narrow streets of Alberobello, a UNESCO World Heritage Site.

# BACKWATERS

Whether you take to the water or stay on dry land, peace and
quiet is guaranteed on these natural and man-made stretches of water.

### ❶ Rideau Canal, Ottawa, Canada

A 125-mile-long (201 km) string of lakes and rivers joined by
man-made canals links Kingston on Lake Ontario with Ottawa.
You could well be joined by a muskrat when passing through one
of the 45 hand-cranked locks, spot terrapins basking on logs, and
hear the cries of loons echoing across the still waters at night.

Planning The canal opens in late May and closes mid-October. Allow a
minimum of three days one way. www.rideau-info.com/canal

### ❷ Boundary Waters, Minnesota

Straddling the United States–Canada border, this wilderness area
of waterways and bogs includes the Boundary Waters Canoe Area
in the Superior National Forest of northeast Minnesota. There are
more than 1,000 lakes and 1,600 canoe routes with portage trails.
Many of the 2,000 campsites are accessible only from the water.

Planning Permits required for overnight stays must be reserved in
advance in summer, when a quota system regulates the number of
canoeists entering the area. www.fs.fed.us/r9/forests/superior/bwcaw

### ❸ Anavilhanas Archipelago, Brazil

This labyrinth of islands and channels on the Negro River in the
Amazon River Basin is the world's largest freshwater archipelago.
In the rainy season, many islands are covered by water, creating
a flooded forest where pink river dolphins swim in the treetops
and fish feed on nuts. The Ariaú Amazon Towers (18 miles/39 km
away) is the world's largest treetop hotel.

Planning The archipelago is 50 miles (80 km) upstream from Manaus.
www.ariautowers.com, www.anavilhanaslodge.com

### ❹ Myall Lakes, New South Wales, Australia

This system of four interconnected coastal lagoons is separated
from the ocean by beaches and sand dunes. You might spot
kangaroos, wallabies, and bandicoots, as well as koalas, in the
southern part of the park. Elegant black swans adorn the lakes,
and watch out for pairs of white-bellied sea-eagles along the
shore and dolphins and humpback whales out at sea.

Planning Reached via Pacific Highway, 117 miles (188 km) northeast of
Sydney. www.environment.nsw.gov.au

### ❺ Kolovesi National Park, Finland

Paddle a canoe or row the 25-mile (40 km) circular route around
the Lake Saimaa archipelago. Motor cruisers are prohibited in
order to protect the rare Saimaa ringed seal that survives here in
fresh water, having been cut off from the sea after the last ice age.
Quartz crystals and 5,000-year-old rock paintings can be seen at
rugged Ukonvuori Hill in the eastern part of the park.

Planning You can start at either Käkövesi or Kirkkoranta boat launch
sites, near Enonkoski. www.finland.fi, www.luontoon.fi

### ❻ La Baïse, Lot-et-Garonne, France

La Baïse is one of several major waterways that converge on Buzet
in southwest France. The tree-lined river passes through gentle
rolling countryside punctuated with vineyards and orchards.
Duck is the mainstay of local cuisine and foie gras a specialty.
Floq de Gascoyne is a local wine-based aperitif (rouge or blanc) and
Armagnac, France's oldest brandy, comes from this region.

Planning By canal, Damazan to Valence-sur-Baïse and return takes
about a week. www.europa47.org/anglais

### ❼ Great Glen Way, Scotland

From Fort William to Inverness, a huge geological fault splits
Scotland in two. It is marked by a string of lochs all connected
by the Caledonian Canal. You can explore the route on foot, or
by bike, car, or boat. For the first section of the 73-mile (117 km)
walking trail from the Old Fort at Fort William, the towpath hugs
the shores of the lochs, while later sections are high on adjacent
hills. By boat, the route is technically an inland waterway, although
a windy day on Loch Ness can be more like a sea crossing.

Planning There are bus and rail services from Glasgow and Edinburgh
to Fort William and Inverness. www.greatglenway.com

### ❽ South Oxford Canal, England

Setting out from the "dreaming spires" of Oxford, the canal
twists and turns through Cotswold countryside, with thatched,
honey-stoned villages, welcoming pubs, woodlands, and water
meadows. Diamond-shaped locks, wooden lift bridges, and the
windmill on Napton Hill are unique to this canal.

Planning The cruise from Oxford to Napton and back takes about a
week. www.waterways.org.uk, www.waterscape.com

### ❾ Llangollen Canal, Wales

The aqueducts at Chirk and Pontcysyllte—the latter 1,007 ft
(307 m) long and supported on high, slender, masonry arches—
are engineering highlights along the canal's 46 miles (74 km)
from Nantwich in Cheshire to the foothills of Snowdonia.

Planning Marinas at Llangollen, Chirk, Ellesmere, Wrenbury,
Whitchurch, and Whittington have narrow boats for rent.
www.waterways.org.uk, www.waterscape.com

### ❿ The Gambia River, West Africa

The river is the lifeblood of the Gambia and the best way to see
this tiny sliver of a country. Highlights upriver include hippos,
Guinea baboons, red colobus monkeys, and Nile crocodiles,
while the mangrove-rich estuary is a key site for wetland birds.

Planning Trips on the lower stretches are from Banjul; those to
the Baboon Islands and the middle and upper stretches are from
Janjanbureh (Georgetown) and Kuntaur. www.hi.accessgambia.com

Opposite: Considered by some to be the prettiest waterway in England, the South Oxford Canal connects the Thames River with the heart of England.

# LAVENDER TOUR OF PROVENCE

Fields of lavender rippling gently in the summer breeze
invite a detour to enjoy this uniquely Provençal fragrance.

EUROPE

ead for the high country, the *arrière-pays de Provence* in southern France, to ramble through seemingly limitless lavender fields stretching to blue-violet horizons. The Romans first brought the aromatic plant to this sunny, arid region, where true lavender grows at high altitudes today. A drought-resistant hybrid, *lavandin,* nods in endless rows east of the town of Manosque and across the sun-drenched Valensole plateau. In fact, the crossroads near the Poteau de Telle offers lavender vistas in all directions. A third and rarer type, spike (wild) lavender, or *aspic,* with longer stems and multiple flowerheads, grows on higher ground, north of Grasse on the Plateau de Caussols. To explore a variety of lavender terrain, begin in the Luberon valley at Apt and ascend into the Haute-Provence uplands around Sault. Linger in this sprawling town on the edge of a high plateau, especially on Wednesdays when local artisans come to sell their wares at the colorful market, just as they have done since 1515. Then take a turn off the beaten track via Aurel, into the foothills of Mont Ventoux (a challenging, steep route of the Tour de France bicycle race), before winding toward Buis-les-Baronnies in the Drôme. You may see fields hand-cut for sachets and bundles late in July, but in mid-August, distillery-destined lavender is harvested by machine. Whether you travel by car, bicycle, or on foot, pause to take a deep breath of the fresh aromas, most intense just before sundown.

**When to Go** Just before budbreak early in June, fields take on a stunning, silken shimmer, but actual blossom time varies, running from late June into August.

**How to Find It** Take the TGV (fast train) from Paris Gare de Lyon to Avignon (2.5 hours). Apt is 33 miles (53 km) east of Avignon. Regional buses run from Avignon Central Station to Apt and Sault.

**Planning** Summers can be sweltering—be sure to rent a car with la climatisation (air-conditioning).

**Websites** www.beyond.fr, www.chateau-la-gabelle.com, www.simiane-la-rotonde.fr

### Essence of Provence

■ Stay a night or a week on Marguerite Blanc's lavender farm, **Château de la Gabelle,** near **Ferrassières.** Time a visit during the Lavender Festival, the first Sunday in July.

■ Don't miss the lavender court in **Simiane-la-Rotonde's** medieval château. This historic hillside town's aromatics cooperative, the largest in Provence, runs workshops on essential oils (book in advance).

■ Celebrate the lavender harvest at one of the many local festivals, each a pageant of dancing, parades, and produce, including lavender-honey tastings.

An almond tree punctuates the serried rows of lavender. The fields will lie bare after harvesting in late July into August.

Sharply pointed Seahorse Rock is one of many curious formations that tell of Madeira's volcanic origins.

MADEIRA

# São Lourenço Cliff Walk

Explore the Portuguese island's craggy eastern tip
for phenomenal 360-degree views.

Bristling with volcanic cones and towering cliffs, this long finger of land stretching into the Atlantic is Madeira's most easterly point. A salty breeze sweeps across the rocky wilderness as you stop to take in the view. There are noticeably no trees growing here, but lichen clings to the rocks and tiny flowers and thistles bloom in the hollows. You make your way along narrow ridges, past dramatic rock formations and precipitous cliffs in shades of green, yellow, ocher, and red. The trail is dizzying at times—there are safety wires in the most precarious spots—and whether you look over the edge is up to you, but far below are isolated coves of black or white sands lapped by a foaming ocean. The well-marked trail leads to the end of the land and a steep volcanic peak with views south to the Desertas Islas and, on a clear day, north to Porto Santo, Madeira's smaller sister island. The fishing village of Caniçal glistens down in the bay and a lonely lighthouse stands on a deserted islet. Sometimes you can spot rare monk seals on the shore and lizards darting in and out of dark crevices. The rangers' house is in a small palm oasis, where rock swallows and goldfinches come to drink from the freshwater tank. You'll see seabirds galore, along with buzzards, kestrels, pipits, and colorful flocks of twittering canaries.

**When to Go** Any time of the year, but the peninsula is green in winter, barren in summer. Spring brings a riot of flowers across the island. Sea breezes keep temperatures bearable even in the height of summer.

**How to Find It** Drive from the capital Funchal to the parking lot at Abra Bay, the start of the walk. There is a bus service from Funchal to Caniçal (around 1.5 hours).

**Planning** Allow three to four hours to complete the 5-mile-long (8 km) walk, with plenty of time for photographs and maybe a picnic on the headland. Sturdy shoes, sunscreen, and weatherproof clothing are essential as the weather can change quickly. Only the final climb is truly challenging.

**Websites** www.madeiratourism.org, www.madeira-levada-walks.com, www.madeira-web.com

## Other Trails

■ A hiking route along part of the island's central mountain chain links **Pico do Arieiro** with Madeira's highest peak, **Pico Ruivo** (6,105 ft/1,861 m). This is a demanding 4.3-mile (7 km) trek through rugged terrain, with steep climbs, dizzying drops, and awesome views.

■ A long but relatively easy trek crosses the island on the old **Royal Path,** where gentlemen once traveled on horseback and ladies were carried in hammocks. The trail weaves along **Nuns Valley,** so-called because nuns used the route to escape pirates, and passes through the **Laurisilva Forest.**

AFRICA

# RAIL JOURNEYS

Cutting a swath through some breathtaking landscapes,
these railways offer a unique window on the world.

### ❶ Cass Scenic Railroad, West Virginia

The steam trains climb the 11 miles (18 km) from Cass to the 4,842-ft-high (1,476 m) summit of Bald Knob, which has spectacular views and bracing mountain air. The line, built in 1901 to haul lumber, uses geared locomotives to overcome its ferocious gradients, which include switchbacks.

Planning Advance booking is advisable. Bring plenty of warm clothing. www.cassrailroad.com

### ❷ White Pass & Yukon Railroad, Alaska/Canada

Built in 1898 during the Klondike Gold Rush, the narrow-gauge WP&YR starts from the Taiya Inlet quaysides of Skagway, Alaska, and climbs 2,880 ft (878 m) over the White Pass into Canada's Yukon territories and some of the north's most rugged terrain. Diesel and steam trains travel to Carcross or Fraser Meadows.

Planning Passports are required. There are places to stay in Skagway, on the South Klondike Highway. Advanced booking is advisable. www.wpyr.com

### ❸ The Old Patagonian Express, Argentina

Departing twice weekly from Esquel in Patagonia's mountainous Chubut province, this antique train—known locally as La Trochita ("the little narrow gauge")—winds through rugged terrain to the small settlement of Nahuel Pan.

Planning The round-trip takes 2.5 hours. Accommodations are available in Esquel, reached by plane or bus from Buenos Aires. www.patagonia-argentina.com

### ❹ The Overlander, North Island, New Zealand

This epic 423-mile (681 km) train journey through the heart of North Island links Auckland in the north to Wellington in the south. Highlights along the way include the ski resort of National Park, the Mount Ruapehu volcano, the Raurimu Spiral, and the Hapuawhenua Viaduct. There is an observation carriage at the back of the train and a viewing platform at the front. On certain Sundays the train is steam-hauled for part of the near 12-hour journey.

Planning The service runs daily in the summer season (except Christmas Day). www.tranzscenic.co.nz

### ❺ The Sunlander, Queensland, Australia

Snaking along the Queensland coast between Brisbane and Cairns, the Sunlander offers a superbly luxurious service with dining and sleeping-car facilities. As Queensland glides past the windows, passengers can enjoy local seafood platters or club and buffet-car fare. The climate becomes increasingly tropical as the train travels north toward Cairns.

Planning The journey takes about 32 hours. www.australian-trains.com, www.railaustralia.com.au/sunlander.php

### ❻ Kandy to Haputale, Sri Lanka

The train south from Kandy, in central Sri Lanka, to Haputale travels past tea plantations, forests, unspoiled villages, and waterfalls. For the five-hour journey, the first class observation car is well worth the extra fare.

Planning Advance booking is essential. Expect high temperatures and humidity. www.slrfc.org/railway-seat-reservation

### ❼ Malnad, Western Ghats, India

Shimoga in India's Karnataka province is the eastern end of the run to Talaguppa in the Western Ghat Mountains. The 46.6-mile (75 km), three-hour journey aboard a small railbus from Shimoga to Talaguppa passes through lush rain forest. The magnificent Jog Falls—India's highest waterfall—can be reached by road from Talaguppa.

Planning An overnight train from Bangalore connects with Shimoga. Facilities on the railbus are limited. The line is being upgraded, so check ahead before traveling. www.indiaprofile.com

### ❽ Sarajevo to Mostar, Bosnia and Herzegovina

Traversing superb Balkan scenery, the train from Sarajevo climbs to its highest point near Konjic, where it joins the Neretva Valley. The descent into Herzegovina passes through dramatic gorges until reaching the town of Mostar, famous for the 16th-century stone bridge that was destroyed during the Bosnian War in the 1990s and rebuilt.

Planning The journey takes about 2.5 hours. There are two trains per day. www.mostar-travel.ba/transportation

### ❾ The Romney, Hythe & Dymchurch Railway, England

Opened in 1927, this miniature steam railway (its rails are just 15 in/38 cm apart) runs from the picturesque resort of Hythe to the shingle foreland of Dungeness, famous for its lighthouse, power station, and wildlife. Stops along the 13.5-mile (22 km) route include the seaside resort of Dymchurch with its miles of sandy beach.

Planning There is a model railway exhibition at New Romney Station. www.rhdr.org.uk

### ❿ Welsh Highland Railway, Wales

Running to Porthmadog Harbour Station from Caernarfon in North Wales's Snowdonia National Park, this spectacular line traverses some of the finest scenery in Wales. Catch dramatic views of Snowdon's 3,560-ft (1,085 m) summit and the precipitous Aberglaslyn Pass from the Pullman observation cars as the train blasts through the mountains.

Planning Porthmadog and Caernarfon both have places to stay. www.welshhighlandrailway.net

Opposite: Passengers experience the romance of steam travel on the Cass Scenic Railroad in West Virginia.

Getaria is known as the *cocina de Guipúzcoa* (the kitchen of Guipúzcoa province).

SPAIN

# Basque Coast Walk

You need never go hungry on a trail that takes
in some of the Basque region's gastronomic highlights.

Three days is ample time to hike this stretch of the northeastern Basque Coast to Hendaye, just over the border in France. Begin in Zumaia with a look around the former home and museum of painter Ignacio Zuloaga, with works by artists including Goya, El Greco, and Rivera. Well-marked GR (Gran Recorrido) hiking trails lead over the hills to the pretty fishing village of Getaria and restaurants where *besugo* (sea bream) and *txuleta de buey* (ox steaks) sizzle over coals. A walk over the vineyard-laden hills brings you to the coastal village of Zarautz, with the longest beach in the Basque country. From here the train zips you to San Sebastián for more culinary highlights, ranging from world-class Arzak to tapas in the Parte Vieja. Delicious fish and seafood await across the bay of Pasajes in the charming fishing village of Pasajes de San Juan, its one winding street lined with historic buildings, including the house where Victor Hugo lived. You spend the night at Caserio Artzu, a traditional Basque farmhouse inn above Hondarribia, a colorful fishing village on the estuary of the Bidasoa River—the border between Spain and France. The *navette* or shuttle boat over to Hendaye beach puts you on the GR-10 trail up to the tiny town of Biriatou perched over the Bidasoa. After a night at the Auberge Hiribarren, walk down to Hendaye for the train back to San Sebastián.

**When to Go** May to June or September to November to avoid rain and summer heat.

**How to Find It** Take the narrow-gauge EuskoTren to Zumaia from Bilbao or to San Sebastián. Or take the overnight train to Zumarraga from Barcelona or Madrid and then a bus to Zumaia.

**Planning** The walk is designed as a day-pack hike from inn to inn. Bring good hiking boots, warm clothing, a day or hip pack, and a sturdy umbrella.

**Websites** www.basquecountry-tourism.com, spainguides.com/sansebastian.html

## Basque Wine

The vineyards above **Getaria** produce the signature Basque wine, *txakolí*, a tart, slightly sparkling wine made from Hondarribi Zuria grapes. Txakolí vines grow on overhead trellises, which were traditionally supported by whale ribs. Cultivated over the rainy Bay of Biscay, txakolí grapes receive little sun and are usually harvested before they are fully ripe, giving the wine its high acidity and low sugar content. Txakolí is normally served as an aperitif (complementing salty hors d'oeuvres, such as anchovies) and drunk within a year of bottling. The wine is poured into tall, wide glasses from a height of up to 3 ft (1 m) to activate carbonation and release the flavor. Getaria's Txomin Etxaniz is generally considered the finest brand of txakolí.

EUROPE

# Glen Affric

"The Monarch of the Glen," Landseer's paean to the romance of the Highlands, was inspired by Affric's rugged beauty.

Tourists flock to Loch Ness with hopes of spotting the eponymous monster, but few venture up one of the side valleys to Glen Affric. This vestige of primordial Scotland is a throwback to the Highlands before the arrival of man, a valley strewn with Caledonian pines, flush with wildlife, and riven by streams the color of the single malt for which this region is justly famous. Home to the Chisholm clan since the early 15th century, the glen supported an ample human population until the forced Highland Clearances of the late 18th century. Although Victorian-era logging and sheep farming took its toll, the valley's extreme remoteness precluded total exploitation. Nowadays, only the lower glen is accessible by car, but walkers can explore the remainder of the region on 15 major trails. They range from an easy one-hour jaunt from the main parking lot along the Affric River to a strenuous 18-mile (29 kilometer) circuit to the summits of Carn Eige and Mam Sodhail peaks, both of them snow-covered in winter and windy and changeable at the best of times. Wildlife sightings are possible on any of these paths, especially around dawn when red deer, pine marten, otter, and other creatures are most often out and about. Another great trail, either on foot or by mountain bike, is the round-trip around placid Loch Affric.

**When to Go** Summer is the best time for long-distance hiking, although like anywhere in the Scottish Highlands the weather is highly changeable—sunny one moment, rainy the next.

**How to Find It** Glen Affric can be reached from Inverness on highways A862 and A831 (via Beauly) or from Drumnadrochit on the western shore of Loch Ness by taking the A831 due west. Cannich village is the gateway to the glen.

**Planning** Places to stay in the immediate area include the Cannich Caravan & Camping Park, the Glen Affric Backpackers Hostel, and the historic Tomich Hotel, once a Victorian hunting lodge. Natural High Guiding offers a wide range of guided day hikes, camping trips, mountain bike rides, and bike rentals.

**Websites** www.glenaffric.org, www.walkhighlands.co.uk/lochness, www.naturalhighguiding.co.uk

### Applecross Peninsula

To the west of Glen Affric, nestling between the mainland mountain passes and the Isle of Skye, lies the **Applecross Peninsula.** One of Scotland's most remote places, it was inaccessible by road until the 1970s. A narrow road now runs along the shore, connecting the dozen or so small fishing villages. But the most spectacular approach is up and over the ancient **Bealach na Ba (Pass of the Cattle),** once used for cattle droving but now a single-track paved road with the steepest gradient (20%) of any road in the British Isles. Road signs prepare motorists for the climb ahead, but not the mesmerizing views at the top.

Remnants of the ancient pine forest that once covered much of Scotland provide a haven for wildlife.

WALES

# Hay-on-Wye to Abergavenny

The gentle rolling landscape of the Black Mountains has long provided spiritual and creative inspiration.

The picturesque market town of Hay-on-Wye just over the Welsh border in the Brecon Beacons National Park is known as the secondhand book capital of the world. Visitors come to browse in the many bookshops, including the unattended Honesty Bookshop on the grounds of the castle, where you pay for books by dropping your money into a box. As you drive southward from Hay toward Abergavenny, the castle-dotted route brims with vistas of the breathtaking Black Mountains. This is the easternmost range of the Brecon Beacons, immortalized by Bruce Chatwin in his novel *On the Black Hill*, about twin brothers living on a remote upland farm on the Welsh border. Along the way, stop at Tretower Castle and Court to admire the imposing ruins of a 12th-century castle that soars skyward and a restored 14th-century courtyard house that still stands tall. You might stop for lunch in Crickhowell, a mecca for walkers, climbers, and other outdoor enthusiasts. A Norman castle rises in the town, commanding wonderful views of the Usk Valley. Just outside the town center, stand on the bridge to gaze down on the sapphire-blue Usk River. Continue on to Abergavenny, a market town surrounded by the majestic natural beauty of Blorenge, Skirrid Fawr, and Sugar Loaf mountains—all easily accessible to walkers.

**When to Go** The Abergavenny Food Festival takes place each September. The annual Hay Festival runs around the last week in May/first week in June, when the town crowds with visitors.

**How to Find It** Hay is situated just off the A438 about 20 miles (32 km) from the historic cathedral city of Hereford. Trains from London to Hereford depart from Paddington. Local bus services run between Hereford and Hay-on-Wye.

**Planning** Every Thursday, there's a traditional market in Hay-on-Wye where you can buy locally baked organic bread, Welsh cheeses, and other produce.

**Websites** www.travelwales.org, www.hay-on-wye.co.uk, www.abergavenny.co.uk

EUROPE

### Sugar Loaf Vineyards

En route from Hay-on-Wye to Abergavenny, oenophiles should stop at the Sugar Loaf Vineyards, at the southern foot of the Sugar Loaf mountain, to sample some of the very best wines produced in Wales. There are four tasty varieties of white, one red, and one sparkling wine.

Take a leisurely tour of the verdant 5 acres (2 ha), or stay in one of the vacation cottages and sip a glass or two from the complimentary bottle of wine offered to overnight guests as you gaze out over the beautiful Usk Valley.

Opposite: A rutted footpath leads from the Sugar Loaf to Crickhowell. Above: The imposing ruins of Tretower Castle

# THE CAUSEWAY COASTAL ROUTE

This dreamy road trip around the Emerald Isle's northern fringes deserves to be taken at a leisurely pace.

EUROPE

Signposts point to places that beg to be explored as you drive along the quiet, narrow road linking Belfast, the Giant's Causeway, Portrush, and Londonderry. On Belfast's fringes, Carrickfergus Castle, built in 1177, is one of Ireland's best preserved Norman fortresses. From here, the road pierces some of Ireland's loveliest hiking territory, the Nine Glens of Antrim, deep valleys formed by gargantuan glaciers at the end of the last Ice Age. Amidst the glens, Glenariff Forest Park gushes with waterfalls. The next stop is the Carrick-a-Rede rope-bridge, a surprisingly sturdy high-wire originally hung every February to enable fishermen to reach their nets on an islet. Now a permanent fixture, the vertiginous 60-foot-long (18 meter) bridge has a dizzying 80-foot (24 meter) drop to the Atlantic. A cliff-top pathway provides intoxicating views. A few miles along the coast, the Giant's Causeway beckons. Legend has it that the unusual basalt columns were built by the giant Finn McCool as stepping stones to reach a Scottish rival. Experience spirits of another kind at Bushmills, Ireland's oldest licensed whiskey distillery, where you can sample peaty tipples, including the 1608, available nowhere else, and hot toddies. Seemingly battling the Atlantic, the 17th-century Dunluce Castle is one of Ireland's craggiest, eeriest ruins. The road winds up at Londonderry/Derry, where you can stroll along the historic city walls.

**When to Go** The best weather occurs from April through October. Even in summer be prepared for cold, wet, and windy conditions. The Carrick-a-Rede rope-bridge is open year-round, weather permitting.

**How to Find It** The main airports are in Belfast and Derry. There are also express buses to Belfast from Dublin airport. Ferries sail to Belfast and Larne from Stranraer in Scotland and Fleetwood in England, respectively. The return journey to Belfast can be made on the faster motorway from Portrush or Derry.

**Planning** There are plenty of hotels, hostels, and B&Bs en route. Guided tours are available by bus, rail, river, sea, horseback, and on foot. A steam train runs from the Giant's Causeway to Bushmills.

**Websites** www.causewaycoastandglens.com, www.discovernorthernireland.com, www.gotobelfast.com

## Belfast's Revival

■ **Belfast's pubs** offer all the historic atmosphere, Irish music, and conviviality (or *craic*, as the Irish call it) of Dublin's, but with fewer tourists. As a starter, the John Hewitt, the Crown, Kelly's Cellars, Whites Tavern, McHugh's, Bittles Bar, Muriels, the Spaniard, and the Cocktail Bar all merit a visit to linger over a Guinness or Irish whiskey.

■ You can learn about the city's shipbuilding history (the *Titanic* was built here, 1909–12) at the **Titanic's Dock and Pump House.**

■ Tours of the city take in areas associated with the Troubles, including the murals along the **Falls Road** and **Shankill Road.** You can also visit the **Crumlin Road Gaol,** where political prisoners were held.

The road twists and turns through some of Europe's most spectacular scenery, peppered with evocative historic sites.

Some of the finest specimens of South Africa's national tree, the Outeniqua yellowwood, can be seen along the trail.

SOUTH AFRICA

# THE TSITSIKAMMA TRAIL

A six-day nature trek along the southern Cape's Garden Route takes you through the heart of the Tsitsikamma Mountains.

Tsitsikamma is a Khoisan word meaning "place where the water rises," and as hikers on this 40-mile (64 kilometer) trail soon discover, rise it certainly does. First in silent and then thunderous volume, many rivers flow from the dark-green mountains along South Africa's southern shore. The Tsitsikamma Trail meanders through these mountains, plunging through granite gorges, rising over grassy saddles, and crossing more than a dozen whiskey-colored rivers on its journey west to east between Nature's Valley and Storms River Mouth. The route is anything but easy. It's not so much the roller-coaster pathway as the river crossings—swift-flowing water that often rises to chest level as you gingerly step across on slippery stones. The trailside landscape alternates between dense tracts of indigenous forest and fynbos, which turns into a floral rainbow each spring. This is also the realm of silent leopards and noisy baboons, nocturnal bushpigs, and the tiny duiker antelope. Even if you don't catch a glimpse of these creatures, you'll certainly see their tracks and often hear them while bunking at one of the five overnight huts spaced along the trail. The cabins (and their wood-fired hot showers) are certainly a welcome touch at the end of each day.

**When to Go**  The driest, coolest months are June and July.

**How to Find It**  The Tsitsikamma region is about a day's drive east of Cape Town along the Garden Route coastal highway.

**Planning**  The closest hotels to the trailhead are in Plettenberg Bay, but hikers often spend the night before they hit the trail at the Kalander Hut in Nature's Valley. The trail and huts are maintained by an ecotourism company called MTO, which also offers a porterage service.

**Websites**  www.mtoecotourism.co.za, www.sanparks.co.za, www.stormsriver.com, www.monkeyland.co.za

## On the Trail

■ The Nature's Valley end of the trail boasts a gorgeous golden-sand beach and the **Monkeyland Primate Sanctuary,** where New and Old-World primate and monkey species (many of them rare and endangered) are captive-bred in huge free-roaming spaces. There are guided walking safaris through the sanctuary.

■ A small boat called the *Spirit of Tsitsikamma* runs daily guided trips through the sheer **Storms River Gorge,** starting from a jetty where the river pours into the Indian Ocean.

■ At nearby **Stormsriver Adventures,** those with a head for heights can crawl into a safety harness and zip along a steel cable that hovers 90 ft (27 m) above the forest floor. The canopy tour takes about three hours, with stops on wooden platforms perched in the upper branches of giant Outeniqua yellowwood trees.

AFRICA

KENYA

# THE GREAT RIFT VALLEY

Flamingos paint the shoreline of Lake Nakuru fuchsia pink—just one of many unforgettable Rift Valley spectacles.

The Great Rift Valley carves a giant scar up the middle of Kenya, more than 40 miles (64 kilometers) wide and 6,000 feet (1,829 meters) deep in places, flanked by jagged volcanoes and spangled with lakes that provide sustenance for millions of animals. Nairobi perches in the cool highlands above the valley's eastern edge, the start of a long and adventurous road trip that runs clear across Kenya through the heart of the rift. Plunging down the steep Kikuyu Escarpment, Highway A104 makes a beeline for Lake Nakuru. In addition to around two million flamingos, the lake harbors fish-eagles, sacred ibis, and hundreds of other species. At Londiani the highway splits, the left fork heading over the Mau Escarpment to Lake Victoria, the right crossing the Equator and climbing to Eldoret, hometown of Olympic track-and-field legend Kip Keino. The highlands between here and Kitale are lush and green, a patchwork quilt of forest and farm with snowcapped Mount Elgon looming in the distance. Finally, the highway falls into the Rift Valley again, civilization gradually giving way to the wilds of the North West Frontier Province. Soon enough the landscape turns to acacia-studded desert, once crossable only by camel but now a breeze on the paved road. At Lodwar is the turnoff to Lake Turkana, the largest of the Great Rift lakes, whose stark beauty will remain etched in the memory for ever.

**When to Go**  The climate in highland Kenya is moderate or temperate for most of the year. Nairobi's mean daily high is a pleasant 80°F (27°C). The region around Lake Turkana is always hot and dry, with daytime temperatures approaching triple digits in hotter months like February and March.

**How to Find It**  The southern part of the Great Rift route (Nairobi to Kitale) is well served by public transport, including train service to Naivasha, Nakuru, and Eldoret. Between Kitale and Lodwar, buses or shared taxis (matatus) are much less frequent and it's better to have access to your own vehicle.

**Planning**  The one-way drive takes a minimum of two days. Due to intermittent bandit activity, police escorts are sometimes provided between Kapenguria and Lodwar. Colonial ghosts linger at the historic Fairmont Norfolk Hotel in Nairobi, now nicely restored. Places to stay in the Turkana region include Lobolo Tented Camp on the western shore and Oasis Lodge near the lake's southern end.

**Websites**  www.tourism.go.ke, www.fairmont.com/norfolkhotel, www.oasis-lodge.com

### My Secret Journey

*I open my eyes to an old woman staring me straight in the face. Her lower lip is pierced by an inch-long metal stud, her ears by at least half a dozen hooped rings; her head is shaven but for a dread-locked topknot and her body clothed in nothing more than a wisp of crimson cloth and gazelle hide. She is a member of the nomad Turkana tribe, the first I have ever laid eyes on. And by the curious look on her face, I could easily be her first tourist.*

*My small party had arrived the night before at Eliye Springs on Lake Turkana's western shore. Lacking any other place to stay, we unfurled our sleeping bags in the sand—although not before double-checking there were no crocodiles in residence.*

*As the sun comes up over the desert mountains, I get my first glimpse of the lake—a huge expanse of jade-colored water in what is otherwise unrelenting desert. For a moment you wonder if you've landed on another planet. But then the Turkana woman comes into view again. This could be nowhere else but Kenya.*
**Joe Yogerst**
**Travel writer**

Opposite: The patchwork fields and farms of the Kikuyu  Above: Flamingos feed on Lake Nakuru's blue-green algae.

# SECRET HISTORY

**F**or travelers whose passion for history extends beyond the world's most famous sites, there are numerous less predictable journeys that open doors into vanished worlds. For a powerful encounter with remote antiquity, you need only travel a couple of hours from the cosmopolitan South African city of Capetown to find an array of 2,500 eerily evocative rock paintings created between 800 and 8,000 years ago. Africa is also the setting for one of the Roman Empire's most dramatic survivals: The magnificent remains of Leptis Magna in present-day Libya. Elsewhere, the sites are as surprising as their locations. The precipitous landscape of Zhejiang in eastern China is home to a collection of elaborately sculpted covered corridor bridges resembling giant centipedes clambering up and down the slopes. And a visit to the catacombs of Savoca in Sicily brings you face to face with the citizens who ruled the community in the 18th and 19th centuries, their mummies still clad in the remnants of their official vestments and accompanied by detailed personal biographies.

The beautiful ruins of the once-flourishing ancient Roman city and port of Leptis Magna in Libya gleam against the deep blue waters of the Mediterranean.

# HIGH BRIDGE TRAIL

A trail through the now tranquil hills of Virginia's
Southside recalls the bloody final days of the Civil War.

NORTH
AMERICA

Carrying the Southside Railroad across the Appomattox River east of the town of Farmville, Virginia, High Bridge was one of the world's largest bridges when completed in 1852—about 2,500 feet (762 meters) long, 125 feet (38 meters) high, and bolstered by 21 brick and quarry stone piers. Thirteen years later, in April 1865, the battered, gray-uniformed troops of General Robert E. Lee's Confederate army retreated across this same structure after their catastrophic defeat at Sailor's (or Saylers) Creek to the east. They were seeking much-needed supplies at Farmville. Lee gave orders for his rearguard to burn the span behind them. Almost as soon as the exhausted Confederates fired the wooden supports, Union cavalry and other troops in hot pursuit doused the flames. Thus preserved, the bridge allowed the Union forces to chase the Confederates out of Farmville without respite for Lee's army, which surrendered two days later at Appomattox Court House. Today, the 22-mile (35 kilometer) High Bridge Trail State Park follows the course of the now disused railroad, creating a stunning pathway through rolling hills, from Pamplin in the west to High Bridge in the east. The trail is suitable for hikers, cyclists, and horseback riders. Whichever mode of locomotion you choose, don't forget to pause awhile at the western end of the bridge and imagine the fiery scene that unfolded there on April 7, 1865.

**When to Go** Spring and fall are best—winters can be very cold and snowy and summers suffocatingly hot. Go in April for commemorations of the battles and other events of General Lee's last campaign.

**How to Find It** Farmville is about 65 miles (105 km) west of Richmond, Virginia—an easy 80-minute drive. High Bridge lies 6 miles (10 km) east of Farmville.

**Planning** The High Bridge Trail is due to be extended southeast to Burkeville, close to Sailor's Creek Battlefield. You will find comfortable modern hotels in Farmville.

**Websites** www.dcr.virginia.gov/state_parks, www.nps.gov/apco, www.civilwartraveler.com

## Campaign Tour

■ Lee's Retreat Driving Tour follows the route taken by General Lee's army during its 100-mile (160 km) retreat west from **Petersburg** to Appomattox Court House. Set your car radio to AM 1610 for descriptions of the various battles that took place along the way.

■ The beautifully restored buildings in **Appomattox Court House National Historical Park,** 30 miles (48 km) west of Farmville, include the McLean House, where Lee met his Union counterpart, General Ulysses S. Grant, on April 9, 1865 (Palm Sunday), to agree the terms of surrender for his Army of Northern Virginia.

The magnificent High Bridge proved to be a strategic landmark in the Civil War. It is now the focal point of a trail through Virginia's Piedmont country.

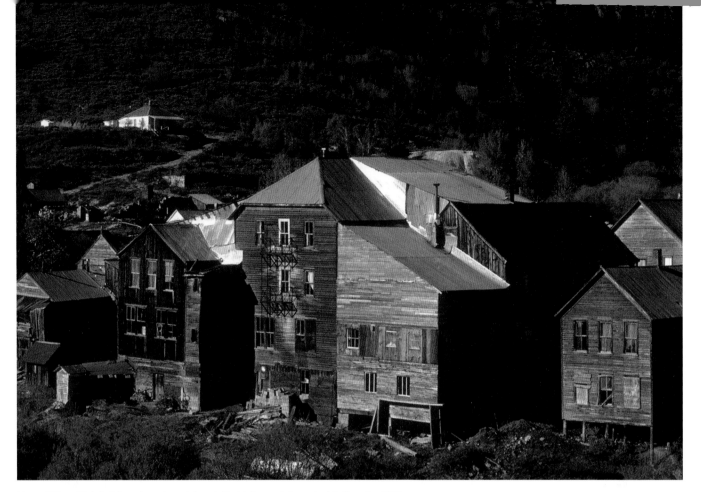

Many of Silver City's buildings, in various states of dilapidation and disrepair, date from the 1860s.

IDAHO

# SILVER CITY

This living ghost town in southwest Idaho provides
a poignant glimpse into the West's wildest days.

Among the American West's multitudinous ghost towns, Silver City is an anomaly, neither wholly moribund nor a retrofitted tourist trap. Rather, it's an unofficial memorial to the heyday of Idaho's great silver rush. Many of the buildings and mining facilities have decayed to a terminal state, but about 70 have been preserved and serve as de facto educational exhibits, modest businesses, or homes for the town's few remaining summer residents. Founded in 1864, after silver was discovered on nearby War Eagle Mountain in the Owyhee range, Silver City boomed with an influx of hard-rock miners, hucksters, harlots, footpads, and itinerant lawmen. At its peak, the town supported 2,500 residents, all involved in moiling for precious metal—or stripping the miners of their pokes once they hit pay dirt. Wandering the unpaved streets, you pass the Masonic Hall, where an annual Mask Ball was held, and buildings that once housed the drugstore, general store, barber shop, and bathhouse. Several cemeteries filled with the graves of miners who lived fast and died hard command nearby slopes. More than 200 mines were founded hereabouts to work the rich lodes of silver and gold. Resist the temptation to explore them, however—they're rife with open shafts and other unmarked hazards.

**When to Go** Plan your trip for June through mid-October, when temperatures range from 37°F (3°C) to 80°F (27°C). Roads can be impassable in winter due to heavy snow.

**How to Find It** From Boise, go west on Interstate 84 to Nampa, then turn south on Idaho 78 to Murphy. About 5 miles (8 km) south of Murphy, take the Silver City Road for about 15 miles (24 km).

**Planning** There is no municipal power service in Silver City and no restaurants. Bring your own food and water. Gas stations are also absent. The Idaho Hotel is open seasonally and provides basic amenities. Greater Boise is a cosmopolitan city and offers a wide range of places to stay and many good restaurants.

**Websites** www.historicsilvercityidaho.com, www.ghosttowns.com

## Town Tour

■ **Our Lady of Tears** Catholic church is one of the best preserved of Silver City's remaining buildings. This wood-frame, Gothic-revival church perches on a hill commanding a panoramic view of the town. Occasional Masses are held here, and weddings can be arranged through the Boise Diocese.

■ Built in 1863, the **Idaho Hotel** was Silver City's main stagecoach stop and is now the town's sole hostelry.

■ The **Schoolhouse,** built in 1892, has a museum on the second floor.

# GHOST TOWNS

With their silent streets, derelict buildings, and remnants of homes and workplaces, abandoned towns offer a haunting view into the lives of once thriving communities.

## ❶ St. Elmo, Colorado

Once a booming mining town and trading post along railroad routes running through central Colorado, St. Elmo was abandoned when the railroad shut down in 1922. Many of the buildings—including stores, houses, and the church—were left intact, filled with the belongings of their former residents.

Planning St. Elmo is in Gunnison National Forest. Numerous trails for hiking and off-road driving are easily accessible from the town. www.st-elmo-colorado.com, www.colorado.com

## ❷ Chaco Canyon, New Mexico

The Chaco civilization thrived from roughly A.D. 800 to 1100. During this period, the canyon served as a ceremonial, civic, and commercial center. Residents built clusters of dwellings and circular ceremonial structures, called *kivas,* from mud brick, sandstone, and wood, many of which remain intact today.

Planning A 9-mile (14 km) paved loop road runs through the canyon. www.nps.gov/chcu/home.htm

## ❸ Bodie, California

In 1879, Bodie was a bustling gold-mining town and home to 8,500 residents known for gunfighting and brawling. Within a decade, the mines had been largely depleted and the population had begun a steady decline that ended in total abandonment. The 150 remaining buildings are much as their residents left them.

Planning Bodie is a California Historic State Park, 7 miles (11 km) south of the town of Bridgeport. www.parks.ca.gov

## ❹ Humberstone and Santa Laura, Atacama Desert, Chile

Home to saltpeter mines, these two company towns in northern Chile were abandoned in 1958. The well-preserved buildings include a theater with its original chairs, houses, a cast-iron swimming pool made from the hull of a ship, a hotel, and grocers' shops complete with price lists.

Planning Humberstone and Santa Laura are close to the town of Pozo Almonte, 30 miles (48 km) east of Iquique, which is the nearest city with places to stay and an airport. www.chilecontact.com

## ❺ Bhangarh, Rajasthan, India

When Bhangarh, a local capital in northwest India, was conquered by the raja of Jaipur in the 1720s, the city was quickly deserted. Dating from the 17th century and before, the ruins—including crumbling temples and pavilions, a fort, and a medieval bazaar—are said to be haunted, and eerie legends surround the city's rise and rapid decline.

Planning Bhangarh is situated 18 miles (29 km) northeast of Jaipur. Tours of the "haunted" city are available. www.rajasthantourism.gov.in

## ❻ Kayaköy, Anatolia, Turkey

When the Greco-Turkish war ended in 1923, roughly a million Greeks living in Turkey were repatriated, and Kayaköy, a Greek village of roughly 2,000 residents in western Turkey, was abandoned. The remains of the village—including hundreds of ruined homes and two Greek Orthodox churches—are preserved as a historic site.

Planning Fethiye, approximately 2.5 miles (4 km) north of Kayaköy, is the closest town. www.gofethiye.com

## ❼ Pyramiden, Svalbard, Norway

This Arctic coal-mining town, owned by the U.S.S.R. since 1927, was an ideal Soviet settlement complete with workers' barracks, a sports center, and a bust of Lenin. The mine is now exhausted, but the buildings, including a library full of books, a theater, and a music hall with the world's northernmost grand piano, have been left as they were when the town was abandoned in 1998.

Planning Stay in Longyearbyen, Svalbard's largest city, and take a day-long boat trip to Pyramiden. Guided tours are available. www.svalbard.net

## ❽ Herculaneum, Naples, Italy

In the summer of A.D. 79, Mount Vesuvius erupted and buried the small, wealthy Roman seaside resort of Herculaneum in searing ash and rock. Archaeological excavations have uncovered private villas, shops, bathhouses, and a fascinating range of everyday objects.

Planning Herculaneum, 5 miles (8 km) south of Naples, can be reached from the city by bus or train (Ercolano station). www.travelplan.it

## ❾ Belchite, Zaragoza Province, Spain

Belchite was the site of a particularly brutal battle during the Spanish Civil War (1936-39). Occupied by Franco's forces in 1937, the town was attacked by the Republican Army. The siege destroyed Belchite, but its ruined buildings serve as a ghostly memento of the intense violence they witnessed.

Planning The remains of the old town are 0.5 miles (0.8 km) from modern Belchite, southeast of Zaragoza city. www.aragonguide.com

## ❿ Kolmanskop, Namibia

Located among the sand dunes of the Namib Desert, Kolmanskop was built to house workers at a nearby diamond mine. The town was abandoned by the mid-1950s and since then the desert has consumed it, almost filling many once grand houses with sand. The interiors of a few buildings, however, are in good condition.

Planning The nearby city of Lüderitz is a good base for exploring Kolmanskop and other abandoned mining towns in the area. www.luderitz.info, www.encounter.co.za

Opposite: The gold-mining town of Bodie in California was once a destination for fortune seekers. The buildings are now preserved in a state of arrested decay.

NEW MEXICO

# Bandelier's Puebloan Ruins

Bandelier National Monument near Santa Fe
contains the remains of ancient Puebloan dwellings.

The American Southwest's mystery people, the ancestral Puebloans, dwelled for centuries in this semi-arid landscape before vanishing about 600 years ago. At the height of their civilization, they built elaborate multiroom cliff dwellings and mastered the arts of hunting and growing crops in a hostile environment. Today, their haunting ruins are scattered across northern Arizona and New Mexico, and one of the best places to see them is Bandelier National Monument, which covers 33,000 acres (13,355 hectares) of ruggedly beautiful canyon wilderness 30 miles (48 kilometers) west of Santa Fe. You can hike the 1.2-mile (2.4 kilometer) Main Loop Trail through Frijoles Canyon, which leads past the ruins of a huge ceremonial *kiva*, a circular stone structure where sacred ceremonies were held, petroglyphs, and man-made caves, called *cavates*, that the Puebloans carved out high in the canyon cliffs to use as winter dwellings. Here, too, are the ruins of Tyuonyi, a Pueblo village that once contained more than 400 rooms. Some hikers follow the beautiful 2.5-mile (4 kilometer) Falls Trail, which descends 700 feet (213 meters) and passes two cascading waterfalls as it winds down to the Rio Grande River. Yet another wonderful hike is the trail to Alcove House, a high cliff dwelling reachable only by climbing 140 feet (43 meters) up the canyon wall on ladders and stairs. Here, on quiet days, the desert stillness rings with the question of what life was like for the people who lived in this remote place centuries ago and what happened to bring an end to their civilization.

**When to Go**  Fall is an ideal time to visit. Spring is also pleasant, with cool evenings and warm but not too hot days.

**How to Find It**  The entrance to Bandelier is on New Mexico 4 between White Rock and Jemez Springs. A paved road leads down to the visitor center in Frijoles Canyon, where the hiking trails start.

**Planning**  This is high desert, so you will need a hat, sunglasses, and sun protection. You can find places to stay in nearby Los Alamos, although most people choose to stay in Santa Fe, an hour's drive from Bandelier, to enjoy the city's legendary fine dining and cultural activities.

**Websites**  www.nps.gov/band, www.lanl.gov/museum

## Los Alamos

Bandelier lies just 10 miles (16 km) from Los Alamos, the town that grew around the ultrasecret World War II Manhattan Project. It was here that J. Robert Oppenheimer led a team of scientists in the creation of the first atom bombs.

Today, the town is still the site of Los Alamos National Laboratory, which has expanded its mandate far beyond top secret nuclear weapons research to include the study of global warming, fuel-cell technology, astronomy, supercomputing, and health research, including the search for a cure for HIV/AIDs.

The **Bradbury Science Museum** is a first-rate attraction charting the history and science of the laboratory through engaging displays and exhibits designed for visitors of all ages.

Opposite: Ancient dwellings pockmark the canyon walls. Above: Zuni Pueblo dancers perform at Bandelier.

Constructed from the local volcanic rock, known as brimstone, the solid walls of the fort are 7 ft (2 m) thick.

ST. KITTS AND NEVIS

# BRIMSTONE HILL FORTRESS

Colonial history and wonderful views across the eastern Caribbean are combined in this well-preserved fort.

The strategic site on top of Brimstone Hill in the north of St. Kitts was discovered in 1690 by British troops searching for high ground from which to bombard the French, who were entrenched below, along the St. Kitts shoreline. Quickly realizing the hilltop's potential, the redcoats constructed an impregnable hilltop citadel that came to be called the Gibraltar of the West Indies. Brimstone has fallen only once, during the American Revolution, when 8,000 French troops besieged the fortress for a month before the 1,000 British defenders were forced to surrender. The island was later returned to the British, who finally abandoned the fortress in the mid-19th century. In recent years, the central citadel and many of the lower, cannon-lined bastions have been restored to their former glory. Tours also include the ammunition store and hospital. Other parts, including the once grand Infantry Officers' Quarters, with its soaring arches and columns, remain in ruins. Inside the citadel is the Fort George Museum, with artifacts and information on the history of the fort and St. Kitts. And don't leave without casting a glance northward across the Caribbean to hazy Statia (St. Eustatius) island in the distance.

**When to Go** St. Kitts is hot and humid year round, although winter can be slightly cooler. The hurricane season runs from late August to early November, and St. Kitts has seen its fair share of major storms.

**How to Find It** Bradshaw International Airport on St. Kitts has daily flights to and from Antigua, St. Martin, Nevis, and San Juan (Puerto Rico). Brimstone Hill is a half-hour taxi ride from the airport.

**Planning** There are no hotels near Brimstone; the majority are clustered along the skinny Frigate Isthmus on the island's south side, or in the capital, Basseterre. Just about the only place to stay on the north side of St. Kitts is Ottley's Plantation Inn, a 17th-century sugar plantation converted into a small hotel.

**Websites** www.brimstonehillfortress.org, www.stkittstourism.kn, www.ottleys.com

## Local High Points

■ Rising close behind Brimstone Hill is 3,800-ft (1,158 m) **Mount Liamuiga.** The volcano is now dormant and guided hiking parties can descend into its 1-mile-wide (1.6 km) crater, nicknamed the "Salad Bowl."

■ Farther south is another volcanic remnant, a remote crater lake called **Dos D'Ane Pond** at the summit of Verchild's Mountain.

■ The **Central Forest Reserve** that encompasses both peaks harbors an array of flora and fauna, including monkeys, hummingbirds, and giant heliconia flowers.

HONDURAS

# Copán Maya Ruins

This city-state was home to 18,000 residents at its peak and it remains a treasure-house of Maya art.

Massive ceiba trees, their canopies teeming with gaudy scarlet macaws, shade the path to the Copán Ruinas Archaeology Park in western Honduras. Entering the site through the Great Plaza, you encounter dozens of animal-shaped altars and well-preserved monolithic stelae, many from the early eighth-century rule of the Maya king, Uaxaclajuun Ub'aah K'awiil, known as 18 Rabbit. Intricate carvings on these 10-to-16-foot-tall (3 to 5 meter) commemorative stone pillars depict the lives and power of Maya royalty. Called Xukpi by the Maya, the site, which is 7 miles (11 kilometers) from the Guatemala border, was a major center of Mesoamerican Maya civilization from the fifth to ninth centuries. Adjacent to the Great Plaza is a richly decorated ball court, its slanted side walls adorned with stone hoops shaped like heads of macaws, the national bird of Honduras. The showpiece of the site, however, is the eighth-century Hieroglyphic Stairway that once led up to a thatched-roof temple. More than 2,000 detailed glyphs chronicling the royal lineage of the Copán Dynasty are inscribed on the 63 steps. Nearby are magnificent temples that were built over the remains of older ones. Curiosity aroused, you can duck into a tunnel dug by archaeologists under the later temples to view the buried, late sixth-century Rosalila Temple and admire its ornate, rose-red stucco exterior.

**When to Go**  The site is open daily year-round. The best time to visit is during the dry season, from December through April. Avoid midday, when the sun is hottest.

**How to Find It**  The site is 0.5 miles (0.8 km) east of the town of Copán Ruinas, which is 100 miles (160 km) by car or bus from San Pedro Sula, the closest international airport.

**Planning**  Give yourself several hours to tour the site. Your admission ticket also includes entry to the ruins of Las Sepulturas, where the Copán aristocracy lived, 1 mile (1.6 km) away.

**Websites**  www.copanruins.com, www.copanhonduras.org

NORTH AMERICA

### Coffee Break

■ The aroma of roasting coffee mingles with the scent of tropical flowers in the highlands around Copán Ruinas, a colonial town of red-tiled roofs and cobblestone streets just west of the ruins. Many small *fincas,* or coffee plantations, can be found in the rain forests around Copán. After visiting the ruins, you can take a tour to see how coffee is cultivated in the shade of the forest canopy.

■ Back in Copán Ruinas, sip a cup at one of the small cafés as *tuk-tuks* (three-wheeled mototaxis) zip past and residents, many descended from the Maya, go about their daily lives.

A statue in the west court depicts the Maya rain god, Chac, holding a burning torch to symbolize his power to create and withhold rain.

# CHOQUEQUIRAO INCA SITE

A strenuous trek takes you to the "other Machu Picchu,"
a ruined city that was never discovered by the conquistadors.

SOUTH AMERICA

Fifteen thousand feet (4,572 meters) above the glacier-fed Apurímac River, the precipitous walls of the Cordillera Vilcabamba climb to a narrow ridge-spur, home to the Inca ruins of Choquequirao. The air is clean and cold up here, and condors circle above the snow line of the jagged Salkantay Mountains. Beyond the small strip of grass that was the central plaza are simple ceremonial temples and administrative buildings, and these give way to a jigsaw of ancient stone that makes up the smaller houses of the workers and artisans below. Cut into the mountainside all around are the intricate zigzagging walls of traditional Inca terracing and, beyond, glimpses of gray stonework in the dense foliage that still covers more than half the site's structures. The ruins are reached from the nearest village, Cachora, by a strenuous 20-mile (32 kilometer), two-day hike on a path that winds through a patchwork of hills and hamlets on lower ground before crossing the Apurímac and climbing steeply through damp, dense rain forest and into the mountains. Your reward is a site often free of tourists and yours to explore with the arrival of the crisp Andean dawn.

**When to Go** The site is open year-round, but the best time is in Peru's dry season, from May to October.

**How to Find It** Treks to Choquequirao can be arranged in Cusco, and packages usually include transportation to Cachora, accommodation, trail guide, and a mule to support your trek. Alternatively, you can take a taxi from Cusco to Cachora (four to five hours) and hire a guide and mule-handler on arrival.

**Planning** You should allow five to six days round-trip from Cusco, which includes an overnight in Cachora and a full day at the ruins. There are a number of cheap campsites and stalls where you can stock up on drinks and chocolate along the trail from Cachora. You will be passing through different climate zones—the lower ground hot and humid, the mountainous regions potentially extremely cold, especially at night—so be sure to pack several layers of clothing.

**Website** www.peru.info

### Hidden History

■ The niches in one of the buildings on the central plaza once held the mummies of dignitaries, positioned so they could look out onto the square.

■ Watch for the llama terraces, where figures of llamas in white stone have been built into the gray walls.

■ A short, steep hike up the truncated peak beyond the central plaza provides 360-degree views over the site, down into the raging Apurímac canyon, and across the peaks of the Salkantay range.

Step terraces, which the Inca built to create flat strips of land for farming, cover the steep hillsides around Choquequirao.

Built in the Ming dynasty, the Wenxing Bridge near the village of Xiao Cun has a span of around 98 ft (30 m).

CHINA

# ZHEJIANG CORRIDOR BRIDGES

In a quiet corner of eastern China, the landscape is dotted with fantastical covered bridges, some several hundred years old.

Five hours west of the coastal manufacturing city of Wenzhou, up a winding mountainous road, lies Taishun county, an area little-known to outsiders and laced with steep, stepped footpaths that link ancient corridor bridges. Some of these bridges are like plain and unpainted houses that have woken from sleep, yawned themselves open at both ends, and stretched luxuriously like cats. Others, which the local people call "centipede bridges," are painted red and rear up dramatically, their two-story central sections topped with writhing golden dragons or ceramic fish. The Bei Jian Qiao (Bei Jian Bridge) at the village of Sixi is a red-skirted bridge whose central roof sports sharply pointed upturned eaves, and on its ridge is a face-off between two lively, lime-green dragons. The Liuzhai Qiao at San Kui consists of two gabled mansions with curly, upturned eaves, connected by a horizontal two-story section, topped with yellow-bodied, blue-headed dragons with large pointed teeth and tails thrashing the air. Xiao Cun's spectacular Wenxing Qiao is truly a centipede in motion. First, there are steep stone steps, then a gradual rise, a leveling out, a swoop to the top, and a steep drop to the stone steps on the other side. As a result, the two-story center section with its upturned eaves has a drunken tilt.

**When to Go** Spring and fall are the best times to go to avoid the heat and humidity of high summer.

**How to Find It** The bridges are within easy reach of Taishun city. Bus services from Wenzhou to Taishun are surprisingly luxurious, with air-conditioned vehicles more than half as wide as the mountain road. Local transport is by battered minibus, often shared with farmers, their produce, and livestock.

**Planning** Places to stay can be found in every village mentioned, but they are mostly very basic, although appropriately cheap. There's no need to book in advance.

**Websites** english.ctrip.com/destinations/RegionDestinations.asp?region=65, www.newpaltz.edu/~knappr/Zhejiang.pdf

### My Secret Journey

*The San Tiao Qiao, or Three Roads Bridge, is perhaps the region's oldest, first erected in the Tang dynasty (618–906). Near the village of Zhouling, about two hours south of Taishun city by minibus, the bridge is reached via a cart track that winds round steep-sided hills and turns into a long, stone staircase dropping steeply past rice terrace after rice terrace. The bridge looks like a long, thin house stretching across a river where three staircase-paths converge. Inside are benches where peasants on the way to market put down their bamboo shoulder poles for a rest in the shade, startled to see a foreigner.*
**Peter Neville-Hadley**
**Travel writer**

ASIA

INDIA

# City of Mandu

Once a thriving city, Mandu's deserted monuments, mosques, and palaces are set like jewels in an emerald-green landscape.

This once great city, with strategic views over the arid Namar plains of central India, was abandoned toward the end of the Mughal period, leaving the area inside Mandu's 28 miles (45 kilometers) of defensive walls a ghost town. Save for the faces of 5,000 local villagers and the appearance of a handful of guesthouses, little has changed here over the past couple of centuries. Most visitors arrive through the Delhi Darwaza, the main entrance consisting of a series of fortified gateways, into what was once known as Shadiabad (City of Joy). The majority of buildings, temples, palaces, and pavilions— rich in pointed arches, cupolas, and intricate latticework and carvings—date to the 1400s and early 1500s, when this was the capital of the Islamic Kingdom of Malwa. In the royal enclave, the Jahaz Mahal (Ship Palace), designed to look like a royal pleasure boat, sits between two man-made lakes, Munj Talao and Kapur Talao. The nearby Hindola Mahal, or Swing Palace, with sloping walls and intricate carvings, was an audience hall. In the center of the city, the multidomed Jama Masjid was inspired by the Great Mosque of Damascus. India's first marble monument—the domed tomb of Hoshang Shah, featuring marble latticework, towers, and courts—is close to the bazaar. Shah Jahan sent architects to study the tomb while planning the Taj Mahal. Sunset Point, near the Lohani Caves (close to the Jahaz Mahal), is a fine place to end a day's exploration.

**When to Go** From December through early February, when daytime temperatures average 70–86°F (in the 20s°C). Water shortages are common during the hot summer months (April and May) that precede the monsoon (June–September).

**How to Find It** Indore, 61 miles (98 km) away, is the closest airport to Mandu. Travelers can take a local bus from Indore, a journey of about three hours. Taxis reduce the journey time to about 2.5 hours.

**Planning** Allow at least a day to visit Mandu's main attractions, longer if you love architecture and its history. Bicycles and rickshaws can be hired to get around the sites. There is a variety of places to stay around Mandu. ATMs can be difficult to find, and hotels usually request settlement in cash, so plan on taking a small reserve of money.

**Website** www.mptourism.com/dest/mandu_ms.html

### Doomed Love

Romantics are drawn to Mandu by the love story of Baz Bahadur, Malwa's last independent sultan, and a shepherdess called Rupmati. According to legend, he was attracted by the shepherdess's singing and was so impressed by her beauty that he wanted to make her his queen. Rupmati agreed, so long as he built her a palace overlooking the Narmada River and allowed her to continue practicing as a Hindu. **Rupmati's Pavilion** is on the crest of a hill, with spectacular views of the river valley and **Baz Bahadur's palace.** Below it, a reservoir, the Rewa Kund, filled by the Narmada, was built to supply the palace with water, via an aqueduct, so that Rupmati could carry out her Hindu rites. The story, however, had a tragic ending: When a Mughal army took Mandu in 1561, Rupmati took her own life and Baz fled.

Opposite: The colonnades around the central court of the Jama Masjid Above: The reservoir beneath Rupmati's Pavilion

# SHEKHAWATI HAVELIS

Take the backroads of northeastern Rajasthan to discover the
exquisite painted havelis (mansions) of the Shekhawati region.

On a rickshaw ride through the narrow streets of several of the region's small towns, you will soon spot the ornately carved wooden gateway and lively painted façade of one of the grand mansions for which the region is famous. Built between 1830 and 1930 by members of the Marwari business community, the *havelis* in towns such as Nawalgarh, Dundlod, Mandawa, Fatehpur, and Lakshmangarh, are symbols of the success and prosperity of families, like the Poddars and the Goenkas, that grew rich on the spice trade. The entryways usually open onto two courtyards, an outer one, used by the men, shielding an inner one for the exclusive use of the women. Intricately carved lattice screens and balconies adorn the interiors, but the real gems are the frescoes. Blues, reds, indigos, maroons, and yellows run riot across the walls, portraying Hindu gods and goddesses, local legends, portraits, animals, wedding processions, and scenes from everyday life—including trains, cars, and early airplanes. Although painted mainly with vegetable pigments, some havelis were decorated entirely with gold leaf as merchants tried to outdo each other in the sumptuousness of their houses. The current haveli owners now live in faraway cities and many of the buildings have fallen into disrepair, but an increasing number are being restored and provide an offbeat glimpse into an exotic way of life.

**When to Go** September to March, although nights can be chilly and central heating can't be taken for granted.

**How to Find It** Jhunjhunu, the regional capital, is 110 miles (177 km) north of Jaipur. The main towns of the region have good road and rail connections.

**Planning** You can get about the region by taxi or rickshaw, and local buses serve many of the towns and villages. The walled fort of Mandawa, with an ornately carved and painted gateway and exquisite frescoes inside, has been restored and turned into a heritage hotel.

**Websites** www.travelrajasthan.net, www.rajasthanindiatravel.com, www.mandawahotels.com

## Haveli Tour

■ The Goenka havelis are the most imposing in **Mandawa.** At the Murmuria haveli you can see scenes of Krishna tending his cows, of Nehru riding a horse, and of Venice.

■ **Nawalgarh** has a decorated fort, havelis of the Poddars, Bhagats, and Dangaichs, and several fine temples.

■ Modi haveli in the main bazaar at **Jhunjhunu** is embellished with some of the best paintings in the Shekhawati area.

■ **Ramgarh** has several Poddar havelis and a Poddar cenotaph with exquisitely painted scenes from the *Ramayana*.

Images at the Goenka haveli in Dundlod include a steam train, a novelty at the time it was painted in the 19th century.

Palmyra's Monumental Arch frames the colonnades of the main street. The ruins are overlooked by an Arab fort.

SYRIA

# PALMYRA

Explore the evocative ruins of a once wealthy Roman city that was located on the caravan route across the Syrian desert.

Beside a palm-filled oasis, the ruins of Palmyra stretch for more than a mile (1.6 kilometers) across a sandy plain. Camels lumber through the sandstone, marble, and granite remains of this ancient city—once among the richest in the Near East. Palmyra's most impressive building is the Temple of Bel, a Babylonian god worshiped as lord of the universe and creator of the world. Within the temple's massive stone walls was a colonnaded courtyard with a sacrificial area at the center. While much of the temple lies in ruin, the sacrificial area and part of one of the colonnades survive. Nearby, the city's main gate, the Monumental Arch, leads onto the main street, which was colonnaded for its entire 0.75-mile (1.2 kilometer) length. On either side of the street are the remains of shops, markets, offices, temples, and fountains. The best-preserved building at the site is the second-century A.D. theater, which has permanent stage scenery and 30 curving rows of seating rising up from the orchestra section. Just beyond the city is the Valley of the Tombs, where the members of wealthy families were buried in multistory towers. Time your visit to end in the early evening, and climb the hill overlooking the valley to watch Palmyra's golden hues change to bronze as the sun sets over the silent desert.

**When to Go** Avoid Palmyra and its relentless desert heat in summertime. The city and the necropolis are always open. The Temple of Bel is open daily from 8 a.m. until one hour before sunset.

**How to Find It** Palmyra is 150 miles (240 km) northeast of Damascus. Tour companies in Damascus offer long one-day trips, but to make the most of the site and take advantage of sunset and sunrise, plan to stay overnight. A regular bus service runs between Damascus and Palmyra and takes around 2.5 hours.

**Planning** There are several hotels with restaurants around the ruins, and fast food and takeout is available in Palmyra town close by. Travelers should check for security warnings before going to Syria.

**Websites** www.syriatourism.org, www.abercrombiekent.co.uk, www.andantetravels.co.uk

## My Secret Journey

*After a few days in Syria, I grew to understand the importance of patience and baksheesh (a bribe), which together can gain you access to places not open to the public. Such was the case with the tomb towers in the Valley of the Tombs. After I had lingered around the locked buildings for a while, a guard wandered by and, in exchange for baksheesh, opened several. Inside, the walls were decorated with frescoes, and rows of niches, each large enough to hold a body, lined the rooms. Each niche was sealed with a stone plaque decorated with a bust of the deceased.*
**Katie Parla**
**Travel writer**

ASIA

# TERMESSOS

This great city occupying the upper slopes of the Taurus Mountains eluded conquest by Alexander the Great.

On the south coast of Turkey, high in the hills to the northwest of Antalya, is a mountaintop strewn with the remains of a once glorious ancient city. Far below is the first hint of its existence. On either side of the main road that twists up through the steep mountain slopes, you catch sight of walls and towers that glint silver in the sunlight: the remnants of a fortified tollgate by which the people of Termessos controlled trade along this stretch of the Mediterranean coast some 2,300 years ago. Reaching the city, which is now at the center of a remote national park, requires a drive up into the clouds along roads with precipitous drops at their sides. The route ends at a small clearing beside a temple with an ornate doorway dedicated to the Roman emperor Hadrian. From here, you have a 40-minute hike up a rocky path shrouded in spiky, shrunken oak trees to the city center. Out of the dense vegetation loom silent structures—baths, a council-house, and gymnasium. The town's theater perches on the edge of a cliff, the curved sweep of its seating distorted by earthquakes into rocky waves. The Termessians, famed for their warlike spirit, withstood an attack by Alexander the Great in 333 B.C. Today, hundreds of their tombs surround the city, eroded by time and scattered asunder.

**When to Go** Spring (mid-April–early June) and fall (September–October) are the best times.

**How to Find It** Termessos is 24 miles (39 km) northwest of Antalya and can be reached by taxi, rental car, or with an organized tour. There is no public transport to the site.

**Planning** There are no services at the site, so take sufficient water and snacks. Wear good footwear, as the ascent and descent are steep and uneven. After rain, the route can be very slippery. Paths are labyrinthine and not especially well marked, and there are no real information boards, so go with a specialist guide who knows the ground and will be able to bring the history to life.

**Website** www.turkeytravelplanner.com

## The Story of Alcetas

One path in the city leads to the **tomb of Alcetas.** Hewn from the limestone, this treasure-trove tomb is decorated with figurines, a funerary couch, and an eagle carrying a snake in its talons. In 319 B.C., Alcetas, a soldier in Alexander's army, took refuge here from Antigonus the "One-Eyed," one of Alexander's leading generals. To avoid capture, Alcetas committed suicide. His body was seized and mutilated by Antigonus but was then retrieved by Termessos's young men, who honored Alcetas with a monumental tomb. You can see the figure of Alcetas carved into the cliff, resplendent in full armor astride a galloping horse.

The theater in the mountaintop city of Termessos provides seemingly endless views to the plains below.

The ruined buildings of ancient Messene are laid out on the slopes of Mount Ithomi.

### Unique Temple

The Temple of Apollo at **Bassae,** north of Messene, provides an unusual detour. It is one of the best preserved ancient Greek temples in the Mediterranean and was one of the more remote. Described in antiquity as a particularly beautiful place of worship, it is also one of the quirkiest, with an unusual alignment, two entrance doors instead of the usual one, and elements of not just one, but all three of the major classical orders—Doric, Ionic, and Corinthian.

EUROPE

GREECE

# MESSENE

The ruins of this fortified capital overlook the Gulf of Messene in the Pelopponese.

The road from the village of Meligalás to the classical Greek city of Messene provides the perfect introduction to this site, passing, as it does, through the only intact city gate—between projecting towers, through the outer gateway, into a circular courtyard, and out through the inner gateway into the city proper. This can be walked or driven, but the latter is recommended as there is still some way to go before you reach the heart of the ancient city. The road continues south and passes the small museum, which displays some of the most beautiful sculptures that have been recovered from the site, before descending to the entrance to the main archaeological zone. Quiet, skillfully maintained, and painstakingly restored, this is one of the most easily understood classical sites in Greece, unencumbered by later construction. The main focus of attention is a large sanctuary of Asklepios, the god of medicine, flanked by a bathhouse, a senate house, the town square, more temples, a theater, and a stadium. The entire core of this once rich city is laid bare for exploration, and the expertly constructed and solemn buildings are neatly offset by the panoramic views of the mountains and valleys that surround it.

**When to Go** Spring is the best season as the area is dotted with wildflowers and the days are long and bright.

**How to Find It** Ancient Messene is next to the village of Mavrommati on Mount Ithomi, about 13 miles (21 km) north of the modern town of Messene (Messíni). There is a daily bus from the nearest major town (Kalamata), but the timetable does not allow for detailed exploration, so you may prefer to rent a car.

**Planning** The site is large and the central part alone takes a couple of hours to explore properly. The area around Messene is packed with historic monuments (ancient Olympia is only about one hour's drive away).

**Websites** www.ancientmessene.gr, en.agrotravel.gr

# ROMAN SITES

When not in Rome . . . The remains of far-flung outposts of the far-reaching Roman Empire lie scattered around the fringes of Europe and North Africa.

## ❶ Sarmisegetuza, Transylvania, Romania

The Dacian fortress at Sarmisegetuza is the center of an impressive ring of six forts that crown the heights of the Orastie and Retezat Mountains. Conquered by Roman armies at the beginning of the second century A.D., the site has a forum and an amphitheater where gladiator shows were held.

Planning Visit in the summer, when temperatures are in the 60s°F (16–20°C), and bring hiking boots. www.romaniatourism.com

## ❷ Pula Coliseum, Istria, Croatia

Far removed from its original bloody purpose, this first-century giant—the sixth largest amphitheater in the world—is now used for such spectacles as large concerts, ballet, and Croatia's International Film Festival. In its prime, the building hosted 20,000 spectators for regular gladiatorial battles.

Planning While in the area, visit the Archaeological Museum of Istria or the nearby Brijuni National Park, which contains some Roman villas. www.pulainfo.hr/en

## ❸ Perge, Antalya, Turkey

On the coastal plains near Antalya, the well-preserved remains of the city of Perge include baths, a stadium, theater, and *nymphaeum* (a fountain with a statue of a river god in the center). The remnants of a massive Hellenistic-Roman gateway are testament to the two civilizations that dominated the city's history.

Planning Perge is 10 miles (16 km) east of Antalya. You could combine it with visits to other nearby Roman sites. www.turkeytourism.org

## ❹ Library of Celsus, Ephesus, Turkey

Built in the second century A.D. to commemorate Celsus Polemaeanus, Roman governor of the Province of Asia, this library once housed about 12,000 scrolls stored in the niches of 30 bookcases. The monumental facade was designed to exaggerate the building's height, and the reading room faced east in order to take advantage of the best light.

Planning Ephesus is close to the village of Selçuk, an hour's drive south of Izmir. A prosperous city in Greek and Roman times, it is rich in ancient remains, including temples, public buildings, and a famous theater. www.ephesus.us

## ❺ Amphitheater, Trier, Germany

Roman ruins decorate the entire city of Trier, but the amphitheater is a unique place to see and imagine the drama of the gladiator games. You can tour the vast space below ground, with its holding areas for wild animals, gladiators, and criminals waiting to do battle in the arena above.

Planning Trier is a three-hour train journey from Cologne and Frankfurt. redaktion.trier.de/praefectus/trier?tourist_en

## ❻ Villa Romana del Casale, Sicily, Italy

Peristyles, courtyards, and *thermae* (baths) are proof of the luxury of Villa Romana del Casale, but the mosaics are the real gem. Providing a glimpse into the lives of an ancient people, subjects include female gymnasts, hunting scenes with riders enthralled in competition, trapped beasts, spritely antelopes, and exotic hippos.

Planning The villa is 3 miles (5 km) from Piazza Armerina in Sicily. www.regione.sicilia.it/turismo

## ❼ Hadrian's Wall, Northumberland, England

This defensive wall, built of stone and turf, stretches the width of England from the North Sea to the Irish Sea. The wall, together with a large ditch and 80 forts, or "milecastles," was designed to secure the Roman Empire's northern border and control trade. The wall's central sector and accompanying forts are well preserved.

Planning You can follow the wall's route from Newcastle-on-Tyne in the east to Bowness-on-Solway in the west along roads A69 and B6318. You can also walk the 84-mile (135 km) Hadrian's Wall Path National Trail, or bicycle along Hadrian's Cycleway (NCN 72). www.hadrians-wall.org

## ❽ Segovia Aqueduct, Segovia, Spain

With 166 arches, the aqueduct spans the entire city, the section through the center having two tiers of arches and reaching 93 ft (28 m) high. No mortar or cement holds the large blocks of granite in place—instead, a careful balancing of forces has kept the arches standing since the aqueduct was constructed in the first century A.D.

Planning Segovia is a great day-trip from Madrid, just 55 miles (89 km) to the south. www.madridinfosite.com, www.spain.info

## ❾ Las Matildes Silver Mines, Cartagena, Spain

Records claim that the mines in this area once yielded an extravagant amount of riches, worth 25,000 drachmas a day to the Roman treasury. This came at the cost of the labor of 40,000 slaves, who worked in harrowing conditions. Visitors can go underground at the Las Matildes mine, which has been restored.

Planning The Mina de las Matildes is at El Beal, off the motorway from Cartagena to La Manga. www.discoveringcartagena.com

## ❿ Bulla Regia's Villas, Tunisia

Villas in Bulla Regia had air-conditioned underground rooms, where the residents could shelter from the summer heat. The rooms also protected extensive mosaics. Although many of the mosaics are now in the Bardo Museum in Tunis, excellent examples remain, including hunting scenes in the House of the Hunt and Venus and Cupid riding dolphins in the House of Amphitrite.

Opposite: Near Housesteads fort, close to the town of Hexham in Northumberland, Hadrian's Wall runs through rolling farmland.

The mummified remains of one of Savoca's former worthies, which reside in the Convento dei Cappucini.

ITALY

# Savoca Catacombs

This beautiful hilltop village harbors a ghoulish
secret—a crypt where rows of mummies line the walls.

Savoca's baroque palaces and churches, in varying states of repair, cling to a volcanic outcrop in Sicily's northeast corner, in view of smoldering Mount Etna. Once an important town, Savoca's prosperity has long since waned, but the legacy of its wealthy patrons lives on in a macabre crypt. Just outside the walls of the village is the Convento dei Cappucini, a Franciscan monastery, where you can climb down a rickety ladder into an underground burial chamber that is home to the mummified remains of 32 of the city's elite from the 18th and 19th centuries. Priests, doctors, abbots, and politicians hang precariously in niches in the crypt, their names and short biographies taped above their resting places. They are decked out in their Sunday best, but what is left of their dry skin barely clings to decaying bone. The tradition of mummifying bodies was used by Franciscan orders as a reminder of the futility of vanity: "What you are, we were, and what we are you will become," the skeletal remains of the order's monks seemed to proclaim. Ironically, the ritual of mummification was adopted by Savoca's nobles to symbolize their enduring

**When to Go** Savoca can be visited year-round, although the summer can be scorching hot. Fall is ideal as the local grapes and olives are harvested and food festivals are held across the region. December 13 is the Feast of Santa Lucia, the town's patron saint, and features elaborate processions.

**How to Find It** Savoca is a 20-minute drive north from Taormina or a 40-minute drive south from Messina. The Convento dei Cappucini is on the main SP 19 road into the village from Santa Teresa di Riva.

**Planning** Savoca's catacombs and its town center can be visited as a half-day excursion from Taormina or Catania. Opening times vary, so check before visiting. A donation is expected. B&B Il Padrino, a restored 17th-century palace in the town center, rents out rooms.

**Website** turismo.comune.savoca.me.it

## The Godfather Connection

In 1971, Francis Ford Coppola came to Savoca to film scenes for *The Godfather*. It was in the **Bar Vitelli** on the ground floor of the elegant 18th-century Palazzo Trimarchi that Michael Corleone, played by Al Pacino, asked Apollonia's father for her hand in marriage, and the church of San Nicolò was used as the backdrop for the procession from the ceremony to the reception.

Visitors to the Bar Vitelli can sit at the table where Al Pacino sat and enjoyed the village specialty, a *granita di limone* (lemon sorbet) with *zuccherata* (a local cookie).

EUROPE

FRANCE

# Crypte Archéologique

Layers of history, from Roman times until the 18th century,
wait to be discovered beneath the streets of Paris.

To explore the ancient heart of Paris, the City of Light, step into the dark, underground streets of the ancient city of Lutetia. Founded by the Roman emperor Augustus in 27 b.c. to manage the local Parisii tribes and territory, Lutetia's remains now lie in the world's largest archaeological crypt, under the square in front of Notre Dame Cathedral. Marvel at the work of Roman urban planners. A network of streets and sewers, traces of monuments and public baths, and even a 1,700-year-old central heating system (a hypocaust) made up of underground furnaces and pipes have been unearthed, along with artifacts that throw light on the resident Romans' lifestyle. From wine jugs brought to northern Gaul from Italy to terra-cotta pots for boiling cereals, everyday items reveal details about the first Parisians. Frescoes of Roman villas and traces of a noblewoman's cosmetic kit are among the layers of life that archaeologists have dug up, dusted off, and analyzed with modern-day scanners. You can also see the only existing stones of Paris's first port, also dating from Roman times and evidence of the important commercial role played by the Seine River. Early medieval remains reveal that streets were widened to allow building materials for Notre Dame Cathedral to be transported along them, while 18th-century layers contain the foundations of a large hospital for foundling children.

**When to Go** The crypt is open year-round except Mondays and public holidays.

**How to Find It** Across the square in front of Notre Dame Cathedral, near the police headquarters, a single marble block marks the entrance to the stairway down to the crypt.

**Planning** Allow at least an hour to tour the site.

**Websites** www.carnavalet.paris.fr, www.franceway.com

EUROPE

### Place Lépine

■ After a visit to the Crypte Archéologique, take a short walk to Place Louis Lépine's **flower market.** The market is vibrant during December, not only for the rare winter birdsong, but also for rows of red and pink poinsettias and the fresh, piney scent of Christmas trees. Many of the flower vendors sell unusual Christmas tree decorations.

■ Watch for the graceful green figures of the **Wallace Fountain** in the square, one of 77 drinking fountains throughout Paris that were financed by the English humanitarian, Richard Wallace, in the 19th century.

Roman remains in the Crypte Archéologique include part of the furnaces and pipes of a central-heating system.

Oradour's ruined houses and church bear the scars of the massacre of the villagers in June 1944.

FRANCE

# ORADOUR-SUR-GLANE

The ruins of this once lively village in central France remind the world of war's most tragic moments.

The rusty remains of daily life in the dying days of the German occupation of France during World War II still strew the streets of Oradour: Bicycles, sewing machines, and a bent baby carriage, all abandoned suddenly on a warm Saturday afternoon in the summer of 1944. You see the barns where some 200 local men were rounded up and gunned down, their bodies then piled up and set alight. In the church, you gaze in horror at the place where a similar fate befell more than 400 women and children. In this French village with no particular history of Resistance activity, many folk had scarcely seen a German soldier in uniform until the afternoon of June 10, when Nazi SS Panzer Division officers arrived and ordered everyone into the central fairgrounds. In addition to local people, more than 100 refugees from Belgium and eastern France who had arrived in Oradour a few years earlier were included. Homes were looted and the village was set on fire. In all, 642 people were massacred. After France had been liberated, the government decided that the village should not be restored. Left as it was after the SS troops departed, ruined Oradour stands as a memorial to all that the French suffered during the occupation.

**When to Go** Weekdays in spring and fall see fewer visitors.

**How to Find It** The ruins of Oradour-sur-Glane lie on a sloping hillside 14 miles (22 km) northwest of Limoges, between St.-Junien and Belloc. They are best reached by car.

**Planning** The village is open to visitors free of charge. Entry is through the striking visitors' center, Centre de la Mémoire, between the new town and the remains of the destroyed village. The cemetery has a huge memorial to the 642 dead, whose names are inscribed on ten tablets of black marble.

**Website** www.oradour.info

### A Massacre Without Explanation

June 10, 1944, began quite normally in Oradour. People gathered in village cafés, children were lined up at school for a medical checkup, and a few radios crackled news of Allied forces landing in Normandy.

That same day, the **SS Division "Das Reich"** was under orders to hasten to Normandy, where the D-Day landings had taken place just four days earlier on June 6. Members of the French Resistance sniped at their tanks and trucks, hindering their progress north.

Why 200 SS troops surrounded and methodically destroyed the village of Oradour-sur-Glane—whose name is derived from the Latin *oratorum*, a place of prayer—remains a mystery. The Nazis' real target may have been **Oradour-sur-Vayres,** 35 miles (56 km) to the south, where an SS officer was thought to be held captive. But confusion between the towns cannot explain the brutality of this carnage.

EUROPE

EGYPT

# Tombs of Beni Hassan

Tombs carved into cliffs above the Nile Valley offer a rare chance to see life in the heyday of ancient Egypt's Middle Kingdom.

AFRICA

Situated about 155 miles (250 kilometers) south of Cairo, and once scarred by political unrest, the village of Beni Hassan is rarely visited by tourists, but cut into the nearby cliffs are 39 tombs richly decorated with frescoes. Most of the tombs date from the 11th and 12th dynasties (2125–1795 B.C.) and were the resting place of provincial governors. The four tombs that are open to the public reveal walls covered with scenes from everyday life. People hunting, fishing, netting birds, farming, gathering papyrus, weaving and spinning, as well as scenes of battle, games, and sports, and funeral rites with traditional boats and offerings, are all portrayed in vivid colors. The ochers and golds look as bright as if they had been painted yesterday, and in the semidarkness you can almost smell the harvest, feel the linen, stroke the gazelles, or imagine yourself bargaining with traders from faraway lands. All is movement and energy. Gaze in wonder at the wrestlers in the tomb of Baqet, scenes of music and dancing in that of his son, Khety, and the elaborate ceiling in Amenemhet's tomb. Amenemhet's tomb also has a false door in the western wall, the direction of the entrance to the underworld. In Khnumhotep's tomb, you'll find a beautiful family scene, plants, animals, and birds, and the deceased's biography on the base of the walls.

**When to Go** Visit in winter, when the sun shines but temperatures are pleasant.

**How to Find It** Beni Hassan is 12 miles (19 km) south of the city of Minya. It may be possible to reach the site by taxi from Minya, but the best way to visit is with a guided tour or as part of a Nile cruise.

**Planning** Security is tight throughout Egypt, and you are likely to be escorted by civilian or uniformed guards, though this is generally discreet and for your own safety. Cruises vary from luxury cruisers to traditional feluccas with billowing sails and basic facilities. Either way, a cruise offers the chance to see historic sites and scenes of contemporary rural life along the river that are strangely reminiscent of those ancient paintings in the tombs.

**Websites** egyptsites.wordpress.com/beni-hasan, www.egypttravelplans.com

### City of the Sun God

Roughly 25 miles (40 km) south of Beni Hassan is the city of **Tell el-Amarna.** For around 14 years in the 14th century B.C., the city was the capital of the pharaoh Akhenaten and his queen, Nefertiti. Parts of temples and palaces remain, as well as 25 cliff tombs with wall paintings reflecting life in the city of the sun god. Among the best are the tombs of Akhenaten's steward, chief servant, fan bearer, chief of police, and the High Priest of Aten. Akhenaten's tomb is tucked away in the Royal Valley, where the sun would always rise. Little remains of the decorations and no body was found, but it is an atmospheric place.

Scenes of daily life fill the walls of Khety's tomb at Beni Hassan.

LIBYA

# LEPTIS MAGNA

Wander the streets of this ancient city on Libya's Mediterranean coast to imagine what life was like in Roman times.

With its sandy beaches, therapeutic baths, extensive shopping streets, plentiful live entertainment, and considerable architectural grandeur, Leptis Magna sounds like the ideal holiday destination. But the labyrinthine Roman city (75 miles/120 kilometers east of Tripoli) lies partly buried under sands blown in from Libya's deserts, and few could find it on a map today. The pillar-lined halls of the spa are now all open to the sky, the blocks of the original domed roof stacked along the walls, wildflowers peeping shyly from among them. Marble-lined shops housed a plethora of outlets, and while some citizens shopped, others drank at the U-shaped bar at one end of the forum. Farther on, men played games of marbles on grids carved in the flagstones while they waited for news of ships arriving at the port just beyond—Leptis Magna was well located to benefit from the brisk trade in goods around the Mediterranean and from the Sahara. But if the entertainment palled, the carving of male reproductive equipment in high relief on a wall nearby indicates that other pleasures were available for a price. At the theater, where the better-educated part of Leptis's population went for its song, the acoustics of the soaring, semicircular bank of 5,000 stone seats are still perfect, accidentally amplifying the birdsong that is now Leptis's loudest sound.

**When to Go**  Leptis Magna's location on the southern shores of the Mediterranean helps to keep its weather mild year-round, and visitors are still so few in number that there's no need to worry about busy seasons.

**How to Find It**  For now, Libya can only be entered on an organized tour, although it can be a hand-tailored organized tour for one if you wish. Local operators, such as Arkno Tours, can provide the invitations you need for a visa to be issued on arrival, and have cars and English-speaking guides, as well as a number of their own small and comfortable hotels.

**Planning**  Visitors to Libya are treated with considerable courtesy. The country is delightfully free of pushy souvenir salesmen, overpricing for foreigners, and other regrettable practices of busier destinations. Passports must show no evidence of visits to Israel or the Occupied Territories or a visa will be denied. An Arabic translation of the passport-holder's details must be supplied.

**Websites**  www.arkno.com, www.alnpete.co.uk/lepcis

AFRICA

## Ancient Customs

■ At **Hadrian's Baths,** the sweat room's marble lining has fallen away to reveal the now cracked and broken slender brick piping–vaguely resembling a church organ–through which hot air circulated, rising and condensing in an ingenious recycling system. While luxuriating in the various pools, receiving massage treatments with olive oil, and making visits to one of the on-site libraries, Leptis's powerful discussed the business of the day.

■ If the bath was a social place, so was the bathroom. Discussions were often continued in the equally luxurious public latrine at rows of marble seats with keyhole-shaped cutouts. In cold weather, slaves would be sent ahead to sit and warm up the stone to spare their masters any discomfort, while musicians provided background music.

Opposite: The remains of Leptis Magna's harbor  Above: A statue in the Severus forum

Manacles hanging from a wall in the Maison des Esclaves are a grim reminder of the trade in human beings along this coast.

SENEGAL

# ÎLE DE GORÉE

A 20-minute ferry ride from the heat and dust of Senegal's capital, Dakar, takes you to an island haven rich in history.

The boat rounds the Île de Gorée's northern headland and sails into a sandy bay, where young people splash and swim joyfully in the waves. Handsome colonial-style buildings line the waterfront, their flaking paintwork displaying a rich palette of pastel and ocher hues. Disembarking from the ferry, you wander along streets and alleys, where colorful swathes of bougainvillea cascade over the tops of high garden walls. On this tiny island—sheltered from the full blast of the Atlantic by the hook of Africa's westernmost point, Cap Vert—there are no cars or even bicycles to dodge. Everything and everyone seem to exude an easygoing charm, worthy of the *signares*—mixed-race matriarchs, famous equally for their beauty, grace, and business acumen—who once lived in the elegant houses around you. But this tropical paradise has a darker side, remembered in the 18th-century Maison des Esclaves (House of Slaves). Here, you will be shown cells where slaves are said to have been confined before being herded through the Porte du Voyage Sans Retour (Gate of No Return) onto ships bound for the Americas. Previous visitors to the Maison des Esclaves have included Nelson Mandela and Pope John Paul II, and it was here in 1992 that the late Pope made an historic apology for the Catholic Church's complicity in the slave trade.

**When to Go** From November through May is best, avoiding the hot summer rainy season.

**How to Find It** Ferries run from the main port of Dakar regularly between 6 a.m. and 11 p.m.

**Planning** The small restaurants by the jetty serve good simple fish dishes. Don't miss Castel Hill with a memorial to the African diaspora and the remains of a former French coastal battery. There are three museums, including the Musée de la Femme (Women's Museum). If you want to spend the night, the Hostellerie du Chevalier de Boufflers has an attractive beachside location.

**Websites** www.senegal-online.com, www.senegal-tourism.com, webworld.unesco.org/goree

## The Age of the Signares

Two narratives are told about the Île de Gorée. According to one, the island was a key link in the transatlantic slave trade. But many historians demur. While the slave trade was an inescapable and horrific reality along this coast, they believe that Gorée's role was comparatively minor. Instead, they tell of the *signares*—from the Portuguese *senhora*, "ladies." Descended from 17th-century Portuguese traders and local African women, the signares were the nucleus of a remarkable matriarchal community that controlled a thriving trade in commodities such as indigo and spices. One of them, Anna Colas Pépin, owned the house now known as the Maison des Esclaves.

AFRICA

SOUTH AFRICA

# SEVILLA ROCK ART TRAIL

A short, easy hike in the Cederberg Mountains takes
in ancient rock art sites left by the San bushmen.

The ibis crossing your hiking trail resembles a strange prehistoric bird—which is
only appropriate when you are on your way to view rock art as old as the Egyptian
pyramids. Less than three hours from modern-day Cape Town, you are entering the
world of the San people, nomadic hunter-gatherers who lived here long before Europeans
arrived. They left a legacy of more than 2,500 rock paintings in the Cederberg region,
many of which can be viewed on the Sevilla Rock Art Trail. The easy 4-mile (6.4 kilometer)
ramble along the Brandewyn River near the small town of Clanwilliam is dotted with
nine individual sites where rock art between 800 and 8,000 years old awaits you. The sense
of otherworldliness is evident even before you reach the first site as starkly beautiful red
sandstone formations, such as the Wolfberg Arch, formed over centuries by the action of
wind and sand, tower over you. And suddenly you come face to face with the surprisingly
vivid paintings. A newborn foal finding its legs, an archer taking aim, long-extinct quaggas
(a variety of zebra), elephants, and a line of dancing women reach out across centuries to
tell the silent story of a lost way of life.

**When to Go**  The trail is open year-round. Go in spring to see the annual blaze of wildflowers for which the
area is famous. Winters are wet, and can be very cold, but can also lend a special beauty to the area when
the Cederberg Mountains are capped with snow.

**How to Find It**  The start of the trail is at Traveller's Rest Farm, 22 miles (35 km) from Clanwilliam on the
road towards Wupperthal.

**Planning**  You may not camp or hike in the area without a permit. Permits, trail maps, and guide booklets
can be purchased at Traveller's Rest Farm, where you will also find self-catering accommodations, which
should be booked in advance. The University of Cape Town Living Landscape Craft Centre in Park Street,
Clanwilliam, sells books, craft items, and a CD on rock art.

**Websites**  www.travellersrest.co.za, www.clanwilliam.info

AFRICA

### Local Highlights

■ The **Clanwilliam Dam** is very
popular for waterskiing. Rent a
chalet or camp near the water's
edge and ski to your heart's
content, or walk the nearby
Ramskop Nature Reserve trail to
experience the richness of the
indigenous flora.

■ The grave of **C. Louis Leipoldt,**
a doctor who became one of
South Africa's best loved poets,
is in the Pakhuis Pass near
Clanwilliam. His grave sits below
more San rock paintings and
provides a perfect excuse
for a sunset drive down the
scenic pass.

Haunting images of people and animals were layered on top of each other by generations of San bushmen.

# SPIRITUAL HAVENS

ncient temples, great cathedrals, and other religious landmarks are ever popular stopping points on the worldwide tourist trail, yet there are still sacred places—some remote, others right in the heart of crowded cities—that have retained an aura of serenity. Who would have thought that one of the world's largest Gothic cathedrals, complete with an awe-inspiring rose window and peacocks strutting on its lawn, stands not in the medieval quarter of an old French town, but in central Manhattan? Equally astonishing is the south Mexican hilltop of Cholula, crowned by one of the many churches built by the Spanish conquistadors. Yet the mound conceals a pre-Columbian pyramid larger than any in Egypt, dedicated to the Aztec deity Quetzalcoatl. Everywhere, places of pilgrimage offer unanticipated rewards. In Japan, a mountainscape of cedar forests and hidden shrines rewards footsore travelers with the chance to bathe in thermal springs. And amid the office blocks of the City of London lie 50 churches—each with its own surprises—packed into one dense square mile.

Built by a king more than 800 years ago, Cambodia's Ta Prohm temple, with its exquisitely carved stonework, was part of a vast city and the focal point for thousands of Buddhist priests, religious dancers, and worshipers.

The cathedral was beautifully restored after a fire in 2001.

NEW YORK

# ST. JOHN THE DIVINE

Experience the soaring spaces of New York's Episcopal cathedral—an oasis of peace in frenzied Manhattan.

Huge bronze doors greet you as you approach St. John the Divine from Amsterdam Avenue. Flanked by 32 carved limestone figures depicting characters from the Old and New Testaments, the doors form part of the cathedral's monumental Portal of Paradise. Step inside the cavernous nave—124 feet (38 meters) high and 601 feet (183 meters) long—and marvel at the sheer immensity. The cathedral has quietly defined the neighborhood of Morningside Heights since its first stone was laid in 1892. In a city now famous for its skyscrapers, St. John the Divine, built in Gothic style on one of the highest points in Manhattan, yields nothing in soaring grandeur to the city's cloud-scratching temples of mammon. And it continues to evolve. In the St. Savior Chapel, pause before the beautiful bronze altar triptych by artist Keith Haring, completed shortly before his death in 1990. Back in the Portal of Paradise, the statues on either side were carved between 1988 and 1997. Take a closer look at the walls beneath them and you will spot sculptures of the Brooklyn Bridge and the Twin Towers.

**When to Go**  The cathedral is open from Monday through Saturday, 7 a.m.-6 p.m., and Sunday, 7 a.m.-7 p.m. Grounds and gardens are open during daylight hours.

**How to Find It**  St. John the Divine is located at 112th Street and Amsterdam Avenue, one block east of Broadway. Buses 4 and 104 stop at Broadway and 112th Street; the 11 stops at Amsterdam Avenue and 112th Street. If using the subway, take the #1 train to 110th Street/Cathedral Parkway station.

**Planning**  Double-deck tour buses give you only enough time for a rapid-fire photo frenzy. Do yourself a favor and hop off for an hour or two to savor the cathedral's unique blend of grandness and serenity.

**Websites**  www.stjohndivine.org, www.sacred-destinations.com

## Window on Eden

■ One of the cathedral's most sublime glories is the **Great Rose Window** above the Portal of Paradise in the western facade. Its 10,000 pieces of glass seem to reflect every hue in the color spectrum.

■ Known simply as **The Green,** the vast lawn that flanks the cathedral is home to a trio of peacocks. The birds were gifts from the Philadelphia and Bronx Zoos and they delight and surprise visitors.

■ Set back from Amsterdam Avenue, the **Biblical Garden** is a veritable Eden, teeming with plants, shrubs, and trees. Many of the flowers and fruits here are mentioned in the Bible.

# GREAT PYRAMID OF CHOLULA

The remains of the largest pyramid ever built vie with lavish baroque churches in the south Mexican city of Cholula.

Approach the small city of Cholula from the north, and you see what looks like an isolated hill rising from the surrounding plain with an impressive-looking church crowning it. Come from the opposite direction, and a portion of restored stonework climbing the side of the apparent hill reveals it as something else: The remains of a pre-Columbian temple pyramid, with the snowcapped volcanic cone of El Popocatepetl, Mexico's second-highest peak, making a spectacular backdrop. While Central America's other temple pyramids are well known, the pre-Columbian site at Cholula, in Puebla state, is generally overlooked. Yet Cholula's great pyramid, devoted to the god Quetzalcoatl, was the largest ever built—bigger by volume than the Great Pyramid of Giza in Egypt, although not as tall. If you have no fear of dark places, explore the 5 miles (8 kilometres) of tunnels excavated by archaeologists. When you have done that, climb up to the Church of Our Lady of the Remedies at the top. At the time of the Spanish conquest, in the early 16th century, the conquistador Hernan Cortes vowed to eradicate the Mixteca-Puebla culture and erect a Christian church over every pagan temple. The saying that Cholula has a church for each day of the year isn't quite true, but its *iglesias* are many and impressive—in the sumptuous Mexican baroque style, brimming with gold and elaborate ornamentation.

**When to Go**  The pyramid can be visited year-round (Tuesday-Sunday).

**How to Find It**  Cholula is 60 miles (97 km) southeast of Mexico City, 90 minutes by bus from Terminal del Oriente, and even quicker by rental car.

**Planning**  Don't miss the local food (*mole poblano, chiles en nogada, tamal de frijoles*), Talavera pottery, and textiles. In the two weeks before Christmas, traditional *posadas*—processions re-creating the journey of Mary and Joseph to Bethlehem—take place in Cholula's churches.

**Websites**  www.aztec-history.com/cholula-pyramid.html, www.mexonline.com/cholula-pyramid.htm

## Gilded Opulence

A short taxi ride from Cholula, the villages of Tonantzintla and Acatepec are essential stops for their superb baroque churches.

■ **Santa María de Tonantzintla** has been called the "Sistine Chapel of indigenous baroque art." Inside, local artists covered the walls with dazzlingly colorful murals, combining pre-Columbian and Catholic motifs.

■ In **Acatepec,** the outstanding features of the **Church of San Francisco** are a facade resembling fine porcelain and a luxuriantly gilded interior.

The domes and towers of the Church of our Lady of the Remedies have capped the ancient pyramid of Cholula since the 1570s.

# SACRED IN THE CITY

In the midst of city hubbub, islands of calm, open to anyone in search
of a quiet moment, can often be found in the most unexpected places.

### ❶ Quiet Garden, Montreal, Canada

The Quiet Garden, or Jardin Tranquille, designed as an extension of the Presbyterian Church of St. Andrew and St. Paul, offers a peaceful green space for reflection in the heart of bustling downtown Montreal. Three hundred such meditation gardens have been created for hospitals, schools, and prisons in cities across the world.

Planning Montreal's Quiet Garden is located across from the Musée des Beaux-Arts. www.standrewstpaul.com

### ❷ Tillman Chapel, New York

Facing the United Nations tower on First Avenue, the Tillman Chapel in the Church Center for the United Nations has a warm, modern, wood-paneled interior. The building belongs to the United Methodist Church, but anyone is welcome in this haven from the storms and stresses of international tension.

Planning The Tillman Chapel, 777 First Avenue at 44th Street, is a discreet setting for intercultural weddings, as well as conferences on worldwide issues. www.gbgm-umc.org

### ❸ Hua Zang Si Temple, San Francisco, California

This startling Gothic-style building with a red-and-silver facade in San Francisco's Mission District used to be a German Lutheran church but is now the Buddhist Hua Zang Si Temple. A nondenominational center for Buddhist study, Hua Zang Si's broad Chinese doors are open daily for meditation.

Planning The temple is at 3134 22nd Street, a five-minute walk from the 24th Street Mission BART station. Arrive about 5 p.m. for the evening chant. www.huazangsi.org

### ❹ Jumeirah Mosque, Dubai, U.A.E.

After shopping, sunbathing, and visiting theme parks—or even spending a day on skis—you may wonder where to find signs of spiritual life in cosmopolitan Dubai. A small-group, morning tour of the old city takes you through the spice market and into the lofty spaces of Jumeirah Mosque, the city's only mosque open to non-Muslim visitors.

Planning In this place of worship, women wear long sleeves, slacks, and cover their heads. A Friday visit, when the mosque is filled with worshipers, is not advised. www.cultures.ae/jumeirah.htm

### ❺ Vanha Kirkko, Helsinki, Finland

The neoclassical simplicity of Helsinki's early 19th-century Vanha Kirkko (Old Church) fits perfectly with the surrounding park. The pastel colors in the interior of this Lutheran sanctuary are uplifting, even on long, gray winter days.

Planning The church is on Lönnrotinkatu Street. Visit on a Tuesday, when organ recitals are on the agenda. www.visithelsinki.fi

### ❻ Santa Maria della Vittoria, Rome, Italy

Within the small baroque basilica's Cornaro Chapel, designed by Bernini in 1646, is one of the sculptor's greatest and most realistic masterpieces, "The Ecstasy of St. Teresa of Avila." White marble carvings on either side of the chapel show members of the Cornaro family watching events from theater-like boxes.

Planning The basilica is at 17 Via XX Settembre, a short walk from Rome's Termini Station. www.romaviva.com

### ❼ St.-Julien-le-Pauvre, Paris, France

The Church of St.-Julien-le-Pauvre in Rue Galande, built in the 13th century, is only a few steps from the bustle of Boulevard St. Michel. This small, rough-stone church, one of the oldest in Paris, now belongs to the Melkite Greek Catholic Church—Orthodox in liturgy, but in communion with Rome. A wonderful collection of golden icons graces its altar.

Planning St. Julien is often the venue for chamber music concerts. www.paris-walking-tours.com/church-of-saint-julien-le-pauvre.html

### ❽ Église Alexandre Nevsky, Biarritz, France

Surf the Bay of Biscay, indulge in artisanal chocolates, play the casino tables—and then what? When Biarritz's glitz loses its appeal, step into the Russian Orthodox Church of St. Alexandre Nevsky, built by Russian aristocrats after the 1917 Revolution. The majestic blue dome prompts both prayer and reflection, especially when a hint of incense lingers after Sunday services.

Planning You will find the church at 8 Avenue de l'Impératrice. www.biarritz.fr

### ❾ Bevis Marks Synagogue, London, England

Dedicated in 1702, Bevis Marks is England's oldest synagogue and has provided a sanctuary for Spanish and Portuguese Sephardic Orthodox Jews for more than three centuries. Its baroque interior retains the original furnishings, including a Renaissance-style ark, a ladies gallery supported by 12 pillars, and seven magnificent candelabra symbolizing the days of the week.

Planning You may like to visit during Hanukkah in December for the candlelit choral service. www.bevismarks.org.uk

### ❿ St. George's Chapel, Heathrow, England

In the heart of one of the world's busiest airports, a multifaith prayer room and, below it, St. George's Chapel serve as havens of peace for travelers and airport staff. A few quiet moments in the nondenominational chapel may chase away flyers' fears.

Planning Travelers in transit can also pause in a chapel at Frankfurt airport, Germany. www.heathrowairport.com

Opposite: The introduction of electric lighting to supplement candlelight is one of the few concessions to modernity at 300-year-old Bevis Marks Synagogue, London.

JAPAN

# KUMANO KODO PILGRIM TRAILS

Follow in the footsteps of emperors to the mystic mountains and sacred shrines of Japan's spiritual heartland.

In ancient times, Japan's emperors journeyed south from Kyoto to the Kii-hanto peninsula in order to purify themselves, pray to spirits dwelling in rocks and trees, and ask for special favors. Their pilgrimage route, a trail network called the Kumano Kodo, crossed wild, waterfall-laced mountains sprinkled with shrines, particularly the three Grand Shrines: Hongu Taisha, Hayatama Taisha, and Nachi Taisha. Today, you can hike the trails or visit the shrines by road. A popular trek is the 4-mile (6.4 kilometer) trail from Hosshinmon-oji to Hongu Taisha. You will pass through cedar forests and mountaintop villages, terraces of tea bushes and mandarin orange trees. At Fushiogami-oji, pilgrims dropped to their knees on sighting Hongu Taisha—marked by the world's largest *torii* (shrine gate)—in the valley far below. The mystical setting of Hongu Taisha is considered to be the spiritual heart of Japan, and many other pilgrimage routes converge on it. After descending to Hongu Taisha, pilgrims paddled down the Kumano River to Hayatama Taisha (you can travel by river from the Kawabune boat center or by road) and then continued on to Nachi Taisha, which centers around Japan's highest waterfall. Hayatama Taisha's red-and-white structures are instantly recognizable. At Nachi Taisha, the buildings, some bright orange, show a fusion of Shinto and Buddhist influences.

**When to Go** The best seasons are spring (April–May), showcasing cherry and plum blossoms, and fall (September–October), with splendid foliage. You may like to visit during the Kumano Hongu Taisha spring festival (April 13–15) or the Nachi-no-Hi Matsuri fire festival at Kumano Nachi Taisha (July 14).

**How to Find It** Takijiri-oji, the trailhead for the Kumano Kodo, is a 14-mile (23 km) drive east into the mountains from the coastal city of Tanabe; Hosshinmon-oji is an additional 22 miles (35 km) away. Buses run daily from JR Kii-Tanabe train station to Takijiri-oji (35 minutes), Kumano Hongu Taisha (110 minutes), and Hosshinmon-oji (two hours).

**Planning** Tanabe city is a good base, with decent hotels and restaurants. You can find maps at the Nanki Tanabe Tourism Information Center in front of the train station. The hike between Takijiri-oji and Hosshinmon-oji is fairly strenuous; the trek between Hosshinmon-oji and Kumano Hongu Taisha is easier.

**Websites** www.tb-kumano.jp/en, www.spiritual-pilgrimages.net

ASIA

### Hot-spring Heaven

At the end of a long day of hiking, why not soak in a hot spring? The Kii-hanto peninsula is famous for its hot springs, which no doubt add to its mystical qualities. The spring known as **Yunomine Onsen,** southwest of Hongu Taisha, is said to have been frequented for 1,800 years and is where pilgrims often stopped for purification rites. You'll find two bathhouses in this quintessential mountain hamlet built beside a gurgling brook. Inside a tiny cabin called **Tsuboyu** is a rocky bath—the only place in the world where you can bathe in a hot spring that is also a UNESCO World Heritage Site. You can get to Yunomine Onsen by road, or by a 70-minute walk from Hongu Taisha.

Opposite: A stone-paved Kumano Kodo trail passes through green woodland. Above: A pagoda at Nachi Taisha

A Buddhist monk finds solace in a niche at Angkor's Ta Prohm temple, built for worshipers more than 800 years ago.

CAMBODIA

# TA PROHM

Entangled by the gnarled roots and branches of banyan trees, a ruined Khmer temple harks back to a golden reign.

One of several archaeological sites in Cambodia's Angkor region, Ta Prohm is regarded as the most atmospheric of the country's ancient Khmer temples. It was built as a Buddhist monastery by King Jayavarman VII in the late 12th century and dedicated to the royal family, soon gaining substantial wealth, including ceremonial parasols and silk beds, diamonds, pearls, and gold plates weighing 1,102 pounds (500 kilograms). In Ta Prohm's golden age, several thousand resident priests and officials, 600 religious dancers, and 80,000 villagers from the surrounding area worked for the king's pleasure. Things are quieter today, especially in the late afternoon when the large tour groups have left and Ta Prohm returns to the jungle, where it lay abandoned for 500 years. Banyan trees soar above the ruins, parakeets screech in the foliage, while roots and creepers cling to the old stones, binding them together like ghostly tendrils from a distant past. This is the best time to explore the buildings of the inner enclosures, such as the Library or House of Fire, or stand by the Echo Wall to hear your heartbeat and catch the last glimpse of a performance by local Apsara dancers. Lizards dart out of the cracks and the carvings come to life as they glow in the setting sun.

**When to Go** From December through January for pleasant temperatures and blue skies.

**How to Find It** Ta Prohm is part of the Angkor Archaeological Park, 5 miles (8 km) north of the town of Siem Reap, and can be reached by taxi or organized tour. An international airport serves Siem Reap, with flights from Phnom Penh (50 minutes), or you can travel by boat from the capital (5-6 hours).

**Planning** Pack a sun hat and sturdy footwear; most areas are exposed and have uneven ground and high steps. For a bird's-eye view of Angkor, you may like to try the anchored hot-air balloon. An Apsara dance show is the perfect complement to a temple visit. U.S. dollars in small denominations are useful.

**Websites** www.cambodia-travel.com, www.tourismcambodia.com, www.angkorwhat.net

### Serenity in Stone

Lying 2.5 miles (4 km) west of Ta Prohm, at the heart of the ancient capital of Angkor Thom, is the Buddhist **Temple of Bayon.** Built by King Jayavarman VII, Bayon's three levels, or terraces, symbolize a holy mountain. The first two levels are square with bas-reliefs depicting battles and everyday scenes—jugglers and acrobats, military parades with elephants and oxcarts, and people playing chess. Most stunning is the circular upper level, where giant stone faces gaze serenely from the towers. Some say they represent the god of compassion, others the great King Jayavarman himself.

ASIA

INDONESIA

# Dieng Plateau

In Java's highlands an ethereal caldera scattered with temple ruins and bubbling volcanic vents lures curious travelers.

This chill volcanic plateau, the highest inhabited area on the island, occupies a powerful position on the spiritual map of Java and maintains the otherworldly ambience of a region whose name is derived, appropriately enough, from the Sanskrit phrase *Di Hyang,* meaning "Abode of the Gods." The profound silence, the mists, and the occasional mysterious death (caused by volcanic carbon dioxide accumulating in depressions) continues to attract shamans, pilgrims, and the curious. In the seventh century, Dieng was home to Hindu priests, many of them itinerant holy men from India, who oversaw the building of 400 temples, the oldest in Java. They transformed the marshy plain into a center for pilgrimage and religious propagation, fostering the spread of Hinduism through most of the island. Only eight of these squat and largely unadorned temples survive; most were destroyed by succeeding generations, who embraced Islam and saw shrines only as a convenient source of building material. Visitors of a less spiritual bent can enjoy lengthy treks through the sparsely inhabited plateau to view bubbling fumaroles, acidic lakes that change hues as the day progresses, and a fascinating land that seems to have changed little since the wandering priests settled the Abode of the Gods.

**When to Go**  April through October, the local dry season, is the preferred time to visit, increasing the chances of viewing a soul-stirring sunrise and lessening the risk of being caught in a highland downpour.

**How to Find It**  Wonosobo, a pleasant town 43 miles (69 km) northwest of Yogyakarta on good, if busy, roads is the usual gateway to Dieng. The area is also accessible from Pekalongan on Java's north coast. Rental vehicles and information about public transport options to Dieng are readily available in Yogyakarta. Avoid a one-day package tour, which allows only an hour or so on the plateau.

**Planning**  Warm clothing is essential if you stay in one of the basic guesthouses. Sturdy hiking shoes are also recommended if you plan a walking tour of the temples and lakes.

**Website**  www.indonesia-tourism.com/central-java/dieng-plateau.html

## Cave Retreat

Tucked into the surrounding hills is a cave named after Semar, a pot-bellied, doddering manservant who is actually the most powerful character in the Javanese *wayang,* or shadow puppet, mythic tradition. The cave is a favored meditation venue for those members of the Javanese elite who, like Semar, prefer to cloak their power and influence in outward modesty and humility. The **Semar cave** is not for spiritual dilettantes, as you must possess sufficient mental and physical stamina to endure the biting mountain chill during the long night.

The extraordinary atmosphere of the Dieng Plateau was not lost on seventh-century Hindu priests, who adopted it as the religious center of Java.

# RELIGIOUS ART

From a guinea pig at the Last Supper to paintings commissioned by the man who may have been the real-life Don Juan, art in the world of worship holds many surprises.

## ❶ Cusco Cathedral, Cusco, Peru

Cusco's majestic 16th-century cathedral holds 400 paintings, but one is quite unusual. In "The Last Supper," Marcos Zapata, a master in the colonial period of painting, portrayed Christ about to dine on roasted guinea pig, chili peppers, and papayas. Local specialties, flora, and imagery clearly found their way into this and other examples of colonial Christian art.

Planning Request an audio guide in English when you buy a ticket to the cathedral. www.cusco-peru.org

## ❷ Kumari Ghar, Kathmandu, Nepal

The temple of Kumari Ghar, in the Hanuman Dhoka Palace area in Kathmandu, is covered with elaborate wooden sculptures and intricate window screens. It is the residence of the Living Goddess, a Hindu child who represents an ancient Nepalese deity. Watch the screens, for she is known to look out and wave.

Planning In September, parades and dancers fill the square for Bijaya Dasami, the harvest festival. www.nepaltravelinfo.com

## ❸ Hadassah Medical Center, Jerusalem, Israel

Twelve glowing stained-glass window panels by Marc Chagall illuminate the Hadassah Medical Center synagogue at Ein-Kerem Hospital west of Jerusalem. Each with a different color theme, the windows were created and donated by Chagall in 1962 to depict the biblical story of Jacob's blessings to his 12 sons.

Planning There is a charge for admission and a tour of the windows. www.hadassah.org.il

## ❹ Scuola di San Giorgio degli Schiavoni, Venice, Italy

Discover Vittore Carpaccio's talent for narrative drama in a dim hall of a former confraternity of Dalmatians (Schiavoni) living in Venice. Nine masterworks illustrate the lives of St. George and St. Jerome. In the backgrounds, Carpaccio portrayed Venetian daily life of the early 16th century in anecdotal detail.

Planning You may need a pocket flashlight to appreciate the paintings' finer points. www.aboutvenice.org

## ❺ Church of San Lorenzo, Borgo San Lorenzo, Italy

North of Florence in the Mugello Valley, the Church of San Lorenzo houses a most striking 13th-century fresco by Giotto, portraying the Virgin Mary with a dark face. Giotto often used the people around him as models, but this fresco may show the influence of dark-faced Byzantine icons.

Planning Borgo San Lorenzo lies 19 miles (31 km) from Florence. If you visit on a Tuesday, market day, you may see people resembling those who probably modeled for Giotto. www.sieveonline.it

## ❻ Our Lady's Church, Bruges, Belgium

Michelangelo's Madonna in Our Lady's Church, Bruges, was originally made for Siena Cathedral in Italy, but two wealthy merchants brought it north in 1506. With sculpted features similar to his famous Pietà in St. Peter's, Rome, the Bruges marble Madonna gazes down as the Christ child stands at her knee.

Planning The Groeninge Museum, a four-minute walk from the church, contains a splendid collection of Flemish religious art, including works by Jan van Eyck. www.trabel.com/brugge/bruges-ourlady.htm

## ❼ Churches of Berry, France

Cherry-cheeked angels and madonnas painted in vigorous early Romanesque frescoes cover entire walls in the village churches of Brinay, Avord, Chalivoy-Milon, Gargilesse, and Nohant-Vicq, in the Berry region of central France. The frescoes were uncovered in the 19th century, and author George Sand, who lived in Nohant-Vicq, fought to protect the rich legacy.

Planning The villages range from 10 miles (16 km) to 45 miles (73 km) south of Bourges. While in Nohant-Vicq, you can also tour George Sand's home. www.bourges-tourisme.com

## ❽ St. James's Church, Nayland, England

The church of St. James in the Suffolk village of Nayland houses a rare altarpiece—one of just three religious paintings by the landscape painter, John Constable. Considered the best of his altarpieces, "Christ Blessing the Elements" is unusual in the haunting expression on Christ's face. It is, in fact, the face of Constable's brother, Golding, who modeled for him.

Planning Take a day to hike along well-marked trails in the Stour Valley, through Constable's landscapes. www.suffolkchurches.co.uk/nayland.htm

## ❾ Hospital de la Santa Caridad, Seville, Spain

A series of works by Bartolomé Esteban Murillo adorn the baroque chapel of Seville's Hospital de la Santa Caridad. Known as the Mercy Paintings, they depict biblical scenes and were commissioned for the chapel in the 17th century by Miguel de Mañara, who supposedly inspired the Don Juan stories.

Planning You will find the chapel at Calle Temprado 3 in the historic Arenal district. www.seville.world-guides.com

## ❿ Hallgrim's Church, Reykjavik, Iceland

Completed in 1986, Hallgrim's Church is a national artistic statement. Architect Guojón Samúelsson designed its concrete tower to simulate basalt coastal formations. In an interior as pure as an ice palace, the Icelandic spirit finds expression in stained glass by Leifur Breidfjord and Einar Jonsson's Statue of Christ.

Planning On a clear day, take the elevator (for a fee) up the tower to survey the coast and city. www.exploreiceland.is, www.visitreykjavik.is

Opposite: The story is biblical, but the setting is unmistakably Venetian in Carpaccio's "The Calling of St. Matthew" in the Scuola di San Giorgio degli Schiavoni.

# Pang Mapha Coffin Caves

Caves and rock shelters in the mountains of northern Thailand house the coffins of a mysterious, long-departed people.

ASIA

Jagged limestone peaks rise high from paddy and farm fields in northwestern Thailand's Mae Hong Son province. Gouged deep into the hills in the Pang Mapha district, along the border with Myanmar (Burma) in the north of the province, are serpentine caves where an ancient unknown people left their dead. More than 60 burial sites are scattered throughout the area, containing coffins carved from giant teak logs, some as long as 30 feet (9 meters). Most of the coffins—some with ornately sculpted ends resembling, for instance, the head of a pig or cat—range in age from 1,200 to 2,100 years old. The terrain is open to adventurers with fit hearts, strong lungs, and no fear of cramped spaces. For a few dollars, you can hire a local guide with a high-beam flashlight. A steep hike and a few belly crawls will lead to dark, dusty caverns littered in rotting wood, human teeth, and bones. In the caves, all is silence. Local hill-tribe villagers believe that the spirits of the dead, known as Phi Maen, live in the rock shelters, and some village elders say they remember the olden days, when the soft, whispery voices of the Phi Maen are said to have been heard in echoes throughout these mountains.

**When to Go** Northern Thailand is at its best during the dry season, November–February. Christmas is pleasantly cool; from March, the temperature heats up and the air grows smoky as farmers burn their fields.

**How to Find It** Many visitors rent a jeep or motorcycle in Chiang Mai and drive the 128 miles (206 km) to the cave region of Pang Mapha (also known as Soppong) using the mountainous loop road through Mae Hong Son. Buses travel this route, though the five-hour drive can be treacherous in the rainy season.

**Planning** Cave Lodge offers food and basic accommodation just a short walk from the area's largest cave system, Tham Lod, where local guides take tourists through the caverns in wooden boats. Ban Rai village, 4 miles (6.4 km) west of Pang Mapha off Highway 1095, offers treks to a rock shelter housing coffins.

**Websites** www.cavelodge.com, www.littleeden-guesthouse.com, www.gt-rider.com, highland.trf.or.th

## Local Delicacies

■ The ethnic **Shans** and hill-tribe farmers have distinctive cuisines. Don't miss the minced meatballs with Shan spices at **Little Eden Guesthouse** in Pang Mapha. **Cave Lodge,** near Tham Lod, offers a Shan dinner with fresh vegetables and spicy tomato and soybean dip.

■ Check out the markets for seasonal produce and explore the villages for noodle shops and colorful varieties of rice.

■ Each tribe holds its own **New Year festivities** (usually between December and March), often with all-night dancing and feasting. Many villages welcome visitors.

The remnants of a coffin, hollowed out of teak and said to be more than 1,000 years old, perch at a cave entrance high on a Thai mountainside.

At festivals in spring and fall, Bhutanese monks wearing animal masks dance and beat their drums to ward off evil.

BHUTAN

# DRAMETSI MONASTERY

Fluttering prayer flags, dancing monks, and an ancient monastery encapsulate the Buddhist spirituality of Himalayan Bhutan.

With golden roofs glistening atop a steep hill, Drametsi—one of the most remote monasteries in eastern Bhutan—seems suspended between heaven and earth. From the bottom of the valley, it takes more than an hour to drive the 12 miles (19 kilometers) of rough, narrow road that climb the steep slopes to reach the *gompa* (fortified monastery buildings). Every bend reveals another view of the Gamri River, with mountains and valleys as far as the eye can see. At 6,890 feet (2,100 meters), you reach Drametsi hamlet, fragrant with chilies and lemongrass, and the gompa, garlanded in prayer flags among tall cypress trees. The monastery was built in the 16th century by a descendant of the Buddhist saint, Pema Lingpa. Inside its temple, incense drifts around banners and paintings, while butter lamps flicker in dark corners. The giant prayer wheel tinkles, and the chanting of monks echoes around the walls. Drametsi owes much of its fame to the sacred drum dance, said to have been revealed in a vision to the son of Pema Lingpa. Today, at festival time, monks perform the dance in a frenzy of yellow skirts and animal masks, pouncing and twirling on the flagstones as they beat their drums with curved sticks to keep evil at bay.

**When to Go** The climate is best for hiking in March through May and September through November.

**How to Find It** Drametsi Monastery is near Tashigang in eastern Bhutan; the international airport is at Paro in the west. Druk Air is the only airline flying to Bhutan (2 hours 40 minutes from Delhi, India).

**Planning** Independent travel is not permitted in Bhutan, and any trip must be pre-arranged by a government-approved agency. Travel is very slow through mountainous terrain and high passes. The visit could be made in three days on a personalized tour from Paro, but it is more usually accomplished as part of a two-week trip, visiting other sights en route, with an operator such as Blue Poppy.

**Websites** www.bluepoppybhutan.com, www.kingdomofbhutan.com, www.bhutan.gov.bt

## Holy Cave

Also in eastern Bhutan, the **Gom Kora** temple lies among golden paddy fields next to a cave where Guru Rinpoche (one of the founding fathers of Buddhism) is said to have subdued a demon snake. The cave is tucked under a huge rock, and locals say that anyone who can run up to the top of the rock will reach paradise. Goats wander the temple steps, while boy monks sit on the grass for lessons, and pilgrims try to crawl through a tight passageway where your sins are said to be revealed if you fail to make it through. Once a year, there is a night-long "romantic festival," when pilgrims are allowed to court the sweetheart of their dreams.

ASIA

The corridors of Rameshwaram temple hold more than 4,000 pillars, each 12 ft (3.7 m) high.

INDIA

# Rameshwaram

On the southern Tamil Nadu coast, visit an island temple commemorating epic deeds from the Hindu scriptures.

Standing on an island off India's southeastern tip, Rameshwaram—the temple of Lord Ramanatha, or Rama—is one of the country's most important Hindu pilgrimage sites, second only to the holy city of Varanasi in the north. The 12th-century temple is where the *Ramayana,* one of Hinduism's sacred epics, is said to come alive for pilgrims, who in times past would walk the 620 miles (1,000 kilometers) from Varanasi to Rameshwaram. Here, you are on the spot where Rama—an avatar (manifestation in visible form) of the deity Vishnu—is said to have paid homage to Lord Shiva and prayed for forgiveness for annihilating the Sri Lankan King Ravana, who had abducted Rama's wife, Sita. Rameshwaram was Rama's first stop in India after his victory over Ravana, and he wished to please Shiva by devising a symbol: The *linga,* or stylized phallus. Legend has it that one of the two lingas in the temple was crafted from golden sand by Sita so her husband could offer worship; the second was brought by Hanuman, the monkey god. A nine-story *gopura,* a spirelike structure decorated with carved figures, stands at the entrance to the temple, connected by a bridge to the colorful, mainland town of Rameshwaram.

**When to Go** From December through February, when temperatures are about 77-86°F (25-30°C).

**How to Find It** You can fly into Madurai, 106 miles (171 km) to the northwest, and rent a car. Trains connect Rameshwaram to Madurai (about a six-hour trip) and Chennai (about 18 hours).

**Planning** Rickshaws and local bus services in Rameshwaram are easy to use, while a network of state buses provides a good service to nearby places. For fun, you could try a ride in a pony carriage or tonga—although from another era, they are part of everyday life in Rameshwaram. Many languages are spoken in the region, but English is understood by most shopkeepers and rickshaw and bus drivers.

**Websites** www.incredibleindia.org, www.tamilnadutourism.org

### Legendary Locations

■ A 37-mile (60 km) drive north from Rameshwaram brings you to **Devipattinam.** Here at low tide you can see nine large stones, the Navapashanam, reputedly positioned by Rama to represent the nine sacred planets.

■ Beautiful **Dhanushkodi Beach,** 11 miles (18 km) southeast of Rameshwaram, is a perfect place to laze in the sun. A chain of reefs, sandbanks, and islets forms an almost unbroken land connection from here to Sri Lanka. It is said to be the remains of a bridge built by the monkey god Hanuman and his followers to enable Rama to cross to Sri Lanka.

ASIA

# JERUSALEM'S ETHIOPIAN CHURCH

The pink-pillared Ethiopian Church is unlike any of the
other sacred sights in the holy city of Jerusalem.

ASIA

Jerusalem overflows with high-profile religious sights, but the Ethiopian Orthodox Tewahedo Church, located in the Debra Gannet (Paradise Monastery) compound on Ethiopia Street, hardly qualifies as one of them. Removing your shoes and entering the building, you find yourself in a largely overlooked landmark. The pastel-colored arches and pillars add to the tranquillity of the side-street setting, while the building's circular layout, with the altar in the center, makes it unusual among churches anywhere in the world. Intricately patterned rugs are strewn around the floors, and murals depicting the Ethiopian Church's most prominent saints cover the walls. Closely associated with Egypt's Coptic Church, the Ethiopian Church has maintained an uninterrupted presence in the holy city of Jerusalem since the conversion of Ethiopia to Christianity in the 4th century A.D. For generations, the Ethiopians contented themselves with a modest monastery built on the roof of the Church of the Holy Sepulchre, but in 1888, Debra Gannet was constructed in the growing neighborhoods lying outside the Old City walls. In keeping with a tradition of remaining separate from their host cultures, Debra Gannet's resident monks and nuns are rarely sighted on the city's streets and do not learn Hebrew or Arabic, speaking among themselves only in Amharic.

**When to Go** The monks hold two-hour services twice daily, starting at 6 a.m. and 4 p.m.

**How to Find It** Ethiopia Street runs north from HaNevi'im in the center of downtown Jerusalem.

**Planning** The visiting hours can change at short notice. If you cannot get to one of the morning or evening services, you may have to make repeated attempts at being admitted. Admission is free, but donations are encouraged.

**Websites** www.gojerusalem.com, www.ethiopianorthodox.org

## Street Life

■ Walking along **Ethiopia Street,** you'll see several houses built in the 1880s that, at various times, have been rented out to prominent intellectuals, including woodcut artist Jacob Pins and trailblazing Hebrew linguist Eliezer Ben-Yehuda.

■ Nearby **HaNevi'im** runs from Davidka Square to the walls of the Old City at the Damascus Gate. It traverses the ultra-Orthodox Jewish enclave known as Geula and winds through the Bikur Cholim medical complex and the contemporary alternative arts hotbed that is Musrara.

Unlike most Western churches, the Ethiopian Church has no nave, just a wide corridor encircling the central altar.

JORDAN

# PETRA'S HIGH PLACE OF SACRIFICE

A steep route winds up the cliff face above Petra to a sacrificial altar as close to the sky as the Nabataeans could build it.

Often, even at the world's most popular historic sites, only a little effort is needed to leave the rest of the tourist crowds behind. In Petra, the broad main route through the ancient Nabataean city leads down from the famous Treasury frontage past the colossal walls of the so-called Palace of the Pharaoh's Daughter. But instead of continuing on, duck into a narrow path that turns off just before the amphitheater. Climbing and doubling back parallel to the colonnaded main street, the path winds past still-occupied caves and into the increasingly narrow Wadi Farasa (Butterfly Valley), carved with more facades and dotted with tumbledown temples. Finally, you zigzag your way up more than 800 steps carved out of the cliff face. From standing beneath the city's towering facades, you climb gradually to look them in the eye and then to peer down on them from above. These high vantage points reveal just how well hidden the buildings are—and that more of the same lies concealed in neighboring valleys. The High Place of Sacrifice is a rocky hilltop leveled to a flat, open space. A sunken court provides seating around a rock-hewn altar with a bowl and groove hollowed out for draining away sacrificial blood. You will likely share the panoramic views with only a few other people, all equally awed into silence by the location.

**When to Go** Summers are furnace-like and winters very cold, so spring and fall are the best times to visit. Tour groups spend merely a day at Petra, but there are weeks of possible exploration in hidden valleys, both here and at nearby Little Petra (Al Beidha), a ten-minute drive to the north.

**How to Find It** Petra (Wadi Musa) is a three-hour drive south from Amman by car or taxi on the Desert Highway and is best seen in at least two visits.

**Planning** If you stay in the comfortable Crowne Plaza, a short walk from the main Petra gate, you will be well-placed to enter the site ahead of the crowds. Tickets for Petra go on sale at 7 a.m., but if you purchase in advance, you can enter an hour earlier. That way, your initial walk down the broad sweep of gravel of the Bab al-Siq, or gateway to the gorge, is likely to be made unaccompanied by other tourists. Later on, the Siq is lined with men offering rides on horseback and in horse-drawn carriages to throngs of visitors.

**Websites** www.visitjordan.com, www.nabataea.net/highp.html

## Petra by Candlelight

Three nights a week, you can experience Petra by candlelight. At 8:30 p.m., a crowd sets off down the slender 3,937-ft-long (1,200 m) entrance canyon, the Siq, which is illuminated by candles shielded from the wind with orange paper.

Hang back from the rest of the group, and you will be able to pass through almost alone. Around you, the combination of candlelight and shafts of moonlight from the slit of sky overhead seem to make the Siq's walls even pinker than in the daytime. The hushed voices and footsteps of the crowd a few bends ahead add a cathedral-like quality to the lofty space.

Outside the Treasury, Bedouin musicians produce haunting melodies on reeds, flutes, and bowed strings, while the facade itself has a movie-star moment, caught in a storm of flashes from the assembled throng. Enjoy the scene, then return the way you came, ahead of the crowd.

Opposite: The remains of an altar crown the High Place of Sacrifice. Above: The 2,000-year-old city of Petra

# HIDDEN VALLEYS OF CAPPADOCIA

Deep in central Turkey, a rugged volcanic landscape
conceals exquisitely frescoed churches hewn out of rock.

ead southeast from Cappadocia's tourist triangle of Üçhisar, Göreme, and Ürgüp, and you reach the isolated upper and lower valleys of Soğanlı with a village of the same name. Set on the side of a tabletop mountain, the village is largely untouched by tourism, with just one pension and a couple of seasonal restaurants. To get to the valleys—the Yukarı (Upper) Valley to the north and the Aşağı (Lower) one to the south—you first pass through lush apple orchards. These give way to rugged terrain, where, between the ninth and 13th centuries, churches were hewn from the rock and decorated with frescoes. In the Yukarı valley, the Kubbeli Kilise (Domed Church) is a two-story structure whose dome was carved from a natural spire of rock, exploiting the volcanic formation to mimic a cupola. The Meryem Ana Kilisesi (Church of the Virgin) has four frescoed chapels, while the Yılanlı Kilise (Snake Church) has an 11th-century fresco of St. George. In the Aşağı valley, the Geyikli Kilise (Deer Church) has a refectory in which you can see the seats and table where the clergy took their meals. Deeper into the valley, the Tahtali Kilise (Church of St. Barbara) has Soğanlı's best-preserved frescoes with scenes from the lives of the saints.

**When to Go** The best seasons to visit are spring and fall, particularly September, when the apple trees bear their fruit. Snowfall in winter often blocks access.

**How to Find It** Soğanlı is 25 miles (40 km) southeast of Ürgüp, but there is no public transport to the village. There are taxis and car rental agencies in Ürgüp, which is served by daily buses from Istanbul (11 hours), or you can take a flight or train from Istanbul to Kayseri, a 90-minute drive from Ürgüp.

**Planning** Allow at least two hours to explore the valleys. Be sure to buy water and snacks before entering the park. Soğanlı's one pension, Emek Pansiyon, is close to the entrance to the valleys. Nearby, Cappadocia Restaurant (open from April through October) serves basic meals in an apple orchard.

**Websites** www.cappadociaonline.com/soganli.html, www.turkeytravelplanner.com, www.kulturgov.tr, www.argeus.com.tr, www.kirkit.com

### Underground Metropolis

For centuries, villagers in Cappadocia made their homes in the tabletop mountains of the region, carving veritable cities on multiple levels within the rock itself. **Mazı,** a 25-minute drive from Soğanlı, is home to one such settlement dating from the Roman period. Take along a flashlight and look for the caretaker at the kiosk next to the entrance; for a small donation, he will guide you through the living quarters, storage areas, wine presses, and streets of this ancient underground city.

Inside, the Yılanlı Kilise (Snake Church) is decorated with snake patterns and frescoes of saints.

The walls and ceilings in Stavropoleos Church are covered with richly colored frescoes.

ROMANIA

# STAVROPOLEOS CHURCH

An 18th-century gem of a church is once again the serene heart of a monastic and choral community.

A diminutive Byzantine throwback, Stavropoleos Church is a precious survivor in Bucharest's Lipscani quarter. Before World War II, this part of the Romanian capital was its commercial center. Today, having been battered by wartime Allied bombing, several earthquakes, and dictator Nicolae Ceauşescu's efforts at "systematization," Lipscani is run-down but still atmospheric. Nowhere is this more true than in the tiny, incense-laden parish church, built in 1724. Here, Romania's troubled history seems to fade away as you trace details of icons depicting scenes from the life of Christ and the sculpted, two-headed eagle of the Byzantine Empire. There are few finer showcases for Romanian Orthodoxy, Ottoman-era Bucharest, or the Brâncoveanu architectural style. Taking its name from Constantin Brâncoveanu, ruler of Wallachia in current-day southern Romania from 1689 to 1714, the style is a glorious fusion of Byzantine and late Renaissance architectural elements with Romanian folk art and lavish stone carving using plant motifs. Originally, the complex around the church contained a monastery and inn. The church, cloisters, and garden survive, and since 2008 the complex has once again been home to a nunnery.

**When to Go** May, June, and September are the best months to visit. In winter, the temperature can fall below freezing. Romanians can be seen at their most devout at midnight Mass on the Saturday of Orthodox Easter.

**How to Find It** The church is located on Strada Stavropoleos, near the southern end of Calea Victoriei and behind the National Museum of Romanian History one block south from Strada Lipscani.

**Planning** Bucharest has no tourist office, but hotel receptionists and taxi drivers are often useful sources of information. Take a dog alarm, available from many pet shops, as strays are a menace in the city.

**Websites** www.stavropoleos.ro, www.romaniatourism.com, www.inyourpocket.com

## Unexpected Pleasures

■ Founded in 1994, after the collapse of communism, the **Stavropoleos Byzantine Choir** performs in Stavropoleos Church and throughout the world, with many albums to its name. To experience the mystical chanting, visit during a service—if you can find space. The choir showcases "psaltic" music, developed in Romania in the 19th century and inspired by Byzantine chants.

■ Restoration of the historic **Lipscani** district is on hold following the discovery of archaeological remains. This old quarter of the city has become a curious mixture of boho-chic pavement cafés, secondhand stores, and artisan workshops that amply repays exploration on foot. Half a day spent here would not be too long.

EUROPE

# QUIET CLOISTERS

Built as tranquil settings for reflection, the earliest cloisters consisted of
a quadrangle of sheltered passages on the south side of a church or abbey.

### ❶ St. Peter Claver, Cartagena, Colombia

The unusual, intimate cloister of the Church of St. Peter Claver is set in a calm, palm-shaded corner just over the wall from Cartagena's old town streets. During the early 17th century, Father Peter Claver, a Jesuit priest, baptized thousands of slaves shipped from Africa to the New World.

Planning The adjacent museum sheds light on the slave trade. www.cartagenainfo.net/saintpeterclaver

### ❷ Church of the Friars Minor, Dubrovnik, Croatia

Slender, paired pillars frame fragrant orange trees in the cloister garden of Dubrovnik's Franciscan church and monastery, built close to the city wall in the 14th century. While relishing the cloister's serene beauty, you can also admire remnants of Romanesque frescoes under the arcades. The friars' pharmacy, still open, is the oldest working apothecary in Europe.

Planning In the adjoining museum and library, discover medieval apothecary tools, rare literary and musical manuscripts, and artworks. www.dubrovnik-guide.net

### ❸ Allerheiligen, Schaffhausen, Switzerland

In the town of Schaffhausen, 32 miles (52 km) north of Zurich, the 12th-century Allerheiligen (All Saints) cloister garden is planted with aromatic and medicinal herbs. During the Middle Ages, honored clergy and other notables were buried here.

Planning The garden forms part of the Muzeum zu Allerheiligen. On May 1, Schaffhausen's wine cellars open their doors, inviting visitors to sample local pinot noir wines. www.schaffhauserland.ch

### ❹ San Marco Monastery, Florence, Italy

Climb to the upper floor of the cloisters in this 15th-century monastery, now a national museum. Here, each of the monks' cells contains a fresco by Fra Angelico or one of his followers. The friar's luminous work also decorates walls, lunettes, and medallions throughout the building. Watch for Fra Angelico's "Annunciation" at the top of the stairs to the cells.

Planning To avoid a long wait standing in line, book tickets to Florence museums in advance. www.florence-tickets.com

### ❺ Santa Maria la Nuova, Monreale, Italy

Monreale, which overlooks Palermo on Sicily's north coast, has what may be the best-preserved cloisters in Italy, adjacent to the Cathedral of Santa Maria la Nuova. They are all that remain of a late 12th-century monastery. Each of the 228 paired columns (some with mosaic inlays) supports ornately carved capitals.

Planning Monreale is 5 miles (8 km) southwest of Palermo. Step out onto the terrace of the cathedral garden for a sweeping vista of Palermo and the Tyrrhenian Sea. www.bestofsicily.com/monreale.htm

### ❻ Abbaye Saint-Pierre, Moissac, France

For centuries, the Abbey of Saint-Pierre in southwest France has provided a refreshing pause for those on the pilgrimage route to Santiago de Compostela in Spain. In the cloister, which dates from 1100, the carved capitals are the oldest and most numerous of their kind in the world. Each is based on a biblical story, with marvelous intertwined patterns of beasts and vines.

Planning Moissac is 43 miles (69 km) north of Toulouse. After the simplicity of the cloister, step inside the cathedral for a jolt of color. www.moissac.fr

### ❼ The Abbey, Iona, Scotland

Much of the abbey on this windswept island off Scotland's west coast dates from medieval times, but the carvings in the cloisters are contemporary. Completed in 1997, they depict, among other subjects, flowers from the Bible and from Scotland, birds of the West Highlands, and the parables of Jesus.

Planning Take a ferry from Fionnphort on the island of Mull. The cloister is a 15-minute walk from the harbor. www.isle-of-iona.com/abbey.htm

### ❽ Gloucester Cathedral, England

You can see some of Europe's earliest and finest examples of elaborate, continuous fan-vaulting in the cathedral cloisters, where light ripples across the delicate, arched tracery. A row of carrels, or desks, where the writing monks would have worked encloses a quiet garden. Scenes from some of the Harry Potter films were set in this 14th-century cloister.

Planning The cathedral also contains the tomb of King Edward II. www.gloucestercathedral.org.uk

### ❾ Convento de Cristo, Tomar, Portugal

The Convent of the Order of Christ opens four of its eight cloisters to visitors. The Cloister of the Cemetery is decorated with 16th-century blue tiles, or *azulejos,* while the Cloister of João (John) III is festooned with elaborate flourishes.

Planning Tomar is 85 miles (137 km) north of Lisbon and is also the site of Portugal's only remaining medieval synagogue. www.igespar.pt/monuments/15

### ❿ Santo Domingo de Silos, Spain

In the Royal Abbey of Santo Domingo de Silos in northern Spain, the Romanesque two-story cloisters have exquisitely carved capitals topping elegant double columns. This is still a working Benedictine monastery, whose monks are famous for their Gregorian chant.

Planning The abbey is about 43 miles (69 km) south of Burgos. Visit in early evening for the light and to hear Gregorian chant at Vespers. www.spain.info

Opposite: Historians believe that fan-vaulting like this was invented by architects and masons working at Gloucester Cathedral in the 1350s.

Towers built in the 15th century guard the Romanesque Church of St. Peter and St. Paul on Reichenau Island.

GERMANY

# Reichenau Island Churches

Wall paintings from the tenth century are testimony to
Reichenau's heyday as a center for art and learning.

In the times of Charlemagne and his successors as rulers of the Carolingian Empire, the Benedictine Abbey of Reichenau—founded in A.D. 724 on an island in Lake Constance in southern Germany—was one of the most influential in Europe. Its abbots were advisers and tutors to emperors and kings, and its school, scriptorium, and artists' workshops enjoyed a fame that stretched far beyond the shores of the lake. Reportedly, there were more than 20 churches and oratories on Reichenau Island, which measures barely 2 square miles (5 square kilometers). Visiting the island today, you will find just three churches, but they offer treasures enough. In the village of Oberzell, admire murals in the Church of St. George that date from before 1000—the earliest wall paintings north of the Alps to have survived almost intact. In Niederzell, the 12th-century Church of St. Peter and St. Paul was redecorated in rococo style in the late 18th century, but medieval wall paintings have been uncovered in the apse. The Abbey Church of St. Mary and St. Marcus in Mittelzell dates from the ninth century. In its treasury, there is a pitcher said to have been used at the marriage feast at Cana, where Jesus is supposed to have turned water into wine.

**When to Go** The churches are open to visitors year-round, though times vary. Try to catch one of the three main religious festivals: St. Markus (April), the Holy Blood (around Pentecost), and the Assumption (August). They are celebrated with movingly beautiful processions and ceremonies.

**How to Find It** Reichenau is 7 miles (11 km) northwest of the city of Constance (Konstanz), off the B33. It is connected to the mainland by a causeway and bridge. Take the No. 7372 bus or a ferry from Constance.

**Planning** You can get around by bike or on foot. Don't miss the view from the island's *Hochwart*, or wine trail, and do sample the Roter-Gutedel, a rare local grape variety.

**Websites** www.schloesser-magazin.de, www.reichenau.de

### Around Lake Constance

Three countries meet in the waters of Lake Constance–Switzerland, Germany, and Austria–providing a rich cultural mix.

■ The Swiss town of **Stein am Rhein,** on the lake's western side, has a beautiful old center of alleyways, elaborately painted facades, and quirky little shops.

■ The pilgrimage church of **Birnau,** on the lake's eastern, German shore, is built in the style of Italian baroque churches. Look out for the organ in a resplendent rococo setting.

EUROPE

# CHAPELLE EXPIATOIRE

Experience the austere, haunting beauty of a Parisian chapel dedicated to Louis XVI and his queen.

An architectural jewel of late neoclassical French architecture, the Chapelle Expiatoire in Square Louis XVI is shielded by trees from the busy Boulevard Haussmann. The name Expiatoire signifies atonement or acts of penance. Architect Pierre Fontaine designed the building in 1816 as a monument to Louis XVI and his wife, Marie-Antoinette. The king and queen were guillotined in 1793, and until 1816 their remains were buried at this site—a cemetery at the time, where some 3,000 other victims of the Revolution were also interred in a separate pit. The chapel, laid out in the form of a Greek cross, was built after the couple's bones had been transferred to the French royal mausoleum in St.-Denis in northern Paris. The light entry hall leads toward an interior courtyard, lined with rosebushes and gravestones. The chapel is reached by a stairway of 12 steps to a domed space, graced by white marble statues of the king and queen. Louis is portrayed on his knees, leaning on an angel to guide him heavenward, while Marie-Antoinette—whose crown has tumbled to the ground—kneels at the feet of a figure representing Religion. The crypt below has a simple altar to mark the spot where the royal couple's remains were said to have been found and disinterred. With its classical dignity and its location above a revolutionary mass grave, this square has been called the "saddest place in Paris."

**When to Go**  Year-round, although greenery around the chapel softens its sober lines in spring.

**How to Find It**  The chapel is in Paris's 8th arrondissement. The closest Métro stop is St.-Augustin.

**Planning**  Chamber music concerts are held in the chapel throughout the year. Each year, ardent royalists hold a Mass in the chapel to commemorate the anniversary of Louis XVI's execution on January 21, 1793.

**Websites**  www.chapelle-expiatoire.monuments-nationaux.fr, www.paris-walking-tours.com

## Swiss Defenders and Roses

■ Two rows of tombs with pointed roofs flank the chapel. They commemorate hundreds of **Swiss Guards,** who were killed by a revolutionary mob while defending the **Tuileries Palace** in 1792. The tombs used to have inscriptions, but these were effaced during the Communard uprising of 1871 and have never been replaced.

■ Pause in the chapel's enclosed courtyard, where roses bloom in spring—just as they did in Marie-Antoinette's gardens at the **Petit Trianon** in Versailles.

Sculptor Jean-Pierre Cortot created the statue of Marie-Antoinette being supported by Religion.

ENGLAND

# CITY OF LONDON CHURCHES

Packed in among the City's high-rises are some 50 churches, each an architectural gem and quiet place of retreat.

EUROPE

London's traditional financial center has always been rich and industrious. To get a feeling of the human scale of this area's past—when lanes were cobbled and business was conducted in coffee shops—visit its churches. The names alone evoke the district's history: All Hallows by the Tower, which overlooks the Tower of London; St. Andrew-by-the-Wardrobe, whose precursor was near the storehouse that housed Edward III's Royal Wardrobe; and St. Boltolph without Bishopsgate, which stood outside the old city walls. There are about 50 churches in the City's square mile, most built, or rebuilt, by Sir Christopher Wren after the Fire of London in 1666. Wren's style was light and airy, the windows plain, the pews set out as in a salon. If you are after pomp, visit his masterpiece, St. Paul's Cathedral, but for a more intimate interior, go to St. Stephen Walbrook, which now has an altar of Roman travertine, sculpted by Henry Moore in 1972, beneath its dome. Many of the City's churches have connections with its craftsmen and guilds: St. Sepulchre-without-Newgate watches over musicians; St. Bride's in Fleet Street is the parish church of printers and journalists, with a museum and a section of Roman pavement in the crypt. Some of the churches from before Wren's day have also survived. The oldest is St. Bartholomew the Great in West Smithfield, founded in 1123 and with a grand Norman nave that has starred in several movies, including *Four Weddings and a Funeral*.

**When to Go**  The City churches are usually open during the day. Many hold regular free concerts, often at lunchtime. Dr. Johnson's House is open Monday through Saturday, 11 a.m.–5 p.m. (until 5:30 p.m. in summer); there is an entrance fee.

**How to Find It**  Take the Underground to St. Paul's station, or bus 4, 11, 15, 23, or 26, or a taxi. Information on the churches is available at the tourist information center in St. Paul's Churchyard, and this is a good place to start your tour. The City's square mile is easy to walk around.

**Planning**  Some churches, such as St. Mary-le-Bow in Cheapside, have cafés in their crypts. When visiting Dr. Johnson's House, be sure to call in at Ye Olde Cheshire Cheese pub on Fleet Street, where the city's famous men of letters once drank.

**Websites**  www.london-city-churches.org.uk, www.drjohnsonshouse.org

### Man of Words

What febrile times there must have been in **Dr. Johnson's House** (on Gough Square, one block north of Fleet Street). Once inside, look at the front door, which used to be secured against clamoring creditors by a vast chain hooked on a twisted spindle, and the barbed window above the door to prevent thieves putting in small children to undo the bolts.

Upstairs, the magnificent withdrawing room has a stained-glass window depicting the house's owner, Dr. Samuel Johnson, compiler of the first reliable English dictionary (published in 1755) and responsible for the saying, "When a man is tired of London, he is tired of life."

The front door at Gough Square was always open to friends—and sometimes strangers, too—and despite Dr. Johnson's occasional cantankerousness, it is the genial conversation that still echoes in this most hospitable of old London homes.

Opposite: Henry Moore's altar is a modern addition to St. Stephen Walbrook. Above: St. Bartholomew the Great

# LA PEÑA DE FRANCIA

The crowning glory of Salamanca's Sierrade
Francia is a monastery built by a French monk.

Perched 5,653 feet (1,723 meters) above sea level on the western edge of central Spain, the Dominican monastery of Nuestra Señora de la Peña de Francia is the world's highest sanctuary dedicated to the Virgin Mary. The peak—the highest point in the province of Salamanca's Sierra de Francia—has been a place of religious significance since the megalithic era, and as you stand there, at the center of the 360-degree view over the surrounding countryside and into the neighboring province of Cáceres, you can see why. Today's monastery was founded in 1437 after a French monk, Simon Vela, discovered a woodcarving of the Virgin Mary hidden in the shale and quartzite rocks of the fortress-like pinnacle that crowns the summit. History, religion, and sublime scenery come together in these mountains. The Sierra de Francia and the Río de Francia that drains the range owe their names to French settlers who lived here during the Middle Ages. Stepping into the 15th-century church built by Simon Vela, you may want to light a devotional candle. If you really wish to absorb the atmosphere, spend a night in the Hospedería, an original 15th-century structure restored in 1956.

**When to Go**  From mid-September through mid-November and from April through June to avoid extreme temperatures. The monastery is open daily from 9 a.m. to 9 p.m (until 6 p.m. in winter).

**How to Find It**  The nearest town is La Alberca, 56 miles (90 km) southwest of Salamanca. There are two buses a day between Salamanca and La Alberca on weekdays, and one each way on weekends (journey time: 90 minutes). If you go by car, you can drive up the recently paved road to the monastery (10.4 miles/17 km).

**Planning**  As well as the Hospedería del Santuario Peña de Francia on the summit, you can stay at the rustic but charming Hotel Antiguas Eras in La Alberca. If walking up from La Alberca, purchase a GR-10 map in Salamanca and bring good walking shoes, sunglasses, water, and binoculars.

**Website**  www.spain.info

### Along the Way

The best way to appreciate the surrounding countryside and panoramic views from the top of La Peña de Francia is by hiking there from the small town of **La Alberca.** The climb forms part of the GR-10, one of Spain's network of **Senderos de Gran Recorrido,** or long-distance hiking trails.

Winding through pine and oak forest for 5 miles (8 km), the ascent from La Alberca—at an altitude of 3,438 ft (1,048 m)—is steep and takes about three hours, whereas the descent, after a leisurely lunch at the Hospedería, can be managed in two.

Nuestra Señora de la Peña de Francia caps the mountain's lonely summit in the sierra of Salamanca province.

A tree-shaded square makes a perfect setting for one of the concerts during Fez's nine-day festival.

MOROCCO

# WORLD SACRED MUSIC FESTIVAL

Once a year the narrow streets and open spaces of old Fez echo to the sounds of spiritual music from a multitude of cultures.

Morocco's spiritual and cultural nerve center, site of one of the world's oldest universities, and one of the world's oldest continuously inhabited cities, Fez makes an ideal setting for a sacred music festival. In late May and early June every year, the World Sacred Music Festival fills the city with performers and music lovers, bringing together Islam, Judaism, Hinduism, Taoism, Christianity, West African animism, Caribbean syncretism, and many other spiritual movements from around the globe. In the old city, or medina, known as Fez el Bali, venues include the Andalusian gardens of Dar Batha Museum, the outdoor auditorium at the Bab Boujloud entrance gate, and the palace at Bab Makina. All these ring out with folk music, Gregorian chant, works from the European classical tradition, and sacred songs from countries as far-ranging as Finland and Vietnam. From England's The Sixteen ensemble and Jordi Savall's Hespérion XXI from Catalonia to Sufi whirling dervishes from Turkey, musical and spiritual tastes meet here in a moving spirit of brotherhood and ecumenical respect.

**When to Go**  The festival usually runs from late May through early June.

**How to Find It**  The journey from Casablanca takes 30 minutes by air, 4.5 hours by train, and 5.5 hours by bus. To visit Meknes, a one-hour drive west of Fez, you can take the bus, train, or a *grand taxi* (agree on a rate beforehand). There are car rental agencies in Fez, but vehicles are not allowed to enter the old city.

**Planning**  Book somewhere to stay well in advance of the festival. The 5-star Sofitel Palais Jamai Fes is well located overlooking the medina, or for local ambience choose a small *riad* (guesthouse) centered around a cool, tiled courtyard. Many have a roof terrace and are hidden behind high walls off one of the medina's alleyways. Concert tickets are available online. Good walking shoes are a must for exploring Fez el Bali, and light clothing is recommended.

**Websites**  www.visitmorocco.com, www.fesfestival.com, www.fez-riads.com

### Imperial City

The city of **Meknes,** 37 miles (60 km) west of Fez, occupies a pivotal position between the Rif and Middle Atlas mountains, the Sahara, and the Atlantic. It owes its importance to the Moroccan ruler **Moulay Ismail,** who made it his capital and fortified it in 1673, building 25 miles (40 km) of walls around the medina. Here he kept 500 concubines, 60,000 slaves, and 12,000 horses. Today, the city's **Bab Mansour** is still one of the most beautiful gates in North Africa. The **suq** (market) and **Bou Inania Medersa** (school) are hauntingly lovely, and the **Royal Granaries** bear witness to the grandeur of Moulay Ismail's imperial city.

# HIDDEN
# TREASURES

The world of travel is now so well charted that serendipitous discoveries can seem hard to find. But the destinations on these pages prove that surprises still lie in wait for those who seek them out. In the quiet backstreets of old cities as well as remote rural locations, doors open into vanished ways of life and hitherto private places. Under the blazing skies of the New Mexico desert, the studio of painter Georgia O'Keeffe reveals the workings of a spectacular location upon that artist's mind. In the leafier landscape of New York State's Adirondack Mountains, the luxurious hideaway of a late 19th-century millionaire provides entertaining insight into a world of rich socialites at play. For those who not only want to see how the other half lives but also to sample these pleasures for themselves, a splendid array of Europe's stately homes and castles open their doors and rent out their beds. Farther east, other formerly locked gates slip open, welcoming the curious into the secret retreats of India's merchant princes or the fortress of 17th-century samurai warriors in Japan.

Superb Portuguese colonial buildings painted in vibrant colors—such as the 17th-century Palace of the Governors (left)—are among the treasures you will discover in the old city of Olinda in northeastern Brazil.

# GILLETTE CASTLE

Enjoy the whimsy of actor William Gillette's mock medieval
castle standing on a high bluff overlooking the Connecticut River.

NORTH
AMERICA

Built by an actor-playwright famous during his lifetime for his stage portrayals of
Sherlock Holmes, Gillette Castle was almost bound to be somewhat fantastical.
The rough-hewn stone fortress, surrounded by 184 acres (74 hectares) of woodland,
was completed in 1919 near East Haddam, Connecticut. Here, William Gillette lived after
his semiretirement from the stage, personally shaping the quirky interior of the home
with the help of local craftsmen. Not surprisingly, the style is theatrical, with hand-
carved woodwork of white oak, massive fieldstone fireplaces, stained-glass windows,
and 47 one-of-a-kind doors. Curious features include cunning door latches, handmade
light switches, and secret passages. Strategically placed mirrors allowed Gillette to
view unsuspecting guests trying to open his cleverly locked bar, and a hidden staircase
allowed him to move unseen around his castle. The view of the Connecticut River from
the south terrace is spectacular, and there are hiking trails through the woods and along
the granite ridge beside the river. Some of the trails follow the route of Gillette's 3-mile
(4.8 kilometer) narrow-gauge railroad, whose miniature train could carry 28 passengers.
The former station still stands, and the electric engine is being restored.

**When to Go** Gillette Castle is open for tours from Memorial Day weekend at the end of May through
Columbus Day (October 12). Goodspeed Musicals offers performances at the Goodspeed Opera House
during this time, but be certain to reserve tickets well ahead as performances usually sell out early.

**How to Find It** East Haddam is about 34 miles (55 km) by road southeast of Hartford, Connecticut.

**Planning** The most romantic way to arrive is with the Essex Steam Train and Riverboat. A steam locomotive
pulling restored cars takes you as far as Deep River Station, where you board a riverboat for the trip up the
Connecticut River to East Haddam. From East Haddam, it's a half-mile (0.8 km) hike uphill to Gillette Castle.

**Websites** www.ct.gov, www.goodspeed.org, www.essexsteamtrain.com

## On the River Front

■ East Haddam's **Goodspeed
Opera House** is a Victorian
gem operated by Goodspeed
Musicals. Originally built in 1877,
William Goodspeed's building
on the Connecticut River
once housed his mercantile
business as well as his theater.
Goodspeed Musicals restored
and reopened it as a theater
in 1963. They present three
musicals each year.

■ Another local highlight is a
ride on the historic **Chester-
Hadlyme car and passenger
ferry** across the Connecticut
River. It gives excellent views
of Gillette Castle perched on its
bluff and the Goodspeed Opera
House on the rivertront.

After Gillette's death in 1937, the castle and its grounds passed to the state of Connecticut and now form Gillette Castle State Park.

Astonishingly lifelike medieval carvings include these beautiful busts of two young women.

NEW YORK

# The Cloisters

Setting and exhibits blend perfectly in an exquisite museum dedicated to the serene beauties of medieval art.

### The Hunt of the Unicorn

The museum's **seven tapestries** known as "The Hunt of the Unicorn" depict in exquisite detail a group of men pursuing a unicorn through a dense forest teeming with wildlife. They find the mythical animal and seem to kill it, but the last panel shows the unicorn alive, encircled by a fence, in a field of flowers.

What does it all mean? No one knows for certain. The two main theories assert that the unicorn's capture symbolizes either Christ's crucifixion and resurrection or a bridegroom's entrapment within marriage. The identity of the artist remains unknown, as does that of the person or persons to whom the tapestries were given. The letters "A" and "E" woven into the scenery in several places only add to the mystery.

NORTH AMERICA

Perched at the top of Fort Tryon Park, overlooking the Hudson River, The Cloisters is just 10 miles (16 kilometers) north of downtown Manhattan but a world away in spirit. The museum—a branch of the Metropolitan Museum of Art—is composed of cloisters reassembled from monastic sites in France. It is also the only U.S. museum dedicated to the art of the European Middle Ages. Wander in and out of the cloisters, galleries, and reconstructed chapels, and relish an atmosphere of contemplative serenity as you take a close-up look at the art that flourished between the 4th and 16th centuries, including paintings, sculptures, metalwork, and ivories. Highlights include 16th-century Flemish unicorn tapestries, brilliantly hued 14th-century stained-glass windows from Austria, and the Bonnefont Cloister Garden, with plants grown and used in medieval times. Traditionally, cloisters provided monks and nuns with a place for rest and meditation; the same can be true for visitors today, as they enjoy the art or recline against the cloister columns and sip coffee in the Trie Café. It adds up to a delightfully unstuffy experience, whether you spend your time scouring the galleries or ensconced in one of the gardens with a good book.

**When to Go**  The museum is open Tuesday through Sunday. It is closed on Mondays, New Year's Day, Thanksgiving, and Christmas.

**How to Find It**  The Cloisters is a ten-minute walk from the 190th Street subway station. Heading north by car along Henry Hudson Parkway, take the first exit after the George Washington Bridge.

**Planning**  Fort Tryon Park is also worth exploring. Designed by Frederick Law Olmsted Jr., son of the codesigner of Central Park, it has lush foliage, impressive rock formations, winding pathways, and inspiring views of the Hudson River.

**Website**  www.metmuseum.org/cloisters

# ODD MUSEUMS

From medieval sorcery in Iceland to forensics in Bangkok, enjoy a sampling of some of the world's most oddly fascinating museums.

## ❶ Museum of Bad Art, Massachusetts

MOBA's curators search thrift stores and Dumpsters for art that transcends the merely incompetent in order to bring the "worst of art to the widest of audiences." The museum's main location—outside the men's room in the basement of a movie theater in Dedham, southwest of Boston—helps keep the collection in the obscurity it deserves.

Planning Entrance is free, but the museum playfully also offers "steep discounts" to students, seniors, and many others. www.museumofbadart.org

## ❷ Salt and Pepper Shaker Museum, Tennessee

Concentrated kitsch in the form of a mind-blowing display of more than 20,000 salt and pepper shakers crowds yard after yard of illuminated shelving in this museum in the mountain resort town of Gatlinburg. There is every shape from pandas to Easter Island *moai* and others that must be seen to be believed.

Planning The $3 admission fee earns an equivalent discount at the gift shop, enticing visitors to start competing collections. www.ludden.com/SandP

## ❸ Erimo Wind Museum, Hokkaido, Japan

Lying on the eastern side of northern Japan's Hokkaido island, Erimo is famous for its nearly perpetual windiness. The smart underground museum features music and light displays driven by windmills and, on rare calm days, a wind tunnel to produce a 56-mph (90 km/h) gale. You can also enjoy wind-free views down to seals basking in the sea below.

Planning Reaching remote Erimo from better-populated western Hokkaido requires a train and two buses. www.jnto.go.jp

## ❹ Beijing Taxation Museum, China

The magnificent 350-year-old Pudu Temple contains very early tax documents with heavy red seals and spidery calligraphy. Dusty old documents of surprising beauty sometimes carry commentary in the vermilion ink reserved for the emperor.

Planning The museum is reached by a pleasant winding walk through recently reconstructed traditional *hutong* (alleys). www.chinaheritagequarterly.org

## ❺ Songkran Niyomsane Museum, Thailand

Of six medical museums housed in Bangkok's Siriraj Hospital, the Songkran Niyomsane Forensic Medicine Museum is by far the most macabre. It offers such attractions as the corpse of a cannibal, the remains of accident victims, and the evidence gathered from murder scenes. Not for the squeamish.

Planning The Siriraj Hospital is on the west side of the Chao Phraya River. www.si.mahidol.ac.th

## ❻ Birdsville Working Museum, Australia

Tours of the clutter in this southwest Queensland museum are given by owner John Menzies, part fairground barker, part vaudeville act. He extracts entertainment from extraordinary material, such as explosive dingo bait and a cardboard record player used by missionaries for broadcasting Bible stories.

Planning Tiny Birdsville boasts a historic hotel with an excellent restaurant. www.diamantina.qld.gov.au, www.outbacknow.com.au

## ❼ National Museum, Nuuk, Greenland

Collections of Inuit and Norse items dating back 4,500 years show the resourcefulness needed to survive in a remote and unforgiving environment. There are displays of kayaks and dogsleds, of clothing and food, and on the harsh lives of the inhabitants both before and after European colonization.

Planning Nuuk, Greenland's capital, is most commonly reached on Arctic cruises or package tours from the Danish capital, Copenhagen. www.natmus.gl

## ❽ Museum of Sorcery and Witchcraft, Iceland

At Hólmavík, about 155 miles (250 km) north of Reykjavík, find out about the wildly inventive sorcery of medieval Iceland. Potions mixing human blood and the brains of ravens were thought to make you invisible. To become rich you needed enchantments that involved catching sea creatures with a net woven from virgins' hair. Or you could wear necropants—made by skinning a dead man from the waist down. Haunting.

Planning Icelandair's transatlantic links are economically priced and often include a stopover with free hotel accommodations in the capital, Reykjavík. www.galdrasyning.is

## ❾ Lumina Domestica, Bruges, Belgium

The exhibits in this museum of interior lighting fill an elegant 15th-century mansion in the picturesque city of Bruges. The collection contains more than 6,000 assorted devices telling the 400,000-year history of domestic illumination, from the crudest Neanderthal cave-lamp to the arrival of electric light.

Planning Also make time for Bruges museums devoted to chocolate, lace, and crossbows. www.brugge.be

## ❿ Museu de Carrosses Fúnebres, Spain

Barcelona's museum of funeral carriages is difficult to find but worth tracking down for its well-lit displays of ornate horse-drawn and motor hearses. Colors range from black to the less obvious white, reserved for children and virgins, all attended by life-sized costumed figures and horses in gloomy harness.

Planning The museum is free and lies at Carrer Sancho de Avila 2, near Metro stop Marina. www.barcelonaturisme.com

Opposite: Seasoning your food will never be the same after visiting the Salt and Pepper Shaker Museum in Gatlinburg, Tennessee.

# LowerEastSideTenementMuseum

A time capsule in what used to be one of New York's poorest
districts opens a window into the lives of newly arrived immigrants.

A single small building on Orchard Street in New York's Lower East Side was home to 7,000 people from 20 countries between 1863 and 1935. In all, 74 different immigrant groups left their mark on its tiny apartments, as on New York City as a whole. Choose the museum's hour-long Getting By tour to understand how two of these groups lived. It focuses on a German-Jewish family weathering the mid-19th-century financial crisis called the Panic of 1873 and an Italian-Catholic family battling through the hard times of the Depression in the 1920s and '30s. As the tour guide explains, showing a patch of wall that has been excavated to reveal successive layers of burlap wallpaper and varnish, "The building itself gives us information." Another tour delves into the story of the Irish Moore family. Like its former residents, the tenement has weathered the storm of time. The neighborhood, too, has emerged thriving. A hundred years ago, each 325-square-foot (30 square meter) apartment in the Orchard Street building rented for $7 per month; the same space might now cost upwards of $1,800 per month. This sticker shock has less to do with inflation than changes in the neighborhood in the past 20 years. Until as recently as the late 1980s, New Yorkers knew the area for drugs, gangs, and dusty shops. Now, art, fashion, food, and nightlife converge to make it one of the city's most buzzing quarters.

**When to Go** The absence of heating or air conditioning in the building makes fall and spring the best seasons to visit. The museum is open year-round except on Thanksgiving, Christmas, and New Year's Day.

**How to Find It** Entrance to the museum is through the Museum Shop at 108 Orchard Street.

**Planning** The museum offers a variety of different tours several times daily, running from mid-morning until 5 p.m. There is also a 90-minute walking tour of the neighborhood visiting different sites that were important to immigrants.

**Website** www.tenement.org

### Past and Present

■ Allow plenty of time to wander the neighborhood around the museum. This will give you a feel for how the past has informed and enriched the area's exciting present.

■ By day, explore the swanky clothing **boutiques** and minimalist **art galleries** that have taken the place of long-gone artisan shops.

■ At night, enjoy the trendy hotels, such as the super-cool **Blue Moon,** and restaurants that light the streets. For a taste of the old-time Lower East Side, stop off in **Katz's Delicatessen** on East Houston Street.

The tenement's apartments appear bright and clean now, but would have felt very different when hundreds were crammed into the same building.

Modern visitors relax outside the chalet where the Vanderbilts once entertained their guests.

NEW YORK

# Great Camp Sagamore

A millionaire's rustic lakeside retreat includes
a dining hall large enough to seat 80 people.

Deep in the slumbering forests of New York State's Adirondack Mountains, near the hamlet of Raquette Lake, the sight of Great Camp Sagamore greets you as it did guests staying there more than a century ago. Developer William West Durant built its centerpiece, a three-story Alpine chalet on the shores of Lake Sagamore, in the 1890s, before selling the estate to railroad heir Alfred Gwynne Vanderbilt in 1901. As with many of the camp's 27 buildings, the chalet's rustic Adirondack-style architecture complements the sylvan setting through the use of indigenous materials, including wood, bark, and stone. Wonder at the sprawling 80-seat dining hall, designed by Margaret Emerson Vanderbilt, Alfred's wife, to host guests for one year's Christmas dinner. Pop into the Playhouse, where billiards and roulette were the games of choice and guests competed on a two-lane wooden bowling alley. In the nearby forest, discover the Wigwam, a lodge covered in cedar bark, where the men enjoyed after-dinner drinks and cigars. Retrace your steps to the chalet to visit the adjacent boathouse, built in 1897, where you can borrow a canoe to paddle the shimmering waters of the lake.

**When to Go**  Overnight accommodations, including meals and guided public tours, are available from late May through mid-October.

**How to Find It**  The only way to reach Sagamore is by car—there is no public transportation. The nearest airports with car rental facilities are at Syracuse and Albany.

**Planning**  Two-hour tours are offered twice daily in summer and on weekends in spring and fall—you need to reserve in advance. Insect repellent, a head net, and bug-proof clothing are recommended if visiting during black fly season, from mid-May through late June.

**Websites**  www.greatcampsagamore.org, www.adirondackexperience.com

## Lakeshore Retreats

■ Board the *W.W. Durant* to tour **Raquette Lake.** As the 60-ft (18 m) vessel cruises the lake, listen to the captain's tales of local history and the lives of the great captains of finance and industry, including J.P. Morgan, Collis Huntington, and the Carnegie family, who owned the secluded great camps that peek through pine thickets along the lake's shore.

■ Visit the **Adirondack Museum** in **Blue Mountain Lake.** Here, exhibits of classic twig and bark furniture, private railroad cars, photographs, and Adirondack guide boats and canoes tell the story of the Adirondacks' Gilded Age, when more than 100 great camps dotted the region. Explore the museum's 20 buildings that interpret 200 years of Adirondack history, including its industry, outdoor recreation, transportation, and community life.

NORTH AMERICA

KENTUCKY

# PLEASANT HILL

Sample the pared-down simplicity of life in a Shaker community, set amid Kentucky's Bluegrass Region.

The guide breaks the stillness as she moves—or, rather, twirls, as she stomps her feet, claps her hands, and raises her voice in song—to the center of the Meeting House, built in 1820. She is re-creating Shaker worship, which was enlivened by song and dance, some of which included movements symbolic of shaking sin out of the body through the fingertips. Many people associate the Shakers almost exclusively with their furniture, but a visit to the Shaker Village of Pleasant Hill in Harrodsburg, Kentucky, deepens your understanding of these people, their faith, their commitment to communal living, their industriousness, their progressive history, and their vow of celibacy. At its height, the community at Pleasant Hill, which existed from 1808 to 1910, was home to nearly 500 "brothers and sisters" living and working in more than 260 buildings. Today, 34 of those structures still stand amid 3,000 acres (1,214 hectares) of rolling countryside bordered by stone fences. The simple elegance seen in Shaker chairs and boxes also found expression in their architecture, from the straw-colored clapboard buildings where craftspeople using 19th-century techniques now make Shaker brooms to the stately, brick Trustees' Office. The latter, with its awe-inducing, three-story, cantilevered double-spiral staircases, welcomed visitors from the "world."

**When to Go**  Year-round, but the silence of an off-season stay makes it that much easier to imagine life as the Shakers knew it. The daily schedule of guided tours, talks, and performances is fuller in summer, and fall color is spectacular. Special events include the Blessing of the Hounds in November.

**How to Find It**  Pleasant Hill is less than 30 miles (48 km) from Lexington.

**Planning**  While day passes are available, try to stay at least one night in the village. Accommodations are in buildings such as the former "family dwellings," where men and women lived on the same floor but across the hall from each other. Brothers and sisters would enter through different doors and continue upstairs using separate staircases. Meals prepared with vegetables and herbs harvested from the village's historic farm garden are available in the Trustees' Office Dining Room. The 40 miles (64 km) of nature trails are a good place for walking off those slices of Shaker lemon pie.

**Websites**  www.shakervillageky.org, www.kentuckytourism.com

NORTH AMERICA

### The Shakers

Formally known as the United Society of Believers in Christ's Second Appearing, the Shakers believed that God was both male and female, and that Ann Lee or **Mother Ann** was the female expression—the second coming—of Christ. Mother Ann was an Englishwoman from the city of Manchester who emigrated to America in the 1770s, founding a community, or "gathering," at Niskayuna, near Albany, New York.

The Shakers had a strong belief in equality, which, after they established communities in the South in the first decade of the 19th century, they extended to African Americans. From 1811, they welcomed African Americans into their gatherings—a radical stance at a time when African Americans were kept as slaves throughout this part of the United States.

The Shakers at Pleasant Hill reached their peak in the 1820s with 491 members. The community went into marked decline in the decades after the Civil War and finally ceased religious activities in 1910. The last of the Pleasant Hill Shakers, Sister **Mary Settles,** died in 1923.

Opposite: Lamps light the way to one of the houses now offering accommodations. Above: Women's bonnets

Biltmore's architect, Richard Morris Hunt, drew inspiration from the 16th-century châteaus of France's Loire Valley.

NORTH CAROLINA

# BILTMORE HOUSE

The Vanderbilts' château-style mansion is well known, but specialty tours open up some of the house's normally hidden treasures.

Built for George Washington Vanderbilt II at the height of the Gilded Age, Biltmore House is the largest privately owned home in North America and one of the most popular tourist attractions in the southeastern United States. What most visitors do not realize is that they are seeing barely 10 percent of this incredible mansion, which has more than 250 rooms. To visit the parts that few people get to see, take one of two little-known tours. The Behind-the-Scenes Tour reveals the inner world of the house, leading you along the narrow hallways of the servants' quarters and showing the remarkably advanced machinery that kept the house functioning. You will get a look at the Vanderbilts' private living and dressing rooms, as well as guest rooms of unrestored grandeur that have stood empty for decades. A second experience, known as the Rooftop Tour, also takes you through unrestored portions of the house but focuses chiefly on the upper floor. Here, staircases lead to hidden rooftop balconies that open to a world of splendid carvings. You will see dozens of gargoyles and statues, each with a different face, and enjoy a panoramic view of the estate and magnificent gardens from George Vanderbilt's private study.

**When to Go**  Summers in the Blue Ridge Mountains are mild, so anytime from April to late October is good for visiting. The most festive times are during spring bloom (May to mid-June) and fall colors (mid-October).

**How to Find It**  Biltmore is about 2.5 miles (4 km) south of the center of Asheville, North Carolina.

**Planning**  The small city of Asheville is well known for its lively arts scene and restaurants that pride themselves on serving local organic foods. The award-winning Biltmore Inn on the Biltmore Estate is an excellent choice for accommodations.

**Websites**  www.biltmore.com, www.exploreasheville.com, www.asheville-mountain-magic.com

## Model Estate

**George Vanderbilt** made his magnificent house—begun in 1889 and completed seven years later—the centerpiece of a working estate that was a model of efficiency.

Shying away from the busy social life of the east coast, Vanderbilt preferred occupations such as travel, art, and education. **Biltmore** was his greatest undertaking.

The estate encompassed 125,000 acres (50,586 ha) and included farming, cattle, and dairy industries that employed hundreds of local workers. Vanderbilt helped pioneer agricultural techniques that benefited farmers throughout the region, and he supported the development of the first forestry school, a forerunner of the National Forestry Service

Vanderbilt's wife, **Edith,** helped to establish craft schools that taught mountain women valuable skills so that they could earn income. The estate still belongs to George and Edith Vanderbilt's descendants.

# GEORGIA O'KEEFFE'S HOUSE

Visit the artist's Abiquiu home and studio along with the
stark landscape northwest of Santa Fe that inspired her art.

The sky, the stars, even the wind are different in northern New Mexico, the artist
Georgia O'Keeffe once noted. "The cliffs over there—you look … it's almost painted
for you, you think. Until you try." Today, O'Keeffe fans make pilgrimages to her 18th-
century adobe home and studio in Abiquiu, which still looks almost exactly as it did when
she moved out in 1984 due to ill health. It is sparsely furnished, its principal beauty being
the views it offers across the region O'Keeffe loved so much because it gave her the space
and freedom she needed. She first visited New Mexico in 1917 and later declared, "When I
got to New Mexico, that was mine." In the absence of the flowers that had inspired her back
east, O'Keeffe painted the animal bones and skulls scattered across the high country desert.
She often set out at 7 a.m. and returned at 5 p.m. after a day exploring on foot or painting
huge canvases in the backseat of her Model A Ford. For a number of years, she lived at
Ghost Ranch near Abiquiu. Then, in 1945, she bought the 5,000-square-foot (465 square
meter) house in the town. Visiting the district, you experience for yourself an extraordinary
landscape where the palette is dominated by parched vistas, red and yellow cliffs, and
cottonwoods growing along the Rio Chama Valley. Here, O'Keeffe created works that
transformed a seemingly austere landscape into art that is spare, yet grandly magnetic.

**When to Go**  Tours of O'Keeffe's Abiquiu home and studio are offered Tuesdays, Thursdays, and Fridays
from March through November, and also on Saturdays from June through October.

**How to Find It**  Abiquiu is about 60 miles (97 km) northwest of Santa Fe.

**Planning**  The hour-long tour is by reservation only. Consider lodging at the Abiquiu Inn, the starting point
for the tour, or at Ghost Ranch, where you can also camp. If you are planning to hike one of the trails
through O'Keeffe's treasured landscape, bring sturdy walking shoes, water, sunscreen, and a hat.

**Websites**  www.okeeffemuseum.org, www.abiquiuinn.com, www.ghostranch.org

NORTH
AMERICA

### Santa Fe's Museums

■ Before you head to Abiquiu
and its surroundings, visit the
**Georgia O'Keeffe Museum** in
**Santa Fe,** opened in 1997. The
museum's holdings now include
2,989 works of art, among
them 1,149 paintings, drawings,
sketches, sculptures, and
photographs by O'Keeffe.

■ Don't miss the museum's
**research center,** a block away.
Its beautiful gardens are
planted with flowers depicted in
O'Keeffe's paintings.

■ For an introduction to the
Native American cultures of
the southwest, visit Santa Fe's
fascinating **Museum of Indian
Arts & Culture.**

Desert light fills the rooms of O'Keeffe's Abiquiu home and plays on the shapes of her sculptures.

# HOUSES WHERE THE PAST COMES ALIVE

Experience life as it used to be in working farmhouses from New Mexico to the west of England, and in grand mansions from Denver, Colorado, to southern Scotland.

### ❶ Joseph Schneider Haus, Ontario, Canada

Restored to how it might have looked in the 1850s, this former farmhouse in Kitchener once belonged to Joseph Schneider, a German Mennonite pioneer, and his family. Interactive events range from "discovery days" for adults to curriculum-based education programs for schoolchildren.

Planning Kitchener has a large German community, making Oktoberfest a good time to visit. www.explorewaterlooregion.com

### ❷ The Norlands, Livermore, Maine

The Washburn-Norlands Living History Center encompasses five buildings belonging to the Washburn family, a 19th-century dynasty of politicians and industrialists. The working farmstead uses 19th-century methods. Tours include a visit to the library to meet with actors playing Washburn family members and a re-creation of an 1853 lesson in the schoolhouse.

Planning For intrepid time travelers, themed overnight packages are available. www.norlands.org

### ❸ Living History Farm, Bozeman, Montana

The farm's focal point is Tinsley House, a family home frozen in the year 1889, where guides in period costume interpret the life of Montana's Gallatin Valley settlers. Part of the Museum of the Rockies at Montana State University, the farm re-creates preindustrial rural pursuits with original tools, most of which were donated by Tinsley family descendants.

Planning The site is open Memorial Day through Labor Day, with various seasonal events. www.museumoftherockies.org

### ❹ Molly Brown House Museum, Denver, Colorado

*Titanic* survivor Molly Brown was a millionairess whose mining-engineer husband had uncovered a substantial gold deposit. Built in 1889, the house looks much as it would have in the early 20th century. There was more to Molly Brown's life than surviving the *Titanic.* The museum also pays tribute to her roles as philanthropist, antipoverty campaigner, and socialite.

Planning Open daily except Mondays. www.mollybrown.org

### ❺ El Rancho de las Golondrinas, New Mexico

Founded in 1710, the "Ranch of the Swallows" was the last staging post along the Camino Real, or Royal Road, from Mexico City to Santa Fe. Nowadays, it is a museum depicting rural life in Spanish colonial times. The 200-acre (81 hectare) site has many of the ranch's original buildings, where guides in period costume grind flour, bake bread, and forge horseshoes.

Planning The ranch is open for self-guided tours between June and September, Wednesday through Sunday. www.golondrinas.org

### ❻ Dennis Severs' House, London, England

In this house in London's East End, each room is a *tableau vivant* from bygone days, complete with the sound of ticking clocks and the smell of cloves and oranges. American-born artist Dennis Severs filled the house from cellar to garret with artifacts from the lives of an imaginary family of silk-weavers named Jervis.

Planning You are expected to be silent throughout the visit. Children are discouraged. www.dennissevershouse.co.uk

### ❼ Mr. Straw's House, Worksop, England

A 1930s time capsule, this modest suburban house in the English Midlands is one of the more unusual properties belonging to Britain's National Trust. Brothers William and Walter Straw inherited the house—built in 1905—from their father, a grocer. The frugal heirs kept it just as it was, buying no TV, telephone, nor radio. One of the lightbulbs, dating from 1932, still works because the abstemious brothers never used it.

Planning To visit, prior reservation is needed. www.nationaltrust.org.uk

### ❽ Acton Scott Historic Working Farm, England

Re-creating life on a Victorian upland farm, with shire horses, dairymaids, and blacksmiths at work, this living museum lies in some of western England's dreamiest countryside. The farm has been part of the Acton family estate since the 12th century. Courses and special events promote rural trades and crafts.

Planning Refurbished estate properties provide bed-and-breakfast or self-catering accommodations. www.actonscottmuseum.com

### ❾ Traquair House, Innerleithen, Scotland

Its earliest parts dating to 1107, this mansion, said to be Scotland's oldest inhabited castle, has belonged to the same family for more than 500 years. Attractions include a domestic brewery, a bed belonging to Mary, Queen of Scots, and a secret staircase used by Catholic priests in times of Protestant persecution.

Planning The house is open to the public daily from Easter to October, and on weekends in November. www.traquair.co.uk

### ❿ Llancaiach Fawr Manor, Wales

Be transported to 1645 and the British Civil War in this semi-fortified manor house in a valley in South Wales. In those days, the owner was Colonel Edward Pritchard, who switched sides from the King to the Roundheads. Costumed "servants" tell you about their work … and if you hear a sudden rustle of petticoats, that'll be Mattie—the ghost of a 19th-century housekeeper.

Planning The house is closed on Mondays between November and February. www.caerphilly.gov.uk/llancaiachfawr

Opposite: Follow the fortunes of the Jervis family in Dennis Severs' House as you move from room to room and through time from 1724 to 1914.

Four boys bound up the front stairs of a brightly painted house typical of the old city of Granada.

NICARAGUA

# Granada's Old City

Life still flows at a stately, leisurely pace
in the New World's third-oldest European city.

Each evening, the residents of Granada drag wicker rocking chairs onto the sidewalk to chat with their neighbors. Around them, bells peal from old Spanish steeples, the aroma of tobacco drifts from a cigar factory, and boys head home with fish they have hooked in the lake that forms the city's eastern edge. Founded in 1524, Granada is the third oldest European city in the New World. Artisans and architects were imported from around the Spanish Empire to create its churches, plazas, and palaces, while its merchants grew rich on trade between the Caribbean and Pacific. This golden age ended when Managua became Nicaragua's capital in 1852. Granada faded from the limelight, a hibernation that spared its buildings and customs. Among the city's architectural gems are the Casa de los Leones, an 18th-century mansion that now serves as a cultural center. Not far away is the Church and Convent of San Francisco. As in so many Hispanic towns, life revolves around the parks and plazas, notably the Parque Central with its shade trees and strolling vendors. Tourism has brought funky cafés and hotels, but not at the loss of any authenticity.

**When to Go**  Christmas and Santa Semana (Holy Week) bookend the best time to visit—the cooler dry season between December and May. The remainder of the year is hot and sticky.

**How to Find It**  Granada is an hour's drive south of Managua along the Pan American Highway. Shuttle buses run frequently between the capital's international airport and Granada; taxis are another option.

**Planning**  Granada flaunts more than a dozen good hotels. The old Alhambra could use a makeover but is still hard to beat for its Spanish colonial ambience, a location overlooking the Parque Central, and an eccentric swimming pool in the courtyard. For more modern digs, try La Bocona, a chic boutique hotel.

**Websites**  www.visitanicaragua.com, www.granada.com.ni, www.thehotelalhambra.com, www.hotellabocona.com

### Nicaraguan Baseball

It would be difficult to find a more dramatic setting for a baseball game than the **Roberto Clemente Stadium** in **Masaya**, about 20 minutes west of Granada. Home of the **Fieras del San Fernando,** the stadium perches on the edge of a steep cliff overlooking **Lake Masaya** and an active volcano on the opposite shore.

Since its introduction by U.S. Marines in 1912, **baseball** has grown into Nicaragua's national sport, and every large city has a professional team. What makes the Nicaraguan experience unique is not so much the game as what takes place off the field.

In Masaya, the San Fernando ball boy sprinkles bats, balls, and gloves with a magic powder that supposedly makes his team play better. A samba band pounds out a steady beat every time a local batter steps to the plate. Vendors with metal trays and plastic buckets balanced on their heads call out the names of various snacks—fried cheese sticks, meat pastries, salted orange slices, even shots of rum.

The San Fernando faithful seem to relish the food and music every bit as much as the game.

BRAZIL

# OLINDA

Once a bustling provincial capital, now an enchanted backwater, Olinda preserves Brazil's colonial past.

It could be the fictional town of Macondo in Gabriel García Márquez's great novel, *One Hundred Years of Solitude*. From Alto da Sé, a short, steep walk from Olinda's town center, you look out over a roofscape of terra-cotta tiles with the spires of baroque churches pointing heavenward, all framed by lush tropical foliage, with the turquoise waters of the Atlantic Ocean beyond. Once the capital of Brazil's northeastern state of Pernambuco, Olinda is undoubtedly the jewel in the country's colonial crown. It was founded by Portuguese colonists in 1537, and the spirit of its original settlers still clings to the winding, cobbled streets, lined by houses with latticed balconies and brightly painted stucco walls. Thanks to a resident artists' colony, Olinda today has numerous galleries and workshops to browse, showcasing regional artworks, including colorful terra-cotta figurines. A citywide restoration project is under way, but many of the historic buildings remain dilapidated, albeit displaying a shabby charm. Of the many churches on street corners and market squares, the Convento de São Francisco is probably the most interesting. Don't be put off by the peeling paint on the building's plain facade. Beyond it lies a gilded stucco interior and some of the most beautiful and intricate *azulejos* (painted Portuguese blue-and-white tiles) to be found in Brazil.

**When to Go** Weather in Olinda is hot and humid throughout the year. Carnival is a moveable feast, depending on the dates of Lent and Easter, so you need to check. The pre-Carnival celebrations in Olinda begin before those in Rio de Janeiro and Salvador.

**How to Find It** Olinda lies just 5 miles (8 km) north of Pernambuco's modern capital, Recife. Flights from Rio de Janeiro land in Recife, and from there it is easy to get to Olinda by bus or taxi.

**Planning** Aim to spend a couple of days in Olinda so you can wander around the town and explore some of the beaches to the north, such as Janga—those closer to town are polluted.

**Websites** www.recifeguide.com, www.virtourist.com

SOUTH AMERICA

### Carnival Madness

Olinda's pre-Lenten Carnival is wild. Unlike the more famous carnivals of Rio de Janeiro and Salvador, there is no sambadrome (an area set aside for samba parades), ticketed entry, or any other system of cordoning off zones. Instead, revelers—from the very young to the very old—throng the town.

Huge papier-mâché puppets, modeled after politicians and celebrities, are carried through the sinuous streets, accompanied by gyrating partygoers and the pounding rhythms of music. You won't sleep a wink, but it is the way that Carnival was meant to be.

Tropical exuberance blends with baroque splendor in a view of Olinda's Convento de São Francisco.

# SMALL MUSEUMS OF TOKYO

From bonsai trees to origami, Japan is known for tiny delights,
not the least of which are the small museums of Tokyo.

Down a narrow lane in eastern Tokyo's trendy Harajuku district, the Ukiyo-e Ota Memorial Museum of Art specializes in traditional wood-block prints—colorful posters created by Japan's finest graphic artists, starting in the early 17th century when the Tokugawa shoguns took power. Another small but fascinating collection in eastern Tokyo is the Mingeikan Museum, founded in 1936 by folk-art aficionado Yanagi Soetsu. While many of its 17,000 items are Japanese, the museum also showcases folk art from China, Korea, and elsewhere. The Ryogoku district is ground zero for everything sumo, including a Sumo Museum on the ground floor of the celebrated Kokugikan Stadium. In addition to displays on the origins and history of Japanese wrestling, the collection features old *banzuke* (ranking lists), ceremonial aprons, and black-and-white photos of sumo legends from the past century. The Kanto Earthquake Memorial Museum on the grounds of the Tokyo Memorial Temple is perhaps the world's only museum dedicated to a natural disaster. It commemorates the 1923 quake and subsequent fire that killed more than 58,000 people and destroyed more than 70 percent of Tokyo. Some idea of the fire's intensity can be gathered from the melted, twisted metal and glass artifacts recovered from the ruins and now on display.

**When to Go** Spring and fall are the best seasons to explore Tokyo. The summers are hot and humid, and winters can be very cold.

**How to Find It** Given Tokyo's vast size, it is best to browse the museums in a given neighborhood on the same day. Obtain a good map of the city's transportation system and plan accordingly.

**Planning** You might combine a visit to the Sumo Museum with tickets to a live match in the adjoining arena. If trying to crowd as many museums as possible into a single day, you should purchase a Tokyo Metro Open Ticket, which gives you a day of unlimited travel on the various subway lines.

**Websites** www.jnto.go.jp, www.ukiyoe-ota-muse.jp, www.sumo.or.jp, www.mingeikan.or.jp

## Japan's Pop Art

Wood-block prints were Japan's brash pop art, mass-produced images of famous people and places that ordinary citizens could hang on their rice-paper walls. The landscape masterpiece *Thirty-Six Views of Mount Fuji* by **Katsushika Hokusai** is the best-known print series today. But in bygone days, Kabuki actors and sumo wrestlers, street musicians and rowdy party scenes were popular subjects. The prints were called *ukiyo-e* because many depicted life in the Ukiyo ("floating worlds")—urban pleasure zones where Kabuki, sumo, geishas, and other traditions thrived.

Housed in a traditional wooden building, the Mingeikan Museum's collections include beautifully displayed kimonos and other robes.

Illuminated at night, the castle keep makes a spectacular centerpoint for Kumamoto city.

JAPAN

# KUMAMOTO SHOGUN CASTLE

A mighty fortress on Japan's southern island of
Kyushu comes close to engineering perfection.

There is a saying that not even a mouse could scale the walls of Kumamoto Castle. Commissioned by the powerful warlord Kato Kiyomasa, the fortress was completed in 1607 after nearly seven years of construction. It is considered one of Japan's outstanding examples of premodern architecture. The original walls rambled for nearly 8 miles (13 kilometers) across rolling terrain, with 49 turrets and 47 gates. Inside, the keep had walls topped by wooden overhangs that were virtually impossible for anyone, even the crafty *ninja,* specialists in unorthodox warfare, to climb. Kumamoto was not immune to treachery, however. During Japan's last civil war, the Satsuma Rebellion of 1877, the castle was torched by the renegade samurai Saigo Takamori. The only major part to survive was the Uto Yagura tower. The rest lay in ruins until the 1960s, when a meticulous reconstruction program began. The task continues as historians and architects resurrect the legendary bastion piece by piece. The Honmaru Goten Palace was opened in 2008 after years of renovation, and there is more to come. A museum displays examples of samurai weapons and armor, and a scale model of what Kumamoto Castle would originally have looked like.

**When to Go**  Located in the far south of Japan, Kumamoto has a subtropical climate, with balmy summers and relatively mild winters. The Kumamoto Castle Festival in October features demonstrations of samurai yabusame (archery on horseback), Noh drama, and concerts inside the walls.

**How to Find It**  The trip from Tokyo to Kumamoto city is around two hours by air or six hours by bullet train. The castle stands on a hill in the city center.

**Planning**  The nearby Kumamoto Castle Hotel offers stunning views of the castle. In addition to Western-style rooms, the hotel offers Japanese tatami rooms with futons and low wooden furniture. Kumamoto city is celebrated for its spring plant markets (February and March), in which bonsai trees are a special feature.

**Websites**  www.jnto.go.jp, www.hotel-castle.co.jp, www.visitkumamoto.com

### My Secret Journey

In his Tokyo studio, **Tetsuro Shimaguchi**—who choreographed many of the fight scenes for the Kill Bill movies—was giving one of his **Samurai Sword Action** workshops. During a two-hour session, I learned the four basic moves of samurai sword fighting as well as a choreographed series of moves. "Speed and timing are much more important than power in sword fighting," says Shimaguchi. "You need stamina because the sword and the armor are very heavy. Balance is also very important, as well as hand-to-eye coordination." I felt ready now to visit the samurai castle at Kumamoto in the south.
**Joe Yogerst**
**Travel writer**

ASIA

# CASTLES WITH ACCOMMODATIONS

Your home may be your castle, but how about enjoying the luxury of someone else's real-life castle, château, *schloss*, *castello*, or palace?

### ❶ Shiv Nivas Palace Hotel, Udaipur, India

Seventeen huge suites offer superb views over Udaipur, the city of lakes. The rooms feature antique furniture and portraits of generations of Udaipur's royal family. In the palace's Paantya restaurant, sit in splendor among the golden latticework and antique chandeliers that surround candlelit tables.

Planning Udaipur lies midway between Delhi and Mumbai—about 435 miles (700 km) from each. www.eternalmewar.in

### ❷ Schlosshotel Hirschhorn, Germany

Incomparable vistas of the Odenwald Mountains and Neckar River Valley set the stage for a leisurely breakfast on the terrace or candlelight dinner. The castle's Gothic architecture pays homage to its builders, the lords of Hirschhorn, who lived here for 400 years until 1632. Take a boat tour on the Neckar to Heidelberg, or stroll through the village of Hirschhorn.

Planning The hotel closes every year from mid-December to mid-February. www.schlosshotel-hirschhorn.de

### ❸ Schlosshotel Rosenau, Austria

Built in the late 16th century and refurbished with baroque magnificence in the 18th, the hotel seems ready-made for romance. A horse-drawn carriage takes bridal couples to the castle's chapel, where wedding bells ring out the happy occasion. Roses are strewn over a four-poster bed in a room filled with antiques and oriental carpets.

Planning The castle also houses the Freemasonry Museum, the only one in Austria. www.schlosshotels.co.at

### ❹ Castello di Ripa d'Orcia, Tuscany, Italy

The castle's central keep stands out against a backdrop of steep hills, with the forests and vineyards of the Orcia Valley spreading out below. The Pentini family have lived here for 400 years, and in enormous guest rooms with rafted ceilings you feel that you have stepped back to the Middle Ages. Stacks of books beckon you to a cozy library with a glowing fireplace.

Planning Florence is two-and-a-half hours away, and Rome is three hours. www.ripadorcia.it

### ❺ Château d'Hassonville, Ardennes, Belgium

Once a hunting lodge of the Sun King, Louis XIV, the château stands in a 136-acre (55 ha) park. Hike nature trails through the countryside and watch for peacocks parading the grounds. A superb gastronomical experience awaits in the restaurant, including wine from the château's Cellier de Bacchus.

Planning The château is set in Belgium's lovely Ardennes region near Aye. www.hassonville.be

### ❻ Château des Briottières, Loire Valley, France

Eighteenth-century period furniture, fresh flowers, and candles grace guest rooms decorated in shades of red, gold, and blue. Aperitifs are served in a pale green drawing room. The château, set in an English-style park, is child-friendly, offering children's games, Ping-Pong, badminton, tennis, and horseback riding.

Planning The château is close to Angers, a two-hour TGV (fast train) ride to Paris's Montparnasse Station. www.briottieres.com

### ❼ Swinton Park, North Yorkshire, England

Red leaf vines cover the home of the Cunliffe-Lister family. The 200-acre (80 ha) eco-friendly estate has won several green tourism awards, which you will appreciate if you visit the huge walled garden, where a plethora of vegetables are grown for the restaurant. Children gravitate toward a playroom full of toys, a birds of prey center, and a cooking course just for youngsters.

Planning The house is about 30 miles (50 km) from the historic cathedral city of York. www.swintonpark.com

### ❽ Dromoland Castle, County Clare, Ireland

Five-star luxury combines with more than 1,000 years of history in the neo-Gothic former home of the O'Brien family, descended from medieval High Kings of Ireland. Retreat to a spa cocoon of soft music, mood lighting, and fresh flowers; take a dip in the heated pool, or play a round on the championship golf course.

Planning The castle is 8 miles (13 km) from Shannon Airport and within easy reach of Limerick and Galway. www.dromoland.ie

### ❾ Parador de Jarandilla de la Vera, Spain

Chestnut and oak trees, terraced hillsides, and stone cottages surround the castle, tucked into the southern slopes of the Sierra de Gredos in central Spain. The *parador* (state-run hotel in a historic building) offers a place of respite where you can hike, play tennis, paddle a canoe, or hop on a mountain bike. The restaurant serves local dishes, such as partridge stew.

Planning The Emperor Charles V spent his last days in the nearby monastery of Yuste, after abdicating in 1556. www.paradores-spain.com

### ❿ Pousada Castelo de Óbidos, Leiria, Portugal

Battlemented walls encircle the village of Óbidos, and rising in its center is a near-perfect medieval castle keep. The *pousada*—a hotel housed in a historic monument—occupies the castle's 16th-century northern portion. Relax in rooms with stone walls and thick wood beams, explore village streets lined with white houses, or take walks or carriage rides into the countryside.

Planning Óbidos is just over 50 miles (80 km) north of the Portuguese capital, Lisbon. www.pousadas.pt

Opposite: The magnificence of the accommodations at Udaipur's Shiv Nivas Palace takes luxury into the stratosphere.

A blend of traditional Indian and European architectural styles is typical of the Chettiar mansions.

INDIA

# Chettiar Mansions

Tour the lavish rural *havelis* (mansions) built by members of a merchant caste in the south Indian state of Tamil Nadu.

Tamil Nadu is famous for its Dravidian temples, but if you are a lover of architecture, the *havelis* of the wealthy Nattukottai Chettiar community offer an intriguing alternative. Scattered throughout 75 villages around the city of Karaikudi in southern Tamil Nadu, these rambling houses mostly date from the late 19th and early 20th centuries. Their builders belonged to a merchant caste, the Nattukottai Chettiars, or Nagarathars, many of whom amassed large fortunes from their trading and banking interests across South and Southeast Asia. The mansions, entered through heavy wooden doors, were both family homes and business premises, which is why the Hindu goddess of wealth, Lakshmi, can be seen adorning the gateways to many of them. Inside, you find yourself in a warren of courtyards and areas of shade sheltering under roofs held up by teak or rosewood pillars. The fortunes of many Chettiar families have waned and several of these grand, privately owned houses now look careworn, but Raja's Palace in Kanadukathan, 5 miles (8 kilometers) from Karaikudi, is still magnificent. The building, completed in 1912, has 126 rooms and covers an area of 40,000 square feet (3,716 square meters).

**When to Go**  The temperate, post-monsoon months of January and February are best for travel in southern Tamil Nadu. Daytime temperatures vary from 70° to 90°F (21° to 32°C).

**How to Find It**  The closest domestic airport to Karaikudi is Madurai. Trains stop at Karaikudi between Chennai and Rameshwaram.

**Planning**  Prebooking is recommended if you want to stay in one of the district's boutique hotels, such as the Bangala or the Chettinadu Mansion, which also serve traditional Chettinad cuisine. Hire a taxi for the duration of your visit to ensure that you have transport to explore the region.

**Websites**  www.tamilnadutourism.org, www.tamilnadu-tourism.com, www.thebangala.com, www.deshadan.com

## Fiery Food

Chettinad food is among the fieriest in India. **Pepper** and **chilies** ensure that its aromatic, oil-rich dishes register as spicy, while **cinnamon, cardamom,** and **star aniseed** add deep flavor. Chettinad chicken and biryani are very popular. Lamb and seafood are also frequently used in the kitchens of the Chettiar mansions.

Members of the Nattukottai Chettiar business community took cooking implements with them when they traveled to make sure that they could enjoy food prepared the way they liked it. One such set of implements is displayed in the **Chettinad Museum** in Kanadukathan.

LITHUANIA

# TRAKAI CASTLE

Like a castle in a fairy tale, this former ducal palace
rises from an island in the middle of a Lithuanian lake.

EUROPE

Little known outside the Baltic states, the 14th-century Trakai Castle is one of Europe's most photogenic fortresses, its red-capped towers reflected in the lake that acts as a natural moat almost demanding that a Rapunzel come and let down her hair. Trakai, which lies 17 miles (27 kilometers) west of the Lithuanian capital, Vilnius, was the latter's medieval predecessor, while its castle was a heavily fortified palace and seat of royal authority in the once-powerful Grand Duchy of Lithuania. Topped with steep roofs of red tile, the redbrick superstructure creates an impression of elegance and domesticity, despite sitting atop broad expanses of forbidding gray stone—these brick upper portions, reconstructed in a 15th-century style, are the result of painstaking restoration work completed in the 1960s. Many of the exterior windows have a defensive squint, yet as you wander through the galleried interior the atmosphere is that of a grand country mansion. Having completed your tour, make your way back across the long, slender bridge to the lakeshore. There, one of your best views of the castle is from a sunset table at Apvalaus Stalo Klubas (The Round Table Club), as you enjoy, perhaps, roasted rabbit terrine with plums soaked in Armagnac, goose breast, and honey ice cream.

**When to Go** The weather is most comfortable between Easter and September, although lows below freezing point are common into April.

**How to Find It** Trains and buses run regularly between Vilnius and Trakai.

**Planning** Places to stay in Vilnius include several hotels in historic buildings, such as the Shakespeare Hotel in a former palace and the Stikliai Hotel in a merchant's residence, both dating from the 17th century. If you have time to spare, fly to Estonia's capital, Tallinn, then drive the 370 miles (595 km) south through the little-visited Estonian and Latvian countryside to Vilnius.

**Websites** www.tourism.lt, www.muziejai.lt, www.stikliaihotel.lt

## Capital Churches

The churches of **Vilnius** make up a memorable architectural collection. Here are two of them:

■ The 16th-century **St. Anne's Church** is a masterpiece of flamboyant, late Gothic architecture. Its pinnacled facade is made from 33 different kinds of brick set out in a dizzying arrangement of ribs, ridges, and three kinds of arch.

■ In the cupola-topped **St. Peter and St. Paul's Church,** the Jesuits created a building in which even the illiterate could read the lives of the saints. The magnificent baroque interior is covered in a riot of around 2,000 life-size, creamy stucco reliefs that would repay days of study.

Now a picture of tranquillity, Trakai Castle was once the hub of one of northern Europe's most powerful states.

HUNGARY

# Béla Bartók Memorial House

Pay homage to one of the 20th century's greatest classical composers in an attractive, leafy suburb of northwestern Budapest.

A pilgrimage to Béla Bartók's last house in Budapest, high up in the Buda hills, still gives a sense of the seclusion and quiet he sought here, far away from the hubbub and prying eyes of the central metropolis. Apart from being one of Hungary's best-loved composers, Bartók was, alongside his friend Zoltán Kodály, one of the founders of ethnomusicology, traveling throughout the Carpathian Mountains and beyond to document the origins of East European and Middle Eastern folk music—a powerful influence in his own compositions. The Memorial House reflects both passions, with exhibits ranging from his Edison phonograph and Bösendorfer piano to a magnificent folk-art collection gathered on research trips. Originally surrounded by forests and exquisite gardens, the three-story villa dates from 1924. Bartók lived and worked here from 1932 to 1940, composing in an upstairs workroom soundproofed with padded doors. Unhappy with fascism, he and his wife reluctantly left Hungary for the United States, where he died of leukemia in 1945. The Budapest house opened as a memorial museum in 1981, the centenary of Bartók's birth, and thanks to successive restorations it closely resembles how it looked in his lifetime. It also displays stamps and works of art inspired by the composer. Fittingly, the house is, as in Bartók's lifetime, an intimate venue for musical recitals, held in the concert room or in the garden.

**When to Go**  The mildest weather in Budapest is usually mid-April through early June and in September. The house is open daily except Monday. Concerts in the house are usually at 6 p.m. on weekdays and on some Saturdays and Sundays at 11 a.m.

**How to Find It**  The memorial house is at Csalán út 29. To reach it, take bus No. 21 from Moszkva tér, bus No. 5 from Pasaréti tér, or bus No. 29 from Szépvölgyi út.

**Planning**  The Budapest Card is a good deal for anyone spending more than a day in the city. It offers free public transport, free or discounted entry to many museums (including the Béla Bartók Memorial House), and discounts in restaurants and on tickets for tours and events. It is available for 48 or 72 hours. The Budapest Spring Festival showcases music by Hungarian and international artists. The town of Szombathely, 141 miles (227 km) west of Budapest by road, hosts a two-week Bartók Festival every July.

**Websites**  www.bartokmuseum.hu, www.budapestinfo.hu, www.hilton.com

### The Castle District

■ In lofty seclusion from Budapest's city center, the Castle District on the right bank of the **Danube** is a wonderfully atmospheric and tranquil place to visit. Sparsely populated compared with the rest of the city, it is a jumble of small houses and narrow alleys that also includes some grandeur, notably the **Royal Palace.**

■ Unusually, the **Hilton Hotel** in the Castle District is a tourist attraction in its own right, built over and around the ruins of a 13th-century Dominican monastery. The Hilton has marvelous views over the mock-Gothic **Fisherman's Bastion** to the Danube beyond.

■ The Castle district also packs in plenty of historic cafés. These include the fun-sized and old-fashioned **Ruszwurm,** running since 1827 in a medieval cubbyhole. It is famous for its cakes and desserts.

Opposite: A bronze statue of Bartók in the memorial house garden. Above: His workroom inside the house

# Castello di Miramare

Opulence and tragic memories make a haunting mix in a royal villa overlooking the azure waters of the Adriatic Sea in northeast Italy.

White crenellated halls and towers, set in a 54-acre (22 hectare) botanical park, rise from a promontory on the Adriatic coast, northwest of Trieste. Built in an eclectic style that blends Gothic, Renaissance, and oriental elements, the Castello di Miramare mirrors its location, close to the modern border of Italy and Slovenia and once part of the Austro-Hungarian Empire. Visiting the huge villa, you cannot escape the poignant story of its builders: Habsburg Archduke Ferdinand Maximilian and his wife, Princess Charlotte of Belgium. A naval theme runs through the royal pair's private rooms on the ground floor, reflecting the Archduke's career in the Austrian navy. Strolling through the gardens and greenhouses, you glimpse exotic plants, birds, and butterflies, reflecting the couple's plans to retire here and spend their remaining days collecting and studying plant and animal species. Unfortunately for them, this was not to be. Ferdinand Maximilian and Charlotte moved into Castello di Miramare on Christmas Eve 1860. Four years later, the Archduke was named Emperor of Mexico and found himself embarked on an ill-fated adventure that led to his death before a firing squad in 1867. His widow survived until 1927, suffering from mental illness and living as a recluse, partly at Miramare.

**When to Go** The villa and grounds are open daily year-round. It is best to avoid winter, which tends to be cold and wet and can be gusty when the Bora wind blows down from the mountains.

**How to Find It** Miramare is 4 miles (6.4 km) northwest of Trieste. From Piazza Oberdan in Trieste, take the 36 bus, which will deposit you at the villa gates.

**Planning** Allow yourself plenty of time to explore Trieste, a fascinating, cosmopolitan melting pot of a city, mingling Italian, Austrian, and Slavic influences. It is famous for its coffeehouses, including the Caffè Pasticceria Pirona, where James Joyce wrote parts of his modernist masterpiece, *Ulysses*.

**Websites** www.castello-miramare.it, www.turismofvg.it

### Emperor Maximilian

Ferdinand Maximilian (1832-67) was a younger brother of the Emperor Franz Josef. Regarded as a liberal, he was a reforming commander-in-chief of the Austrian navy and viceroy of Austria's realms in north Italy. Under pressure from France's Napoleon III, he accepted the throne of Mexico as Emperor Maximilian, arriving in the country in 1864. But the foreign presence was opposed by forces led by Benito Juárez, who later captured the emperor. Back in Europe, Maximilian's wife Charlotte lobbied unsuccessfully for support. Miramare's Throne Room, completed after Maximilian's execution, commemorates his short, tragic reign.

The design of the villa evokes the sumptuous summerhouses built by the Viennese nobility on the shores of southern Alpine lakes.

A statue of Apis, the Egyptian sacred bull, is just one among the museum's thousands of spectacular exhibits.

ITALY

# The Egyptian Museum

In northern Italy, one of the city of Turin's many surprises is the world's second largest collection of ancient Egyptian artifacts.

Entering the neoclassical building that houses Turin's Museo Egizio (Egyptian Museum), you are first struck by its imposing monumental exhibits, such as the reconstructed Temple of Ellesija. As you continue, you grow curious about the charmingly mundane, such as a makeup kit or a drawing of a dancer. From sculpture to weaving, farming to writing, all aspects of ancient Egyptian life are covered in thematically arranged displays. The clever use of spotlighting helps to re-create the darkness in which many of the treasures lay hidden for thousands of years. The arched ceilings, the lighting, and the realization that the bundle of linen in front of you contains the body of a woman called Merit combine to create the sensation of being teleported 6,000 years into the past. The collection—second in size only to the Museum of Cairo—contains more than 30,000 pieces, of which 6,500 are on display. In a city dominated by cutting-edge engineering, the museum is a reminder of human civilization's early millennia. After you marvel at basalt statues and alabaster vessels, a walk under Turin's renowned arcades takes on a new flavor.

**When to Go** The museum is open daily except Monday. Fall is the perfect time to explore the prestigious winemaking areas that surround Turin, such as Langhe—the home of Barolo and Barbaresco.

**How to Find It** The museum is on Via Accademia delle Scienze, about halfway between the Royal Palace and the elegant Piazza San Carlo.

**Planning** To do Turin justice allow for at least two full days. The city has a dynamic dining scene and fabulous wine bars. The CioccolaTÓ each March is a fair dedicated to chocolate. The biennial Salone del Gusto, organized by Slow Food, takes place in late October in even-numbered years.

**Websites** www.museoegizio.it, www.visitatorino.com, www.turismotorino.org, www.langhevini.it

## Mystical Turin

Grimacing gargoyles, Masonic symbols, and dark hovering angels embroider the historical center of Turin, which is steeped in legends of the esoteric and the occult. Even for ultrarational skeptics, the legends offer fascinating insights into Turin's history.

■ According to the city's mystical lore, **Piazza Castello** concentrates the positive energies of Turin, especially thanks to the square's closeness to the Shroud of Turin stored in the nearby cathedral.

■ Negative energies are said to radiate from the **Piazza Statuto,** built on top of an ancient Roman necropolis and above Turin's labyrinthine sewer system—the ill-reputed "Gate to Hell."

■ During the Renaissance, the Savoy royal family—who also started the collection that later became the Egyptian Museum—hired alchemists from around Europe to search for the elixir of youth and knowledge. The legends say that the **Grotte Alchemiche** (Cave of the Alchemists), which connects Palazzo Madama to Piazza Castello, hides the Philosopher's Stone.

EUROPE

MALTA

# CITTADELLA OF RABAT

A mighty 16th-century citadel forms a hidden city within a city on Malta's smaller sister island of Gozo.

EUROPE

Its massive walls hewn from blocks of local honey-colored limestone, the Cittadella (Citadel) stands high on a hill in central Gozo, keeping guard over the island's capital, Victoria—so-named in 1887 for the British queen's golden jubilee, but still known locally by its original name, Rabat. Knights of the Order of St. John built the great fortress in the 16th century, partly as a place where the island's inhabitants could find refuge against marauding pirates and corsairs. To reach it, wind your way up the hill through the skinny alleys and side streets that make up Victoria. When you reach the gates of the Cittadella, step through the huge stone entrance into a piazza dominated by the baroque Cathedral of the Assumption. Due to a lack of funds no dome was added when the church was built in 1697, but Italian artist Antonio Manuele was later commissioned to paint a detailed trompe l'oeil on the flat ceiling, creating the illusion of a resplendent interior dome. Elsewhere within the Cittadella, ancient stone houses shelter small museums with collections showcasing Gozo's archaeology, heritage, folklore, and natural history. As you meander along narrow passageways, the stones worn smooth by centuries of footfalls, you pass the old law courts and prison buildings. From the battlements, gaze out over the island. The sweeping view takes in a patchwork of villages with towering church domes and verdant fields, while beyond are glimpses of a rugged coastline with cliffs and aquamarine bays.

**When to Go** Year-round, although spring (April to June) generally has the most pleasant weather.

**How to Find It** Fly to Malta, then catch the ferry that links Cirkewwa in northern Malta with Mgarr on Gozo. The 25 bus runs between Mgarr Harbor and Victoria, its timetable synched with the ferry's scheduled arrival and departure.

**Planning** Allow at least two hours for a visit to the Cittadella, longer if you plan to tour all the museums. Entrance to the Cittadella is free, but a fee is charged for the museums. Purchase the all-inclusive Cittadella ticket for admission to the Old Prison, Gozo Museum of Archaeology, Natural Science Museum, and Folklore Museum.

**Websites** www.islandofgozo.org, www.visitmalta.com

**Market of Delights**

■ Victoria's main square is **Pjazza Indipendenza,** located outside the Cittadella. Here, **It-Tokk,** an open-air market, is a colorful kaleidoscope of cottons and silks, where bolts of fabric compete for your attention with thick woolen rugs and bulky knitted sweaters.

■ Elsewhere in the market, tables overflow with the local harvest of crimson-red plum tomatoes, deep purple eggplants, and sweet emerald-green peppers. Gozitan women quietly haggle with fish merchants over the price of *lampuki* (the local name for dorado), caught only hours earlier in the Mediterranean. Other vendors peddle sweet Gozo honey and *gbejniet,* a soft goat's milk cheese sold fresh, dried, or pickled.

■ Beyond the hubbub of the busy market square are shops selling traditional craft goods, while lacemakers continue an age-old tradition of weaving intricate designs by hand.

Opposite: The cathedral tower rises above the Cittadella's narrow alleyways. Above: The Cittadella on its hilltop

Sunlight strokes the step-gabled brickwork of one of the houses in the Kortrijk *begijnhof*.

BELGIUM

# Begijniiof of Kortrijk

Deep calm and tranquillity—this is what you still experience in a walled and gated medieval refuge for women.

C lose to the center of Kortrijk (Courtrai) in West Flanders, step through an archway to find a small, tree-shaded square lined by 17th-century, step-gabled houses and a whitewashed chapel. Beyond lies a loop of cobbled streets and a garden, with terraced cottages behind. This is a *begijnhof* (*béguinage* in French). The first *begijnhoven* were founded in the late 12th century as communities for single women as the Crusades had caused a gender imbalance. Many of the women were widows; others could not find a husband but did not like the alternatives of living with married relatives or entering a convent. So they became *begijnen* (*béguines*), taking simple vows of piety and obedience to a Mother Superior. At Kortrijk, they wore black habits with white headdresses, but they were not nuns: They were free to leave if, say, they wished to marry. They lived quiet, communal lives, carrying out good works. The Kortrijk begijnhof is one of the most beautiful, containing about 40 houses, once home to more than 130 begijnen. It includes a small museum in the former house of the Mother Superior, where the lives and work of the begijnen are explained.

**When to Go**  Like most of the begijnhoven of Flanders, the Kortrijk Begijnhof is open to the public daily from sunrise to sunset. Visitors are asked simply to respect the tranquillity of the location and the privacy of the residents. The museum is open 2–5 p.m. daily except Monday.

**How to Find It**  Kortrijk is in northwest Belgium, about 50 miles (80 km) from Brussels.

**Planning**  Sights in Kortrijk include a late Gothic Town Hall, interesting churches, the Broelmuseum of art, and a new and impressive museum called Kortrijk 1302, which commemorates the Battle of the Golden Spurs, a pivotal point in Flemish history. There are plenty of good restaurants and places to stay.

**Websites**  www.kortrijk.be, whc.unesco.org/en/list/855, www.visitflanders.com

## Four of the Best

Numerous begijnhoven were built across the Low Countries, virtually one in every town. Many survive and are now used for private or social housing.

■ In the Brussels suburb of **Anderlecht,** a tiny begijnhof dating from 1252 served just eight begijnen. The two brick cottages now house a museum evoking their lives, told through furniture, pictures, and artifacts.

■ Originally founded in 1244, the begijnhof of **Bruges** has white-painted 17th- and 18th-century houses surrounding a large, tree-shaded green. The ensemble contains a baroque chapel and small museum. Benedictine sisters now live here.

■ **Ghent's Klein Begijnhof** is now used for private housing, but you can still wander around its tranquil streets and the garden that surrounds the baroque church. Most of the houses are 17th-century, but the begijnhof was founded in 1235.

■ In **Diest,** an elaborate baroque gateway is the entrance to a large grid of 16th-century terraced cottages lining cobbled streets. Founded in 1253, it housed some 400 begijnen at its height in the 17th century.

EUROPE

# Château de Fontainebleau

Enjoy the secluded charms of a royal hunting retreat set deep in the heart of a game-rich forest southeast of Paris.

EUROPE

The Château de Fontainebleau started as a 12th-century hunting lodge where medieval kings of France could take a break from the cares of state. Over the centuries, successive rulers left their mark on the building, resulting in a jumble of architectural styles with something for every decorative taste. Stand in the symmetrical Oval Court at the heart of the château and relish the unusual juxtaposition of a 12th-century keep flanked by two Italianate Renaissance wings. In the Renaissance and baroque rooms, gilt opulence embellishes every surface. For a relatively sober style, take a look at Napoleon's private apartments, where he planned and plotted while his family was kept at arm's length from the public eye. To the south are grand gardens and ponds designed by Le Nôtre in the 17th century. To the north, the royal apartments overlook the romantic Garden of Diana (Roman goddess of hunters), where white peacocks roam. Nineteen springs serve the château and its gardens via a system designed by an Italian engineer during the reign of François I in the 16th century. Later that century, Henri IV added the 0.6-mile-long (1 kilometer) Grand Canal for water jousting. This ribbon of water leads the eye to the surrounding forest, nowadays crisscrossed with hiking trails but retaining its ageless sylvan beauty.

**When to Go** The château is open every day except Tuesdays, New Year's Day, May Day, and Christmas Day. The gardens are open every day.

**How to Find It** Trains run every 30 minutes from Paris Gare de Lyon—the journey takes 45 minutes. Buy a ticket that includes the 15-minute bus ride from Fontainebleau-Avon station to the château. Alternatively, get off in Melun and rent a car, allowing you to visit Barbizon and Milly-la-Forêt as well.

**Planning** Make sure to book one of the guided tours of the fascinating Musée Napoléon and Petits Appartements, including the emperor's library and his wife Joséphine's sitting room. These are accessible only as part of a small group tour and are well worth visiting, even if you don't understand the guide's French.

**Websites** www.uk.fontainebleau-tourisme.com, www.courances.net, www.parisbytrain.com

## Painters and Gardens

■ The village of **Barbizon**, 8 miles (13 km) northwest of Fontainebleau, was made famous by the Barbizon School of painters, including Camille Corot, Théodore Rousseau, and Jean François Millet. It makes a good base for a ramble through the Forest of Fontainebleau. If that tweaks your appetite, you'll be ready for lunch at **Le Troubadour** in Fontainebleau, just beside the château.

■ The charming town of Milly-la-Forêt, 12 miles (19 km) west of Fontainebleau, is home to the **Conservatory for Aromatic and Medicinal Plants.** Nearby are the beautifully serene gardens of the **Château de Courances.**

Louis XIII's Salon, like the rest of the palace rooms, is richly embellished with carved wooden paneling, marble, paintings and frescoes, and sumptuous furnishings.

# MUSEUM SECRETS

Every museum worth its salt has a secret. Here are some of them, including a "mouse house"
in Bangkok, an astrologer in Jodhpur, and missing masterpieces in Boston.

## ❶ Isabella Stewart Gardner Museum, Boston

In the early 20th century, wealthy Boston widow Isabella Stewart Gardner turned her mansion into a museum. In 1990, thieves stole $300 million worth of art from the museum. Gardner's will stipulates that the works on display can never be rearranged, so today 13 empty frames mark where the stolen artworks hung.

Planning Despite the missing works, the Gardner Museum has an excellent collection of European paintings. www.gardnermuseum.org

## ❷ The Metropolitan Museum of Art, New York

"Washington Crossing the Delaware" has become central to the cultural identity of the United States, but the painting in the Met is not the original. The first version, painted by German-American painter Emanuel Leutze (who worked in Düsseldorf), was damaged in a fire in Leutze's studio and he made a copy to be sent across the Atlantic. The original remained in Germany until it was destroyed during an Allied bombing raid in 1942.

Planning The Met is open daily, except Mondays. www.metmuseum.org

## ❸ The Jim Thompson House, Bangkok, Thailand

U.S. intelligence officer Jim Thompson arrived in Bangkok in the 1940s but left the intelligence services to work as a silk trader. For decades, he was the social center of the city's foreign community, and his house had a unique attraction to entertain the children of his guests: A 19th-century "mouse house." This glass-fronted mouse mansion was once home to dozens of mice running through their own mouse-sized rooms, hallways, and porches.

Planning The Jim Thompson House also has a superb collection of antique silks made in Southeast Asia. www.jimthompsonhouse.com

## ❹ City Palace, Jaipur, India

The maharajas of Jaipur have long been sponsors of local artists and artisans. Past patronage is documented throughout this palace and museum complex, and current evidence of it is found nearby. A warehouse-like space within the compound is a place for local artists to create, display, and sell their art.

Planning The City Palace has an extensive art collection and breathtaking architecture. www.rajasthantourism.gov.in

## ❺ Mehrangarh Fort, Jodhpur, India

This cliff-top fort, which never fell to invaders, may provide a glimpse into the future. Astrologer and palm-reader Mr. Sharma practices his trade daily in the fort's Moti Mahal Chowk, a reception hall. Astrology was an obsession of many Rajasthani rulers, so Mr. Sharma's presence in the fort recalls its history.

Planning To book a session with Mr. Sharma call the fort. www.mehrangarh.org

## ❻ Summer Palace, Tsarskoye Selo, Russia

The most opulent feature of the Russian tsars' Summer Palace is the Amber Room, covered in engraved amber panels. But the room you see today is a reconstruction, completed in 2003. During World War II, the Germans stole the original panels—a gift from the king of Prussia in 1716—which have not been seen since.

Planning The palace, dripping with gold leaf, mirrors, and marble, is just outside St. Petersburg. www.tzar.ru

## ❼ Prague Castle, Czech Republic

The so-called defenestration window does not offer a beautiful view but did play a role in European history. In 1617, Catholic officials closed down Protestant chapels in Prague, and two were punished by a group of Protestants by being thrown out of a palace window. Although they fell uninjured into a dung pile, the Defenestration of Prague signaled the start of the Thirty Years' War.

Planning Prague Castle offers many wonderful attractions. Spend at least half a day there. www.hrad.cz

## ❽ Vasari Corridor, Florence, Italy

This passage was built in 1564 to link the Uffizi Gallery (then administrative offices) to the Palazzo Pitti, home of Florence's ruling Medici family. Cutting through churches and across the tops of shops on the Ponte Vecchio, it provided a private and efficient way for the Medici to move through the city. It was the work of the artist, architect, and art historian Giorgio Vasari.

Planning Tourists can gain access to the corridor only by appointment and usually with a guided tour. www.polomuseale.firenze.it

## ❾ Stanza della Segnatura, Vatican

Several Renaissance artists received papal commissions to paint frescoes in the Vatican. Images of two are preserved in "The School of Athens" in the Stanza della Segnatura. Raphael painted himself staring out from the lower right-hand corner, while Michelangelo—who was working on the ceiling of the Sistine Chapel next door—is sketching intently in the foreground.

Planning Thousands of tourists visit the Vatican each day. Be there just when the museum opens at 9 a.m. to beat the crowds. mv.vatican.va

## ❿ Victoria & Albert Museum, London, England

Museum study rooms are typically open only to scholars, but the V&A's Prints and Drawings Study Room is open to everyone, and there is no need to book an appointment. Any visitor can see and even handle the museum's extraordinary collection of hundreds of thousands of photographs, prints, and drawings.

Planning The Study Room is located on the fourth floor of the Henry Cole Wing. www.vam.ac.uk

Opposite: The Jim Thompson House in Bangkok is filled with a collection of rare art, antiques and curiosities from southeast Asia.

# TOULOUSE-LAUTREC MUSEUM

A former bishop's palace in southwest France is the surprising setting for works by the chronicler of the Parisian demimonde.

The rooms are spacious and airy, their tall windows carefully shaded to ensure that the bright sunlight does not damage the drawings and paintings in one of France's most highly prized art collections. This is the Palais de la Berbie, a fortress-like former bishop's palace on the banks of the Tarn River in the ancient city of Albi. Gazing out over formal riverside gardens, you can easily imagine esoteric church matters being discussed in times gone by. Now, in contrast, the imposing building houses the lively works of France's much-loved painter of 19th-century Parisian bohemia. Henri de Toulouse-Lautrec was born not far away in the old quarter of Albi, and it was his mother, the Countess Adèle de Toulouse-Lautrec, who donated the collection—the entire contents of his studio—after his death in 1901, aged 36. You can admire a diverse and very personal collection of more than 1,000 drawings and paintings—from childhood sketches, through formal portraits, to the vibrant, colorful posters of the Moulin Rouge dancers, Jane Avril and Louise Weber (La Goulue, "the Glutton"), for which Toulouse-Lautrec is best known. The pictures evoke the risqué milieu of the Parisian clubs in Pigalle and Montmartre, the world of prostitutes and entertainers that held such a fascination for the eccentric provincial aristocrat. Another group of almost 40 pictures features circus performers.

**When to Go**  Spring, fall, and winter are the best times to visit, with fewer tourists.

**How to Find It**  Albi is 48 miles (77 km) northeast of Toulouse by road.

**Planning**  Albi has great food, and wines from the nearby Gaillac AOC are gaining acclaim: Light reds, rosés, and a semisweet, slightly sparkling wine called *perlé*. Le Vieil Alby, a tiny hotel at 25 rue Henri de Toulouse-Lautrec, also has a good restaurant; booking is essential.

**Websites**  www.albi-tourisme.fr, www.aveyron.com, www.musee-toulouse-lautrec.com

### Château du Bosc

Henri de Toulouse-Lautrec spent his childhood summer holidays at the Château du Bosc, at **Naucelle** between Albi and Rodez. The château is still owned by descendants of Henri's first cousin, Raoul, and is open to visitors year-round (by appointment in winter). Memorabilia include a boat Henri built while recovering from a fall at age 14 that left him partly disabled. Look out for the wall on which the heights of the children were recorded—at age 18, Henri was only a little over 4 ft 11 in (1.5 m) tall. The convalescence from his fall, and another down a gully, are thought to have encouraged him to develop the artistic talents that ran through the whole family.

Visitors to the museum in Albi admire Toulouse-Lautrec's famous posters advertising the Moulin Rouge cancan dancer, La Goulue.

Dappled sunlight catches "One and Other" (2000) by the Yorkshire-educated sculptor Anthony Gormley.

ENGLAND

# Yorkshire Sculpture Park

Art and nature stand side by side in this glorious 500-acre (200 hectare) open-air museum in the north of England.

Whether beneath huge brooding skies or on glorious summer days, when leaves glow golden in the fall or winter frosts glisten, no two visits to the Yorkshire Sculpture Park are ever the same. It is not just the foliage that changes, but the sculptures, too, their metal, stone, or wood acquiring different tones in the shifting light. Occupying the grounds of Bretton Hall, an 18th-century mansion, the park's grassland, woods, and central lake are the backdrop for sculptures by Henry Moore and Barbara Hepworth, both Yorkshire-born, as well as contemporary artists such as Andy Goldsworthy and Antony Gormley. Four indoor galleries include the new Underground Gallery. Some of the works on display are whimsical; others are heroic or dramatic; all are thought-provoking. Dawn can bring a particular treat. Although the park as a whole is closed at this hour, four times each year 20 or so visitors are accommodated inside the Skyspace, created by the U.S. artist James Turrell in a former deer shelter. Here, the unfolding dawn illuminates the space through an aperture in the roof with awe-inspiring effect.

**When to Go**  The galleries are open 10 a.m.–5 p.m. year-round. The park opens a little earlier. There are free tours at 2 p.m. on Saturdays and Sundays.

**How to Find It**  The Yorkshire Sculpture Park (YSP) is 1 mile (1.6 km) from Junction 38 of the M1, between Barnsley and Wakefield. Wakefield Westgate is the nearest main-line train station.

**Planning**  The restaurant on top of the Visitor Centre has fabulous views and excellent food. Sunrise in the Skyspace needs to be booked well in advance (check the website); it concludes with a full-scale breakfast. A shuttle bus runs the 1.2 miles (2 km) from one side of the park to the Longside Gallery at the other.

**Website**  www.ysp.co.uk

## Nature and Art

■ The park attracts a great variety of wildlife, from herons, which return each year to nest on islands in the lake, to voles in the woods. Storks have also been seen in the lake. Treecreepers, nuthatches, goldcrests, and woodpeckers inhabit the woods, and you may see hedgehogs or families of weasels gamboling in the grass. There are also foxes and badgers.

■ Lichen creates artful patterns on tree trunks, and in fall more than 50 kinds of fungi have been identified. Spring is the time to visit the **Camellia House** and see the collection of these dramatic flowers started by the former owners of the estate.

■ In nearby Wakefield, **Hepworth Wakefield** is a new gallery dedicated to Barbara Hepworth, born in the town in 1903. She met Castleford-born Henry Moore at art school in Leeds, where the **Henry Moore Institute** today has a series of temporary exhibitions.

# SCULPTURE PARKS AND TRAILS

In woodlands and jungles, along coastlines, and on mountaintops, parks
and trails have been created where you can enjoy nature and art together.

### ❶ DeCordova Sculpture Park, Massachusetts

More than 40 large-scale, colorful, contemporary sculptures are
distributed through a beautiful woodland setting with hiking
trails and picnic tables. Mainly by New England artists, the
sculptures are a mixture of commissioned pieces and works on
loan, and the selection changes from year to year.

Planning The park is 15 miles (24 km) west of Boston and includes an
art museum. Open year-round. www.decordova.org

### ❷ Stone Quarry Hill Art Park, New York

Four miles (6.4 km) of trails meander across 104 acres (42 ha)
of rolling hills, linking site-specific works by emerging and
established artists. Installed in woods and meadows and around
ponds, the sculptures are inspired by the relationship between
art and the environment.

Planning 25 miles (40 km) southeast of Syracuse. Open year-round.
www.stonequarryhillartpark.org

### ❸ Poustinia Land Art Park, Belize

The park is hidden in the Belize rain forest alongside ancient Maya
ruins. A day's hike along a grassy track through the jungle takes you
past more than 30 site-specific works, such as "Returned Parquet,"
part of a 100-year-old parquet floor made from Belize mahogany
and relaid on the jungle floor, and "Downtown," a miniature
metropolis cast in concrete, all being reclaimed by the jungle.

Planning The park is 80 miles (129 km) from Belize City. Visitors need
to make an appointment in advance. www.poustiniaonline.org

### ❹ Naoshima Island, Japan

This tiny fishing island in the Seto Inland Sea is a treasure trove
of modern art, including the giant "Red Pumpkin" that greets
travelers arriving at the harbor. Two-hundred-year-old village
houses have been converted into contemporary installations,
and a Shinto shrine has a flight of glass steps leading from an
underground pool up through the ground.

Planning Naoshima is a six-hour train and ferry journey from Tokyo.
There are two modern art galleries, one of which, Benesse House, also
has guest rooms. www.naoshima-is.co.jp, www.japan-guide.com

### ❺ Connells Bay Sculpture Park, New Zealand

On beautiful Waiheke Island, near Auckland, around 25 sculptures
by leading New Zealand artists are arranged across farmland and
among great sweeps of native trees. Works include "Guardian of
the Planting," two heads reminiscent of those on Easter Island,
and Jeff Thomson's "Three Cows Looking Out to Sea."

Planning The island is 30 minutes by boat from Auckland. The park
is open from October through April. Walks are guided and must be
booked in advance. www.connellsbay.co.nz

### ❻ Artscape Nordland, Norway

Beacons, shelters, huts, human figures, pyramids, and other
monumental sculptures by internationally renowned artists
such as Anish Kapoor and Antony Gormley have been installed
on rocks, beaches, cliffs, and in fields along northern Norway's
beautiful, remote, and sparsely populated Atlantic coast.

Planning The sculptures can be found in 33 of Nordland county's
municipalities. They can be reached by a combination of road, ferry,
and air travel. www.visitnordland.com, www.skulpturlandskap.no

### ❼ Chianti Sculpture Park, Italy

Tree stumps carved in marble, a cypress tree made from layers of
glass that sparkle in the sunlight, a glass labyrinth, and the ribs
of a ship are just some of the sculptures along a woodland trail
in the Tuscan hills. They have been designed to harmonize with
the colors, light, and trees around them.

Planning The park is near the village of Pievasciata, about 7 miles (11
km) northeast of Siena. www.chiantisculpturepark.it

### ❽ Refuges d'Art, France

High in the mountains of Haute Provence, art-loving hill walkers
can enjoy the stunning scenery and a series of art works by
British land artist Andy Goldsworthy. Along 100 miles (160 km)
of ancient paths, Goldsworthy has created three "Sentinelles,"
or stone cairns, and renovated a series of overnight shelters in
deserted buildings, adding an artwork in each one.

Planning The circuit begins in Digne-les-Bains, northwest of Nice, and
takes about five days. Local company Etoile Rando organizes guided
hikes. www.beyond.fr/villages, www.etoile-rando.com

### ❾ Forest of Dean Sculpture Trail, England

A 4.5-mile (7 km) woodland trail links a series of sculptures
that celebrate the life and history of this ancient forest in
Gloucestershire. Set among the trees are swings, observation
towers, and giant acorns, while works resembling mine shafts,
railroad tracks, and charcoal hearths are reminders of the forest's
industrial past, which dates back to pre-Roman times.

Planning The loop trail starts at Beechenhurst Lodge visitor center, west
of Cinderford. www.forestofdean-sculpture.org.uk, www.forestry.gov.uk

### ❿ North Mayo Sculpture Trail, Ireland

The discovery of the most extensive Neolithic site in the world at
Ceéde Fields on the north Mayo coast inspired this trail, which
follows the coast road west from Ballina. The 15 sculptures,
representing figures, refuges, and shelters, celebrate the wild
beauty of the area and its long history of human habitation.

Planning The trail can be followed by car, starting in Ballina.
www.mayo-ireland.ie

Opposite: Naoshima Island's iconic 6-ft-tall (1.8 m) fiberglass "Yellow Pumpkin," one of two created by Japanese artist Yayoi Kusama, sits at the end of a pier.

A fountain plays in the pool of Leighton House's resplendently tiled and pillared Arab Hall.

ENGLAND

# LEIGHTON HOUSE

Behind the austere, redbrick exterior of this London house, a Victorian painter, collector, and orientalist created his "private palace of art."

Stand in the Arab Hall, its walls covered with more than a thousand 17th-century Syrian tiles in a range of beautiful blues and blue-greens, sunlight filtering through carved lattice window screens from Cairo, and the murmur of a small fountain in the background, and be transported into a world of oriental exoticism. A mosaic frieze, made in Venice, runs around the upper walls, displaying mermaids, ships, and peacocks set in gold leaf; the domed ceiling is also covered with gold leaf. This jewel of a house on the edge of Holland Park was created by the eminent painter Frederic, Lord Leighton, as a place in which to work, as a home for his collection of paintings and ceramics, and as a setting for entertaining his many friends, who included the artists Dante Gabriel Rossetti, John Everett Millais, William Morris, and the poet Robert Browning. The opulent theme is continued in the other downstairs rooms, with deep blue tiles, gold leaf, marble, mosaic floors, and oriental ceramics. The real heart of the house, however, is upstairs. Passing the Silk Room, an informal area hung with Leighton's painting collection, you enter his large studio where light floods in through a large window above the model's dais. Here Leighton worked by day and in the evenings held musical soirees that were attended by his friends.

**When to Go** Open daily except Tuesdays; closed Christmas Day, Boxing Day, and New Year's Day.

**How to Find It** Leighton House is on Holland Park Road, on the west side of Holland Park and close to Kensington High Street.

**Planning** Regular programs of courses and talks are held in Lord Leighton's studio.

**Website** www.leightonhouse.co.uk, www.rbkc.gov.uk/museums

## A Victorian Family Home

**18 Stafford Terrace**—the Linley Sambourne House—located on the east side of Holland Park, was the home of *Punch* cartoonist Edward Linley Sambourne and his family in the late 1800s. This lovingly created Victorian family home still has its original decoration and is brimming with beautiful period furniture, textiles, ornaments, and pictures collected by Linley Sambourne and his wife, Marion, over many years. Linley Sambourne's cartoons, drawings, photographs, and glass-plate negatives—he was a keen photographer—cover the walls of the charming, little-known treasure-house.

Costumed tours (led by actors representing Marion Sambourne and her staff) and conventional ones (led by expert, but uncostumed guides) are available.

ENGLAND

# HEVER CASTLE

History comes alive in a castle associated with
Tudor intrigue and restored with American wealth.

Anne Boleyn, second of Henry VIII's six wives and mother of Elizabeth I, spent her childhood at Hever. But the splendid, double-moated castle and gardens that you visit today owe more to William Waldorf Astor, who nearly 400 years after the time of the Boleyns turned the place into a dream playground. The richest man in America, Astor moved to Britain in 1891, declaring, "America is not a fit place for a gentleman to live." His idea of a gentleman's estate must have been taken from a visit to Hampton Court, Britain's best-known Tudor palace. In 1903, he bought a much dilapidated Hever, where he set about restoring the castle and building a half-timber extra wing to live in. The grounds gained a Tudor garden, two mazes, and a loggia by the lake, where an hour-long shore walk now begins. Rowboats, an adventure playground, a shop, and a restaurant ensure that this is a family day out. In summer, you may witness the galloping clash of knights in armor during a medieval-style jousting tournament. But for many, the gardens are the chief attraction: Starting with swathes of snowdrops, crocuses, and daffodils in March and April, then camellias, tulips, rhododendrons, and azaleas. The 3,000 roses are at their best in July and August, continuing through to the fall when dahlias add their rich hues.

**When to Go**  Open daily, April 1 through October 31, 10 a.m. (castle: noon)–5 p.m. Open part of each week at other times of the year.

**How to Find It**  Hever is 30 miles (48 km) southeast of London. Trains run from London Victoria and London Bridge to Edenbridge, where you can take a taxi to the castle. Alternatively, you can continue to the unmanned Hever station, with a 1-mile (1.6 km) rural walk to the castle.

**Planning**  Medley Court, part of the 1903 Astor Wing, is a self-catering property sleeping seven that can be rented for a week–guests have the run of the grounds after day visitors have gone home. The King Henry VIII pub opposite the entrance to the castle dates from 1597 and has rooms where you can spend the night.

**Websites**  www.hevercastle.co.uk, www.kinghenryviiiinn.co.uk

EUROPE

## Historic Neighbors

■ **Winston Churchill** bought his country home, **Chartwell,** 5 miles (8 km) north of Hever, because of its superb views over the Kentish countryside. The garden studio has a collection of splendidly vigorous oil paintings by the wartime prime minister.

■ **Penshurst Place,** also nearby, is a medieval and Tudor gem that has belonged to the Sidney family since 1552. The Elizabethan poet, courtier, and soldier, Sir Philip Sidney, was born here.

■ At moated **Groombridge Place,** the gardens were laid out in the 17th century as "outside rooms" divided by high hedges.

Pink cherry blossoms and a moat-side display of daffodils frame a springtime view of Hever Castle.

# SANTA MARÍA LA REAL

Astonishing historic and artistic riches lie hidden in a monastery in the northern Spanish city of Burgos.

A dazzling mix of architectural styles—Romanesque, Gothic, and Renaissance—is the highlight of the Monastery of Santa María la Real de las Huelgas in Burgos. Nowhere is this more evident than in the Cloister of San Fernando. Constructed by King Ferdinand III of Castile in the late 13th century, the barrel-vaulted cloister has superb tracery in the Mudejar style (Moorish decorative techniques used in Christian architecture) with designs that include early Arabic script, castles, peacocks, and griffins. King Alfonso VIII and his English Queen Leonor (Eleanor) founded the monastery in 1187 as a retreat for female members of the royal family and aristocracy and as a burial place for Castilian monarchs. Its abbesses were figures of high status, endowed with enormous legal and liturgical powers; these privileges survived until as late as 1873, when they were finally revoked by Pope Pius IX. Now, more than 800 years after its founding, the monastery is still the home of Cistercian nuns, which makes the experience of visiting it all the richer. The Museo de Telas Medievales (Museum of Medieval Clothing) has the costumes of different members of the Castilian royal family from the 12th to the 14th centuries. All the items are precisely dated because they all came from royal tombs.

**When to Go**  April through June and September through December are good months in Burgos. Summer can simmer and winter is bitterly cold. The monastery is closed on Mondays.

**How to Find It**  Follow the N-120 west from the center of Burgos. The monastery lies just off the road in the city's western outskirts.

**Planning**  Don't miss the monastery's hinged pulpit, which can be swung around to allow the preacher to address anyone hidden in the choir. There is plenty to see in Burgos, which was one of medieval Castile's richest cities. Bring warm clothing any time of year, as evenings tend to be cool.

**Websites**  www.turismoburgos.org, www.spain.info

### Burgos Sights

■ **Burgos Cathedral** is one of Spain's largest and most magnificent Gothic structures. The body of the Spanish hero, Rodrigo Díaz de Vivar, better known as **El Cid** Campeador, is buried here.

■ The cathedral's octagonal 15th-century **Chapel of the Condestable** is a superb example of the flamboyant, distinctively Spanish, late Gothic style called "plateresque."

■ Opposite the cathedral on the Plaza del Rey San Fernando is the ornate **Arco de Santa María,** one of the 12 ancient gates of Burgos. Inside it, the Sala de Poridad has a fine Mudejar carved ceiling.

The main tower looms above the warren of buildings that makes up the Monastery of Santa María la Real.

Each of the museum's rooms reveals different aspects of Tunisia's astonishing historical legacy.

TUNISIA

# BARDO NATIONAL MUSEUM

Wander through magnificent rooms filled with
treasures from Tunisia's Carthaginian and Roman past.

A maze of beautifully renovated rooms in the former palace of the beys (rulers) of Tunis makes a spectacular setting for exhibits from all over Tunisia. Here, under ornate ceilings, cupolas, and archways festooned in delicate stucco work, you can explore the relics of some 40,000 years of history—above all, those from Carthaginian (Punic) and Roman times. Ancient Carthage, Rome's great rival, stood on the outskirts of modern Tunis, and in the Punic rooms you get close to its culture as you pore over amulets, jewelry, funeral masks, and steles bearing mysterious inscriptions. Haunting this part of the museum are tales of Hannibal and his elephants struggling across the Alps, and of Carthage finally destroyed and plowed with salt by its Roman conquerors in 146 B.C. Roman artifacts include amphorae, urns, and statues, but mosaics steal the limelight. Dating mostly from the 3rd and 4th centuries A.D., they depict life in Roman Tunisia, from everyday routines to festivities and worship. Among the most celebrated are mosaics showing Virgil writing the *Aeneid*, the nine muses, and Venus bathing. Glowing colors and flowing shapes bear witness to the skills of myriad unknown artists whose legacy has survived for almost 2,000 years.

**When to Go** Spring is best for pleasantly warm temperatures and dry weather. The Bardo National Museum is closed on Mondays.

**How to Find It** The museum is in the suburb of Le Bardo, about 2.5 miles (4 km) west of Tunis's city center. You can reach it by tram.

**Planning** Allow at least half a day to visit the museum. The ruins of Carthage are spread over Tunis's northern outskirts. Taxis are usually available at the different sites. If you plan to travel farther afield, consider shared taxis (louage), which are cheap, fast, and popular with locals.

**Websites** www.tourismtunisia.com, www.tunisiaonline.com/mosaics, www.ThomasCook.com/Tunisia

### Ruins of Carthage

■ Take the scenic TGM railroad along Lake Tunis—where thousands of flamingos congregate in winter—to explore the remains of **Carthage.**

■ The ruins stretch from the National Museum of Carthage on Byrsa Hill to the Roman remains down by the sea. Look out for the restored **Theater of Hadrian,** the **Baths of Gargilius,** and the **Baths of Antonine** tucked among pink oleander.

■ The **Roman Villas Archaeological Park** is a jumble of columns, statues, and mosaics, with wonderful views across the Gulf of Tunis.

AFRICA

# UNDISCOVERED VILLAGES

8

Some are no more than tiny dots on the map, located at the far end of a minor road to nowhere. Others lie in the heart of great forests or cling to cliffs. Whatever their location, these villages and small towns represent something very special. They are the last, eccentric survivals from a lost world, reminders of what rural life was like before global brands, suburban sprawl, and high-speed broadband made their marks. For travelers of a romantic bent, a journey into the English countryside leads to places such as picturesque Lavenham, whose half-timber shopfronts and cottages have been watching the world go by since Shakespeare's day. Those who prefer wild remoteness might consider a trek across the Chilean deserts, where San Pedro de Atacama sits on its high plateau, ringed by volcanic lakes. But for an encounter with a rural community that defies all preconceptions, there may be nowhere quite as startling as Hukeng in southeast China, where large, ring-shaped buildings each form a self-contained village housing hundreds of members of the Hakka minority.

A jumble of stone houses piles up the hillside as if supporting the church that illuminates Maratea's skyline. The village straddles the last rocky outcrop before the mountains plunge into the Gulf of Policastro, on Italy's southwest shore.

# QUEBEC TOWNSHIPS

Delectable local produce and postcard-pretty villages
reward the traveler in Quebec's Eastern Townships.

NORTH
AMERICA

Meandering along the back roads of Quebec's Cantons d'Est (Eastern Townships), you pass undulating farm fields and vineyards plump with purple grapes, and through pocket-size villages. The region lies tucked in the Appalachian foothills along the border with Vermont, New Hampshire, and Maine, its character shaped almost as much by its New England neighbors to the south as by the French Canadians and Europeans who settled here in the early 19th century. Sherbrooke is the cultural center with a mélange of museums, art galleries, and historic neighborhoods. Traditions and tasty treats abound, all redolent of the French pioneers' homeland. At Savon Des Cantons, near Magog—17 miles (27 kilometers) to the southwest—you can watch craftspeople make soap, while nearby Bleu Lavande turns acres of lavender into aromatic products. Continuing southwest, you reach Sutton. Stroll its main street to peruse artisanal shops, among them La Rumeur Affamée with a bountiful array of breads, cheeses, and smoked meats, including local Lac Brome duck. To the east, on the shores of Lac Memphrémagog, the Benedictine monks of the Abbaye de Saint-Benoît-du-Lac, near Austin, celebrate the daily round of offices (services) in Gregorian chant. At their shop, look for the abbey's L'Ermite, a tangy blue cheese.

**When to Go** You can visit the townships at any time of year, but summer and the fall foliage season are the most popular periods, when roads and attractions may be more crowded. Expect snow in winter.

**How to Find It** Fly into Montreal, about an hour's drive north of Sherbrooke, and rent a car. Although many communities may be reached by public bus, a rental vehicle will provide greater flexibility.

**Planning** Allow at least a week for your visit. Lodge in a hotel, bed-and-breakfast, or even a yurt.

**Websites** www.easterntownships.org, www.laroutedesvins.ca, www.bonjourquebec.com

### The Wine Route

La Route des Vins follows a circuitous 82-mile (132 km) trail linking wineries in the western part of the Eastern Townships with other small, family-run agricultural enterprises.

■ **Vignoble de L'Orpailleur,** in Dunham, produces a delicious, sweet ice wine made from grapes picked frozen from the vines in winter.

■ Near Frelighsburg, stop at **Domaine Pinnacle,** an orchard and cidery, to sample its ambrosial Pinnacle Ice Cider, or **La Girondine,** where homemade foie gras, duck pâtés, and meat products are for sale.

Fall colors, a lake, and mountain peaks in the background: It all adds up to a perfect setting for the Eastern Townships' Abbaye de Saint-Benoît-du-Lac.

Brightly painted stripes on the road keep this marching band in Bristol's Fourth of July Parade on the correct route.

RHODE ISLAND

# BRISTOL

Passionately red, white, and blue, a small town on the
East Coast prides itself on its celebration of U.S. history.

B ristol, Rhode Island, is a little community making a big claim as the most patriotic town
in the United States. Here, permanently painted down tree-shaded Hope Street, in the
historic heart of town, is a bold red, white, and blue stripe, marking the route of the
annual Fourth of July parade: Bristol hosts the longest continually operating Independence
Day celebration in the United States, going back to 1777. Throughout the downtown area,
history is on display. Many well-kept colonial clapboard residences bear placards denoting
their original owners. A walk along Hope Street takes you past Linden Place, a glorious 1810
Federal-style mansion, now a museum, which has hosted four presidents and was featured
in the film *The Great Gatsby*. Continuing south, Bristol's yachting heritage is celebrated at the
harborside Herreshoff Marine Museum, home to the America's Cup Hall of Fame. A few
minutes beyond, deck dining at its finest may be found at the Lobster Pot, aptly named in that
the two promontories that make up Bristol are shaped like a lobster claw. A five-minute drive
east takes you to Mount Hope Farm: 200 acres (80 hectares) of fields, meadows, woodlands,
and walking trails opening to superb vistas of Mount Hope and Narragansett Bays.

**When to Go** Summer is the best time to take in Bristol, the warm weather allowing for long, leisurely walks.

**How to Find It** Bristol is a 25-minute drive southeast from Rhode Island's capital city of Providence and 75
minutes by car south from Boston. Or you can cycle the East Bay Bike Path from East Providence to Bristol
Harbor (14.5 miles/23 km), with beautiful views of Narragansett Bay along the way.

**Planning** Leave a day for perambulating the attractions. For overnights, Bristol has some of the oldest
B&Bs in the state, including Rockwell House (1809) and Bradford-Dimond-Norris House (1792).

**Websites** www.discoverbristol.com, www.onlinebristol.com, www.lobsterpotri.com

## Rooted in Bristol

■ In the middle of Bristol's
downtown is an elegant
alcove of respect and dignity,
the **War Veterans Honor Roll
Garden.** Here, granite benches
for resting stand alongside a
gleaming black marble slab—
50 ft (15 m) long and 6 ft
(1.8 m) high—bearing the names
of locals who have served in
the nation's wars.

■ When you think sequoia,
you don't think East Coast.
But at **Blithewold Mansion,
Gardens, and Arboretum,** at the
southerly tip of Bristol's eastern
promontory, is a 90-ft (27 m)
sequoia, the tallest east of the
Mississippi. Also here is the
45-room summer home of 19th-
century coal baron Augustus
Van Wickle, with 33 landscaped
acres (13 ha) featuring 3,000
trees and shrubs.

NORTH
AMERICA

# ST. MICHAELS

Savor the old-world allure of a Chesapeake
Bay fishing town turned boaters' paradise.

Crabs, history, and seafaring charm all come together in the nautical town of St. Michaels, standing on the shore of Chesapeake Bay. During the War of 1812, it gained a reputation as the "town that fooled the British" by hanging lit lanterns high in the tree tops at night. The British were misled, and their cannons shot over the rooftops causing little damage. Today, St. Michaels is a romantic yachting haven on the rural eastern shore of the bay. The main thoroughfare, South Talbot Street, is lined with historic buildings that house an inviting collection of boutiques, antiques stores, galleries, and restaurants. The intriguing Chesapeake Bay Maritime Museum showcases the bay's shipbuilding and nautical traditions. Skipjacks, which dredged for oysters, and other craft that once plied the shallow waters are on view, along with exhibits that tell the story of oystering and crabbing on the bay. Children can learn the art of catching crabs, while adults can apprentice for a day in the shipbuilding school and help build a traditional wooden skiff. A cruise on board *Mr. Jim,* one of the original "buyboats" that used to ferry fresh-caught fish from the skipjacks to shore, is a good way to explore the watery landscape. And a visit to the lovingly restored, octagonal Hooper Strait Lighthouse brings alive the world of the lighthousemen whose beam once shone brightly.

**When to Go** The best time to visit St. Michaels is May through September. Cool Chesapeake Bay breezes keep most summer days comfortable. May and September are less crowded, except during the Labor Day weekend festival in early September.

**How to Find It** The town lies 80 miles (129 km) east of Washington, D.C. Follow U.S. 50-E over Chesapeake Bay Bridge. At Easton, take Maryland 322, then Maryland 33 for the last 9 miles (14.5 km) to St. Michaels.

**Planning** The Crab Claw Restaurant on the waterfront is popular for steamed crabs, while St. Michaels Crab & Steak House offers an extensive menu of fresh seafood, as well as local steamed crabs and steak.

**Websites** www.stmichaelsmd.org, www.cbmm.org, www.thecrabclaw.com, www.stmichaelscrabhouse.com

### Chesapeake Crab Feasts

In a ceremony almost as old as the town, locals, visitors, and boaters gather in St. Michaels' **waterfront restaurants** every evening for a leisurely meal of succulent blue crabs. The crabs are steamed to perfection in secret spice mixes and served at tables covered with butcher's paper. Diners crack the crabs with a knife, wooden mallet, and fingers. The blue crab, *Callinectes* ("beautiful swimmer") *sapidus* ("savory"), is Chesapeake Bay's signature crustacean. Here, crabs are steamed, not boiled, which preserves the sweet flavor. The sweet meat is also enjoyed in Maryland crab cakes, crab soup, and hot crab dip.

The Hooper Strait Lighthouse—now part of the Chesapeake Bay Maritime Museum—stands on iron pilings "screwed" into the seabed.

Seafarers' sailboats and artists' houseboats are moored side by side in Apalachicola Bay, on the Gulf of Mexico.

FLORIDA

# APALACHICOLA

To experience the charms of old-time Florida, look no further than this oyster town set on the edge of an exquisite marine wilderness.

Florida visitors often lament that "Old Florida"—the Florida of devil-may-care living, salty fishing towns, and eccentric waterfront characters—has vanished. But don't mention that to anyone who lives in the Florida Panhandle, facing the Gulf of Mexico, for they will be quick to tell you that old-time Florida is thriving in the seaside town of Apalachicola. A bustling cotton port in the 19th century, the town later became a center for the sponge-diving industry. Today, evidence of its wealthy past lies in the 900 or more historic homes that line the tidy streets. Apalachicola is a great place for walking. Along Water Street, you will find the Maritime Museum and a row of houseboats belonging to artists and craftspeople. The downtown area has restored cotton warehouses and other well-preserved buildings containing a funky blend of gift shops, restaurants, and inns. These days, Apalachicola is famous for the huge, sweet oysters that multiply in the pristine waters of Apalachicola Bay. Walk north on Market Street and you will come to the harbor where dozens of oyster boats dock. When you are ready to sample these awesome delicacies, eat where the locals do—at nearby Papa Joe's Oyster Bar & Grill. A table overlooking the water makes the perfect perch to savor dinner and watch the sunset over the wildlife-filled salt marshes.

**When to Go** The most pleasant temperatures coincide with the start and end of oyster season in late fall (October-November) and early spring (March-April). June through September can be very hot and humid.

**How to Find It** Apalachicola lies 80 miles (129 km) southwest of Tallahassee on U.S. 98. A bridge links St. George Island with the mainland, 5 miles (8 km) east of Apalachicola. St. Vincent Island can be reached by private shuttle boat from Indian Pass on County Road 30-B, 22 miles (35 km) west of the town.

**Planning** Apalachicola provides good accommodations and restaurants. Bring sun protection and insect repellent—gnats and mosquitoes can be fierce, especially after the sun goes down.

**Websites** www.apalachicolabay.org, www.anaturalescape.com, www.fws.gov/saintvincent

### Gems in the Bay

■ Apalachicola's oyster-rich bay is formed by a string of sandy offshore islands creating one of the most unspoiled marine estuaries in the United States. On **St. George Island,** a state park preserves one of the finest, wild, Gulf Coast beaches in Florida, where you can stroll for hours along dazzling white sand washed by emerald green surf.

■ At the western end of the chain, **St. Vincent Island** forms part of a national wildlife refuge. Paths lead across the sand-and-pine island to lengthy, shell-strewn beaches. It is home to bald eagles and sea turtles, and is a stop for migratory birds.

NORTH AMERICA

# MUSIC FESTIVALS

Every corner of the world has its musical celebration, whether rock in Denmark, Creole in the eastern Caribbean, or the entrancing sound of the lusheng in remote southwestern China.

## ❶ Sedalia, Missouri

Savor ragtime's catchy rhythms in the Scott Joplin Ragtime Festival, a toe-tapping celebration in central Missouri, held each June since 1980. Scott Joplin lived in Sedalia from 1894 to 1901, honing his syncopated style, and this was where his most famous composition, "The Maple Leaf Rag," was published.

Planning The website gives festival details and information on where to stay. www.scottjoplin.org

## ❷ Hilo, Hawaii

For one week each July, the gentle strumming of ukuleles along with slack key and steel guitars fills the air when the Big Island Hawaiian Music Festival sets up stage in lush Hilo. Falsetto singers join in the serenade with haunting high notes.

Planning Take a trip to Volcanoes National Park, where the Hawaiian goddess Pele is said to work her fiery magic. www.bigisland.org

## ❸ Dominica, Windward Islands

Ringed by coral reefs, Dominica harbors lush mountains, pristine waterfalls, and rain forests, providing a natural setting for the World Creole Music Festival. This less-visited Caribbean isle lies between Martinique and Guadeloupe. Held annually, starting on the last week of October, the festival has attracted musicians from throughout the French Creole-speaking world, including Zouk Machine, Taxi Creole, and Tania St. Valle.

Planning Don't miss Dominica's rain-forest hiking and superb scuba diving. www.wcmfdominica.com

## ❹ Morelia, Mexico

The week-long International Guitar Festival features master classes by skilled guitarists from more than 50 countries, including Italy, Spain, and Paraguay. The celebration takes place in Morelia, capital of central Mexico's Michoacán state, where tall, pink-stoned baroque buildings and historic churches stand alongside a fountain-flanked square.

Planning Morelia is an attractive city with a good selection of places to stay. The festival is usually held in March. www.michoacan-travel.com

## ❺ Guizhou, China

In October or November, members of the Miao ethnic minority gather for a raucous week of music and more at the Miao Lusheng Festival in the province of Guizhou, southwest China. Dancing and singing to the hypnotic tones of lushengs—Miao reed flutes—young women vaunt ornately embroidered costumes and gleaming silver headdresses.

Planning Watch what you eat at this festival; there is always a chance that roast donkey or dog might feature on the menu. www.chinahighlights.com/travelguide/festivals/lusheng-festival.htm

## ❻ Krakow, Poland

Every summer, medieval Krakow's Jewish quarter, Kazimierz, resounds with lively klezmer music, synagogue song, and folk music when the Jewish Culture Festival gets under way. More than 100 events are programmed, including an outdoor grand finale concert, surrounded by the imposing architecture of this World Heritage site and former royal capital.

Planning While you are in Krakow, visit Wawel Hill, dubbed the "Polish Acropolis," with its soaring cathedral, once the site of royal coronations. www.jewishfestival.pl

## ❼ Roskilde, Denmark

Denmark's former medieval capital of Roskilde lies near a narrow sliver of fjord, 19 miles (31 km) west of Copenhagen. The city's week-long, annual festival of rock and other contemporary music has featured musical luminaries from Bob Dylan, Bob Marley, and Santana to Nirvana and Bjork, as well as up-and-coming bands.

Planning Take time out to see Roskilde's Viking Ship Museum and the Gothic, redbrick cathedral. www.roskilde-festival.dk

## ❽ Ljubljana, Slovenia

Druga Godba International Music Festival in Ljubljana lives up to its name, which means "the other music." This summer festival presents musicians from places as far-flung as Mali in West Africa, Trinidad and Tobago, and Brazil, among others. From Afrobeat and funk to steel drums, Druga Godba spans a world of musical genres.

Planning Be sure to visit Ljubljana's old town and castle perched atop a stately hill. festival.drugagodba.si

## ❾ Parma, Italy

Every October, the dramatic notes of *Rigoletto, La Traviata,* and other operas fill the air during the Verdi Festival in Parma's Teatro Regio and other venues. The northern Italian city and its surrounding countryside, including Verdi's hometown of Busseto, provide fitting backdrops for the month-long celebration.

Planning Visit the house where Verdi was born in Busseto, 25 miles (40 km) northwest of Parma. www.festivalverdiparma.it

## ❿ Feakle, Ireland

Each August, the 800 or so residents of the tiny town of Feakle in County Clare welcome music-loving visitors to experience the festive sounds of the Emerald Isle's traditional tunes. Concerts, workshops, fiddle recitals, and dancing are all part of the International Festival of Traditional Irish Music.

Planning Enjoy hearty home cooking at affordable prices during the festival at Pepper's Bar & Restaurant. www.feaklefestival.ie

Opposite: The lusheng, played by Miao musicians in Guizhou, China, is a reed instrument made from bamboo and can measure up to 10 ft (3 m) long.

The clock tower and bandstand were 20th-century additions to Cuetzalán's *zócalo*, or square.

MEXICO

# CUETZALÁN

A heady aroma of coffee pervades the mountain village of Cuetzalán, where the streets are stepped and the caves deep.

High in the Sierra Norte of Puebla state, the morning mist lifts to reveal Cuetzalán, home to Nahua and Totonac people, skilled weavers and keepers of ancient culinary and shamanistic traditions. After a four-hour drive from Mexico City, through the mountains northeast of the capital, arriving in the village is like entering another world, where traffic is almost nonexistent and the cobblestone streets are stairways leading down from the hills to a central plaza. Indigenous people, many of them in traditional dazzling white costumes embroidered with bright flower and bird motifs, gather in the square for the weekly market. Baskets of calla lilies, fruit, herbs, and river shrimp fill the marketplace, interspersed with women making wild mushroom quesadillas over charcoal fires. The aroma of roasting coffee beans permeates the village, which is at the center of a coffee-growing region. At nearly 4,000 feet (1,219 meters) above sea level, the village and surrounding subtropical forest boast views of the Gulf Coast. Beneath Cuetzalán lies an extensive cave system with fantastically shaped stalactites and stalagmites. Nearby, waterfalls cascade into natural bathing pools. Local children are eager guides.

**When to Go**  Cuetzalán's Coffee Festival (first week in October), its patronal fiesta (July 15-18), and Guadalupe Day (December 12) provide opportunities to see the *voladores*—dancers who "fly" from a pole.

**How to Find It**  Buses depart daily from Mexico City's TAPO terminal on the four-hour trip to Cuetzalán, or you can rent a car. Check road conditions before traveling in the rainy season (June-September).

**Planning**  Small family inns and hotels have restaurants, and there are several local dining spots. To see the Totonac pyramids, visit the Yohualichan Archaeological Site, open Wednesday through Sunday, 10 a.m.-5 p.m.

**Websites**  www.planetware.com/mexico/cuetzalan-mex-pue-ctzln.htm, www.ecoturismolatino.com

### Onward to Yohualichan

■ A fine group of **Totonac stone pyramids** rises up out of the deep green vegetation at Yohualichan, 5 miles (8 km) northeast of Cuetzalán. Built in A.D. 400, they continue to be used as a ceremonial dance center by the inhabitants of the small village adjacent to the site.

■ Yohualichan's women's cooperative, **Maseal Siuat Xochitajkitinij**—Indigenous Women, Weavers of Flowers—promotes the conservation of artisanal traditions, especially weaving on a backstrap loom. Visitors can observe the women at work and buy goods from their shop. The community dining spot, **Ticoteno,** serves local dishes with an emphasis on legumes and spices.

NORTH AMERICA

CHILE

# SAN PEDRO DE ATACAMA

Adventure, sport, and extraordinary desert formations await the traveler who ventures to the town across the sands.

SOUTH AMERICA

It seems incredible that human settlements could survive, let alone thrive, in the Atacama Desert of northern Chile. But the oasis town of San Pedro de Atacama has done just that for more than 900 years, first as a pre-Columbian indigenous settlement, then as a Spanish mission town. Almost lost in the desolate landscape, today's San Pedro is a magnet for those who crave archaeology, desert adventure, or just plain solitude. Located 7,900 feet (2,408 meters) above sea level on a high desert plain called the Puna de Atacama, the town is surrounded by dramatic geography: Snowcapped volcanoes, saline lakes that glimmer with thousands of pink flamingos, and arid oddities like the Valle de la Luna (Moon Valley), with giant dunes and wildly eroded arroyos. San Pedro's twin landmarks are the whitewashed San Isidro Chapel and the modern R.P. Gustavo Le Paige Archaeological Museum, showcasing relics of ancient life, including a surprisingly well-preserved Atacameño mummy. On the outskirts of town is Pukará de Quitor, a 12th-century fortress settlement built by the people who occupied this region before Spanish colonial times. There are plenty of ways to work up a sweat in the desert that surrounds San Pedro, including hiking, mountain biking, wildlife-watching, and sandboarding down giant dunes.

**When to Go**  High altitude moderates the desert climate; summer temperatures can reach 90°F (32°C) between December and February. Winter (June–August) is mild, but after dark the temperature can drop below freezing. The Fiesta de San Pedro, honoring the town's patron saint, takes place on June 28.

**How to Find It**  LAN Chile has daily flights between Santiago and Calama, where you can rent a vehicle and drive 60 miles (97 km) southeast along paved roads to San Pedro. Daily buses operate from the coastal town of Antofagasta, 132 miles (212 km) southwest, and Calama.

**Planning**  There are two eco-lodges: Explora Atacama Hotel de Larache, a stylish adventure resort, and Altiplánico, where the adobe bungalows are inspired by the dwellings of the ancient Atacameño people.

**Websites**  www.visit-chile.org, www.sanpedroatacama.com, www.explora.com, www.altiplanico.com

## My Secret Journey

*My driver rouses me in the night. It's surprisingly chilly as we make our way through the empty streets of San Pedro and out into the open desert. Pulling off the main road, we follow a rutted track into the mountains. Two hours later we reach our destination—***El Tatio***—the world's third largest geyser field. In the pitch dark, we can't see a thing. But we know the area's 80-plus geysers are there from the sulfur aroma and the hissing and bubbling that precede each hot-water eruption. The magic starts at dawn, watching sunrise over the Andes through an eerie filter of spray and condensation.*
**Joe Yogerst**
**Travel writer**

A shady café-restaurant in San Pedro de Atacama offers a welcome retreat from the fierce desert sun.

CHINA

# HUKENG

Curious, round, fortresslike buildings pepper the landscape
between Fujian and Jiangxi, each one almost a village in itself.

In nearly 50 counties along the border between China's southeastern provinces of Fujian and Jiangxi stand groups of giant, multistory fortresses called *tulou*, made from sand, lime, and earth. Many are large enough to house hundreds of members of the Hakka ethnic minority who built them. Each tulou is a village in its own right, where some residents rent rooms to travelers. The most easily accessible group is at Hukeng, about 124 miles (200 kilometers) inland from Fujian province's busy port city of Xiamen. Here a variety of tulou of different shapes stand on either side of the river that flows along a narrow green valley. The Zhencheng Lou of 1912 is a vast four-story khaki-colored ring, tiny windows only appearing on the higher floors. Beyond heavy gates, a tunnel leads to a balconied interior with 222 inward-facing rooms, including those in a smaller, two-story inner ring, some of which house livestock, and a hall for worship, weddings, and performances. The oldest fortress here is the Huanxiang Lou, dating from 1550, which still houses about 200 people, all called Li. The square Kuiju Lou dates from 1834. Residents of the Fuyu Lou of 1880 are all called Lin. Built in a shape the Chinese call "Fire-Phoenix," it has multiple axes, beautifully carved beams and pillars, and a five-story tower at the rear. If you opt for a room in a tulou, expect an authentic Chinese experience—your pit toilet will be three unlit stories down, and the nighttime entertainment is listening to crickets and owls.

**When to Go** Spring and fall are the best times to visit. Summers are hot and humid, although Hukeng's mountain location eases summer nights. Avoid travel around the busy Chinese New Year (between late January and mid-February) and the first week of October, which is a national holiday.

**How to Find It** Hukeng can be reached by bus from Xiamen in 4 hours, or by train to Yongding in 6.5 hours and a taxi or minibus for the 23-mile (37 km) drive east to the village.

**Planning** There are simple places to stay in the nearby modern Hukeng village, 3 miles (4.8 km) away, but tulou residents with rooms for rent will persistently approach you. Evening meals cooked over wood fires are available for modest amounts. You can visit several other clusters of tulou from Hukeng using local transport.

**Websites** www.icm.gov.mo/exhibition/tc/fjintroE.asp, traditions.cultural-china.com/18two.html

### A Foreigners' Isle

The vibrant port of **Xiamen** is one of China's more attractive cities and far more than just the departure point for trips inland to Hukeng.

After the city was designated a treaty port in 1843, permitting foreign residents, the new arrivals opted to occupy the tiny island of **Gulangyu,** a short ferry ride from the main port. They covered the island in grand pseudo-European mansions and churches, whose domes, spires, and neoclassical pillars, prettily shrouded in bougainvillea, look startlingly exotic in the sub-tropical setting.

The foreigners were driven out when the communists took power in 1949. But the island's winding, car-free lanes have been retained, and the mansions still stand. A walk around the island's coastline provides views of **Taiwan,** only a few miles away across the water.

Opposite: Fortresslike tulou houses make a pattern of different shapes. Above: Life revolves around a central courtyard.

# CAO BANG PROVINCE

A trek among the pyramidal peaks and evergreen paddy fields
of highland Vietnam will lead you to remote hill-tribe villages.

Secluded in the highlands of northern Vietnam, the Cao Bang region nurtures stunning landscapes and ancient hill-tribe culture. The extraordinary scenery—velvet-green paddy fields and beige cornfields set against dark, jagged, limestone peaks—often takes a backseat to the vibrant garb of the people of the Tay, Dao, and other tribes. Most of the area's menfolk have taken to modern clothes, but their mothers, wives, and daughters continue to don the multihued outfits they have worn for centuries, all handmade at home on simple looms. Village markets overflow with both local produce and household goods imported (often smuggled) across the nearby frontier with China. Many of the settlements are accessible only on foot. The primary trekking region—an area of rice terraces and precipitous karst (limestone) outcrops between Ta Lúng and That Khé—is about 20 miles (32 kilometers) southeast of Cao Bang. Travelers to isolated villages, such as Na Nieng (Tay minority) and Pac Khoang (Red Dao), stay in typical hill-tribe houses built from wood and thatch and raised on stilts above a farm-animal enclosure. Meals are prepared over a smoky hearth in the middle kitchen, and everyone (including guests) sleeps on thin, futon-like mattresses spread across the floor.

**When to Go** Vietnam may be a tropical country, but winters in the northern highlands can be bitterly cold. Rainfall is heavy from May through August. In addition to Tet (the Chinese Lunar New Year), a Tay harvest festival holiday called Long Tong—"Going to the Field"—takes place about a week after Tet concludes.

**How to Find It** Cao Bang town is 169 miles (272 km) north of Hanoi. Daily buses from the capital take about seven hours to negotiate the route, or you can rent a car and driver from a reputable agency in Hanoi.

**Planning** The Bang Giang Hotel in Cao Bang town provides modest accommodation. Hanoi Peace Tour offers a nine-day road trip into the northern highlands. Paradissa runs week-long guided hiking trips.

**Websites** www.vietnamtourism.com, www.hanoipeacetour.vn, www.paradissa.com, www.waytovietnam.com/car.asp

ASIA

### Highland Hideout

It was among these craggy hills that **Ho Chi Minh** and his Vietminh cadres took refuge in the 1940s, during their struggle against French rule. Ho and other leaders established a base at **Pac Bo cave,** 33 miles (53 km) northwest of Cao Bang town. From here they launched the military and political campaign that led to victory over the French and independence for North Vietnam in 1954. Inside the cave is the wood-plank bed where Ho slept. In addition to a small museum, other nearby reminders of those days include **"Lenin" Stream** and **"Karl Marx" Mountain.**

A waterwheel in the foreground and limestone peaks in the background: Both are characteristic elements of the Cao Bang landscape.

Women cook corn in Boti's communal village kitchen.

INDONESIA

# Kingdom of Boti

On the island of Timor, there is a tiny kingdom where the people have forgone modernity to preserve their ancient culture.

The old king of Boti ruled not with a scepter but a garden hoe. He grew his own food and demanded that his 400 subjects do the same. "I have ten fingers," the monarch said at the age of 96. "If I use these ten fingers to get something to eat, I feel better." From 1939 until his death in 2005, Ama Nune Benu fought to save Indonesia's last remaining semiautonomous kingdom from encroaching modernity. His son has since taken the mantle, presiding over this small patch of tree-covered land amid the scrub of West Timor. Boti's greenery is testament to generations of animist and conservationist beliefs. "If you cut the trees," Ama Nune Benu once said, "you kill yourself." But times change. A new road leads into—and out of—Boti, bringing ever closer an alternate world of technology, vehicles, and schools. Yet those who stay in Boti remain rooted in their ancestors' ways. They grow the cotton that becomes the ikat sarongs around their waists. They carve dishes from coconuts. They start fires from flint and eat meals of homegrown sweet potatoes, popcorn, and peanuts. Sometimes, late at night, the men take sacred swords in hand, dancing to gamelan, feet stomping, arms flailing—just as old-time Boti warriors did after battle.

**When to Go** West Timor has two main seasons: Wet and dry. Travel is best during the dry season (May–September). Heavy rains and flooding can make Boti inaccessible during the wet season.

**How to Find It** Begin from the small town of Soe, about 30 miles (48 km) northwest of Boti. Independent travel to the village is not encouraged. Some Indonesian travel companies offer day trips to Boti by road as part of a package tour, or you can rent a guide for a three-hour trek to the village.

**Planning** Spend the night in Boti, get to know the villagers, and enjoy their garden-fresh food.

**Websites** www.floressatours.com, www.photovoicesinternational.org/indonesia/boti.html

### Royal Weavers

Since 1970, the royal women of Boti have run their own weaving corporation. They begin from scratch by ginning and spinning village-grown cotton. Their hand-dyed fabrics, called ikat, are among the region's thickest and most vibrantly colored. "We're happy. This is our profession, our job," says Princess Molo Benu. The women bring their spinning and their blankets and gather each day for communal craftwork and chitchat. They share the work, weaving the stories of their lives into patterns each knows by heart. Normally, it takes one woman six to nine months to finish a blanket on her own; together, the group can complete the task in three months. "We're good friends," Molo Benu says. "It's better that way."

ASIA

Built in 1891, the grand Australian Bank of Commerce building today houses the World Theatre.

AUSTRALIA

# CHARTERS TOWERS

Get a whiff of the gold-fueled frenzy that created Charters Towers in the late 1800s with a stroll around this onetime boomtown.

Stand on the polished floor tiles of the Royal Arcade—once the stock exchange of this northern Queensland town—and a shiver of excitement runs down your spine as you listen to the "Calling of the Card," an audio re-enactment of hectic share-trading at the height of the 19th-century gold-mining boom. In the 1870s, Charters Towers was so fabulously wealthy it was hooked up to the rest of the world by telegraph, electric lights blazed, and the stock exchange operated around the clock. Crowds gathered in the evenings to check the latest deals and prices. To its proud and newly rich inhabitants, the town was known as "The World"—there was no need to go elsewhere. People seeking their fortune arrived from across the globe. Sports and entertainment flourished, and the population peaked at more than 25,000. The magnificent heritage buildings clustered in the area known as the One Square Mile are a lasting monument to those glorious days and can easily be explored on foot: The Stock Exchange, the World Theatre (formerly the Australian Bank of Commerce), and the Excelsior Library (formerly Excelsior Hotel). In the 1880s and 1890s, the town's mines produced a vast quantity of gold from some of the world's richest ores. But it couldn't last forever—by 1916 the boom was over.

**When to Go** Plan to visit during the mild winter months (April–September) as the summer can be very hot. The Stock Exchange (Royal Arcade) is open Monday–Friday, 8:30 a.m.–4:30 p.m., and weekends 9 a.m.–3 p.m.

**How to Find It** Charters Towers lies 84 miles (135 km) inland from Townsville on Flinders Highway.

**Planning** Start with the short film *Ghosts of Gold* at the visitors' center on Mosman Street. From there, pick up a map of the heritage trail. Stay at a pub, motel, or B&B, such as Advent House B&B, or to get the full outback experience, try a farm stay on a working cattle station.

**Websites** www.charterstowers.qld.gov.au, www.nationaltrustqld.org/properties.htm

## Striking Gold

■ Charters Towers took its name from W.S. Charters, the gold commissioner at the time of the discovery of the area's first nugget in 1872, and from the conical shape of the hills near where the strike took place.

■ Take a 2.5-mile (4 km) drive to the **Venus Battery.** Built in 1872, it was the last of the ore-crushing facilities to close, in 1973. Hologram "ghosts" introduce the characters and stories that make up the history of the town.

■ On an early morning wildlife walk around **Towers Hill,** you'll see kangaroos, wallabies, and wedge-tailed eagles.

AUSTRALIA AND OCEANIA

# GALLE FORT

A fortified bastion on the Indian Ocean, Galle Fort displays
an eclectic mix of Portuguese, Dutch, and British influences.

Old Galle assaults all of your senses, but it is the sounds of this ancient walled city that pull you into the past. The cry of a muezzin calling the faithful to prayer, the smash of a ball off a cricket bat, the clink of cups and saucers at high tea, and the gentle whirl of a ceiling fan help to set the mood for a town little changed from a hundred years ago. Galle has gone through several reincarnations since the first Europeans arrived in the 16th century. The Portuguese started the seafront fortifications, but it was the Dutch who built the stout bastions that surround the town today. By 1796, the British were the island's colonial masters and they left their own stamp on Galle. Much of the Dutch and British colonial architecture survives, including landmarks like the Groote Kerk (Dutch Reformed Church), the British-era clock tower, and the iconic lighthouse with its garland of coconut palms. Surrounded by water on three sides, the town is breeched by only two gates and is best explored on foot along lanes that still bear colonial names, such as Queen Street. Several old buildings house relics of bygone days, most notably the Dutch Period Museum. The walls take about two hours to circumnavigate, best accomplished early in the morning when the air is still cool, or late afternoon just before sunset.

**When to Go** The weather is hot and humid year-round. The winter monsoon (December–March) brings drier skies and slightly higher temperatures. Between April and November, pack an umbrella or rainproof clothing.

**How to Find It** Galle lies 71 miles (114 km) south of Colombo. The fastest way to get there from the capital is to rent a private car and driver, a journey that can take as little as two hours. The train makes the Colombo-Galle trip in about 2.5 hours. Air-conditioned express buses take about three hours.

**Planning** The old Dutch administrative building (originally built in 1684) inside the fort has been converted into the luxury Amangalla Hotel, with antique furnishings, holistic spa, and elegant restaurant.

**Websites** www.srilanka.travel, www.amanresorts.com

### Geoffrey Bawa

From author Michael Ondaatje (*The English Patient*) to cricket player Aravinda de Silva, there are many renowned Sri Lankans. But none is more revered at home than Geoffrey Bawa (1919–2003), the island's foremost architect. Bawa's forte was "tropical modernism"—a highly attractive blend of traditional Asian form and Western function that created structures that became landmarks in themselves. His most notable achievement is the national parliament building in Colombo, yet many of his masterworks are found along the coast near Galle, including the chic Ahungalla and Lighthouse Hotels.

A British-style mailbox still stands on a street corner in Galle Fort. Two ladies stride past carrying parasols to ward off the heat of the sun.

# WINE & BEER FESTIVALS

From remote mountain villages to small towns on the plains, wine and beer festivals are an integral part of local life and joyous occasions to eat, dance, and celebrate the fruits of vine and hop.

### ❶ McMinnville, Oregon

Pinot Noir was first planted in Oregon in 1965, and the International Pinot Noir Celebration—held annually at the end of each July—is a chance for producers and consumers alike to celebrate this versatile grape. Expect food from the finest chefs in the northwest, vineyard tours, and a wide selection of wines to taste from all over the world.

Planning The festival takes place on the campus of Linfield College, McMinnville, 52 miles (84 km) southwest of Portland. Purchase tickets in advance. www.ipnc.org

### ❷ Curicó, Chile

The Fiesta de la Vendimia—Grape Harvest Festival—in Curicó's palm-shaded square kicks off with a cowboy parade. During the third week in March, the town square comes alive with costumed folk dancers, brassy music, and empanada vendors. Wineries are on hand with their fine, crisp white wines.

Planning Curicó lies 124 miles (200 km) south of Santiago and is best reached by car to allow visits to wineries. www.winesofchile.org, www.rutadelvinocurico.cl

### ❸ Chisinau, Moldova

Parades, folk dancing, and tastings in wine cellars in Chisinau's wine region are on the agenda for the annual National Wine Day, the second Sunday in October. In between performances, there is time to visit remarkable, extensive underground caves in (and under) nearby Cricova and Milestii Mici, where mines were converted into wine storage in the 1950s.

Planning Chisinau has an international airport and is accessible by train from Bucharest. www.travel-chisinau.com, www.milestii-mici.md

### ❹ Eger, Hungary

The Harvest Day Festival and Wine Show draws wine lovers from across northern Hungary every September. Winemakers in and around this baroque town open their doors to visitors for tastings. Hearty red Egri Bikavér wine is the star of the festival, but some vintners from the Tokaj region are usually on hand, too.

Planning Trains from Budapest take you to Eger and on to Tokaj. www.europeanrailguide.com/maps, www.gastronomy.gotohungary.co.uk

### ❺ Panzano, Italy

On the third weekend in September, Chianti winemakers gather for their Vino al Vino festival in the Tuscan hilltop town of Panzano, midpoint between Siena and Florence. About 20 wineries offer tastings; food stalls sell grilled, roasted, or pickled tidbits; and music fills the air.

Planning The purchase of a tasting glass is your ticket to sample and buy wines from the various vintners. www.panzano.com

### ❻ Diksmuide, Belgium

The little town of Diksmuide, in West Flanders, has been hosting its October beer festival for more than 50 years. Revelers throng the old market square, toasting the selections of top-quality Flemish beers to the blasts of brass oompah bands.

Planning The festival takes place over four Saturdays in October. Diksmuide is 15 miles (24 km) south of Ostend, at the foot of IJzertoren, a 22-story memorial to fallen Flemish soldiers. www.beerfestival.be

### ❼ Riquewihr, France

Riquewihr teems with folk dancers and wine tasters every July, when this small 16th-century town holds its rollicking Foire aux Vins (Wine Fair). In addition, 50 wine villages dotted along the eastern foothills of the Vosges Mountains in Alsace celebrate the grape with smaller-scale fairs between April and November.

Planning Arrive for the weekend in time for Friday's colorful market, and take the little train tour on the old town walls. www.ribeauville-riquewihr.com, www.vinsalsace.com

### ❽ Duras, France

Wine festivals abound in southwest France, but few have a setting as noble as the Côtes de Duras Fête du Vin on the grounds of the Château de Duras. The August wine fair features local products: Prunes from Agen, Périgord walnuts, the region's finest foie gras, as well as superior red and white wines.

Planning Allow time to explore Duras's rolling hillsides of vineyards and gardens. www.cotesdeduras.com

### ❾ Skipton, England

What better than a combination of glorious scenery, an ancient market town (complete with medieval castle), and a fine selection of lovingly crafted English ales? In late April, Skipton, in the North of England, hosts a three-day beer festival showcasing 70 or so "real ales," all made locally in small breweries. Don't miss the offerings of Skipton's own Copper Dragon Brewery.

Planning Skipton is the gateway to the beautiful mountains and moors of the Yorkshire Dales. www.keighleyandcravencamra.org.uk

### ❿ Getaria, Spain

Txakolí Eguna (Txakolí Day) is as eagerly awaited in the Basque province of Gipuzkoa as the arrival of the new Beaujolais is in France. Traditionally celebrated in Getaria on January 17, St. Antony's Day, the first tasting of the tart, slightly fizzy Txakolí white wine barely 100 days after the grape harvest is accompanied by fifes and drums, spontaneous versifiers declaiming Bacchic poetry, and *pintxos* (tapas on toothpicks).

Planning Getaria is 16 miles (26 km) west along the coast from San Sebastián. www.spain-info.com, www.costagipuzkoa.com

Opposite: A bowl of luscious, ripe Riesling grapes marks the start of the harvest on the Pfersigberg vineyard in Alsace, France, in early November.

# Makrinitsa

Walk in the footsteps of the Greek gods to their fabled
summer retreat on the slopes of Mount Pelion in Thessaly.

The noble, eastern Greek village of Makrinitsa clings to the wooded hillside of Mount Pelion as though suspended from it. Founded in the 13th century by refugees from Constantinople, Makrinitsa became a wealthy enclave of artisans, craftsmen, and traders. At street level, their 18th-century homes, embellished with window and wall decorations, have roofs so low that a cat might easily hop onto them. But on the other side, facing the valley, the houses are three stories high. From the lowest to highest point in the village, there is a sharp rise of 1,640 feet (500 meters). Heavy slate roofs keep interiors cool in summer, attracting city dwellers to stay in the village during July and August. The ancient Greek gods were said to summer on Mount Pelion, listening to the same babbling brooks and resting in the same chestnut-shaded glens enjoyed by people today. Stone paths lead walkers through dense woods to discover one small church after another, each with frescoes, icons, and sculpted doors. Walk up to Makrinitsa's highest point, the women's monastery of Agios Gerasimos, or sit under plane trees on the square with a coffee and chestnut sweets. Take in spectacular sunsets over Volos and its bay in the distance. Is it any wonder that Makrinitsa has long been known as "the balcony of Mount Pelion"?

**When to Go** From April into May is a magical time as Pelion's apple trees bloom across the valleys. Winter brings skiers to Mount Pelion in droves, and Athenians escape the summer heat here, so spring or fall are more tranquil. Avoid Makrinitsa on Sundays, when all of Volos seems to arrive for the day.

**How to Find It** Travel to Volos by bus, a five-hour journey north from Athens, then rent a car to explore Thessaly's hidden villages. Steep streets and limited parking in Makrinitsa discourage traffic, so park outside town, or in Portaria, and walk the final mile (1.6 km) on groomed paths up to the village.

**Planning** Bring good walking or hiking shoes to navigate the steep stone paths.

**Websites** www.aroundpelion.com, www.pelion-paths.gr

### Around Pelion

■ **Pelion,** a long mountainous peninsula, stretches like a bent index finger to divide the Gulf of Volos (or Pagasitic Gulf) from the Aegean Sea. Peppered with charming villages, ancient churches, and marked paths, it is a hiker's paradise.

■ Stroll along the marina or shop in the old center of **Volos,** a university town 10 miles (16 km) south of Makrinitsa. Tavernas around the harbor specialize in fish dishes traditionally accompanied by *tsipouro,* a spirit distilled from the residue of the wine press. From Volos, you can take a ferry to two of the islands of the Sporades— **Skopelos** and **Skiathos.**

A shady square in Makrinitsa occupies a rare patch of flat land in the village on Mount Pelion.

In the old town of Gjirokastra, your wake-up call is more likely to be a cockerel than a car.

ALBANIA

# GJIROKASTRA

An Ottoman-era architectural jewel of a town has survived
invasion, siege, and a dictatorial regime largely intact.

After rain, polished ancient cobblestones checkered in a crosshatch of pink and white make a slippery pathway for those exploring the steep, narrow streets of this gray-tiled showcase of Ottoman architecture. But post-precipitation walks are the best time to appreciate the probable Greek origins of this overgrown village's name, Argyrokastro, or "silver city." The birthplace of Albania's Stalinist dictator Enver Hoxha (1908–85) and a center of resistance to Ottoman occupation, Gjirokastra found communism kinder to it, at least aesthetically, than many Albanian towns, gaining museum-city status in 1961. This is a sterling place to enjoy Albanian hospitality, which is based on a code of customary law, the Kanun. In the past, the Kanun also underpinned rigidly observed blood feuds, hence the many *kulle*—fortified towers—erected by landowners to protect their families. They are topped by beautifully decorated, galleried living quarters, such as at the Zekate House (open by appointment). Other Ottoman-era attractions include the magnificent castle, the old bazaar and mosque, the ethnographic museum in Hoxha's reconstructed former home, and "Ali Pasha's bridge," actually the only remaining part of a 19th-century aqueduct.

**When to Go** The best weather is between April and June. July and August can be very hot. Winters are often harsh and roads to Gjirokastra are sometimes closed because of snow. Several festivals take place in September, including the Traditional Cuisine Fair, the National Artisan Fair, and Gjirokastra Liberation Day (September 18). The town plays host to Albania's National Folk Festival once every four or five years.

**How to Find It** Gjirokastra lies 144 miles (232 km) south of the capital, Tirana, about five hours by car or six by bus. A slower coastal road goes via Saranda. It is also accessible from Ioannina in northern Greece.

**Planning** In winter, bring hiking boots to cope with the slippery cobbles. Gjirokastra has a tourist office in the old town's bazaar. A good place to stay is the family-run Hotel Kalemi in the historic Palorto district.

**Websites** www.gjirokastra.org, hotelkalemi.tripod.com

### Ismail Kadaré

As a master of Albanian history, or the Kanun, nobody outshines Gjirokastra's illustrious son, Ismail Kadaré. When the first Man Booker International Prize garlanded him in 2005, many literati were aghast. They had never heard of Kadaré. Other plaudits include a nomination for the Nobel Prize in literature and the Légion d'Honneur. Yet as an interpreter of life under totalitarianism, he is every bit the rival of Solzhenitsyn or Orwell. Kadaré's terse *Broken April* (1978) is no cheery read, dealing with a chilling blood feud, but its masterful prose and hidden layers of meaning compel several re-readings. He also has two works about Gjirokastra: *Chronicle in Stone* (1971) and *Matters of Madness* (2005).

EUROPE

Woodlands surround St. Jakob am Thurn's ancient castle tower, reflected serenely in the lake.

AUSTRIA

# St. Jakob am Thurn

To find peace and solitude in a country setting near Salzburg, look no farther than the hamlet of St. Jakob—until festival time.

Barely 15 minutes south of Salzburg by car lies a little village that could not be more romantic and secluded if it tried. Technically belonging to the town of Puch bei Salzburg, the heart of the village consists of no more than seven houses grouped around a castle tower first recorded in 1238 and a church that enjoyed much popularity as a center for pilgrimage in medieval times. The latter forms part of the Way of St. James, the pilgrimage route across Europe to Santiago de Compostela in Spain, and is worth a visit for its relics and baroque artifacts. Explore the surrounding woodlands to discover natural caves, waterfalls, and extensive opportunities for rock climbing and mountain biking, or enjoy a leisurely stroll by the village's lake and a peek into the private gardens of the castle. Walk in the countryside, where most of the farmhouses have belonged to the same families for at least 200 years and have been lovingly restored in keeping with local traditional style. Join the locals to see the world-renowned performance of the Jakobischützen at the summer festival, or indulge in the Christmas market, arguably the most authentic and atmospheric in the area. It is one of the few markets still to stage the procession of Perchten, when participants don scary folkloric masks and devil's costumes.

**When to Go** Visit in summer, when balconies brim with flowers and village life takes place outdoors. The Christmas market opens on weekends in December.

**How to Find It** St. Jakob is 6 miles (10 km) south of Salzburg. You can take bus 160 from Hauptbahnhof (central train station) to the Haslach stop in Hallein, near Puch, and walk the final mile (1.6 km) to the village.

**Planning** Stroll around the lake to Schützenwirt on the far side, an organic restaurant serving local produce and its own award-winning Jakobsgold beer.

**Websites** www.salzburg.info, www.visit-salzburg.net, www.salzburgerland.com

### Summer Festival

Legend has it that the **Jakobischützen**—the marksmen of St. James (Jakob in German)—who hail from St. Jakob, were formed in 1476 to protect the people against invading Turks. Since then, they have, rather peacefully, been devoted to "piety, charity, and the welfare of pilgrims." Their traditional dance and colorful folkloric costumes have enlivened many a village celebration and are still at the heart of the **Kirtag summer festival,** which takes place on the Sunday following July 25. They have earned an international reputation, performing in folk festivals around the world.

EUROPE

ITALY

# PIENZA

A rare fruit of the ancient utopian dream to create an "ideal city," Pienza is perfectly designed in every way.

EUROPE

As you pass through the gates of Pienza, leaving behind the sinuous curves of the Val d'Orcia, you understand why the town is known as the "ideal city." The elegance of Renaissance geometry, the harmony of shapes and volumes, the balance between the sacred and the secular—that is what the 15th-century Pope Pius II envisioned when he decided to convert his humble hometown of Corsignano into a city worthy of a newly elected pope. A true Renaissance man of impressive intellect and learning, Pius II hired the Florentine architect Bernardo Rossellino to realize his dream. Centuries have passed since the town's inauguration in 1462, yet they have only lightly touched this Tuscan jewel. The embodiment of the Pope's vision is nowhere more apparent than in the main square, Piazza Pio II, where the cathedral faces the town hall and is embraced by the palaces of the Piccolomini and Borgia families. To savor Pienza's colors, flavors, and aromas, step into the narrow streets that lead up to Corso Rossellino. The minuscule *trattorie* and specialty shops—purveyors of juniper, truffles, porcini, marmalades, pecorino, olives— exemplify Val d'Orcia's reputation for gastronomic excellence. Raise a glass of the local Brunello di Montalcino wine to Pius II and his monumental achievement.

**When to Go** From April through October has the best weather. Annual events include the Pienza e I Fiori (flower festival) in May; Fiera di Cacio in September; and, just after Christmas, Torneo del Panforte dedicated to this traditional Christmas sweet.

**How to Find It** Pienza is 77 miles (124 km) south of Florence. It is a 75-minute journey by bus from Siena.

**Planning** Rent a car and allow for at least four to five days to enjoy this voluptuous corner of Tuscany, its superlative wines, hearty food, and rich mosaic of natural beauty.

**Websites** www.pienza.info, www.ufficioturisticodipienza.it, www.valdorcia.it, www.palazzopiccolominipienza.it

### The Big Cheese

Pienza offers many ways to enjoy *cacio pecorino,* its renowned sheep's cheese: Delicate and soft, crumbly and aged, wrapped in walnut leaves—or thrown at a target. In early September, Pienza hosts a festival dedicated to cacio. The crowning event is the **Cacio al Fuso** competition. Under the intent gaze of locals and visitors, six teams, each representing one of the town's neighborhoods, throw disks of cacio, aiming to land them as close as possible to a vertical pole anchored in the pavement of **Piazza Pio II.** This is no leisurely game—the participants will have been preparing for the tournament for months.

Pienza's focal point is the 15th-century cathedral, commissioned by Pope Pius II for his hometown.

ITALY

# Maratea

A group of villages, spread along a dramatic stretch of shoreline in the region of Basilicata, is one of Italy's best kept secrets.

EUROPE

Clinging to vertiginous cliffs and huddling around sheltered coves along Italy's southwest coast are a smattering of beguiling villages that together make up the "town" of Maratea. For more than 19 miles (31 kilometers), pine forests, sandy beaches, and rocky inlets alternate, providing places for swimming, trekking, and yachting that rival the beauty and biodiversity of the more famous Amalfi Coast to the north. Dubbed "the pearl of the Tyrrhenian Sea," Maratea attracts vacationing Italian families and couples, but it is largely ignored by foreign travelers. The villages' anonymity helps keep their sapphire and emerald waters clean and contributes to the area's local feel and authentic atmosphere. Along the coast, Fiumicello, Porto di Maratea, and Marina di Maratea are most lively in the summer months, when their ports brim with yachts and their bars, restaurants, and cafés are abuzz with activity. Uphill, Maratea Paese is the inland old town, with meandering alleyways, pretty squares, and ancient churches—enough to keep a visitor busy for a good afternoon. Farther uphill still, on Monte San Biagio, stands the symbol of Maratea, the 72-foot (22 meter) Redentore, a massive Carrara marble statue depicting Christ the Redeemer with arms outstretched in the form of a cross. He faces east, turning his back on the coastal panorama, seemingly unaware that one of Italy's most astonishing and secret landscapes sprawls behind him.

**When to Go** You can swim from May-June through October, but the coastline is ideal for trekking year-round. Most beach clubs, restaurants, and hotels are only open May through October. The last two weeks in August, when Italians take their summer vacations, are the busiest.

**How to Find It** The closest airports are Naples, 97 miles (156 km) to the north, and Lamezia Terme, 95 miles (153 km) to the south, where you can rent a car for the scenic drive to Maratea.

**Planning** Accommodations and restaurants are mainly located in Fiumicello. As in most southern Italian towns, Maratea's shops close for a long lunch break between 1:30 p.m. and 4 or 5 p.m. Restaurants are open 12:30–3 p.m. and 7:30 p.m.–midnight. The Tourist Office is located at Piazza Gesù 32 in Fiumicello.

**Website** www.aptbasilicata.it

### Saint's Day

If you travel to Maratea in the second week in May, you will witness the **Feast of San Biagio,** a religious festival celebrating the town's patron saint.

On the Thursday of that week, a silver effigy containing the relics of the saint is removed from its chapel in the **Basilica di San Biagio** beside the Redentore statue and covered with a red shroud. Townspeople take turns carrying it down the mountain on their shoulders to the **Chiesa di Santa Maria Maggiore** in Maratea Paese. Here, the cloth is removed, and Maratea's mayor symbolically hands over the keys to the town to the effigy of the saint.

Villagers celebrate with Masses, processions, and celebrations throughout the weekend until the silver statue is returned to its resting place in the basilica high on Monte San Biagio on Sunday.

Opposite: Dusk falls on a Maratea waterfront on the Gulf of Policastro. Above: An alleyway in Maratea Paese

# COLLONGES-LA-ROUGE

To explore Collonges-la-Rouge is to step back in time
to a village where medieval noblemen once summered.

EUROPE

Even when it is raining, the chunky rectangular stones of Collonges-la-Rouge, in southwestern France, glow with a rust-red hue. In sunshine they fairly blaze, set against the lush Limousin countryside, dotted with walnut trees and neat rows of vines. Small châteaus and manor houses, arched gateways, walled courtyards, stone dormers, and soaring chimneys are all fashioned from local red sandstone. The houses are grand for village dwellings for these were the summer retreats of medieval noblemen. Round, pointy, pepperpot turrets and square towers are topped by steep roofs of *lauze*—layer upon layer of flat stones, covered in moss. Don't miss the 16th-century Castel de Vassinhac and the museum of local life in Maison de la Sirène, two of the finest buildings. The market hall at the centre of the village still includes a communal baker's oven, today fired up for the annual La Fête du Pain (Bread Festival). The streets are horse-and-cart narrow and pedestrian-friendly. In spring, flowers festoon the buildings, on walls, in window boxes, around doorways, and in pots. Many houses have walled gardens, shady trees, and potagers for herbs and vegetables. Peer over a wall and you are likely to see a blue-aproned woman tending herbs in the way her forebears have done for hundreds of years.

**When to Go** Spring and fall are the best times to visit, as July and August can be hot and busy. The annual Fête du Pain is held on the first Sunday of August.

**How to Find It** The bus from Brive, 12 miles (19 km) northwest of the village, takes around half an hour. Cars are not allowed in the village, so if you plan to drive you will have to use the pay-and-display parking lot nearby and walk. If that is full, you may have to park on a rural road.

**Planning** There are restaurants and cafés along with shops selling local produce. The Relais de St. Jacques de Compostelle and Jeanne Maison d'Hôtes provide comfortable accommodations.

**Websites** www.les-plus-beaux-villages-de-france.org, www.jeannemaisondhotes.com, www.francethisway.com/places/collongeslarouge.php

### A Church of Two Faiths

The centerpiece of the village, the Romanesque **Church of St. Pierre,** dates largely from the 11th and 12th centuries. Fortified during France's wars of religion in the 16th century, it has both a square tower and a taller round one. It also has two naves, which enabled Catholic and Protestant (Huguenot) worshipers of the 16th century to use the same church—a remarkably tolerant arrangement. The village became a favorite resting place for pilgrims traveling to Santiago de Compostela in Spain. A quiet inspection of the church may be accompanied by classical music—slide a coin donation into the slot meter for lights and music.

Pepperpot turrets and glowing, red sandstone walls characterize the village of Collonges-la-Rouge.

Some of the best views of La Roque-Gageac are to be had from canoes on the Dordogne River.

FRANCE

# La Roque-Gageac

Pause a while in this village, which sits so snugly between river and cliff that it could almost have been hewn out of the rock itself.

Southwest France is renowned for picturesque villages, some rising on ridges, others folded into valleys. One of the most unusual—looking something like an opera set—is La Roque-Gageac. Whether approached by land or by water, this assemblage of toast-colored stone dwellings appears to grow like mushrooms from the base of an immense cliff, wedged against the banks of the Dordogne River. Located on a site inhabited since prehistoric times, La Roque-Gageac was for centuries a busy river port. To capture the boatman's viewpoint, spend an hour on a *gabare,* a replica of the flat-bottomed boats that plied the Dordogne, or rent a kayak or canoe to explore at your own pace. Then fill your afternoon poking around the steep village streets. These are so warmed on their south-facing cliff that you will find tropical plants, including bamboo and palm trees, particularly around the 16th-century church on the eastern edge of the village. On one street, a simple marker tells (in French) of a disaster in 1957, when a part of the rock face fell onto some homes and killed three residents. On another winding street, the old manor house of the Tarde family stands watch over the town, as it has done since the Renaissance, during wars and other disasters as well as more tranquil times.

**When to Go** Travel in Périgord in spring or fall to avoid summer crowds.

**How to Find It** La Roque-Gageac lies 110 miles (177 km) east from Bordeaux and 9 miles (14 km) south of Sarlat. It is best to arrive by car; parking is available on the outskirts of the village.

**Planning** Stay for a weekend to discover castles and gardens on the Dordogne River. Cozy hotel or *chambre d'hôte* (bed-and-breakfast) rooms offer spectacular views. Auberge La Plume d'Oie, on the main street, has four rooms and an inventive chef loyal to local produce; reserve well in advance.

**Websites** www.les-plus-beaux-villages-de-France.org, www.sarlat-tourisme.com, www.aubergelaplumedoie.com, www.marqueyssac.com

## Gardens in the Sky

The promontory of **Marqueyssac Château,** 3 miles (4.8 km) west along the river road to Beynac, is quite a sight from the water. To enter a truly magical world, walk through the cliff-top gardens, preferably just before sunset on a spring evening. Hand-clipped boxwood hedges line paths leading to the belvedere, 427 ft (130 m) above the river, with a heart-stopping panorama of the rolling Périgord landscape. By day, you could stop for an ice cream or lunch on the café terrace to survey the château-studded river valley. In early fall, pink Naples cyclamen carpets the woods. Spring brings pastel wisteria for the annual Easter-egg hunt. The gardens are open April to November.

EUROPE

THE
CROOKED HOUSE
GALLERY

LAVENHAM
paintings · cards · prints

ENGLAND

# LAVENHAM

The intensity of Lavenham's color palette and its crooked timber buildings will bring a smile to the face of any traveler.

If you have never seen woad, head for Lavenham. The plant, used by the ancient Celts to paint themselves blue, was used in this Suffolk town to dye its once famous Lavenham blue broadcloth. In the late Middle Ages, "Lavenham blue" made the town's citizens so rich that they could build what has become the largest collection of half-timber buildings in Britain. Look out for old weavers' cottages with craft symbols in their plasterwork, and visit the garden of the Guildhall of Corpus Christi (1530), where woad and other plants used by the local dyers are still grown. Outside is a shop from Tudor times with two arched windows. You can almost hear a shopkeeper attired in doublet and hose calling out his wares: "Finest Lavenham blue!" Hundreds of years later, Lavenham is still a colorful town. More than 300 of its buildings date from around the 15th century, and many are rendered in washes of different hues, notably Suffolk pink, made from elderberries, sloes, or even ox blood. The only time you are liable to hear raised voices is when there is heated debate about whether beams should be painted—like the whitewashed Guildhall—or not. It is possible to see inside some of the town's historic buildings, such as Little Hall on the main square, built in the 1390s and now a museum. You can stay in others, like the Swan Hotel, built about ten years after Little Hall. The hotel's Old Bar has a wall signed by British and U.S. airmen stationed at Lavenham Airfield during World War II.

**When to Go** Check the National Trust for events at Guildhall (closed late December through early March), including demonstrations of clothmaking. Look out for theater productions and other events at Kentwell.

**How to Find It** Lavenham is 75 miles (121 km) northeast of London; driving will take about two hours. Trains from London go to Sudbury, from where there are buses northward to Lavenham (7 miles/11 km).

**Planning** Call in at the Pharmacy in the High Street and pick up an audio tour with map—it lasts about an hour and a half. On weekends from June through October a guided walk sets off from Lavenham Tourist Information Centre in Lady Street. The Great House restaurant serves French food; it is a boutique hotel, too.

**Websites** www.discoverlavenham.co.uk, www.greathouse.co.uk, www.kentwell.co.uk, www.nationaltrust.org.uk, www.suffolk.gov.uk

EUROPE

### Stars in Their Eyes

■ Take a look at **Shilling Old Grange** on Shilling Street. Jane Taylor, a contemporary and friend of the English landscape painter John Constable, lived here with her father and sister. One clear night in 1810 she looked out of her bedroom window and was inspired to write a few lines that began: "Twinkle, twinkle, little star…"

■ **Kentwell** is an Elizabethan moated mansion in Long Melford, 6 miles (10 km) southwest from Lavenham. Owned by Judith and Patrick Phillips, the 500-year-old manor still has the feeling of a family home. In fact, when you visit you can wander through the rooms used by the enthusiastic couple, who have been restoring the manor since they bought it in 1971. It gives a wonderful idea of life in Tudor times, especially during the summer Great Annual Re-Creation, when hundreds of costumed "re-creators" get into character.

Opposite: Lavenham's Crooked House was built in 1425. Above: The Swan Hotel dates from 1400.

High-backed settles and flagstone floors adorn Great Tew's Falkland Arms, a traditional Cotswold village pub.

ENGLAND

# HIDDEN COTSWOLD VILLAGES

Exploring the Cotswolds is like a game of hide-and-seek, with exquisite, yellow-stone villages secreted off the beaten track.

The Cotswold Hills occupy nearly 800 square miles (2,070 square kilometers) of southwest England, sprawling across six counties. Many of their towns and villages—famous for their architecture of warm, yellow Cotswold stone— are popular tourist traps, but others remain known to few, apart from the residents. One such place is Blockley in Gloucestershire. Halfway between Moreton-in-Marsh and Chipping Camden, the village is hidden in a steep-sided valley and not on a road to anywhere in particular. Silk mills, powered by a forceful brook, once thrived here, and they still stand, among rows of cottages made even prettier by climbing roses, with views to sheep-dotted slopes on the other side of the valley. About 20 miles (32 kilometers) east of Blockley, Oxfordshire's Great Tew is one of the prettiest villages in England, but it, too, is comparatively little-known, despite a prize-winning 16th-century pub, the Falkland Arms. Many of Tew's cottages have thatched roofs with neatly patterned caps, as does the old post office, now a café and store. From the primary school with Elizabethan chimneys to the triangular village green, every view is jigsaw-puzzle-perfect.

**When to Go** English summers can be unpredictable and wet, but when the weather is good you can enjoy the landscape from a garden or bench outside an historic pub. Weekends are often busy.

**How to Find It** Various Cotswold centers, such as Moreton-in-Marsh, can be reached by train from London's Paddington Station (90 minutes). Some villages are accessible by bus, but services are infrequent, and the only reliable way of seeing much of the area, or reaching the lesser-known villages, is by car.

**Planning** Most villages offer attractive B&B accommodations, and the larger ones have historic hotels. The National Trust opens many splendid old country mansions and gardens to the public.

**Websites** www.cotswolds.info, www.cotswoldsaonb.org.uk, www.stanwayfountain.co.uk

### Spouting High

The tiny village of **Stanway** stands at the base of the Cotswolds escarpment, 13 miles (21 km) west of Moreton-in-Marsh. It has a 17th-century manor house of extraordinary beauty, constructed from a warm local stone known as Guiting Yellow. Inside, the manor still contains many of its original furnishings and fittings. Outside, a recently restored water garden, of 18th-century design, is now complemented by the world's tallest gravity fountain. This shoots water 300 ft (90 m) into the air and is visible for miles around when it operates on open-house days in June, July, and August.

SPAIN

# BEGET

Tucked away in a beautiful valley, high in the Catalan Pyrenees of northeastern Spain, is a stone-built village that time forgot.

EUROPE

To the few people who have heard of it, Beget—1,775 feet (541 meters) above sea level in the Pyrenees—has the reputation for being Catalonia's *més bufó* (prettiest) village. A collection of some four dozen houses, Beget (pronounced "buh-JHET") has two medieval bridges, a Romanesque church, and 27 permanent residents. It was entirely cut off from motorized transport until the mid-1960s, when a *pista forestal* (jeep track) was engineered from the road to Camprodon to the southwest. In 1980, Beget was finally connected to the 20th century with an asphalt roadway that links with the road from Camprodón to Prats-de-Mollo in France. Beget's charm comes from its isolation, the golden-ocher stone of its small houses, the rustic wooden doors and balconies, and the humpbacked bridges spanning the pellucid stream that runs through the village. A slender square bell tower rises from the late 12th-century Church of Sant Cristòfol. Inside is a Romanesque baptismal font, a Gothic alabaster statue of the Virgin Mary, and the 6-foot (1.8 meter) Majestat de Beget—Majesty of Beget—a brightly painted wood-carved image of Christ on the cross, dressed in a sumptuous full-length tunic. Since 2003, another jeep track, from the village of Oix to the southeast, has connected Beget to Castellfollit de la Roca in Catalonia's spectacular volcanic hinterland, La Garrotxa.

**When to Go** April through June and September through November have the best weather.

**How to Find It** Beget is just over 10 miles (16 km) northeast of Camprodon, which is nearly 60 miles (97 km) by road northwest of Girona airport.

**Planning** Bring hiking boots and warm clothing. You will need to rent a car to reach Beget. If the church is locked, ask for the keys at Carrer Bellaire 8. There are three restaurants in town, of which El Forn offers rooms, a secluded terrace over the stream, and fine Garrotxa cooking.

**Websites** www.pyreneesguide.com, www.rural-pyrenees-guide.com, www.turismegarrotxa.com

## Towns of La Garrotxa

■ **Besalú** in La Garrotxa is one of Catalonia's best-preserved medieval towns. Its most iconic sight is an 11th-century fortified bridge over the Fluvià River. The *mikvah*, a 13th-century ritual bath used in Orthodox Judaism for attaining physical and spiritual purity through immersion in running water, is the most unusual sight in Besalú's *call*, or Jewish quarter.

■ **Castellfollit de la Roca** clings to the top of a 150-ft (46 m) basaltic cliff carved by the Fluvià and Toronell rivers. Medieval houses built from volcanic stone line the streets. From the edge of the town, relish spectacular views along the Fluvià and Toronell Valleys.

One of Beget's two stone bridges crosses the Trull River, with the tower of the Church of Sant Cristofol silhouetted against a perfectly blue sky.

# CITY SECRETS

9

Atmospheric neighborhoods, hidden gardens where nature is left to run wild, tiny squares unmarked on tourist maps, venerable cafés haunted by illustrious ghosts—these are the places that give a city its soul. So slip away from the crowded thoroughfares, leave behind the famous landmarks, and take a peek behind the scenes. Some of the destinations are so secret that they might even surprise the natives. How many New Yorkers, for instance, know that Central Park is a year-round bird-watcher's paradise? Other journeys lead to places that locals might prefer to keep to themselves, like the tranquil islands in Venice's lagoon, a world away from the camera-clicking throngs on the Rialto. For those prepared to penetrate the backstreets, rewards lie waiting: Tiny but welcoming dance-clubs throbbing with the rhythms of samba in Rio de Janeiro; tantalizingly fresh produce along Bologna's winding alleyways; and in downtown Beijing, a labyrinth of lanes known as *hutong*, enclaves of a traditional way of life that is fast disappearing.

The well-preserved walled city of Pingyao in China retains many vestiges of its ancient and once-prosperous past, offering today's visitor a remarkable snapshot of what life would have been like in the Ming and Qing dynasties.

# BIRDING IN CENTRAL PARK

This green lung in the heart of the city is as
much of a lifeline for bird life as it is for humans.

New York City's Central Park—843 acres (341 hectares) of wilderness, made up of woodlands, vast stretches of lawn, and various bodies of water—is a veritable sanctuary for birds and bird-lovers alike. Nearly 200 different species of bird make the park their home at one time of the year or another. Most are migratory and drop by when journeying between warmer climes farther south and breeding areas in the north, but there are also year-round residents, such as the blue jay, the northern cardinal, and the red-bellied woodpecker. The Ramble, a quiet area overgrown with trees and shrubs between 74th and 79th Streets, is a great place to spot both local and migratory birds. In spring and fall, watch out for small, colorful songbirds, including the yellow-and-gray Canada warbler and the black-throated green warbler. Just to the north, at the Belvedere Castle, spy on sharp-shinned hawks and Cooper's hawks as they travel south each fall—you may even see one feasting on a less-fortunate bird. Other propitious spots include the Reservoir, between 86th and 96th Streets, where mallard, buffleheads, and other duck and geese overwinter. In the dense North Woods between 102nd and 106th Streets, downy woodpeckers chatter and knock against the trees, while hummingbirds such as the soot-colored chimney swift have been known to dart above the Great Hill, off Central Park West on 104th Street.

**When to Go** While you can observe birds in Central Park year-round, fall and spring are when many species migrate between north and south. Most are more active in the early morning and late afternoon.

**How to Find It** A good place to start is the Central Park Conservancy at Belvedere Castle, located mid-park at 79th Street.

**Planning** Free kits containing binoculars, a guidebook, and maps are available on loan from the Central Park Conservancy, 10 a.m.-4:30 p.m., Tuesdays through Sundays, April-October, and Wednesdays through Sundays, November-March.

**Website** www.centralpark.com

### Pale Male and Lola

Meet Pale Male, a red-tailed hawk and a true New York City celebrity. Since the early 1990s, he has resided in a nest on the ledge of a Fifth Avenue building across the street from Central Park. In 2004, he and his current mate, Lola, faced temporary eviction when the building's residents voted to have his nest removed, but protests ensued and the birds were ultimately welcomed back.

Today, as Pale Male's progeny raise offspring of their own and other red-tailed hawks migrate to the city, a glimpse of these majestic birds is no longer a rarity, but is still nothing less than thrilling.

A black-crowned night heron visits Harlem Meer at the northern end of Central Park.

In late April and May, the Arboretum's thousands of azaleas explode into a riot of vibrant color.

WASHINGTON, D.C.

# NATIONAL ARBORETUM

This glorious expanse of trees, meadows,
and floral plantings is truly America's garden.

Hidden away on the east side of Washington, D.C., the National Arboretum was launched in 1927 with a mandate to "conserve and display trees, shrubs, flowers, and other plants." But it got its real start in 1935 during the Depression, when the Civilian Conservation Corps dedicated thousands of man-hours to create the roads, ponds, greenhouses, trails, fountains, and plantings that make up today's 446-acre (180 hectare) site. The result of their efforts is a horticultural wonder, where you can easily spend a day and still see only a fraction of what is on offer. Well-tended paths lead you to out-of-the-way treasures, such as the quirky National Capitol Columns—a sunny plaza and fountain created around a group of columns donated after a renovation of the U.S. Capitol. Spring is heralded by the mass blooming of azaleas, while the pastel colors of the Dogwood Collection are another early delight. Not to be missed is the Bonsai Collection, considered one of the finest in the world, with scores of meticulously tended miniature trees, some of which are almost 400 years old. Alternatively, relish the tranquil Herb Garden, the colors and fragrances of the Asian Collection, the deep green splendor of the Holly and Magnolia Collections, or the near-mystical serenity found in the stand of dawn redwoods.

**When to Go**  Go late April through June to enjoy floral displays, or mid-October for fall colors.

**How to Find It**  The main entrance is on R Street, two blocks north of Bladensburg Road. The National Arboretum is located in the heart of an old and somewhat shabby section of the city, so it is best to arrive by car. Take the Metrorail train to Union Station, then a cab to the Arboretum. Staff will be glad to call you a cab for your return.

**Planning**  A 35-minute narrated tram tour is available several times daily on weekends and major holidays, mid-April through mid-October. There are no restaurants in the Arboretum, so bring a picnic.

**Website**  www.usna.usda.gov

### Water Lily Paradise

**Kenilworth Aquatic Gardens,** in northeastern Washington, D.C., is the only U.S. National Park dedicated to the cultivation of water lilies, lotuses, and other water-dwelling plants. Surrounded on three sides by the extensive Kenilworth Marshes, the 12-acre (5 ha) park is a place of lush beauty and peacefulness, where meadows surround a series of still ponds. In late spring and summer, these burst forth with the multihued blooms of flowering water plants from around the world. On many days you can stroll in near solitude among the grassy, willow-shaded spaces and beside the flower-filled ponds.

NORTH AMERICA

Office workers in the downtown concrete jungle find lunchtime solace in the Yerba Buena Gardens.

CALIFORNIA

# SoMa, San Francisco

If the city's other districts remain rooted—however charmingly—in the past, the SoMa District represents the future.

Once the town's skid road, the South of Market (SoMa) District reinvented itself in the 1990s, helped along by well-funded redevelopment initiatives. The gritty warehouses that once served the area's industrial past have been gradually transformed into hip and happening spaces for work, living, art and music, and the pursuit of pleasure. In the early years of this century, SoMa was the center of the city's dot. com boom—and subsequent bust. While business has suffered, the good times endure, at least in the social sense, with a plethora of restaurants serving food that ranges from the sophisticated to the idiosyncratic and a pulsating night scene that runs the gamut from plush discos to blues clubs to S&M fetishistic grottoes. The district is multiracial and multicultural, though its denizens also share some common bonds: For the most part they are young, highly educated, and involved in media or information technology. SoMa doesn't have any center to speak of—its restaurants, clubs, and bars are scattered over a couple of square miles of flat, rather drab cityscape. An urban oasis can be found at the Alice Street Community Gardens, where younger disabled people and seniors from the neighborhood tend flower and vegetable plots beneath a huge hand-painted mural.

**When to Go** Spring and fall bring the most comfortable temperatures.

**How to Find It** SoMa is bounded by Market Street to the north and northwest, San Francisco Bay to the east, Townsend Street on the south and southeast, and Highway 101 on the west-southwest.

**Planning** Visitors can take a picnic to the Alice Street Community Gardens. A sample of restaurants includes: So (Asian Fusion), Pazzia Restaurant and Pizzeria (rustic Sicilian), Fringale (French bistro).

**Websites** www.sfgate.com/neighborhoods/sf/soma, www.sanfrancisco.com

### Cartoon Museum

While SoMa's signature museum is the **San Francisco Museum of Modern Art,** located in the Yerba Buena Center on Mission Street, art of another kind is showcased at the **Cartoon Art Museum,** which began as a collective of local artists intent on sharing their work with each other and the general public. In 1987, a generous endowment from *Peanuts* creator Charles Schulz allowed the museum to move to its current location on Mission Street. It now houses 6,000 pieces in a permanent collection and supports rotating exhibitions that cover everything from newspaper comic strips to Japanese manga.

NORTH AMERICA

# THE SOUNDS OF RIO

Set your feet tapping as you follow the music and dance trail through Brazil's most exotic city, Rio de Janeiro.

SOUTH AMERICA

With its conical mountains and miles of beaches, Rio has a setting that a surrealist might have conceived. In this city of carnival, the background is always musical. If you have spent the day with "The Girl from Ipanema" playing in your head, grab a *chopp* (or *chope*), a Brazilian draft beer, at Garota de Ipanema. This is the bar in the Ipanema district where composer Tom Jobim and lyricist Vinícius de Moraes penned the song back in 1962, introducing the world to the infectious rhythms of bossa nova. Across the street is Vinícius Piano Bar, where live bossa nova acts keep the flame alive. A block away is Toca do Vinícius, a virtual temple of bossa nova, where fans can browse a trove of CDs and catch impromptu evening concerts by singers such as Claudia Telles. After that, head to the Lapa neighborhood in the center of the city. Cariocas (Rio's inhabitants) like to say that it does not matter whether you are rich or poor in Lapa, because everyone comes for the same things: Music, dancing, and a well-made *caipirinha*, the national cocktail of sliced limes, sugar, ice, and *cachaça*, a sugarcane liquor. Among Lapa's best clubs is Rio Scenarium, an eccentric *boite* (club) jammed with antiques as well as partygoers. You can also dance and hear music at Estrela de Lapa and Carioca da Gema, both filled with lovers of samba and bossa nova every night.

**When to Go** You'll either love the crowds and chaos of Rio de Janeiro's pre-Lenten Carnival, or you'll hate them, so plan accordingly. Otherwise, the city's music scene knows no season.

**How to Find It** To navigate the nightlife of Rio, plan on taking taxis.

**Planning** In most bars, cafés, and restaurants, a 10 percent service fee is included with the bill, so there is no need to tip further. In taxis, you can round up the amount of the ride for the tip.

**Websites** www.embratur.gov.br, www.barcariocadagema.com.br, www.jazzrio.com

## Music with a View

■ One of Rio's headiest musical events is jazz night at **The Maze**, on the first Friday of every month. This warren of concrete rooms is set high above the city in the **Tavares Bastos** favela. The sounds may be jazz, bossa nova, or samba, served up with a jaw-dropping view of Rio's lights.

■ If you are keen for the cutting edge, make for the neighborhood around **Praça Tiradentes**, a once forgotten area coming back to (night)life. This is largely due to the **Centro Cultural Carioca,** which is both a club and a place to take samba lessons—perhaps the ultimate musical souvenir of Rio.

Bands at the Lapa district's Rio Scenarium specialize in samba and *chorino*, a distinctive 19th-century Brazilian blend of polka, waltz, and samba.

# CITY CAFÉS

Exploring a new city can't be all sightseeing. Knowing the best places to sit down with a coffee or hot chocolate and perhaps a bite to eat is one of the secrets of pleasurable travel.

## ❶ Hell's Kitchen, Minneapolis, Minnesota

Start your day with a steaming bowl of wild rice porridge. At Hell's Kitchen, breakfast menu delights also include saucy frittatas and lemon ricotta pancakes with fresh blueberries. On the popular weekend brunch menu, try your luck with the bison Benedict—the carnivore's riff on eggs Benedict.

Planning Reserve in advance for "Salvation Sunday" brunch with live music and for weekend suppers. www.hellskitcheninc.com

## ❷ Espresso Vivace, Seattle, Washington

Cafés perch on nearly every corner of this city of coffee roasters and java aficionados. To narrow the choice, look for Espresso Vivace cafés. At establishments that include their Blix Café, Gran Bar, Alley 24, and Sidewalk Café, virtuoso barista performances are all part of the cappuccino ritual.

Planning Leave space in your suitcase for a packet or two of Espresso Vivace blends to take home. www.espressovivace.com

## ❸ Tree House, Santa Fe, New Mexico

Light floods across the tables and open kitchen of the Tree House Pastry Shop and Café, where cupcakes seem to bloom in the desert. All pastries and salads for breakfast and lunch are made on the spot, supporting local agriculture—and in tune with the changing seasons. Look for the mouthwatering special dietary options on the menu.

Planning Located in the Lofts, at 1600 Lena Street, Tree House is just off Second Street. www.treehousepastry.com

## ❹ Café Zambra, Hong Kong

The finest coffees from around the globe find their way to this bright, modern café located in Hong Kong's Wan Chai business district. Gaze out (and up) at the high-rise cityscape outside. Soft seating on the mezzanine invites you to linger a while over your coffee or tea. Don't leave without trying Zambra's cappuccino cheesecake.

Planning Zambra is a block from Gloucester Road. On weekdays, it is open from 7:30 a.m. until 10 or 11 p.m. www.zambra.net

## ❺ Konditori Valand, Stockholm, Sweden

Aromas of cardamom and ginger tickle your nose as you step inside the traditional Konditori Valand for a ritual Swedish afternoon coffee break. Classic 1950's décor, with the warmth of wood paneling and teak chairs, is the backdrop for an array of freshly baked cinnamon buns, almond cream pastries, fruit-topped cheesecakes, and tempting open-faced sandwiches.

Planning Summer brings a plethora of coffee choices, with cafés popping up all along Stockholm's seafront. www.stockholmtown.com

## ❻ Palmenhaus, Vienna, Austria

Caught touring Vienna's Burggarten on a rainy, cold day? Sip a cup of *café mit schlagsahne* (coffee with whipped cream) in the garden's spacious conservatory, the Palmenhaus. Sitting under tropical plants and palms, you will find the experience so relaxing that you may be tempted to stay for lunch.

Planning When ordering lunch, be warned: Portions are generous. In sunny weather, seating outside on the plaza offers prime people-watching. www.palmenhaus.at

## ❼ Flat White, London, England

A haven of calm among the busy clothing and food stalls of Berwick Street Market, this tiny Soho gallery and café draws fans of the Aussie "flat white" style, a cappuccino with less foam. When the weather is fine, take your coffee on a bench outside and watch the hip world go by.

Planning In the afternoons, Flat White can be crowded, so the overflow heads to its sister café, Milk Bar, a couple of blocks away on Bateman Street. www.trustedplaces.com

## ❽ Café Martini, Paris, France

Find comfort in a cup of hot chocolate as you settle into a cozy corner of Café Martini and survey the tempting menu of snacks, tapas, and different kinds of hot chocolate. Located just a few steps off the Place des Vosges, Café Martini redefines café traditions in the City of Light.

Planning Bastille is the nearest Métro stop. The café stays open until 2 a.m. www.chocoparis.com/le-cafe-martini

## ❾ Café de la Paix, La Rochelle, France

In the ancient seaport of La Rochelle, duck under the arcade facing Place de Verdun into the belle epoque Café de la Paix. Mystery writer Georges Simenon, who had a house near La Rochelle, used to frequent its gilded salon. It has been freshened up a bit since his time, but otherwise the café has remained remarkably little changed.

Planning Weekday lunchtimes are best. Closed on Sundays. www.ville-larochelle.fr

## ❿ Café es Faro, Sóller, Mallorca, Spain

A wooden train, the Ferrocarril, winds through the mountain landscape between Palma and Sóller. Once in Sóller, you are ready for a lunch of tapas and sangria at Café es Firo in shady Plaça Constituçio. Local valley citrus fruits are squeezed to produce a refreshing orange ice cream. Take one along on the antique tram, the Orange Express, to Sóller's natural harbor.

Planning Avoid Easter vacation, as cyclists swarm across the island and can cause train and traffic delays. www.sollernet.com

Opposite: Take an elegant break in Vienna's Art Nouveau Palmenhaus (Palm House), located in the former private gardens of the Habsburgs.

You may not need to find a salon. For Santiago's musicians, a street bench is often venue enough.

CUBA

# Music Salons of Santiago

Experience the contagious rhythms of Cuba's second largest city, where music is the lifeblood of daily existence.

Guests pour into the Casa de la Trova with the reverence normally reserved for church. They take their seats in folding chairs and chat among themselves as the band sets up. But this composure is short-lived—in fact, it doesn't even last through the first song. Soon, people are on their feet, clapping, dancing, and crooning. Santiago de Cuba is known for many things, including its role as the birthplace of the 1959 revolution. But nothing trumps its sultry affair with music. Although you can catch everything from mambo to salsa in its myriad music clubs, Santiago is best known for *trovas*, ballads that blend Spanish guitar and African percussion with passionate lyrics, mirroring the trials and tribulations of daily life on the spicy Caribbean isle. Casa de la Trova is a national institution, an atmospheric venue that has hosted every Cuban music star of the last hundred years and that presents solo artists or groups every afternoon and evening. The sounds pour out of the open windows and doors onto Calle Heredia, known as Cuba's Bourbon Street because of its many clubs and its unbreakable bond with the local music scene.

**When to Go** November through February is best, when the hurricane season is over and there is a steady sea breeze to keep down the temperature and humidity.

**How to Find It** There are at least three flights per day from the capital, Havana, a trip that takes around 90 minutes. Other transportation options from Havana are the overnight train or a 15-hour bus ride.

**Planning** Plan on at least three nights. The elegant old Hotel Casa Granda sits on the corner of Calle Heredia and the Parque Céspedes in the heart of the old town. For more modern digs, try the Meliá Santiago in suburban Vista Alegre, where the 15th-floor terrace bar offers endless views and live music.

**Websites** www.gocuba.ca, www.santiago-de-cuba.net, www.gran-caribe.com, www.solmeliacuba.com

## Salons, Festivals, and Wrecks

■ Among other music salons, try the **Patio de Artex,** also on Calle Heredia. Additional venues include **Café Cantante Niágara** at the Teatro Heredia, the **Patio de los Dos Abuelos** on Plaza de Marte, the **Casa del Caribe** on Calle 13, and the **Casa de Las Tradiciones** in the Tivoli district. No matter where you end up, there is absolutely no way your feet will keep still.

■ Santiago's calendar overflows with music-centered events, including a **rumba festival** in January and the **Carnaval Santiaguero** in July with bands, floats, and sinuous conga lines.

■ If you like scuba diving as well as music, the wrecks of four Spanish warships lie off the coast near Santiago and can be easily explored on diving trips. The *Vizcaya, Pluton, Furor,* and *Almirante Oquendo* were all sunk by U.S. warships in the Battle of Santiago de Cuba during the **Spanish-American War** of 1898.

NORTH AMERICA

CHINA

# Hutong of Beijing

For an authentic taste of life in the capital, slip away from the wide streets into a maze of animated lanes and alleyways.

ASIA

The 13th-century Mongol founders of Beijing built a rigid grid of roughly north-to-south and east-to-west avenues, which the Chinese Ming dynasty preserved when it restored the city's capital status in 1403 and remodeled it. Over the centuries, a mesh of winding alleys, still known by the Mongolian-derived word *hutong*, gradually and organically filled in the grid. Modern maps offer only the vaguest sketch of these labyrinths. The best way to discover them is simply to take a randomly selected side turning and then be prepared to be mesmerized by the sights and sounds that lie ahead. In these alleys, cars are relatively few and far between compared with bicycles. Small guardian lion statues or drum stones sit on doorsteps. Carved lintels and roofs of ancient tiles give clues to the antiquity of houses. Walls have been knocked out to turn rooms into tiny shops. Seamstresses bend over wedding-dress commissions. A young woman in a slit traditional dress and vertigo-inducing high heels stands at the entrance of a dubious-looking hairdressing salon. Nearby an old woman sits patiently by her speak-your-weight machine. Piles of bamboo steamers sit on miniature coal-fired stoves, offering tasty and filling dumplings for delectably low prices. This is where you find real Beijing life.

**When to Go**  The best times to visit are late September and October, when days are warm and dry and high-level winds add some blue to the sky. April and early May are the second choice, although there are occasional sandstorms. Northern Chinese winters are bitter, and the summers hot and wet.

**How to Find It**  Map books bought locally are often helpful, mainly for directions when regaining main thoroughfares after a period lost in the maze of alleys. Their description of the hutong themselves is imaginative or nonexistent.

**Planning**  There are increasing numbers of small hutong hotels, often in traditional courtyard houses or mansions. Check guidebooks and travel websites for details. In some areas, organized tours via cycle-rickshaw are available, but these are overpriced and second-best to wandering at your own pace.

**Websites**  www.instanthutong.com/hutong.htm, www.hutongphotography.com, en.bjchp.org

## Last Days

It is estimated that there were around 2,000 hutong under the Ming dynasty (1368-1644), rising to 3,000 during the Qing dynasty (1644-1912) and perhaps 3,200 in the 1940s.

Nowadays, hundreds of acres of traditional courtyard residences are destroyed every year, although this sometimes reveals and results in the restoration of tiny temples and guildhalls that may have been used as sewing workshops or pharmaceutical storehouses or for light industry. If you see a ringed Chinese character roughly daubed on a wall, this is probably *chai* ("demolish") and within a week the entire alley may be gone.

Hutong are disappearing fast, so reflect as you walk that you are looking at the last days of old Beijing.

# CITY GARDENS

Gardens aren't just for the country. Some of the world's most fascinating
gardens lie hidden, like little-known oases, in the middle of busy cities.

## ❶ Sun Yat-Sen Garden, Vancouver, Canada

For the largest Chinese garden outside China visit Vancouver.
Opened in 1986, the Dr. Sun Yat-Sen Chinese Garden was
designed in the style of a Ming-dynasty scholar's residence and
named for Chinese republican leader Sun Yat-Sen. Relish ever
changing views through latticework frames, or "leak windows."

Planning Spring, when blossoms unfurl, is a beautiful time to visit.
The garden is closed on Mondays. www.vancouverchinesegarden.com

## ❷ Conservatory Garden, New York City

This 6-acre (2.4 hectare) oasis is the only formal garden within
Central Park, offering seasonal color from spring bulbs to Korean
chrysanthemums in fall. Enter on Fifth Avenue and 105th Street
via the wrought-iron Vanderbilt Gate, then take your pick from
sections offering French, Italian, and English garden styles.

Planning Open from 8 a.m. to dusk each day. There are free tours
most Saturdays. www.centralpark.com

## ❸ Foster Botanical Garden, Honolulu, Hawaii

Want to escape bustling downtown Honolulu? Stroll through this
mature, tropical garden, whose noteworthy specimens include
24 trees judged to be "exceptional" due to factors such as age or
rarity. Many were planted in the 1850s by the man who started
the garden, Dr. William Hillebrand, a German-born physician.

Planning There are tours led by volunteers, Monday through Saturday.
www.honolulu.gov/parks

## ❹ Botanic Gardens, St. Vincent and the Grenadines

A warm breeze carries the sound of birdsong and the exotic
fragrances of the rare plants growing in 20 well-tended acres
(8 hectares) on the edge of the Caribbean nation's capital,
Kingstown. Locals are justly proud of the gardens, probably
the oldest of all the numerous botanic gardens created by the
former colonial powers across the tropics.

Planning Don't miss a breadfruit tree, descended from a specimen
brought here from the East Indies by Captain Bligh of HMS *Bounty*
fame. www.stvincent.com.vc

## ❺ Botanic Gardens, Singapore

A key attraction is the National Orchid Garden, whose
buildings range from a colonial bungalow housing VIP orchids,
such as the hybrid *Dendrobium* "Margaret Thatcher," to mist and
cool houses for rain-forest and highland species. The Botanic
Gardens also includes a section of tropical rain forest—take the
walkway suspended over the top of it for a bird's-eye view.

Planning The Botanic Gardens is free and open daily from 5 a.m. to
midnight. There is a $5 charge for the Orchid Garden. www.sbg.org.sg

## ❻ Hanging Garden, Mumbai, India

Take an early morning or evening stroll through this terraced
park, originally laid out on the western slopes of Malabar Hill
in 1881. You will get a welcome breeze, and in the evening you
can watch the sunset over the Arabian Sea.

Planning The park is easily reached from all parts of Mumbai by bus,
taxi, or local train. www.mumbai.org.uk

## ❼ Musée Rodin, Paris, France

Before he died in 1917, the sculptor Auguste Rodin donated a
collection of his work to the French state. The Musée Rodin
opened in 1919, and its garden was restored in 1926. A redesign
of the garden in 1993 has made room for more statues. Must-
sees include "The Thinker" in the rose garden and the Garden
of Orpheus, with a statue of Orpheus emerging from plants
chosen for their symbolism.

Planning Closed Mondays. The nearest Métro stations are Varenne
and Invalides. www.musee-rodin.fr

## ❽ Royal Botanic Garden, Edinburgh, Scotland

A mile (1.6 km) from the center of the Scottish capital, the
garden extends over 70 acres (28 hectares). Take your pick from
attractions that include the new John Hope Gateway visitor
center, a huge collection of Chinese plants, a rock garden with
5,000 Alpine plants, and the Victorian Temperate Palm House.

Planning Entry to the garden is free, but there is a charge for the
glasshouse. Open daily from 10 a.m. www.rbge.org.uk

## ❾ Chelsea Physic Garden, London, England

London has many well-known public parks, but this 3.8-acre (1.5
hectare) garden in upscale Chelsea is a well-kept secret. Founded
in 1673 by the Worshipful Society of Apothecaries, the garden has
a warm microclimate, so many tender specimens—including
the largest olive tree in Britain—can grow outside. The early
interest in natural remedies continues today with the Garden
of World Medicine laid out in 1993.

Planning Open to the public from midday several days a week, April
through October. www.chelseaphysicgarden.co.uk

## ❿ Jardin Majorelle, Marrakech, Morocco

Jacques Majorelle was a French painter who settled in Marrakech
in 1919. He made an inspired choice of Berber blue for his studio
and as a motif running through the iconic garden where he
cultivated his large collections of cacti and palms. The garden was
restored in the 1980s by fashion designer Yves Saint Laurent.

Planning Aim to visit early to avoid the crowds. Open daily from 8 a.m.
(9 a.m. during Ramadan). www.jardinmajorelle.com

Opposite: The vibrant color contrasts of the Jardin Majorelle make the garden look like a painting by one of Majorelle's friends of the Fauvist school come to life.

# PINGYAO

Spend an hour or so walking around the walls of
this remarkably well-preserved medieval Chinese city.

In 1370, the Ming dynasty's Hongwu Emperor gave Pingyao in northern China a military upgrade to defend it against Mongol raiding parties. Walls standing 33 feet (10 meters) high and with six fortified gates, corner towers, and 72 projecting bastions for flanking fire were erected around the 0.8 square mile (2 square kilometer) city. Amazingly, these fortifications still stand, enclosing narrow streets squeezed between vast Ming-era mansions, once the homes of merchants and bankers. The gray two-story walls are scarred with the scraping of flatbed tricycles, which make deliveries and provide mobile sales and services of various kinds. Access to the courtyards tucked behind the walls is through studded entrance doors with elaborate canopies of carved wood and brick. The doors are usually left ajar and often double as blackboards for children—traces of their chalked English homework are still sometimes visible. From inside come rhythmic chopping sounds, as the ingredients for meals are prepared, mingled with the cries of infants at play. Swallows dart past at ankle level, and an itinerant peachseller may pause to dust off his produce with a clothes brush.

**When to Go** The bitter winters in Pingyao make even Beijing's seem cozy, so late spring through early fall are the best times to visit. Avoid Chinese New Year in late winter, when transportation is hard to come by, and the national holiday in the first week of October, when Pingyao is packed with domestic tourists.

**How to Find It** You can reach Pingyao by train from Beijing, but there is a more rapid service from Beijing to the nearby Shanxi provincial capital of Taiyuan, with a frequent minibus service from there. En route you pass the vast Qiao Jia Dayuan, a wilderness of interlocking mansions within a single walled structure—well worth hopping off the bus to visit.

**Planning** The Rishengchang and Baichuantong, vast ornate multicourtyard mansions that were two of China's original banks, both now contain excellent museums.

**Websites** whc.unesco.org/en/list/812, www.worldheritagesite.org/sites/pingyao.html

## City of Bankers

In the 19th century, merchants from Shanxi province, with fortunes made in bean curd or tea, needed ways to get their money safely through bandit-ridden countryside.

The owners of a Pingyao dye shop, whose business had expanded to other provinces, found a solution: They created a remittance system allowing payment at one location and collection at another. In 1823, they established **Rishengchang** ("sunrise of prosperity"), China's first bank. It grew rapidly to 57 widely scattered branches and began to handle the payment of officials' salaries and other Qing government transactions.

One of four fierce guardian statues at the entrance to the Daoist Qingxu Temple, now a museum of Pingyao's history

Most of Po Toi's small population lives around the main cove in the fishing hamlet of Tai Wan.

CHINA

# HONG KONG ISLANDS

Slip away from the clamor and bustle of Hong Kong's present for a spiritually uplifting hike around this remnant of its bucolic past.

It is now almost impossible to imagine the sparsely populated, barren rockiness that greeted the first British settlers when they annexed Hong Kong nearly 170 years ago, unless you voyage less than 2 miles (3.2 kilometers) from Hong Kong Island's southeast corner to the tiny, peaceful, and still car-free island of Po Toi with its single fishing village. Here, as the noise of the departing ferry's engine dies away, birdsong rather than traffic noise strikes your ears. From the village you climb up crumbling steps, partly overgrown with hibiscus and flowering ginger, their blossoms a magnet for butterflies. As you ascend, the throaty rumble of frogs and the buzz of crickets join the birdsong. The hillside is studded with armchair graves that face out to sea, most showing signs of maintenance, some studded with tiles and some with photographs of the deceased. At the top, you enjoy views to a spectacularly blue bay. A side path winds down to the roar of the sea and to rock carvings possibly dating back to the local Bronze Age, about 2,500 years ago. A little farther on, Palm Rock turns out to be fingers of stone running up the cliff side. Turtle Rock does, indeed, seem to have dragged itself up a hillock to give its quite distinct "head" a view over the ocean, while Monk Rock leans over the path, as if to give a blessing to passersby.

**When to Go** November to February are the least humid and most comfortable months, but Chinese New Year, which may be any time from late January to mid-February, is very busy. Hong Kong's typhoon season is May through September, so keep an eye on the forecasts and be prepared for suspension of services.

**How to Find It** A battered wooden ferry from the Aberdeen Typhoon Shelter plies during the week. Services do not run every day, so check with the Hong Kong Tourism Board for the latest schedules.

**Planning** Avoid Sundays, when boatloads of day-trippers descend, including bird-watchers in search of elusive black-naped orioles and narcissus flycatchers.

**Websites** www.discoverhongkong.com, www.hkoutdoors.com/outlying-islands/po-toi.html

## A Meal and a Walk

**Ming Kee**—a simple concrete-floored restaurant jutting on piles into the sea and open on three sides—is famous for its chili squid and steamed fish, and during the week is the only restaurant likely to be open on Po Toi. After selecting a fish from the tank, there is just time while it is being cooked for a brisk five-minute walk through the village to the headland. This takes you to a temple trimmed with a riot of gaudy ceramic figures and giant ceramic fish, tails a-thrash. Its dim, smoky interior is dedicated to Tin Hau, a Daoist protector of seafarers immensely popular all around the South China coast, whose shining effigy sits behind piles of offerings at the rear.

ASIA

JAPAN

# THE MOSS GARDEN OF KYOTO

A mantle of velvety moss of many subtly different shades
of green cloaks one of Japan's oldest surviving gardens.

During cherry-blossom season in spring and when the turning leaves are in full view in fall, visitors throng the temples of central Kyoto, but at Saiho-ji, a Zen temple tucked into a peaceful corner to the west of the city, the crowds are absent. Here, the vibrant green of more than 120 different types of moss predominates. More commonly referred to as Kokedera, or Moss Garden, this was once a more traditional Zen garden, with rocks surrounded by white stones, but during the Meiji era (mid-19th to early 20th century), the monastery lacked the money to maintain the garden, and moss took over. Today, the garden is laid out in two parts—an upper section where three tiers of rocks form a "dry waterfall," and a lower section carpeted with moss and thickly wooded with acers and bamboos. A circular walk takes you around a central pond (said to be designed after the Chinese character for heart) that has several small islands, and bridges that rise out of nowhere. The job of keeping the moss looking pristine is a labor of love, as it needs plenty of moisture to flourish but is overtaken by an unattractive-looking kind of lichen if it becomes too damp. Monks regularly trim and clean the moss with small hand brooms, and clip the tree branches overhead to ensure it gets enough light. The garden is somehow at its most beautiful on a rainy day, when mist rises off the water and the green carpet becomes more vibrant. The moss muffles the sound of the raindrops and the overwhelming silence adds to the feeling that this place is ancient, out-of-time, forgotten.

**When to Go** The moss covers the ground year-round, but the garden is particularly beautiful in fall.

**How to Find It** Local buses run regularly between all Kyoto temples. The stop for the Moss Garden is Kokederamich. The main station in Kyoto is a good place to pick up buses.

**Planning** Be warned: This is not an easy temple to visit. You need to write at least three weeks in advance, with your preferred date and the number of people. Don't forget to include an address so the monks can get in touch with a confirmation. Wear soft-soled shoes without heels so you do not damage the moss. You will be asked to chant or meditate (a ritual known as a *zazen*) before going into the garden.

**Websites** www.pref.kyoto.jp/visitkyoto/en, www.japan-guide.com

ASIA

### Tranquil Pleasures

■ For a contemplative stroll, try the Philosopher's Walk, a delightful 1.2-mile (2 km) walk along the canal close to **Ginkaku-ji** (the Silver Pavilion) in northeastern Kyoto. Once you head away from this popular temple, there are numerous hidden, quieter corners and serene temples to explore, including the beautifully secluded **Honen-in Temple** with its thatched gate. The path is lined with hundreds of cherry trees, so spring and fall are popular times to visit.

■ Well off the tourist beaten track is **Otagi Nenbutsu-ji Temple** in an area known as Oku-Saga, in the Arashiyama district of Kyoto. Here in serried rows on the hillside are hundreds upon hundreds of moss-daubed stone statues known as *rakan*. They were all carved by students of the renowned sculptor Kocho Nishimura and all have different expressions, some serious, many others laughing and jovial. Some can be seen standing on their head, while elsewhere there are tipplers, surfers, musicians, and photographers—all guaranteed to put a smile on your face.

Opposite: The green blanket of moss contrasts with the fall colors of the acer trees. Above: A traditional washbowl

# HIDDEN GEMS OF DAMASCUS

Tucked away in a corner of Syria's sprawling capital, the ancient al-Salihiye quarter boasts superlative Islamic architecture.

Muslim refugees fleeing the Crusader occupation of the Holy Land in the 12th century built Damascus's al-Salihiye neighborhood at the base of the hill of Jebel Qassioun. At that time, al-Salihiye was an independent village separated from the walled city of Damascus by more than a mile (1.6 kilometers) of plain. Today, it is tightly woven into the fabric of the Syrian capital. Here, you can walk streets laid out almost a millennium ago and admire monuments built between the 12th and 16th centuries, when Islamic architecture was at its height. Al-Salihiye's original settlers established schools, hospitals, charity centers, *hamams* (baths), and mosques, many of which still stand, at least in part. Even the present-day suq (market) incorporates medieval fragments among its shops and stalls—look for the telltale white and black inlaid stones that form waves of two-tone masonry, still undulating across walls. The most visited site is the tomb of the 13th-century Sufi mystic Ibn 'Arabi, enclosed in a glass case and surrounded by glowing green lamps. Close by is the Imaret Sultan Süleyman, a 16th-century soup kitchen built to feed pilgrims to Ibn 'Arabi's tomb and still in use today as a bakery. The stone building's central court is topped by two elegant cupolas and surrounded by service rooms, where food was stored and prepared. On al-Salihiye's main street, the Maristan al-Qaymari was a 13th-century hospital, whose vaulted hall, or *iwan*, has carved stucco decorations and inlaid stonework. Enjoy gorgeous views over the city from the hall's window.

**When to Go** Visit between September and May to avoid the oppressive summer heat. The city's Jasmine Festival (celebrating the beautifully fragrant flower) is in April. There is a film festival in the fall.

**How to Find It** An inexpensive taxi ride is the easiest way to get to al-Salihiye.

**Planning** Women should bring a head cover for visiting mosques and in general dress conservatively. Travelers to Syria must obtain an entry visa or transit visa issued by the Syrian embassy or consulate in their home country or place of residence.

**Websites** www.syriatourism.org, www.discoverislamicart.org

### Dura Europos Synagogue

Damascus's **National Museum** houses a hidden polychrome treasure: The third-century synagogue of Dura Europos, a city in eastern Syria. After its discovery in 1932, the 46 ft by 10 ft (14 x 3 m) single-room structure was reassembled in a remote wing of the museum, where you can see it upon special request.

Three tiers of framed images depicting scenes from the Jewish Bible (Old Testament) cover the walls right up to the ceiling in warm reds and oranges. Below the images are marble seats to accommodate 90 worshipers. The synagogue shows how Jews in antiquity adapted Roman motifs and art forms to fit their decorative and didactic needs.

The mausoleum housing the tomb of Ibn 'Arabi was designed by Sinan, known as the "Michaelangelo of Ottoman architecture."

These Armenian merchants' houses face the town's main market square.

POLAND

# Zamość

Tucked away in Poland's southeast corner and untroubled by tourist hordes is one of Europe's finest examples of a Renaissance city.

In 1590, Polish nobleman Jan Zamoyski had a vision for a new town on the important trade route linking western and northern Europe with the Black Sea in the picturesque region of Roztocze. With Renaissance Italy as his inspiration, he commissioned Italian architect Bernardo Morando to design what would come to be regarded as the Padua of the North. Zamość soon developed into a multicultural city, its population of Armenians, Jews, Hungarians, Greeks, Germans, and other nationalities served by six Catholic churches, a synagogue, and an Orthodox church, all ringed by formidable fortifications. Renaissance architecture with a Polish twist is on display in the main market square, where elegant arcaded merchants' houses are adorned with friezes, reliefs, frescoes, and false fronts. Dominating the square and fronted by an imposing fan staircase is the Town Hall, where each day at noon the bugle is sounded from the soaring clock tower. Other must-sees include the Academy, the Zamoyski Palace, the cathedral, and the Arsenal. The summer months bring a feast of cultural events worthy of a Renaissance city, including open-air theater and classical-music concerts. Still in business 400 years on is Rektorska, Poland's oldest pharmacy. Upstairs there's a museum and in the basement, a jazz café where you can sample an unusual ginger beer.

**When to Go** Any time of year, although summer brings the best weather and numerous festivals and cultural events.

**How to Find It** Fly to Rzeszow and then take the bus to Zamość (three hours). By bus, Zamość is five hours from Warsaw, seven hours from Kraków.

**Planning** Zamość is a good base for exploring the surrounding scenic countryside, including the Roztocze National Park. Outside the city there are great routes for horseback riding, cycling, and walking. The open-air heritage park in the picturesque village of Guciów is worth a visit.

**Websites** www.zamosc.pl, www.zamosc.wonder.pl

### German Occupation

During World War II, the Zamość region was earmarked by the Nazis for German resettlement. The city itself was to be renamed Himmlerstadt (Himmler City), and a planned 60,000 Germans would be settled there by 1943. Many Polish people lost their lives and the Jewish community of more than 12,000 was virtually wiped out, but a combination of fierce local resistance and the arrival of the Red Army in 1944 meant that, ultimately, the German plan was thwarted.

Although the city's **synagogue** was looted and even used as a carpenters' workshop during the Nazi occupation, the beautiful Renaissance building survives as an important monument to Jewish heritage in Poland.

EUROPE

# Markets & Bazaars

From canaries in Beijing to felt skullcaps in Tunis, relish the sheer variety
of the world's marketplaces and the produce and wares on offer.

### ❶ Sololá Market, Guatemala

Red with white stripes is the dominant fashion among sellers and customers at this weekly market in the Guatemalan highlands. Many women arrive with sacks on their heads filled with goods ranging from tortillas to live chickens as well as the handwoven costumes of the Kaqchikel Indians. There is barely a tourist trinket in sight, and traditional dress is the rule.

Planning Friday is Sololá's market day. www.atitlan.net

### ❷ La Vega Central, Santiago, Chile

The Chilean capital's joyously chaotic La Vega Central market, beside the Mapocho River, positively drips South American culture. For the less squeamish—and the large stray dog, cat, and fly population—pigs' heads, tripe, and intestines are a draw. Other delicacies on offer include sopaipillas (fried pumpkin bread), *caldo pata* (hoof soup), and *pastel de choclo* (corn pie).

Planning The market is busiest on weekends. www.visit-chile.org

### ❸ Namdaemun Market, Seoul, South Korea

South Korea's largest traditional market, Namdaemun—"great south gate"—owes its name to its location near a former gate in Seoul's long gone city wall. More than 1,000 stores and stalls purvey an array of produce, including clothes, flowers, ginseng products, street food, leather goods, toys—and live turtles.

Planning Namdaemun is open nonstop except Sundays. The best bargains are after midnight. www.visitseoul.net

### ❹ Flower, Bird, Fish, and Insect Market, Beijing, China

Chirruping canaries, caterwauling kittens, and chirping crickets create a quintessentially Chinese sound track at Beijing's Guan Yuan Hua Niao Yu Chong Shi Chang (Flower, Bird, Fish, and Insect Market). Shoes, scorpions, and smoking pipes are among the finds, alongside kites and insects. Much of Beijing may have been sanitized in a frantic rush to modernize, but this old-style market remains refreshingly authentic.

Planning The nearest subway station is Fu Cheng Men. www.cnto.org

### ❺ Grand Bazaar, Kashgar, China

Two thousand years of history have not dented exotic Kashgar's importance as a market town on the ancient Silk Road. Its Grand Bazaar has long attracted merchants from throughout Central Asia and western China, trading in livestock, carpets, handicrafts, clothes, and food. Barter remains common.

Planning The market is open daily but busiest on Sundays. Consult your travel adviser as Kashgar has experienced periodic civil disturbances. www.farwestchina.com, www.orientaltravel.com

### ❻ Pak Khlong Talat, Bangkok, Thailand

Head from Memorial Bridge toward Bangkok's Chinatown and your nose will guide you to the city's largest wholesale flower, spice, fruit, and vegetable market, open round the clock. Orchids, jasmine, roses, and myriad other eruptions of color and fragrance compete for visual and olfactory attention.

Planning The market is liveliest from around 2 a.m. to dawn, when boats deliver fresh cargo. www.bangkoktourist.com

### ❼ Mercato della Pignasecca, Naples, Italy

At its brash best, Naples is one of Italy's most exuberant cities. A superb place to experience its vibrant soul and top-notch street food is the Pignasecca Market. Culinary favorites include calzone, *panzerotti* (potato croquettes), *taralli* (Italian-style pretzels), *pizza fritta* (deep-fried pizza), and *sfogliatelle* (filled pastries).

Planning Beware of pickpockets in Naples. www.comune.napoli.it

### ❽ Isle-sur-la-Sorgue, Provence, France

This island in the fast-flowing Sorgue River was once a water-milling center producing silk, wool, and paper. The traditional industries went into decline in the 1960s, and a new one arose: Antiques-selling. The town now has more than 300 permanent antiques dealers, and its flea market is France's largest outside Paris. Musicians create a carnival mood on market days, while stalls sell Provençal food and handicrafts.

Planning The market takes place daily in summer, on Sunday and Thursday mornings in winter. www.oti-delasorgue.fr

### ❾ Mercado da Ribeira, Lisbon, Portugal

Founded in 1882 and housed in its current riverside building since 1930, this is Lisbon's largest food market. On the ground floor, stalls sell everything from fish and seafood to flowers, meat, fruit, and vegetables, while the upper story is a center for local art and gastronomy. Star buys include honey and hand-painted tiles, a Portuguese specialty.

Planning The market is open daily (except Sunday), 5 a.m.–2 p.m. On Sundays, it makes way for a collectors' fair. www.visitlisboa.com

### ❿ Souk des Chéchias, Tunis, Tunisia

Dedicated to the *chéchia,* a felt skullcap with tassels or a tuft, this suq (market) full of 19th-century shops is perhaps the most interesting—yet endangered—in Tunis. Traditionally associated with Andalusian Moors exiled from Spain between 1609 and 1614, the handmade chéchia became part of the Tunisian national costume. Nowadays, a mere handful of craftsmen remains.

Planning Hardcore haggling is in order. Don't call a chéchia a fez. www.tourismtunisia.com, www.tunisia.com

Opposite: A food vendor in Seoul's Namdaemun Market presides over a tempting array of dishes for stall-side eating.

Leipzig's Old City Hall, much altered over the centuries, was built in just nine months between 1556 and 1557.

GERMANY

# Art and Fairs in Leipzig

Formerly cut off behind the Iron Curtain, Leipzig has reclaimed its preeminence as one of Germany's booming cultural centers.

An artsy buzz infuses the old Saxon city of Leipzig, symbolized by the internationally acclaimed group of young artists called the Neue Leipziger Schule (New Leipzig School), all of whom trained at the city's venerable Academy of Visual Arts. Plunge yourself into the thick of it as you follow a cobbled street in the city's western side that leads to the Baumwolls-Spinnerei, once the largest cotton mill in continental Europe. In the 1990s, the mill's 23 buildings were converted into a mammoth arts complex. Here, you will find shops, galleries, theaters, and a restaurant among studios and workshops for painters, architects, jewelers, furniture-makers, and dance groups. Farther east, the 16th-century Altes Rathaus (Old City Hall), presiding over the Market Square, is a reminder of Leipzig's centuries-old importance as a commercial center, known for its great trade fairs. Visit some of the restored former fair buildings, including Barthels Hof—hiding an elegant 18th-century interior behind a 19th-century front—and Specks Hof, whose courtyards and glass-roofed arcades are now home to lively bars, restaurants, and shops.

**When to Go** Clear blue skies and warm weather make June through September an ideal time to visit. If you prefer a nip in the air, around Christmastime is good, allowing you to enjoy the Christmas market.

**How to Find It** Leipzig is two hours by road from Berlin. Alternatively, you can reserve a seat on ICE (Germany's high-speed train) and go from Berlin to Leipzig in almost half the time.

**Planning** Look into the Leipzig Welcome Card, which offers free travel within the city limits on all trams and buses. You will also receive generous discounts for museums, restaurants, and events such as performances at the Gewandhaus concert hall and the Leipzig Bach Festival.

**Websites** www.leipzig.de, www.ltm-leipzig.de, www.cometogermany.com

## Music, Coffee, and Christmas

■ For a glimpse into Leipzig's musical heritage, visit the **Thomaskirche** (St. Thomas Church), whose 800-year-old Thomanerchor, a boys' choir, counts Johann Sebastian Bach among its past choir masters. The composer is commemorated outside the church with a statue, along with Felix Mendelssohn, who also lived in Leipzig.

■ One of Europe's oldest coffee houses, **Zum Arabischen Coffe Baum** (The Arabian Coffee Tree), a couple of blocks west of the Altes Rathaus, draws you in on aroma alone. Enter under a sandstone carving showing an Ottoman Turk offering Cupid a cup of coffee, and join the list of notables who have sipped their coffee here, including the poet and playwright Goethe and the composers Bach, Liszt, Wagner, and Grieg. On the third floor, a small museum showcases all things coffee.

■ Leipzig's **Christmas market** is one of the most famous of these festive fairs. From late November until a couple of days before Christmas, the Market Square fills with 200 stalls, an ice rink, and the world's largest Advent calendar, measuring 9,225 sq ft (857 sq m).

EUROPE

# RIVERSIDE IN MUNICH

Be sure to pack a bathing suit when visiting landlocked Munich
so you can join the locals and get in the swim around town.

On a hot summer's day, join the throngs of Munich natives flocking to the banks of the Isar River to picnic, sunbathe, and swim. The place to be is a stretch of the river near Prater Island in the center of town. Sun yourself on the wide pebbled banks, then splash in the shallow jade-green water. As the day draws to a close, barbecues and wine bottles come out and the party goes on. Offering further aquatic action is the English Garden just off Prinzregentenstrasse, only a short walk away, with an artificial river called the Eisbach ("Ice Brook") flowing through flower-strewn meadows. As the water rushes into the garden from the Isar River, its fast-flowing current creates a perpetual wave—a lure for neoprene-clad surfers, who take turns to ride the wave before they wipe out and the next surfer jumps in. On hot days, it's tempting to plunge in and let the cool waters pull you along, but the current and rocks make this a risky activity and signs—often ignored—remind people that it is illegal. For a river trip where the beer flows nearly as fast as the water, head 21 miles (34 kilometers) southwest of Munich to the town of Wolfratshausen. Here, you board a traditional log raft for a six-hour ride down the Isar back to the outskirts of Munich. Steered by leiderhosen-clad boatmen, the raft rolls past rocks and splashes down three low waterfalls to the sound of an onboard oompah band.

**When to Go** To swim and sunbathe, go during the summer months. To watch a few hardy surfers on the wave or visit the Müller'sches Volksbad, visit in December when the Christmas markets are in full swing.

**How to Find It** The wave is in the English Garden, just behind the Haus der Kunst art museum. Walking and cycling paths run alongside the Isar; Prater Island is near the Deutches Museum.

**Planning** Bring an open mind to the English Garden and the banks of the Isar: Many places are clothing-optional. For the Volksbad, bring flip-flops or shower sandals—the floors in the sauna rooms are red-hot.

**Website** www.isarflossfahrten.biz, www.munichtoday.de

### A Jewel of a Pool

For year-round swimming, go to the **Müller'sches Volksbad,** an elegant Art Nouveau bathhouse opposite the Deutches Museum. In the enormous 102 ft x 43 ft (31 m x 13 m) main pool, you can swim under the watchful gaze of a water-spitting gargoyle.

There are a number of smaller, warmer swimming pools and a Roman-style complex of steam rooms and plunge pools, as well as saunas, massage facilities, and a beer garden.

It's the perfect place to unwind after a day of sightseeing (open every day except Monday, until 11 p.m.) or even to take a nap in a private cabin.

It's not a Mediterranean beach, but the banks of the Isar River in Munich make a buzzy, easy-to-reach, summer alternative.

ITALY

# VENICE'S LAGOON ISLANDS

Give Venice the time it deserves. Enjoy the lesser-known islands in its lagoon as well as the world-famous sites, such as St. Mark's Square.

Most of the 3 million people who visit Venice each year trudge around on foot and spend less than a day in the city, sticking to the central islands that are home to St. Mark's Square, the Doge's Palace, and the Rialto Bridge. But La Serenissima, as Venice is known, is built in a marshy lagoon, teeming with more than 100 islands. If you really want to understand the city, take to the water to reach the lagoon's farther-flung corners, navigating by boat as Venetians do. In the northeast, the small, scarcely populated island of Torcello (best reached by ferry via the island of Burano) is one of the most magical places in the whole of Venice. Its Cathedral of Santa Maria Assunta has 12th-century mosaics that undulate in ripples of gold and glass, attesting to Torcello's importance in the Byzantine era in which it was built. Nearby, the islands of Mazzorbo and Burano, with boxy, pastel-painted houses, have been famous for lacemaking since the 15th century. Even more out of the way, and accessible only by private boat, is Sant'Ariano, northeast of Torcello, where from the 17th to the 20th centuries the bones of long-deceased Venetians were dumped to make room for the new dead in the city's crypts. Farther south, Sant'Erasmo is one of the lagoon's largest islands, noted for its calm residential feel and fertile farms where *castraùre* (the young buds of globe artichokes) and asparagus are raised. Contemplate the rich culture and varied land- and waterscapes on the way back to central Venice on a vaporetto.

**When to Go** Venice can be visited year-round, but midsummer can be swelteringly hot and humid (as well as crowded), and in winter a biting wind often blows from the north.

**How to Find It** Domestic and international flights arrive at Venezia Marco Polo Airport. From there, the Alilaguna waterbus routes take you to the Fondamente Nuove, the Lido, St. Mark's Square, the Rialto, and the railroad station. There are trains to Venice from most major Italian cities.

**Planning** Be sure to plan ahead during the busiest times, from Easter to late October and during special events like the pre-Lenten Carnival, the Venice Film Festival, and the Biennale. Allow at least a full week to explore all that the lagoon has to offer.

**Websites** www.actv.it, www.turismovenezia.it, www.contexttravel.com/venice, www.veniceconnected.com, www.labiennale.org

### San Lazzaro degli Armeni

In 1717, the Venetians donated a former leper colony on the tiny island of **San Lazzaro** (St. Lazarus, the patron saint of lepers) to Armenian monks fleeing persecution by the Ottoman Turks.

The monks—belonging to a Catholic Benedictine order known as the Mekhitarists—transformed their new abode into a center of learning, art, and literature, attracting a distinguished list of visitors, including the poet Lord Byron.

Today, the monks still welcome the few tourists who land on their island, which lies between central Venice and the Lido. They offer tours of the monastery once a day, just after the arrival of the 3 p.m. vaporetto.

Opposite and above: It is a custom for islanders on Burano to paint their houses in a palette of cheerful colors.

# CITY RIVER WALKS

Many of the world's great cities are built on waterways, and waterside walks
often provide an intriguing and enlightening route for exploration.

## ❶ Calzada de Amador, Panama City, Panama

Built from rocks dug out to make the Panama Canal, this 3-mile
(4.8 km) causeway links the mainland with four islands at the
canal's Pacific entrance. Stroll past restaurants, shopping arcades,
and hotels to reach the Smithsonian Tropical Research Institute's
Marine Exhibition Center and Panama's Museum of Biodiversity,
designed by architect Frank Gehry.

Planning The causeway is easily reached from Panama City center by
taxi ($5-10). www.pancanal.com

## ❷ Chao Phraya River, Bangkok, Thailand

The heart of ancient Bangkok is Rattanakosin Island, wedged
between the Chao Phraya River and canals built when the city
was founded. From the National Museum, a 20-minute riverside
walk leads to Thanon Phra Athit, a street of old buildings housing
restaurants, small shops, and cafés. The walkway affords a good
look at life on the river.

Planning The National Museum stands by Phra Pin-klao Bridge, a good
starting point for several walks. www.bangkok.com

## ❸ RiverWalk, Brisbane, Australia

Brisbane loves its river of the same name, and walking the
riverbank is the best way to appreciate the city. Starting at Victoria
Bridge, head downstream through South Bank Parklands. Either
cross the footbridge to the Botanic Gardens Path or stay on the
south side to reach Kangaroo Point Cliffs, a picnic spot where
rock climbers practice—even at night, when it is illuminated.

Planning The RiverWalk can be accessed from all parts of the city, and
guided tours are offered. www.brisbane.qld.gov.au

## ❹ Neva River, St. Petersburg, Russia

Built around canals and the Neva, St. Petersburg is made for
waterside wandering. The Palace, Admiralty, and English
embankments run between Leitenanta Schmidta and Troitsky
Bridges on the Neva's palatial south bank. In between is Dvortsovy
Bridge. Cross here for the best views of the Winter Palace.

Planning From May through November, the Dvortsovy Bridge is raised
between 1:35 and 4:55 a.m. to let water traffic through; despite the
hour, the event draws an enthusiastic crowd. www.saint-petersburg.com

## ❺ Limmat River, Zurich, Switzerland

There is more to Zurich's waterside than the lake. Lake Zurich
(Zürichsee) is the source of the Limmat River, and Limmatquai
on the river's right bank is one of the city's oldest parts, with
elegant 17th- and 18th-century guildhouses, now inhabited by
smart shops and restaurants.

Planning From May through October you can rent a bike free from the
city and enjoy the bike paths by the river. www.zurichtourism.ch

## ❻ Tiber River, Rome, Italy

Shaded by sycamore trees, the embankments (lungoteveri) that
line the Tiber make Rome's river an easy stroll. The tranquil Isola
Tiberina (Tiber Island) is a good starting point. From here, Ponte
Fabricio, Rome's oldest bridge, leads to the attractive Ghetto
district. Turn left to pass by splendid 16th-century palaces.

Planning In summer, enjoy the evening outdoor cinema on Isola
Tiberina. www.rome.info

## ❼ Merseyside, Liverpool, England

Liverpool's Pier Head, with its trio of iconic buildings—the
Cunard Building, Port of Liverpool Building, and Royal Liver
Building—is a reminder of the great days of transatlantic travel.
To its south, Albert Dock houses the Tate Liverpool art gallery, a
maritime museum, and The Beatles Story museum.

Planning Any visit to Pier Head should include a ferry across the
Mersey or a river tour. www.visitliverpool.com

## ❽ Regent's Canal, London, England

Canal towpaths were needed for horses to draw barges. Today,
they let you walk across much of London. An attractive stretch
of the Regent's Canal runs for 2 miles (3.2 km) from Camden
Lock in north London around Regent's Park to Little Venice. On
the way, you pass the gardens of the wealthy and may hear the
song of nightingales mingling with roars from London Zoo.

Planning Camden is the Underground station for Camden Lock,
Warwick Avenue for Little Venice. www.canalmuseum.org.uk

## ❾ Les Berges du Rhône, Lyon, France

In Lyon two great rivers—the Rhône and the Saône—converge,
both with highways racing along their banks. Cars are now
banned from the Berges du Rhône (Banks of the Rhône),
providing a pleasure promenade on the Rhône's left bank. This
is good news for strollers, inline skaters, and picnickers, while
traditional barges have found new life as restaurants and cafés.

Planning Visit in the cool of the evening, when the Rhône bridges are
magically lit. www.en.lyon-france.com

## ❿ Tagus River, Lisbon, Portugal

It is more than 5 miles (8 km) along the Tagus from Praça do
Comércio, Lisbon's regal waterside square, to Belém, where Vasco
da Gama and other 16th-century explorers set sail. A shorter walk
is from Doca de Santo Amaro, a marina beneath Ponte 25 de Abril.
In Belém, shops and cafés selling pastéis de Belém (custard tartlets) and
the Jerónimos monastery, where da Gama is buried, await you.

Planning Frequent bus and train services link Cais de Sodré station,
Doca de Santo Amaro, and Belém. www.golisbon.com

Opposite: The curiously named Church of the Savior on Blood, completed in 1907, watches over a quiet stretch of St. Petersburg's Griboedov Canal.

One of the historic port's many alley stalls selling the freshest of fresh produce

ITALY

# ALLEYS OF GENOA

Hit the labyrinth of narrow streets early in the morning
to maximize your snacking—and drooling—opportunities.

There can be a certain pleasure in getting lost in a strange place, and in Genoa getting lost is a near certainty. A multitude of narrow alleys, called *caruggi* in the local dialect, snake through the city, creating a Byzantine map with umpteen ways to get from point A to point B. In honor of La Superba's (the Proud's) maritime heritage, start your visit in the area around the Porto Antico (Old Port). The city was, after all, the birthplace of Christopher Columbus, and in its heyday was among the greatest sea powers in history; it is still one of Italy's two largest ports. Near the Porto Antico, you will find the unmistakable aquarium (the second biggest in Europe) and the glass-domed biosphere. Working inland from the vast Piazza Caricamento, stroll down the long walkway called Via Sottoripa, flanked by vendors hawking everything from fish so fresh that its skin sparkles to crispy, golden *panisse* (chickpea fries) and herb-flecked fritters called *frisceu* (think savory doughnut holes). Shops called *sciamadde*—literally "flames" in Genoese, for their wood-burning ovens—have long marble countertops arrayed with these two treats and a panoply of others. A pit stop at one, or better yet, a slow crawl to snack at many, fuels you for a stroll down Via Garibaldi as day fades to night. This quiet street is lined on either side by no fewer than 14 grand palaces.

**When to Go** Genoa has a mostly mild climate year-round, although winter can bring chilly north winds.

**How to Find It** The most atmospheric way to arrive in the Porto Antico is by the NaveBus (water bus) that links it with the seaside suburb of Pegli, where many of the hotels are located.

**Planning** The baked and fried foods typical of this area will be at their freshest earlier in the day, and the shops offering them often close around sundown. The narrow alleys are best avoided at night if you are alone.

**Websites** www.genova-turismo.it, www.civiltaforchetta.it/Stampa/HowtoeatinGenoa_s.html

## Culinary Treats

Genoa has always been home to a multitude of eateries, tempting sailors and explorers of old to return to dry land. A favorite local dish is *farinata,* a thin, crispy-topped pancake that gets its richness from chickpea flour and its bewitching aroma from fruity Ligurian olive oil, widely considered the finest in Italy. One of the best places to eat this traditional treat may also be one of the oldest: **Antica Sciamadda,** whose wood-burning ovens have been flaming hot for more than 200 years.

After that, make your way to **Pietro Romanengo fu Stefano,** the second-oldest candy shop in Europe, where you'll find fruit jellies of every hue and tiny candied violets, as deliciously sweet as they are expensive.

EUROPE

BELGIUM

# Le Châtelain

Designers, artists, and artisans of every description continue to gravitate to this art deco and art nouveau-influenced district.

The trendy area around the Place du Châtelain in the Ixelles (Elsene in Dutch) district of southern Brussels bursts with cultural diversity. To see it at its liveliest, come here on a Wednesday afternoon, when market stalls fill the square and nearby Rue du Bailli. Don't miss Rue du Bailli's chocolate- and candy-makers, Irsi, famous for their sugar almonds and their *manons*, delectable confections filled with fresh cream, vanilla, and coffee or chocolate mousse. Feast your eyes as well. Art nouveau architects Victor Horta and Paul Hankar were both active in this neighborhood in the 1890s and after. Two blocks away from Place du Châtelain, the Horta Museum in Rue Américaine comprises Horta's home and studio. Hankar's house in Rue Defacqz lies to the north. For further art nouveau and art deco delights, cross the elegant, chestnut-shaded sweep of Avenue Louise, lined with designer boutiques, art galleries, and antiques, textiles, and jewelry shops. Here, at No. 346, is Horta's recently restored Hotel Max Hallet—an elegant residence built for the lawyer Max Hallet. Beyond Avenue Louise, in the western part of Ixelles, the park surrounding the two Étangs d'Ixelles (Vijvers Elsene in Dutch, Ponds of Ixelles) forms an oasis of greenery. In Place Sainte-Croix (Het Heilig-Kruisplein), admire the art deco former headquarters of Belgian radio, now a cultural center, built by Joseph Diongre in the late 1930s.

**When to Go** Temperatures are mild from May through October. Summertime brings a lively assortment of festivals and performing arts programs. December brings the dazzling Christmas market and ice rink.

**How to Find It** Châtelain is a 30-minute walk from Brussels' Grand-Place, one of the loveliest squares in Europe. Alternatively, you can take trams 91 or 92 from Louise metro station.

**Planning** Other offbeat Brussels attractions include the Belgian Comic Strip Center, housed in a fine 1906 building designed by Victor Horta on Rue des Sables. Or you might want to pay a visit to the family-owned Cantillon Brewery on Rue Gheude—the 5-euro tour includes a free glass of *geuze*, the classic Brussels beer.

**Websites** www.visitflanders.us, www.visitbelgium.com

EUROPE

### Spice Cookies

Even the name "speculoos" sounds fun and enticing. Speculoos are addictive spice cookies that are cut into different shapes. They were traditionally made using hand-carved wooden cutters shaped like the image of St. Nicholas and doled out to good children on the saint's feast day, December 6. Nowadays, they are widely available in markets and served year-round. The crunchy delights linger on the palate with hints of dark brown sugar, cloves, cinnamon, ginger, nutmeg, and blanched almonds. They go particularly well with a steaming cup of coffee, and some locals serve them with ice cream.

The lake in pretty Square Marie-Louise is one of just a handful of remaining ponds out of the 48 that once cut across the city.

# Sand Dunes, The Hague

The Netherlands is a flat and densely populated country, but some signs of ever shifting wilderness remain.

W hile The Hague may be better known for war-crime tribunals, international organizations, and a bicycling monarchy, it also holds a remarkable natural phenomenon more associated with Africa than Europe. The city was built on three sand dunes, and near-pristine vestiges of each remain. One of them, Meijendel, is 4 miles (6.4 kilometers) long and 2 miles (3.2 kilometers) wide and stretches from The Hague to Wassenaar. The constantly seaward-bound sand deposits play an important role in the local ecosystem and are a habitat for more than 250 bird species, as well as field mice, rabbits, bats, foxes, deer, wild horses, and weasels. The dunes even have wetlands that shelter toads, bright green-and-red tree frogs, and the rare sand lizard. For the human population, Meijendel serves as a sea-defense, a source of exceptionally pure, sand-filtered drinking water, and a largely local recreational attraction. Several paths traverse this weird, desolate wilderness and are open to hikers, cyclists, and horse riders. There is, however, a dark reason behind the barbed wire that seals off parts of Meijendel. In World War II, the country's Nazi occupiers not only built a network of bunkers and trenches—now part of a NATO communication center—but also used the dunes as a secret execution range for resistance members, and they are still treated as a burial ground today.

**When to Go** The weather in The Hague is changeable, but generally mild year-round. The warmest months are July and August. Many hotels offer discounts in winter.

**How to Find It** The 43 bus to Meijendel leaves from The Hague's central railroad station. Alternatively, go Dutch and explore Meijendel and The Hague by customized tour with local bicycle-rental outfit Totzo!

**Planning** Meijendel has three main hiking routes, marked with yellow, red, and blue posts, and various bicycle and bridle paths. Some trails require a walking permit from the DZH, the water company in charge of the dunes, which also arranges regular guided tours. The Delflandse Kust visitor center is a good place to learn more about the dunes' environmental value. Refuel at the typically Dutch pancake house.

**Websites** www.holland.com, www.kustgids.nl/meijendel-en, www.totzo.org, www.denhaag.com

### Chic Resort

Ten minutes by car from the center of The Hague—and with its own sand dunes—is the beach resort of **Scheveningen.** In warmer weather, its windswept promenade buzzes with café society and its beach draws water-sports enthusiasts. Spar with scavenging seagulls at harborside stalls selling deep-fried seafood with fries and homemade mayonnaise, a Dutch culinary triumph.

In The Hague, don't miss the **Panorama Mesdag,** a 360-degree landscape painted around the inside walls of a circular building. It depicts Scheveningen's outlook as it was in the 19th century. Surprisingly, much remains unchanged.

The Hague's third surviving sand dune is at the quiet resort of **Kijkduin.**

Empty beaches and miles of unspoiled sand dunes are a stone's throw from The Hague's bustling center.

La Bagatelle's famous roses in full bloom. The orangerie beyond was built by the château's mid-19th-century English owner, the Marquess of Hertford.

FRANCE

# LA BAGATELLE, PARIS

An English-style garden combines with Parisian elegance to create a haven of charm amid the green spaces of the Bois de Boulogne.

This 18th-century château and garden were originally created by the Count d'Artois, younger brother of King Louis XVI. AS a result of a bet with his sister-in-law, Marie Antoinette, the count built the house within two months as a bagatelle, or trifle. In the 230-odd years since then, the 59-acre (24 hectare) enclave in the middle of the Bois de Boulogne has been further embellished by succeeding owners and gardeners, and it continues to delight. Each part of the garden has a different theme. In one corner, irises grow in glorious profusion, peaking in May. Elsewhere, pear and apple trees form a protective barrier around a kitchen garden filled with rows of vegetables. Paths and footbridges lead to grottoes, cascading waterfalls, and a crystalline reflecting pool brimming with water lilies and other aquatic plants. In spring, clumps of daffodils flutter in any passing breeze. In summer, orange trees in planter boxes line the pathways. Climbing roses and clematis vines drape themselves over a brick wall facing a long, narrow garden of perennials that bursts with color from spring through fall. The rose garden, with more than a thousand varieties of rose, is most spectacular in early June. Make your way across an immaculate lawn to a shady alley and a restful bench, where you can sit and contemplate the beauty of it all.

**When to Go** The garden is open from 9 a.m. year-round, closing at 8 p.m. May through August, and 7 p.m. September through April.

**How to Find It** Take the Métro to Porte Maillot, then the 244 bus from Porte Maillot.

**Planning** You can take a guided tour of the château. The Bois de Boulogne is large—3.2 square miles (8.3 sq km)—and one of the best ways of exploring it is on two wheels. You can rent bicycles by the entrance to the Jardin d'Acclimatation at the north end of the park. Avoid the Bois de Boulogne late at night—it is a well-known open-air red-light area.

**Websites** www.parisinfo.com, www.franceguide.com

### Plays and Paintings

The **Bois de Boulogne** was laid out in the 19th century, loosely modeled on London's Hyde Park.

■ Inspiration from across the English Channel continues in the **Jardin Shakespeare,** in the Pré Catelan in the center of the park. The plants you see growing here are all mentioned in Shakespeare's plays. In summer, performances are staged in the open-air **Théâtre de Verdure.**

■ In a quiet street near the eastern edge of the Bois de Boulogne, the **Musée Marmottan** has a superb collection of Impressionist paintings, notably by Claude Monet and Berthe Morisot.

EUROPE

# FAR FROM THE MADDING CROWDS

Surprises abound when you go off the beaten city track, including an exquisite coastal garden in Tokyo and Berlin courtyards hiding trendsetting galleries and cafés.

### ❶ Garfield Park Conservatory, Chicago

This is an unexpectedly cozy corner of the Windy City: A huge hothouse surrounded by gardens and produce. Designed to resemble midwestern haystacks, the greenhouse stands in a 184-acre (74 ha) park, home to projects such as the City Garden and the Monet Garden, based on the original at Giverny in France.

**Planning** The conservatory is a short walk from Conservatory-Central Park Drive Station on the CTA Green Line. www.garfieldconservatory.org

### ❷ Museo Casa de la Bola, Mexico City, Mexico

This sumptuous villa is a cornucopia of good taste, with paintings, sculptures, and curiosities that caught the eye of Don Antonio Haghenbeck y de la Lama, who lived here from 1942 until his death in 1991. Admire the Salón Versailles ballroom and the private chapel, then take a stroll in the large, delightful garden.

**Planning** Open Sundays 11 a.m.-5 p.m., or weekdays by appointment. www.mexicocity.gob.mx

### ❸ Parque Enrique Lage, Rio de Janeiro, Brazil

With an elegant patio and colonnade around a pool, the mansion at the heart of this subtropical wonderland of a park was remodeled in the 1920s for its owners, mezzo soprano Gabriella Besanzoni and her shipbuilder husband Enrique Lage. The building is now an art school, but you can be a guest at the Café du Lage and sit on cushions around low tables or by the pool.

**Planning** The Park is at No. 414 Rua Jardim Botânico, on the south side of the city. www.ipanema.com

### ❹ Hamarikyu Gardens, Tokyo, Japan

On Tokyo Bay, beyond the skyscrapers of the Shiodome district, the Hamarikyu Gardens are the former duck-hunting grounds of the Tokugawa shoguns. Today, they still have a tidal saltwater lake and freshwater carp ponds. Black pines, plum trees, cherries, and myrtle grow alongside camellias, hydrangeas, and peonies. Take tea on the verandah of the elegant Nakajima Teahouse.

**Planning** The best way to arrive is by boat. There is a landing stage inside the gardens for the Asakusa waterbus. www.japan-guide.com

### ❺ Lake Sihwa, Ansan, South Korea

A sewage-disposal plant may not be your idea of a day out, but Lake Sihwa Reed Wetland Park is the place to find unadulterated wildlife among reed beds whose real purpose is to purify foul water the natural way. A mile-long (1.6 km) walkway allows you to look out over the reeds and ponds and to see birds and flowers that come and go with the seasons.

**Planning** From Seoul, you can reach the park in just over an hour by subway (line 4) and bus (No. 52). www.visitseoul.net

### ❻ Fairfield Park, Melbourne, Australia

If you want to drift in a slow boat through city bushland, head for Fairfield Park Boathouse. This Edwardian survivor on the Yarra River was opened in 1908. The boathouse has an open-air fish and meat barbecue, but it is best known for its "Devonshire teas" of scones and cream. For elegant boating, take to the water in one of the locally built wooden "gentleman's rowing skiffs."

**Planning** There are wood fires in winter. www.fairfieldboathouse.com

### ❼ Banganga Tank, Mumbai, India

Above the mayhem of Mumbai is this holy, man-made, rectangular pool fed by underground water. It is one of the most revered sites in the city, the silence of its unruffled waters broken only by ringing bells and chanting from the Hindu temples and shrines around it. Stone steps descend on all four sides to the pool, where you may spot fish and even turtles.

**Planning** Banganga Tank is a short walk from Walkeshwar Bus Depot at the south end of Malabar Hill. www.maharashtratourism.gov.in

### ❽ Lobkowicz Palace, Prague, Czech Republic

Be sure to get the audio guide when visiting this corner of Prague Castle. The U.S. narrator is William Lobkowicz, whose family has owned the palace since the 16th century, except for a 40-year-period under Communist rule. The family collections include works by Breughel, Velázquez, and Canaletto, and signed scores by Beethoven and Mozart.

**Planning** Starting at 1 p.m. every day, a trio performs a program of classical music in the Concert Hall. www.lobkowiczevents.cz

### ❾ Hinterhöfen, Berlin, Germany

The courtyards (*hinterhöfen*) of the blocks of flats built for Berlin's workers are always worth ducking into. While many are rundown, you may find a funky gallery or nightspot, a charming café, or a small museum. Visit Sophienstrasse 21 for Barcomi's trendy café and deli and the Sophie Gips Höfe gallery.

**Planning** The Kreuzberg district is home to a cutting-edge arts scene, in courtyards such as Aqua Carré's in Lobeckstrasse. www.visitberlin.de

### ❿ Jermyn Street, London, England

The oldest shop on this street dedicated to shirts, boots, jewelry, and sundry (mainly male) requisites is the perfumers Floris at No. 89. Dating from the mid-18th century, the shop still belongs to the family of its founder, Juan Famenias Floris. Beckoning on the street's north side are the jewel-box shops of the covered Princes and Piccadilly Arcades.

**Planning** Places to dine include Rowley's Restaurant (No. 113), with generous portions of steak and chips. www.jermynstreet.net

Opposite: An elderly pilgrim sits in the lotus position as he relishes the sacred calm of Mumbai's Banganga Tank.

Pont Valentré, the most elegant structure in Cahors, spans a serene meander of the Lot River, west of the city.

FRANCE

# SECRET GARDENS OF CAHORS

Always famous for arts and music, Cahors in southwestern France also offers a *ville fleurie* (city in bloom) trail of secret gardens.

There are many ways to explore a city—especially one with an ancient cathedral, churches, an imposing medieval bridge, and grand riverside houses—but few are more enjoyable than by following a route dotted with more than 30 secret gardens, each celebrating the city's rich history. In Cahors, you will find gardens that have existed for centuries, new gardens, a Moorish garden, an Italian garden, a sculpture garden, and many more. The starting point, at the eastern end of the Pont Valentré, is the Jardin de l'Ivresse (Inebriated Garden), which, being a vineyard, salutes the city's role as the hub of a wine region. In the herbarium at the Hôpital de Grossia, medicinal plants—some brought back by soldiers returning from the Crusades—have been grown since the Middle Ages. In the Courtil des Moines, Benedictine monks *(moines)* planted sorrel, borage, and flowering artichokes in a vegetable patch *(courtil)* tended for their cooking pot. The Jardin Bouquetier (Flower Garden) provided altar flowers for the cathedral, while the cathedral cloister, the Préau Céleste (Heavenly Courtyard), features neat box hedges and clumps of vibrant lavender. The Place des Épices (Square of Spices) dates back to the Midlde Ages, when Cahors was an important staging post on the spice route between Asia, Spain, and northern Europe.

**When to Go** Late spring and early fall are best, as summers are hot and humid. Go early on market day; two markets are held each week, on Wednesdays and Saturdays.

**How to Find It** Cahors is about 70 miles (113 km) north of Toulouse.

**Planning** Allow at least two hours for the walk. Le Balandre restaurant at the Hotel Terminus is legendary for its fine food and cellar. Less expensive but top quality is L'O à la Bouche in Rue St. Urcisse.

**Websites** www.quercy-tourisme.com, www.frenchentree.com/france-lot-quercy

## The Devil's Bridge

Begun in 1306, the **Pont Valentré** is regarded by many as Europe's finest remaining fortified bridge. Its three towers are so imposing that it was rarely attacked and never breached. It is also known as the Pont du Diable (Devil's Bridge), because of a legend dating back to its construction. Progress was so slow—it took 70 years to complete—that the builder is said to have made a pact with the devil in order to finish it. But as the bridge neared completion, the builder had second thoughts and reneged on the deal. In revenge, each night the devil stole the final stone placed in the central tower, which then had to be replaced the next day. And the next night, the devil removed it again. A small statue of the devil, added during restoration work in the 1870s, is visible on the east face of the central tower, just below the tiled roof.

# MACKINTOSH BUILDING

Be guided around the masterwork of Glasgow-born architect Charles Rennie Mackintosh by those who use it daily, the art students.

A janitor's lodge floating like a Japanese lantern in a stairwell is just one of the visual surprises that await you in Glasgow School of Art's Mackintosh Building. With its eclectic blend of influences—Scottish baronial, art nouveau, and a touch of Japanese—the structure made use of brilliantly innovative light and startlingly original furnishings when it opened in 1899. Mackintosh's passion for interior detail is seen in the corridors outside the studios, where niches, each intended for a vase containing a single, inspirational rose, were incorporated into the paneling. Sadly, the budget for this battered but much-loved building no longer supports fresh roses. The top floor, often bathed in northern light and known as the "hen run" as it was originally frequented by female students, overlooks the main glass-topped exhibition gallery and gives magnificent views across Glasgow. The casement windows have helped generations of students frame those views as they draw on foldout desks beneath. One of the last areas to be completed was the library, the quiet hub of the school, with bay windows that soar three stories high. The light filtering past dark wooden beams, a minstrel gallery, and the high-backed furniture give the study space the feeling of a forest clearing.

**When to Go** Year-round. From April through September, there are seven tours daily between 10 a.m. and 5 p.m; from October through March, there are tours at 11 a.m. and 3 p.m.

**How to Find It** The school is a 5-minute walk from Cowcaddens subway station, including a short toil up a very steep hill, the Garnethill, off Sauciehall (pronounced "socky-hall") Street. For tours, use the building's side entrance at 11 Dalhousie Street.

**Planning** The Mackintosh Building has a shop, furniture gallery, and exhibition space, which you can visit any time during normal opening hours. The rest of the building can be visited only with a guide, usually a third-year student. It is best to book your ticket in advance.

**Websites** www.gsa.ac.uk, www.crmsociety.com, www.seeglasgow.com

## Mackintosh Trail

■ For insight into Mackintosh's close collaboration with his wife, the artist Margaret MacDonald, visit the **Mackintosh House** in Glasgow University's Hunterian Museum and Art Gallery. This consists of reconstructions of the principal rooms of the couple's Glasgow home, furnished with their original furniture.

■ Other sites include **The Willow Tea Rooms** on Sauchiehall Street, the **Mackintosh Church** at Queen's Cross, and two newspaper buildings—**the Daily Record Building** and the **Lighthouse,** formerly the offices of the *Glasgow Herald*.

This detail from an oak bookcase, now housed in the Mackintosh Building, was originally designed around 1897 for the schoolroom of a private residence.

# Inns of Court, London

These peaceful enclaves in the capital's legal quarter have stood for centuries, a world away from the tumult of central London.

EUROPE

Tucked away among great halls, chapels, libraries, treasuries, and lawyers' chambers are lovingly tended gardens that open during the week to give office workers lunchtime respite. Within a short walk of the Royal Courts of Justice on the Strand, the four Inns of Court, founded in medieval times, exclusively train and accommodate England's barristers—lawyers qualified to plead cases in court. Closest to the Courts of Justice are the Tudor-style brick buildings of Lincoln's Inn. Here, in the inn's elegant New Square, the splashing water of the Jubilee Fountain, completed in 2004, breaks the silence of a capacious lawn edged with flowers. Farther east, Gray's Inn has an avenue of plane trees in a 5-acre (2 hectare) lawn known as The Walks. Most intriguing are the Middle and Inner Temples, which meld in a warren of courts and alleys between Fleet Street and the River Thames. The two inns owe their name to the medieval Knights Templar, who founded their English headquarters here in the 11th century. It was the knights who built the Temple Church, now shared by the Middle and Inner Temples, to mimic the Church of the Holy Sepulcher in Jerusalem. Nearby are the fragrant cottage-garden flowers of the Middle Temple's Elm Court, while Fountain Court—a paved square with benches dappled by mulberry trees—is truly a place for reflection and contemplation.

**When to Go** Year-round, though the gardens are at their most colorful in spring and summer. The inns are open weekdays only, and the lawns only at lunchtime.

**How to Find It** The nearest Underground stations are Temple, Holborn, and Chancery Lane.

**Planning** If you want to take something to eat, go to Fuzzy's Grub, 62 Fleet Street, for a rare roast beef with horseradish sandwich or roasted tomato and mature English Cheddar cheese. The Inner Temple garden is open 12:30-3 p.m. on weekdays. The Soane Museum is open 10 a.m.-5 p.m. Tuesday to Saturday.

**Websites** www.graysinn.info, www.lincolnsinn.org.uk, www.innertemple.org.uk, www.middletemple.org.uk, www.soane.org

### Lincoln's Inn Fields

■ On the north side of London's largest public square is **Sir John Soane's Museum,** a remarkable collection of art and classical antiquities bequeathed to the nation by architect and avid collector Sir John Soane (1753-1837). Only 70 visitors are allowed in at a time, all the better to marvel at exhibits that include the sarcophagus of Seti I in the crypt and Hogarth paintings in the picture gallery.

■ Just off the square is the **Old Curiosity Shop,** a quaint half-timber shop built in the 16th century and thought to have been the inspiration for the novel of the same name by Charles Dickens.

The Great Hall in Inner Temple stands on the site of one of the ancient halls of the Knights Templar.

The Museo Sorolla has been left just as it was when Sorolla was alive, with his last unfinished canvas still on the easel.

SPAIN

# SMALL MUSEUMS OF MADRID

Intrepid art-lovers explore the city's smaller, more intimate venues for top-notch collections—without the crowds.

Madrid's famous "art mile"—the Museo del Prado, Museo Thyssen-Bornemisza, and Centro de Arte Reina Sofía—may represent the planet's densest concentration of great paintings, but the Spanish capital's lesser-known collections are also irresistible and often more manageable. From the north end of the Paseo del Prado, a 30-minute walk up the Paseo de la Castellana brings you to the Museo Sorolla, the onetime home and studio of Spain's finest Impressionist painter, Joaquin Sorolla (1863–1923), on Avenida General Martínez Campos. Known for sea- and beachscapes in full, glowing sunlight, Sorolla was a master of the light of the Levante, Spain's Mediterranean coast around Valencia. The nearby museum of the Fundación Lázaro Galdiano—in the former home of financier and publisher, José Lázaro Galdiano (1862–1947)—is famous for its ivory and enamel collection and for works by Hieronymous Bosch, El Greco, Zurbarán, Murillo, and Goya. On Calle Alcalá near Puerta del Sol, the Real Academia de Bellas Artes de San Fernando houses an astonishing collection of works from 500 years of Spanish painting, from José de Ribera and Murillo to Sorolla, with Goya as the star of the show represented by a dozen paintings and 30 engravings. Also near Puerta del Sol is the 16th-century Monasterio de las Descalzas Reales, crammed with masterpieces by, among others, Brueghel the Elder, Titian, and Zurbarán.

**When to Go** From October through June are the best months in Madrid, when temperatures are low, the air dry and crisp, and the sun welcome.

**How to Find It** Walking is the way to get around the city. Distances that may seem too long are surprisingly manageable on foot.

**Planning** Bring good walking shoes and both light and warm clothing. The air on the 2,100-ft (640 m) *meseta* (Spain's central plateau) is dry, so bring lip balm and ski cream (sun cream for high altitudes).

**Websites** www.madridcard.com, www.gomadrid.com

## Unexpected Treasures

■ The **Church of San Antón** on Calle Hortaleza in the Chueca neighborhood is another of Madrid's hidden gems. Hanging discreetly in the gloom of a side altar on the right side of the nave, you will find what is believed to be Goya's last major liturgical painting, "The Last Communion of San José de Calasanz" (1819)—or at least a study for it or possibly a copy.

■ The **Museo Nacional del Romanticismo** is another interesting visit, featuring Goya's "San Gregorio Magno," works by his disciple Leonardo Alenza, and art and objects tracing the 19th-century Romantic Movement.

EUROPE

# Index

# Credits

## Authors

Jeremy Allan
Jane Anson
Aaron Arizpe
Jacqueline Attwood-Dupont
Derek Barton
Michael Bright
Katie Cancila
Karen Coates
Marolyn Charpentier
Danielle Demetriou
Liz Dobbs
Helen Douglas-Cooper
Ellen Dupont
Kay Fernandez
Stuart Forster
Paul Franklin
Ellen Galford
Diana Greenwald
Lisa Halvorsen
Solange Hando
Karen Hursh Graber
Ben Jacobson
Paul Kandarin
Laura Kearney
Andrew Kerr-Jarrett
Tom Le Bas
Miren Lopategui
Glen Martin
Antony Mason
Michael Metcalfe
Peter Neville-Hadley
Barbara A. Noe
Katie Parla
Everett Potter
Joost van de Putten
Agata Radkiewicz
David St Vincent
Sathya Saran
George Semler
Joyce Slayton Mitchell
Peter Sommers
Barry Stone
Linda Tagliaferro
Jenny Waddell
Johanna-Maria Wagner
Joby Williams
Roger Williams
Joe Yogerst

## Picture Credits

**1 Left to right:** Boris Stroujko; Shutterstock; jerl71/Dreamstime.com; Jamie Robinson/Shutterstock; age fotostock/SuperStock; Ian Cameron; Bruno Perousse/age fotostock/www.photolibrary.com. **2–3** Ariadne Van Zandbergen/Oxford Scientific/www.photolibrary.com; **4** Ernesto Burciaga/www.photolibrary.com; **5** Jon Arnold travel/www.photolibrary.com (1); Michele Falzone/age fototstock/www.photolibrary.com (2); Steven Vidler/Eurasia Press/Corbis (3); Roderick Edward Edwards/Animals Animals/www.photolibrary.com (4); Anne Conway/Cubo Images/Robert Harding (5); Kevin O'Hara/age fototstock/www.photolibrary.com (6); Wolfgang Kaehler/Corbis (7); Massimo Borchi/4Corners Images (8); Kevin O'Hara/age fototstock/www/photolibrary.com (9); **6** Jean-Baptiste Rabouan/Hemis/Corbis; **8–9** Jon Arnold/www.photolibrary.com; **10** Kleinhenz/F1 Online/www.photolibrary.com; **11** South Carolina Department of Parks Recreation & Tourism; **12** age fotostock/SuperStock; **13** Miles Ertman/First Light Associated Photographers/www.photolibrary.com; **14** John Warburton-Lee/www.photolibrary.com; **15** Jarno Gonzalez Zarraonandia/Shutterstock; **16** Alexandre Cappi/Getty Images; **17** Rob Blakers/www.photolibrary.com; **19** Michele Falzone/JAI/Corbis; **20** Chad Ehlers/www.photolibrary.com; **21** Yan Ping/XinHua/Xinhua Press/Corbis; **22** Diehm/Getty Images; **23** © 2008 Ajit Pal Singh; **24** © 2007/Jerry Redfern; **25** age fotostock/SuperStock; **26** Fergus Kennedy/John Warburton-Lee Photography/www.photolibrary.com; **27** Gavin Hellier/Jon Arnold Travel/www.photolibrary.com; **29** Zanchika/Shutterstock; **30** Antonio Real/age fotostock/www.photolibrary.com; **31** World Pictures/Photoshot; **33** Brian Lawrence/SuperStock/www.photolibrary.com; **34** Robert Frerck/Getty Images; **35** Jane Sweeney/Lonely Planet Images; **36** Fred Hoogervorst/Panos Pictures; **37** Gerald Cubitt; **38–39** Michele Falzone/age fotostock/www.photolibrary.com; **40** Frank Guiziou/Hemis/Corbis; **41** Parcs Nunavik Parks; **42** Alan Majchrowicz/age fotostock/www.photolibrary.com; **43** George D. Lepp/Corbis; **44** Sebastien Burel/Shutterstock; **45** Mark File; **47** EcoPrint/Shutterstock; **48** Sylvain Grandadam/SuperStock/www.photolibrary.com; **49** Dana Carrier; **50** Joshua Roper/Alamy; **51** Altrendo Nature/Getty Images; **52** Dietmar Nill/naturepl.com; **53** Michael Eudenbach/Getty Images; **54** Pete Oxford/naturepl.com; **55** Vincent Munier/naturepl.com; **56** Danita Delimont/Alamy; **5 7** TAO Images Limited/www.photolibrary.com; **58** Bert de Ruiter/Alamy; **59** Roger Arnold/Alamy; **60** N.Selje/Still Pictures; **61** Herbert Kehrer/imagebroker.net/www.photolibrary.com; **62** Orien Harvey/www.photolibrary.com; **63** Sylvain Grandadam/Robert Harding Travel/www.photolibrary.com; **64** David Wall/Lonely Planet; **65** Gerald Cubitt/NHPA/Photoshot; **67** Roy Toft/National Geographic/Getty Images; **68** Andy Rouse/NHPA/Photoshot; **69** Pavel Dunyushkin/Shutterstock; **70** Pablo Galan Cela/age fotostock/www.photolibrary.com; **71** Ecobo/Dreamstime.com; **72** Niall Benvie/naturepl.com; **73** Pawel Wysocki/Hemis/www.photolibrary.com; **75** Henry Ausloos/age fotostock/www.photolibrary.com; **76** Loop Images/Corbis; **77** Ariadne Van Zandbergen; **78–79** Steven Vidler/Eurasia Press/Corbis; **80** Stephen Saks/Lonely Planet Images; **81** Katja Kreder/imagebroker.net/www.photolibrary.com; **83** Tom Pepeira/Iconotec/www.photolibrary.com; **84** age fotostock/SuperStock; **85** Michael Melford/National Geographic Images; **86** Nicholas Pitt/Getty Images; **87** Andre Seale/age fotostock/www.photolibrary.com; **88** John Elk III/Lonely Planet Images; **89** Roy Mangersnes/naturepl.com; **90** George Steinmetz/Corbis; **91** Michele Falzone/Jon Arnold Travel/www.photolibrary.com; **93** Georgette Douwma/Imagestate/www.photolibrary.com; **94, 95** John Pennock/Lonely Planet Images; **96** ©JNTO; **97** Holgs/Dreamstime.com; **98** Image Quest Marine; **99** age fotostock/SuperStock; **100** Michail Kabakovitch/Shutterstock; **101** Frank Chmura/Nordic Photos/www.photolibrary.com; **102** Onne van der Wal/bluegreenpictures.com; **103** Rick Tomlinson/bluegreenpictures.com; **104** McPHOTO/Still Pictures; **105** www.scottishviewpoint.com; **107** David Clapp/Oxford Scientific/www.photolibrary.com; **108** Camille Moirenc/Hemis/Corbis; **109** Guido Alberto Rossi/Tips Italia/www.photolibrary.com; **110** Still Pictures/U. Katz; **111** Still Pictures/Dani-Jeske; **112** George Osodi/Panos Pictures; **113** Aquavision/Getty Images; **114–115** Roderick Edward Edwards/Animals Animals/www.photolibrary.com; **116** George Hunter/SuperStock; **117** Pat & Chuck Blackley/Alamy; **118** Dennis Frates/Alamy; **119** Stephen Saks/Lonely Planet Images; **120** Robert Shantz/Alamy; **121** Ralph Hopkins/Lonely Planet; **123** Stefano Scata/Getty Images; **124** Eduardo Juárez; **125** Reuters/Corbis; **126** Damien Simonis/Lonely Planet; **127** Japan Travel Bureau/www.photolibrary.com; **128** Lisa McKelvie/www.photolibrary.com; **129** Andrew Bain/Lonely Planet Images; **131** Alaska Marine Highway Systems; **132** © Österreich Werbung/Weinhaeupl W./Austrian National Tourist Office; **133** Targa/age fotostock/www.photolibrary.com; **134** Pep Roig/Alamy; **135** Imagebroker.net/Photoshot; **137** nagelestock.com/Alamy; **138** Brigitte Merle/Photononstop/www.photolibrary.com; **139** T.W.P./Mauritius/www.photolibrary.com; **141** Cass Scenic Railroad State Park; **142** Juan Carlos Munoz/age fotostock/www.photolibrary.com; **143** Peter Lewis/Oxford Scientific/www.photolibrary.com; **144** David Cheshire/Alamy; **145** Chris Howes/Wild Places Photography/Alamy; **146** Cameron Davidson/www.photolibrary.com; **147** Chris Mattison/age fotostock/www.photolibrary.com; **148** Images of Africa Photobank/Alamy; **149** Sébastien Boisse/Photononstop/www.photolibrary.com; **150–151** Anne Conway/Cubo Images/Robert Harding; **152** High Bridge Trail State Park/Virginia State Parks; **153** Pierre Perrin/Corbis Sygma; **155** Robert Dayton/age fotostock/www.photolibrary.com; **156** altrendo travel/Getty Images; **157** Ernesto Burciaga/Tips Italia/www.photolibrary.com; **158** Gavin Hellier/Robert Harding Travel; **159** Robert Francis/Robert Harding; **160** Rodrigo Torres/Glowimages/Photoshot; **161** View Stock/www.photolibrary.com; **162** Amar Grover/John Warburton-Lee Photography/www.photolibrary.com; **163** Wayne and Miriam Caravella/www.photolibrary.com; **164** Anders Blomqvist/Lonely Planet Images; **165** Hugo Canabi/Iconotec/www.photolibrary.com; **166** Prisma/SuperStock; **167** Styve Reineck/Shutterstock; **169** World Pictures/Photoshot; **170** Vincent J.Musi/Aurora Photos; **171** NRT-Travel/Alamy; **172** Martin Richardson/Alamy; **173** Sandro Vannini/Corbis; **174** Kevin O'Hara/age fotostock/www.photolibrary.com; **175** Bruno Perousse/age fotostock /www.photolibrary.com; **176** Maggie Steber/National Geographic Stock; **177** Richard Du Toit/Minden Pictures/National Geographic Stock; **178** Kevin O'Hara/age fotostock/www.photolibrary.com; **180** Tina Fineberg/AP/Press Association Images; **181** Jerl71/Dreamstime.com; **182** Art Directors & TRIP/Alamy; **184** Nobuaki Sumida/Aflo Foto Agency/www.photolibrary.com; **185** Floris Leeuwenberg/Corbis; **186** Stuart Westmorland/Getty Images; **187** Walter G.Allgöwer/imagebroker.net/www.photolibrary.com; **189** "The Calling of St. Matthew" (oil on canvas), Carpaccio, Vittore (c.1460/5-1523/6)/Scuola di San Giorgio degli Schiavoni, Venice, Italy/The Bridgeman Art Library; **190** © Jerry Redfern; **191** Solange Hando; **192** Dinodia/age fotostock/www.photolibrary.com; **193** Shai Ginott/Corbis; **194** Rick Strange/World Pictures/Photoshot; **195** Sonia Hal'iday Photographs; **196** Michael Short/Robert Harding Travel/www.photolibrary.com; **197** More'eaze Tropicana/Alamy; **199** E & E Image Library/In agestate/www.photolibrary.com; **200** Markus Keller/imagebroker.net/www.photolibrary.com; **201** "Marie Antoinette (1755-93) held by the Religion," 1825 (marble), Cortot, Jean-Baptiste (1787-1843)/Chapelle Expiatoire, Paris, France/© Clement Guillaume/The Bridgeman Art Library; **202** tim gartside London/Alamy; **203** Priory Church of St Bartholomew the Great; **204** © Heinz Hebeisen/Iberimage; **205** Betrand Bechard/MAXPPP/Photoshot; **206–207** Wolfgang Kaehler/Corbis; **208** J.schultes/Dreamstime.com; **209** Birgit Pohl/Nonstock/www.photolibrary.com; **211** Lynette Andreasen; **212** Dan Herrick/Lonely Planet Images; **213** Jeff Greenberg/Alamy; **214** age fotostock/SuperStock; **215** Michael Snell/Robert Harding; **216** Paul M. Franklin; **217** Herbert Lotz © 2010. Photo Georgia O'Keeffe Museum, Santa Fe/Art Resource/Scala, Florence; **219** James Brittain/View Pictures/www.photolibrary.com; **220** age fotostock/SuperStock; **221** Sebastien Boisse/Photononstop/www.photolibrary.com; **222** ©JNTO; **223** Prisma/SuperStock; **225** John Wilson/Robert Harding; **226** Paule Seux/Hemis/www.photolibrary.com; **227** Wojtek Buss/age fotostock/www.photolibrary.com; **228** Jonathan Smith/Lonely Planet Images; **229** Attila Kisbenedek/AFP/Getty Images; **230** Jerl71/Dreamstime.com; **231** Egyptian Museum Turin/Gianni Dagli Orti/The Art Archive; **232** Imagebroker.net/Photoshot; **233** Lionel Coates/World Pictures/Photoshot; **234** catherine lucas/Alamy; **235** Sandro Vannini/Corbis; **237** Luca Tettoni/Robert Harding Travel/www.photolibrary.com/www.photolibrary.com; **238** ©François Pons, Musée Toulouse-Lautrec, Albi, France; **239** Anthony Gormley, "One and Other," 2000. Photo: Jonty Wilde; **241** Iain Masterton/Alamy; **242** Leighton House Museum, Royal Borough of Kensington and Chelsea; **243** Hever Castle; **244** Turespaña; **245** Japan Travel Bureau/www.photolibrary.com; **246-247** Massimo Borchi/4Corners Images; **248** Paul Laramee; **249** Art Fleury/Alamy; **250** Daniel Dempster Photography/Alamy; **251** Paul M.Franklin; **253** Christophe Boisvieux/Corbis; **254** Berndhard Lang/F1 Online/www.photolibrary.com; **255** Imagebroker.net/Photoshot; **2 56** Best View Stock/www.photolibrary.com; **257** Chrisian Kober/John Warburton-Lee Photography/www.photolibrary.com; **258** Meobeo/Dreamstime.com; **259** © 2002/Jerry Redfern; **260** Barry Goodwin/Courtesy of Tourism Queensland; **261** John Hicks/Corbis; **263** Mick Rock/Cephas; **264** terry harris just greece photo library/Alamy; **265** Wolfgang Kaehler/Corbis; **266** Regina Hofmann; **267** Mike Kipling/The Travel Library/www.photolibrary.com; **268** Kaos03/SIME/4Corners Images; **269** Stefano Amatini/4Corners Images; **270** Michael Busselle/Robert Harding; **271** Nicholas Thibaut/Photononstop/www.photolibrary.com; **272** Travel Library Limited/SuperStock; **273** Rod Edwards/Britain on View/www.photolibrary.com; **274** Andy Williams/Britain on View/www.photolibrary.com; **275** Jordi Cami/Alamy; **276–277** Kevin O'Hara/age fotostock/www.photolibrary.com; **278** Cal Vornberger/Still Pictures; **279** Ping Amranand/SuperStock/www.photolibrary.com; **2 80** Creatas/Comstock/www.photolibrary.com; **281** Balthasar Thomass/Alamy; **283** Martin Siepmann/imagebroker.net/www.photolibrary.com; **284** Benjamin Rondel/First Light/ Corbis; **285** Best View Stock/www.photolibrary.com; **287** Jean-Pierre Lescourret/Corbis; **288** Japan Travel Bureau/www.photolibrary.com; **289** Charles Bowman/www.photolibrary.com; **290** Frank Carter/Lonely Planet Images; **291** Robert Essel NYC/Corbis; **292** John Wreford; **293** Walter Bibikow/Jon Arnold Travel/www.photolibrary.com; **295** dbimages/Alamy; **296** Japan Travel Bureau/www.photolibrary.com; **297** Barry Blitz; **298** Mike Kipling/The Travel Library/www.photolibrary.com; **299** Radius Images/www.photolibrary.com; **301** Fet/Dreamstime.com; **302** Ian Armitage; **303** Oliver Knight/Alamy; **304** Reso/www.photolibrary.com; **305** René Mattes/Hemis/Corbis; **307** Richard T.Nowitz/Corbis; **308** Michael Busselle/Robert Harding World Imagery/Corbis; **309** Mackintosh Building at The Glasgow School of Art; **310** Julian Love/John Warburton Lee-Photography/www.photolibrary.com; **311** Visions of America, LLC/Alamy.

**Front Cover**
**Background image:** Chad Ehlers/www.photolibrary.com.
**Picture strip, left to right:** Boris Stroujko; Shutterstock; jerl71/Dreamstime.com; Jamie Robinson/Shutterstock; age fotostock/SuperStock; Ian Cameron; Bruno Perousse/age fotostock/www.photolibrary.com.

**Back Cover**
**Background image:** Chad Ehlers/www.photolibrary.com.
**Picture strip, left to right:** : Zanchika/Shutterstock; Roy Toft/National Geographic/Getty Images; EcoPrint/Shutterstock; Chris Howes/Wild Places/Alamy; Michele Falzone/age fotostock/www.photolibrary.com; Stuart Westmorland/Getty Images.

**Spine:** Alaska Marine Highway Systems

## Secret Journeys of a Lifetime

### Published by the National Geographic Society

John M. Fahey, Jr., Chairman of the Board and Chief
Executive Officer
Timothy T. Kelly, President
Declan Moore, Executive Vice President; President,
Publishing
Melina Gerosa Bellows, Executive Vice President, Chief
Creative Officer, Books, Kids, and Family

### Prepared by the Book Division

Barbara Brownell Grogan, Vice President and Editor in Chief
Jonathan Halling, Design Director, Books and Children's
Publishing
Marianne R. Koszorus, Director of Design
Barbara A. Noe, Senior Editor
Carl Mehler, Director of Maps
Lawrence M. Porges, Project Editor
Melissa Farris, Design Consultant
Olivia Garnett, Mary Stephanos, Contributors
R. Gary Colbert, Production Director
Jennifer A. Thornton, Managing Editor
Meredith C. Wilcox, Administrative Director, Illustrations

### Manufacturing and Quality Management

Christopher A. Liedel, Chief Financial Officer
Phillip L. Schlosser, Senior Vice President
Chris Brown, Technical Director
Nicole Elliott, Manager
Rachel Faulise, Manager
Robert L. Barr, Manager

### Created by Toucan Books Ltd

Ellen Dupont, Editorial Director
Helen Douglas-Cooper, Senior Editor
Jane Chapman, Jane Hutchings, Andrew Kerr-Jarrett,
Editors
Victoria Savage, Editorial Assistant
Leah Germann, Designer
Christine Vincent, Picture Manager
Sharon Southren with Mia Stewart-Wilson, Picture
Researchers
Marion Dent, Proofreader
Michael Dent, Indexer

The National Geographic Society is one of the world's largest
nonprofit scientific and educational organizations. Founded
in 1888 to "increase and diffuse geographic knowledge," the
Society's mission is to inspire people to care about the planet.
It reaches more than 400 million people worldwide each
month through its official journal, *National Geographic,* and
other magazines; National Geographic Channel; television
documentaries; music; radio; films; books; DVDs; maps;
exhibitions; live events; school publishing programs; interactive media; and merchandise. National Geographic has
funded more than 9,600 scientific research, conservation and
exploration projects and supports an education program
promoting geographic literacy. For more information, visit
www.nationalgeographic.com.

For more information, please call 1-800-NGS LINE
(647-5463) or write to the following address:

National Geographic Society
1145 17th Street N.W.
Washington, D.C. 20036-4688 U.S.A.

Visit us online at www.nationalgeographic.com

For information about special discounts for bulk purchases,
please contact National Geographic Books Special Sales:
ngspecsales@ngs.org

For rights or permissions inquiries, please contact National
Geographic Books Subsidiary Rights: ngbookrights@ngs.org

ISBN: 978-1-4262-0646-7

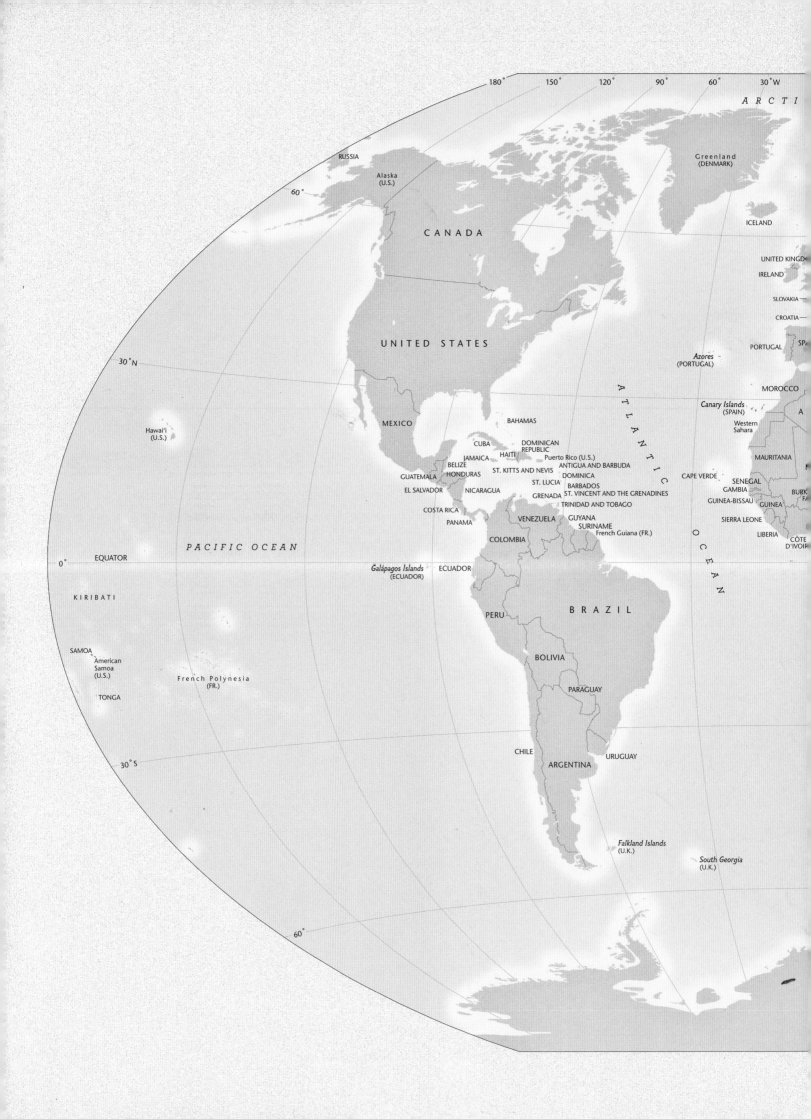

ARCTI

180°    150°    120°    90°    60°    30°W

RUSSIA

Alaska
(U.S.)

60°

CANADA

Greenland
(DENMARK)

ICELAND

UNITED KINGD

IRELAND

UNITED STATES

SLOVAKIA

CROATIA

PORTUGAL          SP

30°N

Azores
(PORTUGAL)

MOROCCO

Hawai'i
(U.S.)

MEXICO

BAHAMAS

CUBA          DOMINICAN
              REPUBLIC

Canary Islands
(SPAIN)

Western
Sahara

A

JAMAICA     HAITI

Puerto Rico (U.S.)

MAURITANIA

BELIZE                      ANTIGUA AND BARBUDA

GUATEMALA   HONDURAS   ST. KITTS AND NEVIS   DOMINICA

CAPE VERDE

SENEGAL

GAMBIA

BURK

EL SALVADOR   NICARAGUA   ST. LUCIA   BARBADOS
                           GRENADA  ST. VINCENT AND THE GRENADINES

GUINEA-BISSAU          GUINEA           FA

COSTA RICA                         TRINIDAD AND TOBAGO

SIERRA LEONE

PANAMA        VENEZUELA   GUYANA
                          SURINAME

LIBERIA

CÔTE
D'IVOIR

COLOMBIA                 French Guiana (FR.)

EQUATOR

PACIFIC OCEAN

A
T
L
A
N
T
I
C

O
C
E
A
N

Galápagos Islands   ECUADOR
(ECUADOR)

KIRIBATI

PERU                    B R A Z I L

SAMOA

American
Samoa
(U.S.)

French Polynesia
(FR.)

BOLIVIA

TONGA

PARAGUAY

30°S

CHILE          URUGUAY

ARGENTINA

Falkland Islands
(U.K.)

South Georgia
(U.K.)

60°